# THE NEW SOUTHERN GARDEN COOKBOOK

# The New Southern Garden Cookbook

ENJOYING THE BEST FROM

HOMEGROWN GARDENS, FARMERS' MARKETS,

ROADSIDE STANDS, & CSA FARM BOXES

SHERI CASTLE

The University of North Carolina Press   Chapel Hill

Library of Congress Cataloging-in-Publication Data
Castle, Sheri.
The new southern garden cookbook : enjoying the best from homegrown gardens,
farmers' markets, roadside stands, and CSA farm boxes / Sheri Castle.
p. cm.
Includes index.
ISBN 978-0-8078-3465-7 (cloth : alk. paper)
1. Cooking, American — Southern style. 2. Cookbooks.  I. Title.
TX715.2.S68C385 2011    641.5975 — dc22    2010038338

15  14  13  12  11    5  4  3  2

TO MY PRECIOUS DAUGHTER, Lily Castle Tidwell

THE MOST EXTRAORDINARY PERSON I KNOW

# Contents

# Acknowledgments

I've tested and developed the recipes for several fine cookbooks and written for several more. Based on that, I thought that writing my own cookbook would be pretty easy. Nope. Full authorship is to writing for hire what parenting is to babysitting.

This book would not have been possible without the support of more people than I can ever thank adequately, but I must try to specifically thank these few.

My husband, Doug Tidwell, not only put up with me through all of this but maintained his enthusiasm and constant support. He did everything from fixing computer problems (and cocktails) to proofreading to listening to me fret over every detail. He never declined a request, no matter how many times I asked him to read something or handed him a spoon and said, "Taste this and tell me whether it's bookworthy." Doug is the wittiest, funniest person I know.

My unflappable agent, Michael Bourret, of Dystel & Goderich Literary Management, patiently answered all my questions and consistently looked after my best interests. He knows his stuff, and I'm so glad he's in my corner.

I am grateful to everyone at the University of North Carolina Press. In particular I want to thank Elaine Maisner and Paula Wald, my editors. Elaine shepherded this book from day one, when it was nothing more than a dream I mentioned over lunch. When all was said and done, Paula made sure it was all said and done. I appreciate their patience, editorial insight, and friendship. Many thanks to everyone on the team who helped bring this cookbook to fruition.

Stewart Waller's beautiful photographs made the food I put on the plate come alive on the page. Thanks for sharing my vision of the food and for being so easy to work with.

Many thanks to Julie Walker for her expert prop styling and cheerful support during the photo shoots, not to mention sharing her enviable collection of art, fabric, and dishes. Thanks to Anne Dusek and Touchwood Antiques for lending lovely objects as well.

To my friends at the Carrboro Farmers' Market: If you grow it, I will come. Thanks also to my cohorts in the Southern Foodways Alliance. I am proud to be a member of such a smart, cool, hardworking, and well-fed group.

Many of my friends will never know how much they helped while I was immersed in this book. They listened and they listened and they listened a little more as I prattled on and fretted more than a bit. Blessings to Elizabeth Beal, Sarah Blacklin, Sharon Brody, Kelly Clark, Anne and Alex Dusek, Anne Fairchild, Marcie Ferris, Kathleen Fitzgerald, Susan Gilpin, Nancy Halberstadt, Alex and Betsy Hitt, Ted Lee, Catherine Linford, Sheila Neal, Carol O'Laughlin, Sara Roahen, Bill Smith Jr., Julie and David Walker, Laura Werlin, and all the rest.

My beloved Domino is the best dog and truest pal ever. He has a pure soul and good outlook on life. He makes me happy every day. Thanks to Daddy Lynn and T. Mom for giving their granddaughter and our grand dog a summer place while I finished the book.

And to everyone else who did good things along the way: Thanks to each and every one of you from the bottom of my heart.

THE NEW SOUTHERN GARDEN COOKBOOK

# Introduction

Southerners are renowned for dishing up all sorts of good things to eat, but if you want to see a southerner's face really light up, ask about the last time they enjoyed fresh vegetables and fruits from the garden. *The New Southern Garden Cookbook* celebrates the pleasures of fresh, local, seasonal food. And it celebrates how much easier it is becoming to find produce grown in our communities. This cookbook promotes the delicious, healthful home cooking made possible by the diverse array of seasonal fruits and vegetables grown in the South—and in most of the rest of the nation as well. These pages hold good food for omnivores and vegetarians alike.

The history and art of southern cookery were built on seasonal and mostly homegrown vegetables. No other component—not even the barbecue, fried chicken, or hot biscuits—more clearly conveyed the southern approach to meals. Weekday meals usually included at least three vegetables or fruits. A proper Sunday dinner offered twice that. The dishes soared to a dozen or more on holidays and special occasions. Produce figured into the entire meal, not just the side dishes. With all that carefully prepared garden-fresh food, not to mention the jars of pickles, relishes, and preserves, traditional southern meals offered endless combinations of textures, nuanced flavors, and aromas. Such meals could give the fortunate eaters the feeling that no one anywhere was eating better at that exact moment.

The story is told that Eden, a garden, was paradise itself. The same is not said of fast-food joints. To quote an old song, "We got to get ourselves back to the garden."

## WHAT CONSTITUTES A GARDEN THESE DAYS?

A garden doesn't have to be a plot of ground out back. We can grow a few things in deck boxes, in patio pots, or in a square of a community garden. We can pick our fresh produce from local farmers' markets and roadside farm stands. We can join a Community Supported Agriculture (CSA) program to have a farm box of local fare delivered to our door each week. We can accept an armload of produce handed across the fence from a generous neighbor. Even supermarkets sometimes feature locally grown food. With all these options, it's possible for many of us to eat from a bountiful garden without having to personally grow that garden.

The common thread among all these definitions of "garden" is that the food is local and seasonal, two ideas as old as the ages in southern cooking. Our good cooking always began with good growing.

Garden food is obviously local, because there is no place more local than our own backyards, farmers' markets, and CSAs. Left to her own devices, Mother Nature insists that garden fare be seasonal because things can grow only when they are supposed to. There is no better time to eat a food than when it is ready, in the place it is ready. Each season, even each week within a season, brings something new. The appearance of a certain food on the table can be as true a mark of a season as the position of the sun in the sky. There are certain everyday smells in the kitchen, but there are others that turn the page of the calendar, telling us that a new season is beginning and another is closing until next year, when it all comes around again.

It is estimated that the average American meal travels about 1,500 miles. That's far from fresh. Local and regional produce enjoyed at the height of its natural season delivers better value and can cost less than when it is shipped across the globe year-round. A three-dollar basket of luscious, local, sun-ripened strawberries enjoyed on the same warm spring day as they are picked is a better value than a three-dollar basket of hard, bland, gassed berries shipped across many time zones in the dead of winter. Perfectly ripe berries picked from homegrown perennial plants cost pennies. When it comes to flavor, freshness trumps, and it shows on our plates.

Gardens, farmers' markets, and CSAs offer us variety that most supermarkets and mega-marts cannot. Large markets must focus on produce that meets requirements for shipability, uniformity, and shelf life—regardless of season or flavor. In contrast, local food outlets can reflect local tastes and preferences, giving us more variety in our familiar favorites and introducing us to new things along the way.

> "A three-dollar basket of luscious, local, sun-ripened strawberries enjoyed on the same warm spring day as they are picked is a better value than a three-dollar basket of hard, bland, gassed berries shipped across many time zones in the dead of winter."

Local food can bridge the gap between producers and consumers, letting us know exactly where our food comes from, who grew it, and how. Home gardening closes that gap altogether. That is one of the reasons that, for the first time in decades, the popularity of home gardening and cooking is sharply on the rise. Farmers' markets and CSA subscriptions are experiencing similar growth. Gardeners, conscientious shoppers, and discerning eaters are realizing that turning a blind eye to food production and distancing ourselves from our food supply isn't wise or sustainable.

There are plenty of economic and environmental reasons to eat local, seasonal food, but it doesn't have to be an all-or-nothing proposition. It's scalable and flexible, depending on what's available and what's practical. We don't have to give up everything that comes from around the world. Embracing the glory of a homegrown tomato doesn't mean that we should no longer buy bananas for our pudding. But when it comes down to choosing between produce grown and picked as close as possible to when and where we eat it versus a long-hauled, flimsy knockoff of the same thing, local and seasonal make sense.

## WHAT'S GROWING IN OUR NEW SOUTHERN GARDENS?

Southern gardens have always been as diverse as the gardeners wanted them to be and the land allowed them to be. The South is a mosaic of micro climates, which means just about everything will grow somewhere in the South. The new southern garden can include venerated heirloom items and the newest cultivars. Some gardens contain plants so common that they seem universal, while others are intensely local. A typical garden, farmers' market, or CSA farm box in New Orleans will look considerably different from one in Asheville, but both are equally, authentically, and sufficiently southern. Like our dinner tables and recipes, our gardens are shaped by a mixture of circumstances and customs, history and habits.

The earliest southern gardeners were the Native Americans who cultivated our indigenous foods. Everything else was added because someone couldn't imagine life without it and found a way to grow it. Starting with the earliest explorers and colonists, new vegetables and fruits arrived in the South with each wave of newcomers. People tried to bring a little of what they had, what they knew, and what they anticipated they would need in the most unknown and foreign of places. One of the surest and most soothing ways to get our bearings in a new place is to cook and eat something we

"The new southern garden can include venerated heirloom items and the newest cultivars."

"When we can't go home to eat, we can eat to go home."

recognize and find familiar, something that tastes of home. When we can't go home to eat, we can eat to go home.

## WHAT IS SOUTHERN COOKING?

Authentic southern cooking is as diverse and multicultural as the regions in the South and the families who live there. Southern cooks have always creatively drawn upon the mix of cultures that compose the South, starting with Native Americans, Europeans, and Africans. Sure, southerners tend to like what granny made, but those grannies didn't come from the same place, so they didn't cook the same way, even when presented with the same ingredients. If what we see as southern depends on where we stand, then what we eat as southern depends on who stirs the pot.

A universal southern dish is more often just a universal southern idea. Each community or family can have its own convictions about what a certain dish should contain and how it should be made. And each is darn sure its way is the best way. But go fifty miles in any direction and there will be another set of equally heartfelt convictions that its version is better. A bite of a dish in each place is a culinary GPS — one taste and you'll know where you are. Context and pride of place are as crucial to the integrity and authenticity of a southern dish as any recipe or cast-iron skillet. If there is no *there* there, it will never taste right.

Loyalty to local customs remains a southern culinary cornerstone. At the same time, southern cooking is a dynamic art, with each generation making its own contributions and adaptations. Southern food has a threshold for the familiar that must be crossed, but the ways to do that are ever-expanding. We can find exquisite southern food in the humblest of home kitchens, in no-frills meat-and-three eateries, in white linen restaurants, and passed through the window of a street food truck. It's possible to get passionate, immutable, authentic southern food in kitchens that aren't even in the South, prepared by cooks who were neither raised in the South nor versed in that tradition. Southern food can embrace ethnicity and ethnic cooks can embrace southern ingredients. That's why we can find tamales in the Delta, sauerkraut in a Smoky Mountain hollow, and collards cooked in a wok. Southern food is a balance of enduring and evolving foodways.

Southern food is also evocative. It makes us southerners talk because it makes us remember. Before we tell you how a thing tastes, we need to tell you how it makes us feel and what it reminds us of. We cannot tell of the

"Context and pride of place are as crucial to the integrity and authenticity of a southern dish as any recipe or cast-iron skillet. If there is no *there* there, it will never taste right."

food without telling of the people who made it for us, and why, and how well they did or didn't do. Southern is on the tip of our tongues.

This isn't to say that all southern food memories are good because, of course, not all southern food and cooking are good. On the other hand, some southern meals are so exalted that we are sure it's what the angels eat on Sunday. Whether good or bad, food memories are hard to shake. There is no more tenacious nostalgia. One bite of food or one whiff of an aroma from our past is swift transport to somewhere. The persuasion of a food memory is association, not accuracy. Memories are rarely drawn to scale.

## HOW TO USE THIS BOOK

The garden has always been an extension of the kitchen. Cooks tended most gardens, or at least orchestrated them. That is why this cookbook is organized by type of vegetable or fruit. This book is built on the premise that when cooking with fresh fruits and vegetables, the ingredient, not the recipe, is the wiser starting point. When we start with the best of what's currently available in our garden, our neighborhood farmers' market, our CSA farm box, or even our grocery store, the cooking and the recipes follow easily.

Some cooks have never lost their feel for the produce-driven cooking that forms the core of southern cooking. Others are feeling around for it. Many cooks are adventurous, looking for new ideas. That's why the recipes in this cookbook—a mixture of new and familiar, original and classic, contemporary and traditional, ethnic and down-home—aim to offer possibilities to all these cooks, southern or otherwise.

This book features the fruits and vegetables that most people are likely to find in abundance and in good form, not only in the geographical South but across much of America. There are also a few items (such as ramps and field peas) that are not as widespread but are so iconically southern that they could not be omitted.

Whenever possible, I offer substitutions for the main ingredient, so that cooks have other options when that ingredient isn't available in peak seasonal form or can take advantage of an ingredient that is even more appealing than what they set out to find.

In the index, besides listing the recipes by main ingredient, I sort them by meal categories: appetizers, soups, salads, entrées, side dishes, and desserts. These categories are handy if you're planning a meal or if the type of recipe is as important as the ingredients.

"One bite of food or one whiff of an aroma from our past is swift transport to somewhere. The persuasion of a food memory is association, not accuracy. Memories are rarely drawn to scale."

Two things conspired to turn me into a storytelling southern cook: my mama and Italy.

My mama was my grandmother, Madge Marie Reece Castle. She lived all her days way up in the Blue Ridge Mountains, but she never turned down a chance to travel and get a look at what was out there. She was curious. She loved to laugh. She was my sanctuary.

Mama was one of those storybook southern women who could flat out cook and keep a garden. When she tied on her apron every morning, it was like Superman tying on his cape. Her huge garden was bordered by fruit trees, grapevines, and berry patches. The slap of the screen door as she headed out there was the starter pistol for her day. Like many rural families of the time, the garden fed us. We ate all we could hold while it was fresh, and she put up the rest to eat through the winter. She pickled, preserved, and canned. Many summer days she didn't sit down once until she heard the last bright ping from a sealing Mason jar, her vesper bells. I didn't know that Mama was raising me on food rich with cultural heritage. I just thought it was supper.

I have always cooked. I wrote my first recipe when I was four years old. It was for a far-flung beverage concoction made in the avocado green blender that Mama got with Green Stamps. I called it something like Hawaiian Sunset Delight. I mailed my recipe to one of those daytime homemaker shows popular in the early 1960s. The show came on between two of Mama's stories: *Search for Tomorrow* and *The Guiding Light*. I'd sit under the kitchen table and watch with her. I saw enough of those stories to conclude that fancy people ate dinner at night, when my people ate supper. My recipe revealed my intentions. I planned to rise into the world of those who ate dinner every night, not just after church on Sunday. Hawaiian Sunset Delight was my first step away from my family's table.

I eventually fell deeply back in love with the food I grew up with, but as they say in the mountains, I had to go around my elbow to get from finger to thumb.

About ten years back, I was at a joyful table in a farmhouse kitchen perched on a steep hillside. From the windows I could look over at mountaintops in ten shades of blue and look down at tobacco fields and orchards. We were sharing laughter, telling stories, and passing plates. We were eating greens cooked in pork stock, fresh shell beans, stewed apples, homemade sausage, and hearth bread for sopping. I was in Umbertide, Italy, and I had an epiphany. If this food mattered in Italy, it mattered back home. If this food told a story of these people in this place, it told a story of my people in our place. Sometimes the obvious isn't obvious until something points it out.

I went to Italy to become a better Mediterranean cook and came home a better southern cook, too. I found strong similarity between traditional, authentic southern cooking and traditional, authentic Italian cooking. Both rely on the freshest locally grown produce harvested at its peak of seasonal freshness. Both are masterful at using a little meat, often pork, as a seasoning condiment. Both southern and Italian cooks have strong loyalties to the way a dish is made in their home or their town, a method obviously superior to how it's done up the road. Both merge bits of wit, style, and respect for heritage into a pleasurable whole. And in both the South and Italy, the best examples of the cuisine pay homage to storied home cooking. And mamas. So I got myself back to my southern garden.

## A WORD ON INGREDIENTS

Good cooking relies on good ingredients. Choose foods that are as fresh as possible, minimally processed, and inherently delicious. The more flavor something has, the less you need to do to it. When you start with the highest-quality ingredients you can find (which aren't necessarily the most expensive), it's easy to cook well.

Although this book welcomes creativity in the kitchen, especially when it enables cooks to take advantage of the best seasonal ingredients, there are times when it's best to stick with a recipe. Here are some guidelines on selecting basic ingredients that will help the recipes turn out successfully.

- Black pepper should be freshly ground. Kosher salt is my preferred all-purpose salt. If a recipe calls for sifting salt (or if you need a salt with grains small enough to flow through old-fashioned salt shakers), use fine sea salt. Old-fashioned "table salt" contains several additives that most pure kosher and sea salts do not.

- Eggs are large and preferably from free-roaming chickens with an all-vegetarian diet.

"Choose foods that are as fresh as possible, minimally processed, and inherently delicious. . . . When you start with the highest-quality ingredients you can find (which aren't necessarily the most expensive), it's easy to cook well."

- Unless otherwise specified, butter can be salted or unsalted, depending on your personal preference. I like unsalted butter in most cakes but prefer salted butter on vegetables. Margarine is not a substitute for butter.

- Unless otherwise specified, milk, yogurt, sour cream, and other similar dairy products should be whole. If you want to reduce the amount of fat, you can use low-fat alternatives, but do not use nonfat products. Many nonfat products are so altered that they cannot function as dairy products in most recipes.

- Buttermilk is liquid only, never reconstituted from powder. The best buttermilk comes from local farmsteads, often in glass bottles.

- When possible, use very fresh cream from a local dairy that has been pasteurized but not ultra-pasteurized. It will have better flavor and better volume when whipped.

- Cornmeal is stone-ground and very fresh.

- Unless otherwise specified, flour is all-purpose bleached flour. Whole grain flour will perform differently in recipes and isn't necessarily an even swap.

- Use thin, light metal baking pans, preferably aluminum. Dark, heavy, or nonstick pans usually make the crust of baked goods too thick and dark.

- Always preheat the oven, preferably for at least 20 minutes. Most ovens are not fully preheated even when the indicator says they are.

- When baking, measure carefully and do not substitute ingredients. Baking is chemistry, with each ingredient performing a specific task, especially sweeteners. Sugar plays roles that exceed sweetness, functions that sugar substitutes cannot provide, particularly in baked goods. Real cane sugar is a reliable choice.

- Vanilla is pure vanilla extract, not flavoring.

- Spices and dried herbs must be very fresh and aromatic. Pungent aroma is an indication of fresh flavor, so give your spices a sniff test from time to time. Most spices should be replaced annually. Store your spices in a cool, dark spot, such as the pantry. Spice racks over the stove are pretty but not practical.

- Olive oil is extra-virgin, although when heated, it can be modest, affordable oil from the grocery store. Save expensive extra-virgin oil for vinaigrettes and other recipes where it is not heated.

- Vegetable oil is the best choice for recipes where the flavor and aroma of olive oil are not appropriate. Grapeseed oil is an excellent choice, especially when cooking at high temperatures.

- Lemon, orange, and lime juice should come from fresh fruit. The exception is key lime juice, which is almost always better when bottled. Citrus zest should be freshly grated from fruit that has been scrubbed to remove any wax.

- For the best flavor, freshly grate cheese just before adding it to a recipe.

- Humanely raised and minimally processed meat—especially pork—tastes best. Free-range, organic poultry—especially chicken—that has never been frozen works best in recipes. If you are using fish or shellfish that has been frozen, do not thaw it until you are ready to use it.

- Use dry measuring cups for dry ingredients and liquid measuring cups with pour spouts for wet ingredients. Not only is it easier to make accurate measurements when using the right type of cup, but the amounts can vary considerably between the two types. When measuring something sticky (such as honey or sorghum), give the measuring cup or spoon a light mist of vegetable oil spray.

- Read through a recipe before you begin. Make sure you have all of the ingredients and do as much chopping and measuring as possible up front. Getting halfway through and realizing you don't have something you need is a real spirit breaker.

- More than anything, taste as you go and trust your instincts.

It's time for supper. Now let's go eat.

# APPLES

**At one time, at least 1,500 different kinds of apples** flourished in the
South. Other than a few wild crab apples, none of those apples were native, but they grew rapidly and well from Old World rootstock and seeds
brought over by European settlers, starting as early as 1629. The diversity of apples was crucial because different apples were suited to different purposes, depending on their texture, sweetness, acidity, availability,
and growing season. Although there are far fewer varieties available today,
apples are still task specific, particularly in recipes. Some apples are best
eaten raw, some stay firm when cooked (for pie), and some collapse when
cooked (for sauce).

Local or regional apples that are grown and cherished for their flavor
and purpose are almost always preferable to commercial apples that have
declined into uniform vagueness. That's why apple connoisseurs are working to rediscover and restore apple diversity, which means that we can
look forward to more outstanding antique varieties returning to our gardens and local markets. ■

# Apples in Spiced Ginger Syrup

2 tablespoons thinly sliced fresh ginger

2 cinnamon sticks

8 whole cloves

1 tablespoon whole allspice

4 cups apple cider, preferably unfiltered

6 large very crisp apples, peeled, cored, and cut into ½-inch-thick wedges

Cooked apples are elemental food where I grew up in the mountains of North Carolina. When someone mentioned cooked fruit, it usually meant cooked apples. To this day, if you go to a little meat-and-three joint around there, cooked apples will be one of the choices of sides. Instead of the traditional technique of stewing the apples until they are soft, these are gently poached until barely tender, then refrigerated overnight in the cooking liquid. The next day, the apples are infused with the spices, so the result is somewhere between cooked apples and spiced apples. You can play with the shape of the apples. Sliced is obvious, but you can also cut them into rings or carve out little balls with a melon baller.

You can reuse the poaching liquid. Store it covered and refrigerated for up to one week. It can also be simmered until reduced and used as syrup. If you use red apples, save the peelings and simmer them in the liquid as it reduces. The peelings add flavor and give the syrup a beautiful blush. The syrup is good on pancakes, stirred into hot tea, or drizzled over good cheese to serve with the apples.

I usually use full-sized apples, but this is lovely made with a pound or two of sweet crab apples or lady apples. If you use small apples, cut them in half to remove the tiny cores but do not peel them.

MAKES 6 SERVINGS

1. Tie the ginger, cinnamon sticks, cloves, and allspice into a square of cheesecloth or place in a tea ball. Place in a large saucepan and add the cider. Bring to a simmer and cook for 15 minutes. Add the apples, bring to a boil, reduce the heat, and simmer just until the apples are tender, 15 to 20 minutes.

2. Set the apples aside to cool to room temperature in the liquid. Remove and discard the spice bag. The apples can be served now, but for best flavor cover and refrigerate in their liquid overnight. Strain the apples, saving the cooking liquid for another use. Serve the apples lightly chilled or gently reheated.

VARIATION: You can use this recipe to poach fresh quinces. Because quinces are hard as rocks, increase the cooking time to 1 to 2 hours.

## Slow Cooker Apple Butter

5 ½ pounds apples,
such as a mixture
of Rome, Granny
Smith, Cortland,
and McIntosh

3 cups sugar

4 teaspoons ground
cinnamon

¼ teaspoon
ground cloves

½ teaspoon
ground allspice

½ teaspoon
ground ginger

¼ teaspoon kosher salt

2 tablespoons balsamic
vinegar or unfiltered
organic cider vinegar

Apple butter used to be an all-day affair, simmering apples and seasonings until they collapsed into sweet, spicy preserves. Old-timers cooked gallons of the stuff in copper cauldrons or black wash pots over the coals, stirring for hours with long wooden paddles known as horse heads. Whole communities would gather for "the make." My grandmother and her friends made gallons of apple butter in the huge pots they used to seal canning jars, adding dishpan after dishpan of pared apples to the bubbling stew. Whether made by the gallon or by the quart, the key to good apple butter is low, even heat—just what you'll get from an electric slow cooker. This method is very easy and requires no stirring. Your house will smell divine, as though serious cooking has been deftly done.

Be sure to use apples that fall apart into thick sauce when cooked. A mixture of apples is almost always preferable to any one variety, because each brings its own flavor and characteristics to the pot. I've suggested apples that are available almost anywhere, but do take advantage of any heirloom apples that grow where you live. Anyone who grows heirloom apples can describe their taste and use.

When I was a little girl, I was taught this old wives' tale about apple peels. If you manage to peel an apple while keeping the peeling in one long, continuous spiral, you should drop it over your left shoulder and let it fall to the ground. The twisting, looping peel will form the first letter of the name of your true love. I can assure you, if you are a moony-eyed romantic who wants to see a particular letter, you'll see it.

MAKES ABOUT 8 CUPS

1. Have ready two 1-quart jars, four 1-pint jars, or eight half-pint jars that have been sterilized in boiling water or run through the dishwasher on the hottest cycle. The jars should have sterilized tight-fitting lids. The jars and lids do not have to stay hot, but they must stay sterile.

2. Peel, core, and thinly slice the apples. Toss them with the sugar, cinnamon, cloves, allspice, ginger, and salt.

3. Pack the mixture into a 5- or 6-quart slow cooker. Be sure that your cooker is at least two-thirds full of raw apples to ensure that they will cook properly. Likewise, don't fill the cooker so full that the lid does not sit flat on the rim.

4. Cover and cook on high for 1 hour. Reduce the heat to low and cook until the apples are completely soft and broken down, 8 to 12 hours. Remove the lid, increase the heat to high, and cook until almost all of the liquid has evaporated, about 1 hour. Stir in the vinegar.

5. Purée in a blender (working in batches to not fill the blender more than half full) or purée directly in the cooker with an immersion blender.

(6) Ladle the hot apple butter into the prepared jars and cover tightly. Set aside to cool to room temperature, and then refrigerate for up to 6 weeks.

VARIATION: To make apple and sweet potato butter, replace 2 pounds of the apples with peeled and sliced sweet potatoes. To make pear butter, substitute Kieffer pears.

## Ozark Pudding

¼ cup all-purpose flour

2 ½ teaspoons baking powder

2 large eggs

½ teaspoon kosher salt

1 ½ cups sugar

1 tart cooking apple, peeled, cored, and cut into ½-inch pieces (about 1 cup)

1 cup pecan pieces

1 teaspoon pure vanilla extract

Lightly sweetened whipped cream, for serving

This is a very simple traditional recipe, just the thing when you want to whip up something quick, easy, and comforting. It's an odd dessert that seems to be made up of parts from other desserts. The filling is gooey, like pecan pie with bits of apple. The outer edge is bubbly and chewy, like pralines. The top forms a thin, crisp crust that is like a sticky meringue or macaroon. In other words, this is not pudding-cup pudding but pudding in the English sense of the word, meaning dessert in general.

There is a strong similarity between Ozark pudding and the Huguenot tortes made around Charleston. I've read all sorts of stories about the provenance of this dessert. One account says that Bess Truman invented it to cheer up homesick Harry in the White House. Another tale reports that French Huguenots fleeing persecution brought this recipe over. Another story is that a Charleston cook tasted Ozark pudding on a trip to the Midwest, brought the recipe home, and prepared it to serve in the Huguenot tavern where she worked. No matter which version you believe, it's obvious that good recipes get around.

MAKES 6 TO 8 SERVINGS

(1) Preheat the oven to 325°F. Butter a 9-inch square baking dish.

(2) Whisk together the flour and baking powder in a small bowl. In a large bowl, whisk the eggs and salt until blended and frothy. While whisking vigorously, slowly add the sugar and whisk until thick. Stir in the apples, pecans, and vanilla. Stir in the flour mixture, stirring well to incorporate the dry ingredients.

(3) Scrape the batter into the prepared dish and smooth the top. Bake until the top crust is browned and the filling is bubbly around the edges, about 40 minutes. Let cool at least 10 minutes before serving hot or at room temperature with the whipped cream.

## Apple and Fennel Slaw

- ¼ cup mayonnaise
- 1 tablespoon honey
- 2 teaspoons fresh lime or lemon juice
- 2 teaspoons whole-grain Dijon mustard
- Kosher salt and ground black pepper, to taste
- 2 small fennel bulbs, cored, halved lengthwise, and thinly sliced (about 2 cups)
- 1 small tart green apple, cored and cut into matchsticks (about 1 cup)
- 1 small sweet red apple, cored and cut into matchsticks (about 1 cup)
- 2 tablespoons chopped scallions (white and tender green parts)
- ½ cup pecan pieces, toasted

This colorful slaw combines sweet apple, tart apple, aromatic fennel, and crunchy pecans. The slaw is lightly coated with honey and lime dressing, so it is simple, yet very flavorful. This is fantastic with sandwiches, such as ham or rich grilled cheese.

MAKES 4 TO 6 SERVINGS

1. Whisk together the mayonnaise, honey, lime juice, and mustard in a large bowl. Season with salt and pepper.
2. Add the fennel, apples, scallions, and pecans and toss to coat with the mayonnaise mixture. Season with salt and pepper. Let sit at least 10 minutes to give the flavors time to blend, stirring occasionally.

VARIATION: To turn this slaw into a simple salad, toss the fennel, apples, scallions, and pecans with 4 cups of leafy greens and dress with Apple Cider Vinaigrette (recipe follows). You can also add crisp bacon, slivers of country ham, or grilled chicken.

WHAT ELSE WORKS? You can replace the fennel with finely shredded red cabbage or grated celery root.

## Apple Cider Vinaigrette

- 2 cups unfiltered apple cider
- ¼ cup unfiltered organic cider vinegar
- 6 tablespoons extra-virgin olive oil
- 2 teaspoons honey
- 1 teaspoon kosher salt
- ½ teaspoon ground black pepper

1. Simmer the apple cider in a saucepan over medium heat until reduced to ¾ cup. Pour into a glass jar with a tight-fitting lid. Add the vinegar, oil, honey, salt, and pepper and shake vigorously to combine.
2. Use soon or cover and refrigerate for up to 1 week. Return to room temperature, shake vigorously, and check the seasoning before serving.

## Skillet Apples

6 small firm apples

3 tablespoons bacon drippings or butter

2 to 6 tablespoons sugar

This is what many southerners call fried apples, but they are not deep-fried (not that there's anything wrong with that). Traditional southern recipes often used the word "fried" to mean anything cooked in a skillet in a bit, or a lot, of fat. Fried apples are usually breakfast food, so they are often cooked in the drippings du jour left in the skillet from frying the breakfast meat, such as bacon, country ham, or sausage. They are also delicious in butter. Most people add a little sugar. My grandmother's aunt seasoned her fried apples with sugar, salt, and a pinch of hot pepper. (She also swabbed the inside of her lower lip with a birch twig brush dipped in snuff and cursed like a sailor back when few folks uttered so much as an expletive.)

Small, firm apples work best. I'm partial to puckery-sour green apples, but I'm also happy with old-fashioned sweet yellow transparents. Avoid apples that are mealy or ruined by commercial success. Cook them slowly to coax out their natural juices.

These apples cry out for hot biscuits (page 393 or 394).

MAKES 4 TO 6 SERVINGS

1. Peel the apples only if they are blemished. Cut the apples into quarters, remove the cores, and cut each wedge into 3 or 4 slices.

2. Heat the fat in a large, heavy skillet (preferably cast-iron) over medium heat. Add the apples and stir to coat. Cover the skillet and cook, stirring once or twice, until the apples begin to soften, about 5 minutes. Taste a slice and add sugar as needed. Stir gently to coat the apples and continue cooking until the apples are tender and the juices thicken into syrup, 5 to 8 minutes more. The outsides of the apples should be warm and sticky, but the insides should remain a little firm. Serve warm.

# Apple, Chestnut, and Cornbread Dressing

8 tablespoons (1 stick) butter

2 medium onions, chopped (about 2 cups)

2 celery stalks, thinly sliced (about 1 cup)

1 sweet apple, cored and cut into ½-inch dice (about 1 cup)

1 tart apple, cored and cut into ½-inch dice (about 1 cup)

2 tablespoons chopped fresh thyme

1 tablespoon chopped fresh sage

3 tablespoons finely chopped flat-leaf parsley

1 cup roasted or steamed chestnuts, crumbled

4 cups 1-inch cubes Italian or French bread

4 cups crumbled cornbread (page 391)

2 large eggs

1 ½ to 2 cups turkey or chicken stock, warmed

1 teaspoon kosher salt, or to taste

½ teaspoon ground black pepper, or to taste

This is my house dressing, a certainty at Thanksgiving and a good idea to serve at other times with roasted chicken, game birds, or pork. I call this dressing because I bake it in a dish instead of inside a bird or butterflied chop, which would make it stuffing. If someone in your family expects stuffed turkey for Thanksgiving, then lightly pack some into the bird and bake the rest in a dish, an approach that satisfies the innies and the outies. My advice is that if there is a specific food or practice that defines a holiday for a loved one, even if it's some cockamamy thing from *that* side of the family, just put it on the table and keep your opinions to yourself.

Chestnuts are native to North America and once flourished in our forests and served as a major source of food for Native Americans and frontiersmen. A devastating blight that began in 1904 nearly wiped out the native trees, so most chestnuts we have now come from European or Asian rootstock. It's fine to use jarred or packaged chestnuts that are already cooked and peeled, but if you want to roast your own, follow the directions on page 60.

MAKES 12 SERVINGS

1. Preheat the oven to 350°F. Generously butter a 9 × 13-inch baking dish.

2. Melt the butter in a large skillet over medium-high heat. Add the onions and celery and a pinch of salt and cook, stirring often, until the vegetables begin to soften, about 10 minutes. Stir in the apples and cook, stirring often, until softened, about 3 minutes. Stir in the thyme, sage, parsley, and chestnuts and cook, stirring often, for 2 minutes. Transfer into a large bowl. Stir in the bread and cornbread.

3. Whisk the eggs in a small bowl until the whites and yolks are blended, then stir into the bread mixture.

4. Stir in enough warm stock to make the dressing quite moist but not so much that there is standing liquid in the bottom of the bowl. Season with the salt and pepper.

5. Spoon the stuffing into the prepared baking dish, cover with aluminum foil, and bake for 20 minutes. Remove the foil and bake until the stuffing is hot and lightly browned on top, about 25 minutes longer. Serve warm.

MAKE-AHEAD NOTE: You can prepare the stuffing up through Step 4 up to 1 day ahead. Cover with foil and refrigerate. Bake just before serving.

# Fresh Apple Cake with Caramel Glaze

3 cups unbleached
all-purpose flour

1 teaspoon baking soda

2 teaspoons ground
cinnamon

½ teaspoon freshly
grated nutmeg

½ teaspoon fine sea salt

1 cup firmly packed
light brown sugar

1 cup granulated sugar

1 ½ cups vegetable oil

3 large eggs

5 cups peeled,
cored, and diced
baking apples

1 ¼ cups black walnuts
or English walnuts,
coarsely chopped

2 teaspoons pure
vanilla extract

### GLAZE

4 tablespoons (½ stick)
unsalted butter

¼ cup firmly packed
light brown sugar

¼ cup granulated sugar

Pinch of kosher salt

½ cup heavy cream

My family has been making this cake for more than fifty years, a recipe that proves that a stunning cake doesn't have to be made in layers. This is one of those old-fashioned oil-based cakes, so it's very moist. There is barely enough batter to hold the apples and nuts together. The warm cake is poked and bathed in a sticky caramel glaze that firms up into something like toffee as it cools. It's simply fantastic.

MAKES 12 SERVINGS (IN THEORY)

1. For the cake: Position a rack in the center of the oven and preheat the oven to 325°F. Grease a 9 × 13-inch light metal baking pan. (A dark metal or nonstick pan will make the crust very dark and thick.)

2. Sift together the flour, soda, cinnamon, nutmeg, and salt into a medium bowl.

3. Beat the brown sugar, granulated sugar, and oil until smooth in a large bowl with an electric mixer. Add the eggs, one at a time, beating well after each addition. With the mixer set to low speed, slowly add the flour mixture, beating only until it disappears into the batter. Use a rubber spatula to fold in the apples, nuts, and vanilla. Scrape the batter into the prepared pan.

4. Bake in the center of the oven until a toothpick inserted into the center of the cake comes out clean, 1 hour to 1 hour and 15 minutes. Place the pan on a wire rack while you make the glaze.

5. For the glaze: Melt the butter in a heavy saucepan over medium heat. Add the brown sugar, granulated sugar, and salt. Stir until blended and cook over medium heat for 2 minutes. Stir in the cream and bring to a boil over medium-high heat. Boil until the glaze begins to thicken, about 5 minutes, stirring constantly.

6. Poke holes all over the cake with a wooden skewer or chopstick. Slowly pour the glaze evenly over the cake, letting it seep down into the holes. Let the cake cool to room temperature before serving.

# ASPARAGUS

**Asparagus is native to the Mediterranean.** Imported by early colonists, asparagus growing in beds is described in records from Virginia as early as 1737. Sometimes asparagus escaped the kitchen garden and ran wild along sandy riverbanks and seashores. In some rural areas, the word was corrupted into "sparrow grass," "spare grass," or "sparrow guts."

Almost all eighteenth-century cookbooks advised serving asparagus with toast, butter, and lemon, a combination that remains popular now. Thomas Jefferson recorded harvesting asparagus multiple times at Monticello. He described eating it battered and deep-fried and also in "the French way," presumably in vinaigrette. How to cook asparagus is often discussed more passionately than how to grow it. Even the earliest cookbooks promoted the idea of gently cooking asparagus. As one book put it, "by overboiling they will lose their heads."

Some cooks figure that thin spears are younger and more tender than thick spears, but that's not necessarily true. Some varieties of asparagus are always thin and some are always thick. The key to succulence and good flavor is freshness. Asparagus should be cooked as soon as possible after it is cut, while the heads remain tightly closed and the ends are moist. The difference between green and white asparagus is in how it is raised. White asparagus grows covered by earth or thick tarps that block sunlight so that green chlorophyll cannot form in the plant. The white spears must be peeled, but their tender interiors and subtle flavor make the time and effort worthwhile. ■

## Blasted Asparagus

1 ½ pounds asparagus spears

1 tablespoon extra-virgin olive oil

Kosher salt and ground black pepper, to taste

This is the easiest way to cook asparagus. It's fast, too. The dry, searing heat preserves the flavor and nutrients. This hot, crisp asparagus is fantastic served with a spoonful of Romesco Sauce (page 320) or Roasted Garlic Mayonnaise (page 148).

MAKES 4 TO 6 SERVINGS

1. Preheat the oven to 475°F.
2. Snap off and discard the tough ends of the asparagus. Arrange the spears in a single layer on a rimmed baking sheet. Drizzle with the oil and roll the spears back and forth to coat. Sprinkle with salt and pepper.
3. Roast until crisp-tender and browned in spots, about 5 minutes, depending on the thickness of the spears. Serve hot or at room temperature.

VARIATION: You can also grill the spears over medium-high heat. To keep them from falling through the grate, place them in a vegetable basket or on a mesh grilling screen. Lightly brush with oil and grill, turning and rolling with tongs as needed, until they are crisp-tender, about 5 minutes, depending on the thickness of the spears. It's fine if the tips get a little charred. For an extra treat, cut a couple of lemons in half. Place them on the edge of the grill, cut-side down, until they get a little smoky and show grill marks. Squeeze the warm lemons over the asparagus (or any grilled vegetable) just before serving.

WHAT ELSE WORKS? You can replace the asparagus with whole tender green beans. You can also use ramp bulbs, scallions, or baby leeks; increase the roasting time to 10 to 15 minutes.

## Skillet Asparagus

1 to 1 ½ pounds asparagus spears

2 tablespoons vegetable or extra-virgin olive oil

Coarse or kosher salt, to taste

I'm not a fan of cooking asparagus in water because this method often makes the asparagus spongy and dilutes the flavor. In this recipe, the flavor is concentrated as it cooks slowly in a skillet. This recipe makes enough for four people, but an asparagus devotee could easily finish off the whole pan, using her fingers instead of a fork.

MAKES 4 SERVINGS

1. Snap off and discard the tough ends of the asparagus. Cut the spears into bite-sized lengths.
2. Heat the oil in a large, heavy skillet (preferably cast-iron) over medium heat. Add the asparagus and stir to coat. Cook, stirring often, until the asparagus is quite tender and browned in spots, 15 to 25 minutes. Sprinkle with salt and serve warm or at room temperature.

WHAT ELSE WORKS? You can replace some or all of the asparagus with fiddle-heads, the newly emerged, tender, tightly furled shoots of the edible ostrich fern. Fiddleheads got their name because their coiled shape looks like the scroll of a fiddle. Fiddleheads should be no larger than a half dollar. Rub off the scaly green or brown chaff. Cook them in boiling, salted water for 20 seconds and immediately transfer into a bowl of ice water to stop the cooking and set the color. Drain and pat dry. Cook in the hot oil over medium heat, stirring often, until barely tender, about 5 minutes. Season with salt and pepper and serve warm. You can use fiddleheads in other recipes that call for young asparagus.

## Asparagus with Wild Mushroom Ravioli, Browned Butter, and Walnuts

Smart, time-strapped cooks recognize when it's time to take advantage of high-quality packaged products that make recipes come together quickly. Here, fresh asparagus is cooked in the same pot as packaged ravioli and then is tossed with nutty, aromatic browned butter. In about fifteen minutes, this elegant, delicate dish is ready to serve.

MAKES 4 SERVINGS

| | |
|---|---|
| 1 ½ | pounds asparagus spears |
| 12 to 16 | ounces fresh or frozen wild mushroom ravioli |
| 4 | tablespoons (½ stick) unsalted butter |
| ½ | cup coarsely chopped walnuts |
| 2 | garlic cloves, finely chopped |
| | Kosher salt and ground black pepper, to taste |
| ¼ | cup crumbled goat cheese or coarsely grated Parmesan cheese, for serving |

1. Snap off and discard the tough ends of the asparagus. Cut the spears into bite-sized lengths.
2. Cook the ravioli according to package directions. When the ravioli are 5 minutes short of the recommended cooking time, add the asparagus to the pot and continue cooking until both are done. Drain.
3. Melt the butter in a large skillet over medium-low heat. When the butter is no longer foamy, add the walnuts and cook, gently swirling the pan, until the butter is golden brown and smells like toast, about 3 minutes. Add the garlic and cook for 30 seconds.
4. Stir in the asparagus and ravioli and heat through. Season with salt and pepper and serve hot, sprinkled with the cheese.

# Raw Asparagus and Fresh Orange Salad with Orange Vinaigrette

1 teaspoon finely grated orange zest

2 tablespoons fresh orange juice

2 tablespoons white wine vinegar

1 shallot, finely chopped

1 teaspoon honey

½ teaspoon kosher salt, or to taste

¼ teaspoon ground black pepper, or to taste

¼ cup extra-virgin olive oil

2 tablespoons walnut oil

SALAD

8 ounces thick asparagus spears

2 seedless oranges

¼ cup chopped scallions (white and tender green parts)

4 cups watercress (about 3 ounces)

1 small piece of Pecorino Romano cheese (about 2 ounces)

⅔ cup walnut pieces, toasted

During a segue of seasons, when some things are winding down and others are just cranking up, it's a great time to create a recipe that uses ingredients from both seasons. This one features winter citrus and spring asparagus. The asparagus isn't cooked, so the salad must be made with freshly cut asparagus that is very tender without one bit of woody interior or wrinkled skin. The asparagus is shaved lengthwise into ribbons, which makes this a very pretty and very unusual salad.

MAKES 4 SERVINGS

1. For the vinaigrette: Whisk together the orange zest, orange juice, vinegar, shallot, honey, salt, and pepper in a small bowl. Let sit for 5 minutes. Whisk in the olive oil and walnut oil. Whisk again before using.

2. For the salad: Snap off and discard the tough ends of the asparagus. Working with one spear at a time, place it on a cutting board. Starting at the tip, use a sharp vegetable peeler to shave the asparagus lengthwise into long, thin ribbons. You'll get 4 or 5 slices from each spear. Transfer the ribbons into a large bowl, moisten with some of the Orange Vinaigrette, and let stand until the asparagus is slightly wilted, about 5 minutes.

3. Use a serrated knife to peel the oranges, following the contour of the fruit to preserve the shape while removing all the bitter white pith. Working over the bowl of asparagus, cut in between the membranes to release the sections and the dripping juice into the bowl.

4. In a large bowl, toss the scallions and watercress with enough of the remaining Orange Vinaigrette to moisten. Divide among serving plates and top with equal portions of the asparagus and oranges. Use a vegetable peeler to shave curls of cheese over the salads and sprinkle with the walnuts. Serve at once, with any remaining Orange Vinaigrette on the side.

WHAT ELSE WORKS? You can replace the watercress with other peppery spring salad greens, such as arugula, mâche, or dandelions. You can also replace the oranges with other types of citrus, such as tangerines, clementines, blood oranges, or Meyer lemons.

## Asparagus in Crisp Ham
## with Lemony Deviled Eggs

24 thick asparagus
   spears (about
   1 pound)

12 paper-thin slices
   of country ham,
   prosciutto, speck,
   or Serrano ham

2 teaspoons extra-
  virgin olive oil

  Lemony Deviled
  Eggs (recipe follows)

  Zest of 1 lemon cut
  into very thin strips

  Kosher salt and
  ground black
  pepper, to taste

This classic combination of asparagus, hard-cooked eggs, and lemon is a tribute to asparagus mimosa. The components can also stand alone, served separately. Country ham is my first choice for this recipe, but it can be difficult to buy country ham sliced into paper-thin sheets, so I often turn to prosciutto, speck, or Serrano ham because they are similar in texture. Large asparagus spears are easiest to wrap, but if you have very slender spears, just wrap up two together.

MAKES 4 SERVINGS

1. Preheat the oven to 475°F.
2. Snap off and discard the tough ends of the asparagus. Cut the ham slices in half crosswise. Wrap a slice of ham around the center of each spear, like a wide belt. Arrange the wrapped spears in a single layer on a foil-lined rimmed baking sheet. Brush with the oil.
3. Roast until the ham is crispy and the asparagus is barely tender, 8 to 10 minutes. Divide the asparagus and eggs among 4 serving plates or arrange on a platter. Sprinkle with the lemon zest, salt, and pepper. Serve warm.

VARIATION: You can serve the asparagus with eggs fried in butter or poached eggs topped with butter. Squeeze a few drops of fresh lemon juice over the finished dish, particularly if the yolks are soft. When the lemon mixes with the yolks and butter, it tastes like hollandaise.

## Lemony Deviled Eggs

6 large eggs

½ cup mayonnaise,
  preferably homemade
  (page 317)

4 tablespoons (½ stick)
  butter, at room
  temperature

2 teaspoons fresh
  lemon juice

½ teaspoon finely
  grated lemon zest

¼ teaspoon dry mustard

  Kosher salt and ground
  white pepper, to taste

  Paprika, for dusting

As a southerner, I consider good deviled eggs to be essential. There are many deviled egg recipes, but this is my favorite of all. (Other than my daughter's, but she's not sharing her secret recipe. When she was only five, deviled eggs were the first food she made all by herself. I love that kid.) Light, airy sieved yolks make the filling incomparably smooth and creamy. Don't skip that step.

It's a southern tradition to dust deviled eggs with paprika. Alas, some cooks have used the same tin of paprika since the war. Fresh paprika has bright flavor and pungent aroma. If yours has neither, buy new.

MAKES 12 HALVES

1. Place the eggs in a single layer in a large saucepan and cover with cold water. Bring to a boil over high heat. As soon as the water begins to boil, remove the pan from the heat, cover, and let sit for 12 minutes.
2. Immediately pour off the hot water, fill the pan with cold water, add a handful of ice cubes, and set aside until cool enough to handle. Peel the eggs and cut in

half lengthwise. Remove the yolks and use a spatula or your fingertips to rub them through a fine-mesh strainer into a medium bowl. Add the mayonnaise and butter; mix gently until smooth. Stir in the lemon juice, lemon zest, and mustard. Season with salt and white pepper. The flavors dull slightly when the eggs are chilled, so be a little bold with the seasoning.

③ Spoon or pipe the filling into the egg whites, sprinkle with paprika, and chill until ready to serve.

### TIPS AND TECHNIQUES

Boiled eggs aren't actually boiled. The secret to hard-cooked eggs that are not rubbery and have no green ring around the yolk is to cook them gently in very hot water rather than let them bounce around at a rolling boil.

Eggs that are at least one week old are more likely to peel easily and cleanly. As the eggs age, their liquid interior evaporates enough to create a wee bit of air space between the egg and the shell. An old-fashioned way to determine the freshness of an egg is submerge a whole uncooked egg in a bowl of water. If it lies flat on its side on the bottom of the bowl, it's fresh. If it stands upright, it's a little older and a good candidate for hard cooking. If it floats, it's a very old egg and should be discarded.

## Roast Beef, Boursin, and Asparagus Bundles

24 slender asparagus spears

1 large red, orange, or yellow bell pepper

24 thin slices of premium deli roast beef

10 ounces Boursin herbed cheese, at room temperature

1 tablespoon finely chopped chives, to garnish

I cannot guess how many of these I've rolled up for Quick and Easy Party Food classes. These tasty bundles are light yet filling, so they make great heavy hors d'oeuvres that can be formal or quite casual, depending on the serving piece.

Success lies in the roast beef. It should be the highest quality deli roast beef, never that slick pressed and formed stuff. The roasted eye of round carried at high-end markets and delis is ideal. The slices should be thin but not so flimsy that they shred when you try to pick them up. Slices the thickness of a nickel work great.

MAKES 2 DOZEN

① Trim the asparagus spears to about 5 inches long. Fill a large bowl with ice water. Bring a large saucepan of water to a boil. Add ½ teaspoon kosher salt per cup of water. Add the asparagus. Cook until crisp-tender, about 2 minutes. Use a slotted spoon or strainer to immediately transfer the asparagus into the ice water to stop the cooking and set the bright green color. Drain and pat dry with paper towels.

(2) Cut off the top and bottom of the pepper. Set the pepper upright on the cutting board. Looking down from the top, cut the sides of the pepper away from the core. You should have 3 or 4 large, flat pieces of pepper. Trim away any remaining ribs. Cut the flat pieces into a total of 24 long, thin strips about ¼-inch wide. This is easiest if the pieces of pepper are skin-side down. Finely dice any remaining pepper, including the trimmed top and bottom, to use as garnish.

(3) The slices of beef should be no more than about 4 ½-inches wide so that the tips of the vegetables are exposed when rolled, so trim the slices if necessary.

(4) It's easier and less messy to assemble these in batches instead of one at a time. Arrange 12 slices of beef on a work surface. Use your fingers to spread about 2 rounded teaspoons of Boursin down the center of each slice. Place 1 asparagus spear and 1 pepper strip on top of the Boursin, letting the tips stick out past the beef so that they'll show. Gently roll up each slice into a small, tight bundle, like a little log. Repeat with the remaining beef, Boursin, and vegetables.

(5) Arrange the bundles on a serving platter. To garnish, sprinkle with the chives and the finely diced pepper. Serve lightly chilled or at room temperature.

WHAT ELSE WORKS? You can replace the asparagus with blanched slender green beans (fillet beans) or wax beans. For a meatless variation, wrap the asparagus and Boursin in wide pieces of roasted red pepper.

MAKE-AHEAD NOTE: You can make the bundles up to 1 day ahead. Store in an airtight container in the refrigerator.

# BEETS

**Beets are an ancient food that can be traced back** to a wild seashore
plant that eventually grew in wide swathes over the Northern Hemi-
sphere. Beets came over with settlers who were accustomed to relying on
root vegetables as a source of food, fodder, and sugar. Perhaps sugar beets
never held the appeal in the South that they did in the North because
most southerners had relatively ready access to cane sugar, sorghum,
and other sweeteners.

Southerners usually favored the beet greens and chard over the roots.
Appreciation for the roots has come slowly, but as more cooks discover
that fresh beets are easy to cook, they are more popular than ever. Beets
have an earthy sweetness like no other vegetable, especially when roasted.
Beet and pickle lovers alike sing the praises of beets pickled in sweet,
tangy brine the color of fine red wine. We're seeing more beet variety in
our gardens and markets, with yellow, orange, white, and striped beets becoming almost as common as the red ones. Unless their brilliant magenta
color is important to a dish, beets of any color can be used interchangeably
with the red ones. ■

# Lentil Salad with Beets

1 pound small to medium beets, peeled and cut into ½-inch cubes

1 tablespoon extra-virgin olive oil

5 tablespoons sherry vinegar or red wine vinegar, divided

1 ¼ cups French green lentils (about 8 ounces)

1 small onion, quartered

1 bay leaf

4 small thyme sprigs

3 thick bacon slices, cut crosswise into ¼-inch strips (about 3 ounces)

1 cup chopped leeks (white and tender green parts)

½ cup finely chopped celery

1 cup finely chopped carrot

2 teaspoons chopped fresh thyme

2 teaspoons walnut mustard or Dijon mustard

½ cup chopped walnuts, lightly toasted

1 to 2 tablespoons walnut oil or additional olive oil

Kosher salt and ground black pepper, to taste

4 ounces cubed semi-aged goat cheese (such as Bucheron) or crumbled soft, fresh goat cheese (chèvre)

This salad is made with French green lentils (*lentilles du Puy*), which stay firm when cooked. Lentils are rather drab, but cubes of colorful roasted beet and pieces of white goat cheese make this salad pretty. If the greens are still attached to your beets, cut them into thin strips and cook them along with the leeks, celery, and carrot.

Because the beets are peeled before they are roasted, your hands will not be stained by peeling them.

MAKES 4 TO 6 SERVINGS

1. Preheat the oven to 375°F.

2. Place the beets on a rimmed baking sheet lined with aluminum foil. Drizzle with the olive oil and season with a little salt and pepper. Cover with aluminum foil and roast for 20 minutes. Uncover and continue roasting until the beets are tender, about 30 minutes more. Transfer to a plate, sprinkle with 1 tablespoon of the vinegar, and set aside to cool.

3. Put the lentils into a medium saucepan and cover with cold water by 2 inches. Add the onion, bay leaf, and thyme sprigs. Bring just to a boil, reduce the heat, and simmer gently until barely tender, about 25 minutes.

4. Meanwhile, cook the bacon in a large skillet over medium heat, stirring often, until crisp, about 15 minutes. Transfer with a slotted spoon to paper towels to drain.

5. Stir the leeks, celery, and carrot and a pinch of salt into the bacon drippings. Cook, stirring often, until the vegetables are tender, about 8 minutes. Add 2 tablespoons of the vinegar and stir to scrape up the browned bits from the bottom of the skillet. Keep warm over very low heat.

6. Drain the lentils and discard the onion, bay leaf, and thyme stems. Add the lentils to the skillet and stir gently to coat. Stir in the remaining 2 tablespoons of vinegar, the thyme, and the mustard. Stir in the bacon, beets, and walnuts. Stir in enough walnut oil to moisten. Season with salt and pepper. Sprinkle the cheese over the top and serve warm or at room temperature.

WHAT ELSE WORKS? You can replace some or all of the beets with cubes of roasted sweet potato. Follow the directions on page 329 to roast the potatoes.

## Russian Salad

2 small beets, peeled and cut into ½-inch cubes (about 1 cup)

6 small waxy potatoes, scrubbed and cut into ½-inch cubes (about 3 cups)

2 small carrots, peeled and cut into ½-inch cubes (about 1 cup)

1 cup shelled garden peas

½ cup mayonnaise

1 garlic clove, finely chopped

2 tablespoons lemon juice

½ teaspoon Worcestershire sauce

¼ teaspoon hot sauce, or to taste

3 tablespoons finely chopped cornichons or dill gherkins

1 teaspoon kosher salt, plus more to taste

½ teaspoon ground black pepper, plus more to taste

This salad is to Italy what potato salad is to the South. It's everywhere in Italy during hot weather, sold in takeout deli cups and spooned onto plates to accompany sandwiches and grilled meats. (No one could tell me why this Italian favorite is called Russian salad.) Like any potato salad, there are countless versions of Russian salad, but all of them feature very small, uniform cubes of vegetables instead of chunks. Any variety of beets will work, but the red ones will turn the salad a striking shade of magenta, which I rather like. Be sure to use a waxy potato that will hold its shape when cooked, such as Yukon Gold, Finn, Red Bliss, or Rose Gold.

MAKES 4 TO 6 SERVINGS

1. Place the beets in the bottom of a steamer basket and then layer on (in order) the potatoes, carrots, and peas. Place the basket over a large saucepan of boiling water, cover, and cook until the vegetables are just tender when pierced with the tip of a knife, 8 to 10 minutes. Spread the vegetables on a baking sheet to cool until there is no longer steam rising from them.

2. Meanwhile, whisk together the mayonnaise, garlic, lemon juice, Worcestershire, hot sauce, cornichons, salt, and pepper in a large bowl.

3. Add the vegetables to the dressing and stir gently to coat. Season with salt and pepper. Serve at room temperature or lightly chilled.

## Quick Pickled Beets

1 pound small to medium beets, all but ¼ inch of their greens trimmed away

1 cup distilled white vinegar

½ cup water

½ cup sugar

1 teaspoon pickling salt

1 tablespoon pickling spice

At my grandmother's house, most every night for supper, and certainly for Sunday dinner, there were jars of pickles and preserves huddled in the middle of the table, next to the vinegar cruet and salt and pepper shakers. The prettiest pickles were the brilliant red pickled beets that sparkled in the jar like rubies. Although red is traditional, you can pickle beets of any color. I love the look of the Chioggia beets, the ones that look like a bull's-eye when cut into thin slices.

It is traditional to use pickling salt in brine because it dissolves quickly in liquid and does not contain iodine, which can discolor preserved vegetables. You can substitute another iodine-free salt.

MAKES 4 CUPS

(1) Have ready a 1-quart jar that has been sterilized in boiling water or run through the dishwasher on the hottest cycle. The jar should have a sterilized tight-fitting lid. The jar and lid do not have to stay hot, but they must stay sterile.

(2) Simmer the beets in a large saucepan of water until tender, about 30 minutes, depending on their size and freshness. Drain and rinse under cold running water until cool enough to handle. Peel and trim the beets. Leave very small beets whole or cut them in half. Cut larger beets into ¼-inch slices or thin wedges. Put the beets into the prepared jar.

(3) Stir together the vinegar, water, sugar, pickling salt, and pickling spice in a small saucepan. Bring to a boil, reduce the heat, and simmer for 15 minutes, stirring until the sugar dissolves. Pour the hot brine over the beets, making sure they are submerged. Let sit undisturbed until they cool to room temperature. Cover the jars tightly and refrigerate for at least 2 days before serving. They will keep in the refrigerator for up to 1 month.

VARIATION: Seasoning cooked beets with ginger is an old southern custom. To make Ginger Pickled Beets, make the brine from ½ cup thinly sliced fresh ginger, 1 ½ cups rice wine vinegar, ½ cup sugar, and 1 teaspoon pickling salt.

WHAT ELSE WORKS? You can replace the beets with carrot sticks, radishes, or Japanese turnips. Depending on their size, leave the round vegetables whole or cut them into bite-sized wedges. Blanch very hard vegetables for 2 minutes before adding them to the brine.

## Red Pickled Beet Eggs

I have always loved pickled beets, but as a child I loathed the eggs that were pickled in the beet brine, especially around Easter time when production revved up to a fever pitch. Perhaps I begrudged those pickled eggs because it was the cruel fate of my Easter eggs come Monday morning. The magenta brine turned the egg whites deep pink, but the yolks stayed bright yellow, creating an egg that would give Dr. Seuss pause. For a real conversation starter, use pickled eggs to make your favorite deviled eggs. To paraphrase a familiar poem:

Gather ye eggs while ye may,
Beet brine is still a-flying:
And this same egg that hides today
To-morrow will be dyeing.

To make pickled eggs, submerge whole, peeled, hard-cooked eggs in red pickled beet brine. (See page 24 for tips on hard-cooking eggs.) Cover and refrigerate for at least 1 day and up to 1 week.

## Roasted Beets with Sour Cream, Horseradish, and Sumac

4 to 6   medium beets, all but ¼ inch of their greens trimmed away (about 2 pounds total)

1   tablespoon vegetable oil

¾   cup sour cream

¼   cup freshly grated or drained prepared horseradish

1   tablespoon fresh lemon juice

2   tablespoons chopped fresh dill or chives

1 to 2   tablespoons ground dried sumac

Kosher salt and ground black pepper, to taste

In this recipe, I'm treating beets like baking potatoes by roasting them until tender, splitting them open, and spooning in sour cream spiked with horseradish and herbs. This is a fantastic side dish for steaks, brisket, or pot roast; the combination of beets, sour cream, and beef tastes like borscht.

It might seem odd to see ground sumac in a southern recipe, but it's been used in the Appalachians forever, starting with the Native Americans. Sumac tastes like lemon, a flavor found in practically nothing else in that region, so it's what mountain cooks used to add the tang of citrus to a recipe. It was most commonly used on fresh trout and in a drink that looks and tastes remarkably like pink lemonade. In this recipe, the cherry-red sumac is gorgeous with the green herbs atop the snow-white sour cream. You can find ground sumac in well-stocked grocery stores and Mediterranean markets. Do not pick wild sumac berries unless you are an expert in wildcrafting.

MAKES 4 TO 6 SERVINGS

1. Preheat the oven to 400°F.
2. Rub the beets with the oil and set them in a medium baking dish. Cover the dish tightly with aluminum foil. Roast until tender when pierced with the tip of a knife, 45 minutes to 1 hour 15 minutes, depending on the size of the beets. Remove the foil and let the beets cool enough to handle. Trim the greens and rootlets from the beets and slip off their skins.
3. Whisk together the sour cream, horseradish, lemon juice, and dill in a small bowl.
4. Cut the warm beets in half or into large wedges. Top with the horseradish mixture, sprinkle with the sumac, salt, and pepper, and serve warm.

# Salmon and Roasted Beet Salad with Creamy Herb Dressing

1 pound small beets, all but ¼ inch of their greens trimmed away

½ small red onion, halved lengthwise and cut into thin strips (about ½ cup)

8 ounces snow peas or sugar snaps, tough strings removed (about 1 ½ cups)

6 cups bite-sized pieces of romaine lettuce

Creamy Herb Dressing (recipe follows)

1 crisp apple, cored and thinly sliced (about 1 cup)

1 pound cooked salmon, skinned and broken into large pieces

This is one gorgeous entrée salad. You can swap ingredients to take advantage of seasonal availability, but the combination of sweet beets, tart apples, and fantastic dressing should stay put. In the spring, when the first small beets come in, I use snow peas or sugar snaps in the salad. In the fall, when the second harvest of beets comes around, I replace the peas with cubes of roasted sweet potato. The cooked salmon can be grilled, roasted, poached, or smoked.

MAKES 4 TO 6 SERVINGS

1. Preheat the oven to 400°F.
2. Place the beets in a single layer on a double thickness of aluminum foil. Fold the foil around the beets to make a snug pouch. Roast the beets until they are tender when pierced with the tip of a knife, 45 minutes to 1 hour. Open the foil pouch and let the beets cool enough to handle. Trim off the greens and rootlets and slip off the skins. Cut the beets into thin slices or wedges.
3. Fill a medium bowl with ice water. Add the onion and let sit until needed. The ice water will leach out some of the strong, eye-watering aroma, leaving milder, pure onion flavor.
4. Bring a medium saucepan of water to a boil. Add ½ teaspoon kosher salt per cup of water. Add the peas. Cook until crisp-tender, about 2 minutes. Use a slotted spoon to immediately transfer into the bowl of ice water (with the onions) to stop the cooking and set the color. Drain the peas and onions and pat them dry with paper towels.
5. Place the romaine in a large bowl, drizzle with enough dressing to moisten, and toss well to coat. Divide the romaine among serving plates or arrange on a serving platter. Top with the beets, apple, peas, onion, and salmon. Drizzle with a little more dressing and serve at once with any remaining dressing on the side.

WHAT ELSE WORKS? You can replace the peas with cubes of roasted sweet potato (page 329).

## Creamy Herb Dressing

1 cup plain yogurt

½ cup sour cream

¼ cup fresh lemon juice

½ cup chopped
flat-leaf parsley

2 tablespoons
chopped fresh dill

2 tablespoons
chopped fresh chives

2 tablespoons
chopped fresh basil

3 garlic cloves, chopped

1 tablespoon whole-
grain Dijon mustard

1 ½ teaspoons drained
and finely chopped
anchovies or
anchovy paste

⅓ cup extra-
virgin olive oil

1 teaspoon kosher
salt, or to taste

½ teaspoon ground
black pepper, or
to taste

The star of this recipe is the dressing: creamy, herby, and versatile. This bright green concoction has become my house dressing. Clearly it's great on salad, but it also works as a dip, sandwich spread, or binder for chicken salad, tuna salad, or potato salad. It's easy, too; just dump the ingredients in the blender and give it a whir.

This is similar to what used to be called Green Goddess, a dressing that has been around since the 1920s although few people recognize it by name anymore. It was among the most popular creamy dressings in the days before Ranch, and it's time to bring it back.

MAKES ABOUT 2 CUPS

1. Place (in the order listed) the yogurt, sour cream, lemon juice, parsley, dill, chives, basil, garlic, mustard, and anchovy in a blender. Blend until the herbs are very finely chopped. With the blender running, add the oil in a slow, steady stream. Season with the salt and pepper.

2. Use soon or cover and refrigerate for up to 5 days. Return to room temperature, stir well, and check the seasoning before serving.

# Winter Beet Salad

1 pound baby beets, preferably a mix of golden, Chioggia, and red, all but ¼ inch of their greens trimmed away

1 tablespoon raspberry or sherry vinegar

¼ cup extra-virgin olive oil, divided

Kosher salt and ground black pepper, to taste

2 blood oranges

2 Cara Cara oranges or other sweet, juicy oranges

1 fennel bulb, stalks and fronds removed

1 ripe but firm Hass avocado

2 tablespoons finely chopped flat-leaf parsley

2 tablespoons thinly sliced scallions (white and tender green parts)

¼ cup salted shelled pistachios (not dyed red)

This salad is quite refreshing in winter as a bright foil to heavy comfort food. It's made with citrus fruits that are at their sweetest in winter, along with beets that overwinter well. I make this salad around Christmas, based on my lifelong association of oranges with the holidays. Even my grandparents had oranges for Christmas when they were children in the 1910s and 1920s, exotic treats indeed for Blue Ridge Mountain families back then.

This is a composed salad, which means the ingredients are arranged in colorful rows on a serving platter. It's a scene stealer on a buffet.

MAKES 6 SERVINGS

1. Preheat the oven to 375°F.

2. Place the beets in a single layer on a double thickness of aluminum foil. Fold the foil around the beets to make a snug pouch. (If using more than one color of beets, wrap each color separately.) Roast the beets until they are tender when pierced with the tip of a knife, about 45 minutes. Open the foil pouch and let the beets cool enough to handle. Trim off the greens and rootlets and slip off the skins. Cut the beets into thin wedges and transfer into a medium bowl. Toss with the vinegar and 1 tablespoon of the oil and season with salt and pepper.

3. Use a serrated knife to peel the oranges, following the contour of the fruit to preserve the shape while removing all the bitter white pith. Working over a medium bowl, cut in between the membranes to release the orange sections and dripping juice into the bowl. Set the membranes aside. Toss the orange segments with 1 tablespoon of the oil and season with salt and pepper.

4. Cut the fennel bulb in half lengthwise and trim away the tough core. Slice the bulb as thin as possible. Transfer into a medium bowl, toss with 1 tablespoon of the oil, and season with salt and pepper.

5. Halve and pit the avocado. Use a large spoon to scoop the flesh out of the shell. Cut each half into thin slices and place in a medium bowl. Squeeze the juice from the orange membranes over the avocado, add the remaining 1 tablespoon of oil, season with salt and pepper, and toss gently to coat.

6. To assemble the salad, arrange the beets, oranges, fennel, and avocado in separate rows on a large rectangular platter. Scatter the parsley, scallions, and pistachios over the salad and serve straightaway.

WHAT ELSE WORKS? You can use other types of citrus in place of the oranges, such as grapefruits or tangerines. You can use fresh pomegranate arils in place of the pistachios.

# BLACKBERRIES

**Blackberries are native to the South.** At first their twisty, thorny insistent canes were so abundant that they were considered to be nuisance weeds. Over time, several types were collectively and affectionately called blackberries, from wild varieties to carefully crafted hybrids, including loganberries, boysenberries, dewberries, youngberries, and olallieberries. Some people also put mulberries on this list, but they are quite different botanically and grow on deciduous trees instead of canes.

Even when blackberries are plentiful, they aren't easy pickings. Picking ripe blackberries is sweaty, scratchy work aggravated by the constant threat of vindictive insects, snakes, and skin-ripping thorns, making each full bucket well earned.

A fully ripe blackberry is sweet and juicy. In marked contrast, an unripe berry could be called a thought berry, because after you've tasted one, you'll think twice before doing it again. ■

## Blackberries and Peaches in Sweet Basil Syrup with Cornmeal Pound Cake

1 cup sugar

½ cup water

½ cup off-dry white wine (such as Riesling)

½ vanilla bean

1 cup lightly packed basil leaves

Juice of 1 lemon (about ¼ cup)

1 cup fresh blackberries

4 cups peeled, pitted, and sliced peaches (about 2 pounds)

Cornmeal Pound Cake (recipe follows)

This is a lovely dessert made up of things that are familiar, but perhaps not familiar together. The fruit mixture is a great example of how other herbs, not just mint, can be used in desserts. I first used fresh basil with fruit one day during a cooking demo challenge at my farmers' market. I was presented with a basket of the day's best ingredients and I had to use them on the spot. I had no idea whether the flavor combination would work, but did it ever. You can reuse the syrup. It keeps up to one month if you store it in a tightly covered glass jar in the refrigerator. It's also great in iced tea. Green basil is fine, but purple basil makes the syrup blush.

MAKES 8 SERVINGS

1. Combine the sugar, water, and wine in a medium saucepan. Split the vanilla bean in half lengthwise. Use the tip of the knife to scrape out the seeds, add them to the pan, and drop in the bean pod. Bring to a boil, stirring until the sugar dissolves. Remove the pan from the heat and stir in the basil and lemon juice. Cool to room temperature. Strain the syrup into a large bowl.

2. Add the blackberries and peaches, cover, and refrigerate for at least 3 hours and up to 3 days. The basil flavor gets stronger each day.

3. To serve, place slices of cake in shallow serving bowls or soup plates. Spoon the fruit and a little of the syrup over the cake and serve soon, before the cake gets too soggy.

WHAT ELSE WORKS? You can replace the peaches with other stone fruit, such as nectarines, plums, or apricots, or with a mixture of fruit. It's also nice with all blackberries. You can use ¼ cup finely chopped fresh rosemary in place of the basil.

# Cornmeal Pound Cake

1 cup all-purpose flour

½ cup stone-ground cornmeal

1 teaspoon baking powder

½ teaspoon baking soda

½ teaspoon fine sea salt

8 tablespoons (1 stick) unsalted butter, at room temperature

Finely grated zest of 1 lemon

1 cup sugar

2 large eggs, at room temperature

½ cup sour cream (regular or low-fat)

1 teaspoon pure vanilla extract

Pound cake is an essential southern dessert. Cornmeal is an essential southern ingredient. They join forces in this tender cake that has just enough cornmeal to give it a little crunch. Cut any leftovers into thin slices, spread with butter, and toast in a cast-iron skillet for a wonderful breakfast.

Many southerners are adamant that real cornbread does not contain sugar; otherwise, it would be cake. For all you people who think cornbread should contain sugar, here you go. See, it *is* cake.

MAKES 8 SERVINGS

1. Preheat the oven to 350°F. Grease and flour a deep 9-inch cake pan, tapping out the excess flour. (For best results, use a light metal pan for this cake. A dark metal or nonstick pan makes the crust very thick and dark.)

2. Whisk together the flour, cornmeal, baking powder, baking soda, and salt in a medium bowl. Set aside.

3. Beat the butter and lemon zest until fluffy in a large bowl with an electric mixer set to high speed. With the mixer running, slowly add the sugar and beat until light and fluffy, about 5 minutes. Scrape down the sides of the bowl with a rubber spatula. Add the eggs one at a time, beating well after each addition. Beat in the sour cream and vanilla. With the mixer set to low speed, add the flour mixture in three additions, beating each time only until it disappears into the batter.

4. Scrape the batter into the prepared pan and smooth the top with a spatula. Bake until a tester inserted into the center comes out clean, about 35 minutes. Cool in the pan on a wire rack for 10 minutes. Run a thin knife around the inside edge of the pan to loosen the cake. Invert onto another rack or a large plate and then back onto the rack, so that the top side is up. Cool to room temperature.

## Blackberry and Buttermilk Sherbet

4 cups fresh
  blackberries

2 cups sugar

2 cups well-shaken
  buttermilk

This frozen confection is addicting and soothing. Once you start eating, it's hard to stop until it's gone. This is one of those foods that restores one's will to live on stifling hot and humid summer days.

Since this is made with buttermilk instead of cream, it is sherbet instead of ice cream. The buttermilk is crucial, and only fresh liquid buttermilk will do, not reconstituted powdered buttermilk, which is more like an artificial flavoring than an actual dairy product. If you have access to local, farmstead buttermilk that is full of flavor, use it. Buttermilk is prevalent in many old southern recipes because it kept better than regular milk (once known as sweet milk) in the days before refrigeration.

MAKES ABOUT 1 QUART

1. If the berries are full of tough seeds, remove the seeds by forcing the berries through a food mill or mesh sieve into a large bowl. If the berries are mostly seedless, place them in a large bowl. Stir in the sugar and let stand at room temperature for 30 minutes. Purée the mixture in the bowl of a food processor fitted with the metal blade. Pour into a large glass or metal bowl.

2. Whisk in the buttermilk. Cover and refrigerate until the mixture is very cold (40°F or lower), at least 4 hours, then stir well. Churn the sherbet in a small electric ice cream freezer according to the manufacturer's instructions. The sherbet will be soft, like a thick milk shake. To freeze hard enough to scoop, transfer into an airtight container, press plastic wrap directly onto the surface, and freeze until firm.

WHAT ELSE WORKS? You can replace the blackberries with strawberries.

## Orange Cream Pie with
## Quick Blackberry Compote

PIE

1   (9-inch) pie shell
    (page 396 or
    store-bought)

1   cup sugar

2   teaspoons finely
    grated orange zest

5   tablespoons
    cornstarch

¼   teaspoon kosher salt

5   large egg yolks

½   cup fresh orange juice

2   cups whole milk

4   tablespoons (½ stick)
    unsalted butter, cut
    into 1-tablespoon
    pieces and chilled

½   teaspoon Fiori Di
    Sicilia extract or
    2 teaspoons pure
    vanilla extract

COMPOTE

1   cup seedless
    blackberry or red
    currant jelly

1   tablespoon Grand
    Marnier or other
    orange liqueur
    (optional)

4   cups fresh whole
    blackberries

This is a variation of the classic cream pies beloved across the South. The filling tastes exactly like a Creamsicle, the frozen orange-flavored ice cream treat often bought from an ice cream truck or corner market. The filling is flavored with Fiori di Sicilia, a divine orange and vanilla extract from Italy, although pure vanilla extract will also work. You can find Fiori di Sicilia in some gourmet markets and online.

Old recipes for cream pies and other custards always call for a double boiler. The air space between the simmering water and the bottom of the upper pan insulates the delicate egg mixture from direct heat, which helps prevent curdling. This technique was crucial in the days when most cooks used thin aluminum pots and pans. These days, if you have a heavy saucepan (such as one with an aluminum core clad in stainless steel) and use low heat, you can make the filling without a double boiler. If you don't have a heavy pan or a double boiler, cook this filling in a large metal bowl set over a pan of simmering water. The bottom of the bowl cannot touch the water because the air space is what insulates the filling from the high heat.

It's also a good idea to push the egg yolks through a mesh sieve into the saucepan. This removes any bits of egg white or membranes that cling to the yolks, which are the parts of the egg most likely to curdle. Be vigilant with the smooth and steady stirring while the filling cooks. After the ingredients are incorporated, switch from a whisk to a heatproof spatula that covers more of the pan with each stir.

MAKES 8 SERVINGS

1.  For the pie: Bake and cool the pie shell according to the instructions on page 398.

2.  Combine the sugar and orange zest in a medium bowl. Use fingertips to rub them together until the sugar is moist and grainy. Whisk in the cornstarch and salt. Whisk in the egg yolks, followed by the orange juice.

3.  Warm the milk in a large, heavy saucepan over medium-high heat. As soon as the milk begins to steam and form small bubbles around the edge, whisk it into the sugar mixture in a slow, steady stream. Pour this mixture back into the saucepan and cook over medium heat, stirring slowly and continuously with a heat-proof spatula, until it comes to a boil and is thick enough to coat the back of the spatula, about 5 minutes.

4.  Remove the pan from the heat and whisk in the butter one piece at a time, waiting until it is incorporated before adding the next. Whisk in the Fiori Di Sicilia. Strain the filling through a mesh sieve into the pie shell. Press plastic

wrap directly onto the surface of the filling and refrigerate until well chilled, at least 2 hours.

5. For the compote: Melt the jelly in a medium saucepan over low heat. Stir in the liqueur, if using. Add the berries and stir gently to coat.

6. Serve the pie slightly chilled, topped with the compote.

WHAT ELSE WORKS? You can replace the blackberries with other fresh berries or a mixture of berries. Change the jelly to match the berry or use red currant jelly, which goes with everything.

## Blackberry Barbecue Sauce

2 cups fresh
  blackberries

¼ cup ketchup

¼ cup packed light
  brown sugar

2 tablespoons
  whole-grain
  Dijon mustard

¼ cup sherry vinegar

1 teaspoon
  ground ginger

1 teaspoon kosher salt

1 teaspoon ground
  black pepper

¼ teaspoon
  ground allspice

1 teaspoon
  habanero pepper
  sauce, or to taste

I live in a state that believes that "barbecue" is a noun, not a verb. We assert that good barbecue is pork only. (You can make a reasonably accurate guess about where a southerner lives if you know what he recognizes, much less accepts, as barbecue.) No one in my state would ever put this sauce on barbecue. Having said this, maybe they won't revoke my driver's license for including something called Blackberry Barbecue Sauce, because it's meant to be used as a finishing sauce or dipping sauce with grilled or roasted birds, from chicken to quail to duck.

Habanero chiles are near the top of the Scoville scale, which means they are incredibly hot. But underneath that heat they are fruity, which is why I use a tiny bit of habanero pepper with the blackberries.

MAKES 2 CUPS

1. Place the berries in a large saucepan and crush with a potato masher or the back of a spoon.

2. Stir in the ketchup, brown sugar, mustard, vinegar, ginger, salt, pepper, allspice, and pepper sauce. Bring to a boil, reduce the heat, and simmer until thickened, about 5 minutes. Serve warm or at room temperature. Store covered and refrigerated for up to 2 weeks.

WHAT ELSE WORKS? You can use a fresh habanero or other very hot chile instead of the pepper sauce. Pierce the chile in one or two places with the tip of a toothpick, add it whole to the sauce, and remove it before serving. Wear gloves or wash your hands well after handling hot chiles.

## Dewberry Roll

2 cups all-purpose flour

2 teaspoons baking powder

1 teaspoon fine sea salt

2 tablespoons sugar

2 tablespoons butter, cut into small cubes and chilled

2 tablespoons vegetable shortening or lard

1 large egg

½ cup milk

2 tablespoons butter, at room temperature

2 cups fresh dewberries or other blackberries

¾ cup sugar

1 large egg beaten with 1 tablespoon cold water, for an egg wash

Sweet Corn Custard Ice Cream (page 108), vanilla ice cream, or whipped cream, for serving

This is a very old recipe that illustrates yet another of the basic forms of southern cobbler: fruit wrapped in pastry. In this recipe, whole berries are scattered over buttered sweet biscuit dough that is then rolled up like a jelly roll and baked. Because of the shape, this technique goes by many names, including Valise Pudding, *Bourrelet*, or Dolly in a Blanket.

Dewberries are a type of trailing blackberry that grows on long canes along fence rows and trellises. Some people find them superior to all other blackberries.

MAKES 8 SERVINGS

1. Preheat the oven to 400°F.

2. Whisk together the flour, baking powder, salt, and sugar in a large bowl. Add the butter cubes and drop the shortening in bits over the flour mixture and toss to coat. Use your fingertips to work them in until the pieces are the size of garden peas. In a small bowl, whisk together the egg and milk, pour over the flour mixture, and stir with a fork or your fingertips until the dough comes together.

3. Pour the dough onto a lightly floured sheet of parchment and gently knead until the dough is smooth, about 5 turns. Roll or pat the dough into a rectangle that is ½-inch thick, turned so one of the long sides is at the bottom. Spread the soft butter evenly over the dough. Scatter the berries over the butter, leaving the bottom 2 inches bare. Sprinkle the sugar over the berries. Starting at the top, roll up the dough toward you, making sure it is tight enough to hold the berries in place. It should look like a jelly roll. Pinch the seam and the ends closed. Transfer the roll (still on the parchment) to a rimmed baking sheet. Brush the top and sides with the egg wash.

4. Bake until the pastry is browned and any escaped juices are bubbling, about 35 minutes. Cool on a wire rack for 10 minutes before slicing and serving with ice cream or whipped cream.

## Blackberry and Oatmeal Breakfast Brûlée

4 cups freshly
cooked oatmeal

½ cup coarsely chopped
walnuts, toasted

1 teaspoon pure
vanilla extract

½ teaspoon ground
cinnamon

2 cups fresh blackberries

1 tablespoon gran-
ulated sugar

1 cup sour cream, at
room temperature

½ cup light
brown sugar

Berries and oatmeal make this a healthy breakfast. A thin, crunchy, brown sugar crust makes this a decadent breakfast. You can broil the topping or use a kitchen torch if you have one, which means you get to play with fire before breakfast.

For the best results, use steel-cut or stone-cut oatmeal cooked according to the package directions. In lieu of that, use old-fashioned rolled oats. Instant oatmeal is not an option.

MAKES 4 SERVINGS

1. Preheat the broiler.
2. Cook the oatmeal according to package directions. When it is ready, remove the pan from the heat and stir in the walnuts, vanilla, and cinnamon. Divide the oatmeal among 4 shallow gratin dishes or heatproof bowls and top with the berries.
3. Stir together the granulated sugar and sour cream in a small bowl and spread evenly over the berries. Sprinkle the brown sugar evenly over the top.
4. Place the dishes on a rimmed baking sheet. Broil until the brown sugar caramelizes and forms a crisp shell, about 3 minutes. Serve at once, keeping in mind that the dishes are extremely hot.

WHAT ELSE WORKS? You can replace the blackberries with fresh figs, stems removed and cut into halves or quarters, depending on their size.

# BLUEBERRIES

**Blueberries and huckleberries are native to North America.** They once
grew so profusely that there was no need to cultivate them, and they were
not domesticated until the early twentieth century. Most southern blueberries are now harvested from carefully tended wild stands or from cultivated varieties descended from the original wild ones.

Plentiful berries were sustenance food for Native Americans and the
earliest explorers and colonists. Native Americans knew how to dry blueberries in the sun and used them in pemmican. Later, they sold dried fruit
to English settlers, who used them in place of currants in their recipes.
For decades, blueberries and huckleberries retained their association with
wildness, exploration, and pioneering. In fact, some people think that's
why Mark Twain gave the name Huckleberry to his spirited, adventure-
seeking character. ■

## Blueberry Shortcakes with Lime Curd Cream

1 cup whipping cream, chilled

1 cup Lime Curd (recipe follows)

Shortcake Cream Biscuits (page 297)

4 cups fresh blueberries (about 1 pound)

This is old-fashioned shortcake, but the whipped cream is perked up with tangy lime curd. It's possible to buy lime curd and lemon curd, but these don't compare to the buttery richness of easy-to-make homemade curd. If you decide to buy the curd, read the label on the jar. Look for one that contains the same ingredients as homemade: juice, sugar, eggs, butter, and not much else. Avoid any brands that have an unnatural neon glow because they taste like artificially flavored candy.

MAKES 6 SERVINGS

1. To make the lime curd cream, whip the cream until it forms stiff peaks in a large bowl with an electric mixer set to high speed. Use a rubber spatula to fold in the lime curd.

2. To assemble the shortcakes, split the biscuits and place the bottoms on serving plates. Divide the lime curd cream among the biscuits, top with the berries, replace the biscuit tops, and serve.

VARIATION: To make bite-sized tartlets, spoon about 1 teaspoon of lime curd into 1 ½-inch baked tartlet shells or phyllo cups. Top with a dab of whipped cream and a single berry.

WHAT ELSE WORKS? You can replace the blueberries with other berries or a mixture of berries.

## Lime Curd

½ cup sugar

2 teaspoons finely grated lime zest

⅓ cup fresh lime juice

4 large egg yolks

5 tablespoons unsalted butter, cut into small cubes and chilled

Curd is an intensely flavored citrus and butter sauce that resembles thick, creamy jam. See pages 38 and 57 for tips on cooking egg-based sauces and custards.

MAKES ABOUT 1 CUP

1. Whisk together the sugar, lime zest, and lime juice in a heavy medium saucepan. Whisk in the yolks. Drop in the butter. Cook over medium-low heat, stirring continuously with a heatproof spatula until the mixture is thick, smooth, and beginning to form small bubbles just around the edge of the pan, about 8 minutes.

2. Remove from the heat and pour through a fine sieve into a small glass bowl. Press a piece of plastic wrap directly onto the surface of the curd to prevent a skin from forming. Refrigerate until chilled, at least 4 hours.

WHAT ELSE WORKS? You can use this recipe to make lemon curd or orange curd by changing the juice and zest.

## Fresh Blueberry Parfaits
## with Pistachio Crumble

1 cup blueberry or
red currant jelly

2 cups fresh blueberries

4 ounces all-butter
shortbread cookies

½ cup shelled raw
pistachios (not dyed
red), coarsely chopped
(about 3 ounces)

½ teaspoon ground
cardamom or
ground cinnamon

2 tablespoons
butter, melted

½ cup sour cream

1 tablespoon raw
cane sugar or lightly
packed brown sugar

This recipe is extremely simple and quite impressive. The sour cream is key because it keeps the dessert from being too sweet, plus it tastes fantastic with the brown sugar. Look for raw pistachios because the little bright green pieces are gorgeous with the blueberries.

I often combine fresh berries and jelly to make a quick compote or sauce. I used to make compote by sweetening berries with sugar and thickening their juices with cooked cornstarch slurry. Melted jam is already thick, sweet, and glossy, so it's a one-step solution. I usually match the berry and the jelly, but red currant jelly goes with everything.

MAKES 4 SERVINGS

1. Melt the jelly in a small saucepan over low heat. Remove the pan from the heat and gently stir in the berries. Cover and refrigerate until chilled, at least 30 minutes.

2. Crush the cookies into coarse crumbs and place them in a small bowl. Stir in the pistachios and cardamom. Drizzle in the butter and toss to coat.

3. Just before serving, stir together the sour cream and sugar in a small bowl.

4. Spoon the berry mixture into serving dishes. Top with the cookie mixture and a generous dollop of the sour cream mixture and serve lightly chilled.

# Venison Medallions with Blueberry and Red Wine Sauce

1 tablespoon butter

1 medium onion, cut in half lengthwise and sliced into thin julienne strips

1 teaspoon light brown sugar

½ cup fruity red wine

¾ cup blueberries

½ cup chicken stock

2 tablespoons balsamic or sherry vinegar

2 teaspoons chopped fresh thyme

1 teaspoon cornstarch

1 tablespoon cold water

1 teaspoon kosher salt

½ teaspoon ground black pepper

VENISON

1 ½ to 2 pounds venison tenderloin, trimmed and cut crosswise into 1-inch medallions

1 teaspoon kosher salt, or to taste

½ teaspoon ground black pepper, or to taste

1 tablespoon vegetable oil

1 tablespoon butter

This sauce is fruity without being too sweet, just the thing to go with venison. Tiny, somewhat tart wild blueberries or huckleberries are a great choice.

If the thought of venison gives you Bambi flashbacks, use pork tenderloin instead. The sauce is also good with game birds.

MAKES 4 TO 6 SERVINGS

1. For the sauce: Melt the butter in a large saucepan over medium heat. Add the onion and brown sugar and a pinch of salt and stir to coat. Cook, stirring often, until the onions are very soft and golden brown, about 20 minutes.

2. Add the wine and stir up the glaze from the bottom of the pan. Stir in the berries, stock, vinegar, and thyme. Bring to a boil and cook until the liquid reduces by half, about 10 minutes.

3. Whisk together the cornstarch and cold water in a small bowl until smooth. Add to the boiling liquid and cook, stirring, until the sauce is thick enough to coat the spoon. Season with the salt and pepper and keep warm over low heat, stirring occasionally.

4. For the venison: Pat the medallions dry with paper towels and sprinkle both sides with the salt and pepper. Heat the oil and butter in a large skillet (preferably cast-iron) over high heat. Add half of the medallions and cook undisturbed until seared on the bottom, about 3 minutes. Turn and cook until the other side is seared but the meat is still rare in the center, about 2 minutes more. Transfer to a plate and tent loosely with foil to keep warm while you cook the remaining medallions. (Do not wrap the foil tightly around the plate or the trapped steam will overcook the meat.) Serve at once with the warm sauce.

## Jumble Berry Breakfast Crisp

1 cup granulated sugar

½ teaspoon ground cinnamon

1 teaspoon pure vanilla extract

1 teaspoon fresh lemon juice

¼ teaspoon fine sea salt

2 cups fresh blueberries

2 cups fresh raspberries, blackberries, and/or sliced strawberries

1 cup all-purpose flour

1 cup granola

½ cup walnut pieces

¼ cup sweetened flaked coconut

½ cup packed light brown sugar

½ cup Cope's Dried Sweet Corn (optional)

8 tablespoons (1 stick) butter, cut into small cubes and chilled

Plain or vanilla yogurt, for serving

Starting with the colonists, southerners have long enjoyed pie for breakfast, meaning fruit with some sort of pastry. A descendant from these roots, this breakfast crisp is a great way to start the day. A jumble of juicy berries is capped with crunchy, buttery topping. Although any single berry is good, this crisp is best with a mixture of berries.

In the past, some families preserved part of their sweet corn crop by parching the corn. The corn was dried over low heat, which toasted and concentrated the corn's natural flavor and sweetness. The practice has nearly died out, but you can still buy John Cope's Dried Sweet Corn, produced by a small family business. The sweet, slightly chewy dried corn is fantastic in the crisp topping. Cope's corn is available in some gourmet food markets and online at farmstandfoods.com.

To serve this crisp as a dessert, top it with the Sweet Corn Custard Ice Cream (page 108). The flavor pairing is especially nice if you've used Cope's in the topping.

MAKES 6 TO 8 SERVINGS

1. Preheat the oven to 350°F. Butter a shallow 2 ½-quart gratin dish or 11 × 7-inch baking dish.

2. Stir together the granulated sugar, cinnamon, vanilla, lemon juice, and salt in a large bowl. Add the berries and toss to coat. Pour into the prepared dish.

3. Stir together the flour, granola, walnuts, coconut, brown sugar, and corn (if using) in a medium bowl. Add the butter and toss to coat, then use your fingertips to work it in until the pieces are the size of garden peas. Squeeze about one-third of the topping into balls the size of marbles, but leave the rest crumbly. Sprinkle the topping evenly over the berries.

4. Bake until the topping is golden and the juices are bubbling, about 30 minutes. Set aside for at least 5 minutes before serving warm, topped with the yogurt.

# Blueberry and Pecan Snack Cake

Vegetable oil spray

1 cup all-purpose flour

3 tablespoons stone-ground cornmeal

1 teaspoon baking powder

½ teaspoon kosher salt

8 tablespoons (1 stick) unsalted butter, at room temperature

1 cup granulated sugar

2 large eggs

⅓ cup whole or low-fat milk

2 teaspoons pure vanilla extract

Finely grated zest of 1 lemon

2 cups fresh blueberries

2 tablespoons coarse sanding sugar, raw sugar, or additional granulated sugar

1 cup chopped pecans

This is a welcome change from a muffin but just as handy for breakfast, snacks, and lunchboxes. If you nibble on it all through the day, just a sliver at a time, just a wee slice to even up the edge, you can pretend to be startled that evening when the pan is somehow empty.

MAKES 8 SERVINGS

① Preheat the oven to 350°F. Mist the inside of a 9-inch square light metal baking pan with the spray. (A dark metal or nonstick pan makes the crust very thick and dark.)

② Whisk together the flour, cornmeal, baking powder, and salt in a small bowl and set aside. Beat together the butter and granulated sugar until light and fluffy in a large bowl with an electric mixer set to high speed. Scrape down the sides of the bowl with a rubber spatula. Add the eggs one at a time, beating well after each addition. Add the flour mixture and beat only until it disappears into the batter. Beat in the milk, vanilla, and lemon zest. Use a rubber spatula to gently fold in the berries.

③ Scrape the batter into the prepared baking pan and smooth the top. Sprinkle the sanding sugar over the batter, followed by the pecans. Bake until a tester inserted into the center of the cake comes out clean, about 40 minutes. Cool on a wire rack for at least 15 minutes before serving warm or at room temperature. The cooler the cake, the more neatly it will cut.

WHAT ELSE WORKS? You can replace some or all of the blueberries with finely diced peaches.

# BROCCOLI

**Broccoli, which began life in the Mediterranean** as a descendant of a type of wild cabbage that produced more tight buds than full leaves, was cultivated in the South as early as 1720. About forty-five years later, in what is believed to be the earliest American book on kitchen gardening, *A Treatise on Gardening by a Citizen of Virginia*, Williamsburg resident John Randolph wrote that broccoli stems will eat like asparagus and the heads like cauliflower. After the Civil War, broccoli nearly disappeared from southern gardens until it was reintroduced in the early twentieth century. Although a few folks might wish that it had stayed away, broccoli has turned into one of the most popular and reliable fresh vegetables around, especially when creative cooks go beyond basic steaming. Broccoli can be stir-fried, roasted, swirled into soups, tucked into comforting casseroles, and bathed in creamy cheese sauce. ■

# Broccoli and White Cheddar Soup

2 tablespoons butter

½ cup chopped carrot

½ cup chopped celery

¾ cup chopped
red onion

1 cup diced red-
skinned potato

2 large broccoli stalks,
florets cut into bite-
sized pieces, stems
peeled and finely
chopped (about
4 cups)

3 tablespoons instant
or all-purpose flour

2 cups chicken stock

1 tablespoon fresh
or 1 teaspoon
dried thyme

1 ½ teaspoons dry mustard

1 ½ teaspoons kosher salt

2 cups whole milk

1 ½ cups grated sharp
or extra-sharp white
cheddar cheese

2 teaspoons cornstarch

Broccoli-cheese soup has become ubiquitous, which isn't necessarily a good thing because the less-than-stellar versions can distract us from how great this soup can actually be. This one is creamy, comforting, and chock full of colorful vegetables nestled in flavorful white cheddar cheese.

MAKES ABOUT 2 QUARTS

1. Melt the butter in a large saucepan or small soup pot over medium heat. Add the carrot, celery, onion, potato, and broccoli and a pinch of salt and stir to coat. Cook, stirring often, until the vegetables begin to soften, about 10 minutes. Sprinkle the flour over the vegetables and cook, stirring, for 2 minutes. Reduce the heat if the flour starts to brown.

2. Gradually stir in the stock and cook, stirring, until the liquid begins to thicken, about 1 minute. Stir in the thyme, mustard, salt, and milk. Simmer until the vegetables are tender, about 20 minutes.

3. Meanwhile, toss the cheese and cornstarch together in a small bowl. Remove the pan from the heat, add the cheese mixture, and stir until the cheese melts. Check the seasoning and add more salt, if needed. Serve hot.

MAKE-AHEAD NOTE: You can make the soup up to 3 days ahead. Cool, cover, and refrigerate. The soup thickens as it cools. If it is too thick when gently reheated, add a little more stock or milk. Do not let it boil.

# Turkey Divan

4 cups broccoli spears or florets

3 cups bite-sized pieces of roasted turkey (about 12 ounces)

3 tablespoons butter, at room temperature

3 tablespoons instant flour or all-purpose flour

1 ½ cups whole milk

1 ½ cups grated sharp white cheddar cheese

1 teaspoon kosher salt

½ teaspoon ground black pepper

⅛ teaspoon paprika

1 ½ cups soft, fresh bread crumbs (page 389)

2 tablespoons butter, melted

Never question the contents of your neighbor's mail, trash, or casserole. Turkey Divan, once a regular on many family dinner tables, fell out of favor during the blight of bad casseroles, the ones that jumbled together whatever with a can of Cream of Something soup. For some people, canned cream soup is indispensable; for others, it is intolerable.

I like this simple Turkey Divan because it predates canned soup. It's easy, filling, and open to variations. You can use leftover turkey or roasted turkey breast from the deli (the real thing, not slick sandwich meat). You can change the kind of cheese. You can use dry stuffing mix in place of the bread crumbs. To make this a one-dish dinner, spread 2 or 3 cups of cooked rice in the bottom of the dish before you add the broccoli.

By the way, if there is no time to make the whole dish, the cheese sauce (Step 3) is great poured over cooked broccoli.

MAKES 4 TO 6 SERVINGS

1. Preheat the oven to 350°F. Butter a shallow 2 ½-quart baking dish.

2. Place the broccoli and ¼ cup of water in a large glass bowl. Cover tightly with plastic wrap and microwave until crisp-tender. (You can also cook the broccoli in a steam basket set over a saucepan of simmering water.) Drain in a colander and rinse under cold running water to stop the cooking and set the bright green color. Pat the broccoli dry with paper towels and spread it across the bottom of the dish. Scatter the turkey over the broccoli.

3. Melt the butter in a medium saucepan over medium heat. Add the flour and cook, whisking, for 2 minutes. Reduce the heat if the flour starts to brown. Whisk in the milk and cook, stirring slowly, until the sauce is smooth and thick enough to coat the back of the spoon, about 5 minutes. Remove from the heat, add the cheese, and stir until smooth. Season with the salt, pepper, and paprika. Pour the cheese sauce over the broccoli and turkey.

4. Toss the bread crumbs with the melted butter in a small bowl and sprinkle over the dish. Bake until the crumbs are browned and the sauce bubbles around the edge, about 30 minutes. If the crumbs start to brown too quickly, lay a flat sheet of aluminum foil over the top. Serve hot.

## Pasta with Creamy Broccoli Sauce

2 cups diced baked ham (about 12 ounces)

1 cup heavy cream or plain Greek yogurt

1 cup chicken stock

¼ cup grainy Dijon mustard

1 pound penne pasta

3 cups small broccoli florets

2 large roasted red bell peppers cut into bite-sized strips (about 1 cup) (page 314 or store-bought)

Kosher salt and ground black pepper, to taste

Freshly grated Parmesan cheese, for serving

This warm, creamy, comforting dish is hearty enough to be a satisfying meal. You can use leftover baked ham or a thick slab of deli ham. Any shape of short pasta will do, even macaroni. The mustard adds great flavor and helps thicken the sauce, but be sure to use Dijon, not yellow ballpark mustard. Not only is that flavor wrong, but the alarming neon color would outshine a school bus.

MAKES 4 TO 6 SERVINGS

1. Cook the ham in a very large skillet or large saucepan over medium-high heat until lightly browned and sizzling, about 3 minutes. Add the cream, stock, and mustard. Stir up any browned bits from the bottom of the skillet and cook, stirring, until the sauce thickens slightly, about 5 minutes. Keep warm over low heat, stirring occasionally.

2. Cook the pasta according to package directions. When the pasta is 5 minutes short of the recommended cooking time, add the broccoli to the pot and continue cooking until both are done. Drain well and pour into the cream mixture. Add the roasted peppers and mix gently. Season with salt and pepper. Serve immediately, topped with a sprinkling of cheese.

VARIATION: To make this meatless, use sliced fresh mushrooms in place of the ham.

## Blasted Broccoli

1 to 1½ pounds broccoli crowns, cut into 2-inch florets

3 tablespoons extra-virgin olive oil, divided

1 teaspoon kosher salt

¼ teaspoon ground black pepper

Generous pinch of crushed red pepper flakes

Juice of 1 lemon (about ¼ cup)

Broccoli florets take on a whole new personality when roasted at high temperatures. They remain firm with crisp edges, and the flavors are concentrated instead of diluted by water. This is a very quick and easy way to serve broccoli.

MAKES 4 TO 6 SERVINGS

1. Preheat the oven to 425°F.

2. Pile the florets in the center of a rimmed baking sheet. Drizzle with 1 tablespoon of the oil and toss to coat. Spread the florets into a single layer. Roast for 15 minutes.

3. Meanwhile, stir together the remaining 2 tablespoons of oil and the salt, pepper, and red pepper flakes. Remove the pan from the oven, drizzle the oil mixture over the broccoli, and stir to coat.

4. Continue roasting until the stems are crisp-tender and the tips are lightly browned, about 5 minutes more. Squeeze the lemon over the broccoli and serve hot.

VARIATION: Sprinkle the broccoli with ½ cup coarsely grated Parmesan cheese or other hard grating cheese when you add the oil and crushed pepper mixture.

# Forever-Cooked Broccoli

2 pounds broccoli

½ cup extra-virgin olive oil

3 garlic cloves, sliced

Generous pinch crushed red pepper flakes

4 finely chopped anchovy fillets, 4 teaspoons anchovy paste, or 2 teaspoons Worcestershire sauce

1 teaspoon kosher salt, or to taste

½ teaspoon ground black pepper, or to taste

Like some traditional southern cooks, many Italian cooks do not believe in crisp-tender green vegetables. They contend that vegetables should either be fully crisp or fully tender, which means that crisp-tender misses both targets. Even if you usually prefer crisp-tender broccoli, this recipe is a delightful change of pace. The broccoli is cooked slowly until it is soft, comforting, and full of flavor. It makes a great side dish or pasta topping. It's also great spooned atop crisp garlic bread to make bruschetta.

The recipe calls for fresh broccoli, but it's also a great way to reinvent steamed broccoli left over from another meal.

Don't omit the anchovy in this recipe. When used properly, anchovy adds tremendous depth of flavor without being too fishy or strong. Anchovy should be noticed when it's missing, not when it's used. If you will not use up a small jar or tin of anchovies once opened, open a tube of high-quality anchovy paste instead. Squeeze out what you need, close the tube, and stash it in the fridge. Worcestershire sauce, another savory fish-based seasoning, is also an option.

MAKES 4 TO 6 SERVINGS

1. Trim the broccoli crowns into large florets. Peel the stems and cut into ½-inch-thick slices. Bring a large saucepan of water to a boil. Add ½ teaspoon kosher salt per cup of water. Add the broccoli. Cook for 5 minutes and drain well.

2. Warm the oil, garlic, red pepper flakes, and anchovy in a large skillet over medium heat. Stir in the broccoli and season with the salt and pepper. Cover, reduce the heat, and cook very slowly until the broccoli is very soft but not dissolved into mush, about 1 ½ hours, stirring occasionally. Check the seasoning and serve warm or at room temperature.

WHAT ELSE WORKS? You can replace the broccoli with snap beans that have thick, sturdy pods, such as Romano beans.

## Crunchy Broccoli and Kohlrabi Salad

½ cup mayonnaise

3 tablespoons sugar

3 tablespoons cider vinegar

½ teaspoon kosher salt, or to taste

¼ teaspoon ground black pepper, or to taste

4 cups bite-sized broccoli florets and thinly sliced stems (about 12 ounces)

1 cup peeled, quartered, and thinly sliced small green or purple kohl-rabi (about 4 ounces)

1 small sweet onion, halved lengthwise and cut into thin strips

¼ cup dried cranberries or golden raisins

½ cup diced cooked bacon

½ cup roasted and salted cashews

This is a twist on the tried-and-true broccoli salad that is often among the first things to be gobbled up at a potluck party. Because the flavor and texture of raw kohlrabi is very similar to raw broccoli stems, it fits right in. The bright green broccoli is not cooked, so the acidic vinegar does not turn it drab.

Kohlrabi is unfamiliar to many people, although it's been grown for centuries. It is a member of the cabbage family, and it tastes like a cross between cabbage and broccoli stalks. A good strategy for dealing with an unfamiliar vegetable is to decide what it looks or tastes like and go from there. You don't necessarily have to know what it *is* if you know what it's *like*.

MAKES 4 TO 6 SERVINGS

1. Whisk together the mayonnaise, sugar, vinegar, salt, and pepper in a large bowl until smooth. Set aside for 5 minutes to let the sugar dissolve, then whisk again.
2. Stir in the broccoli, kohlrabi, onion, and cranberries and mix well. Cover and refrigerate until well chilled, at least 3 hours, stirring occasionally.
3. Just before serving, stir in the bacon and cashews. Serve chilled.

WHAT ELSE WORKS? You can replace some or all of the kohlrabi with additional broccoli.

# CABBAGE

**Cabbage has long been an important garden vegetable** because it can survive cold weather and is suitable for long storage through pickling, fermentation, and burying. Most Europeans who settled in the colonies brought along a taste for cabbage. Most of them cooked or fermented their cabbage, but Dutch immigrants also ate it raw in salads. Their *koosla* sparked the southern love affair with coleslaw. Some of the earliest written southern cabbage recipes describe coating cabbage in creamy dairy-based or cooked dressings.

An eighteenth-century Williamsburg newspaper mentioned twenty-two different kinds of cabbage offered for sale in local markets. The good news is that cabbage diversity is still available, giving us easy access to the right cabbage for our recipes. Beyond the familiar compact or conical heads of green, white, and red cabbage, there are the looser heads of napa, savoy, *cavolo nero*, and Asian cabbages. As their appearance suggests, Brussels sprouts are tiny members of the cabbage clan. Raw cabbage is crisp, sweet, and successful in fresh salads. The secret to cooked cabbage lies in restraint, stopping while it's tender and sweet, well short of the point when it just gives up. ■

# Vegetable Soup

4 tablespoons (½ stick) butter

½ cup chopped onion

½ cup chopped celery

2 teaspoons dried Italian blend herbs or 1 teaspoon each dried basil and oregano

½ teaspoon ground allspice

⅛ teaspoon ground cloves

½ teaspoon paprika

½ cup dry white wine

3 cups chicken or vegetable stock

2 cups vegetable juice (such as V-8) or tomato juice

1 cup cola

1 teaspoon kosher salt

2 cups fresh or canned chopped tomatoes with their juices

3 cups chopped cabbage

1 cup peeled and diced potato

4 cups assorted chopped vegetables (such as snap beans, corn, garden peas, butter beans, carrots, okra, and mushrooms)

2 teaspoons hot sauce

1 teaspoon ground black pepper

¼ cup finely chopped flat-leaf parsley

2 tablespoons red wine vinegar

A book that celebrates fresh produce has to include a straightforward vegetable soup. Not meat soup with vegetables, but vegetable soup, pure and simple. Soup is never perfected because the cook learns something new with each pot. I am very lucky to have learned something about vegetable soup from a soup master in Jackson, Mississippi. He taught me to add cola, and I've done it ever since. When I asked why he uses cola, he said he learned it from a man who always put a little in his Bloody Mary mix because it did good things for the tomato juice. It does. However, it must be real cola, preferably sweetened with cane sugar, and never diet cola. I use a vintage cane cola in a glass bottle that tastes like the "cold drink" of my childhood.

Like the proverbial stone soup, you can put nearly any vegetable in the pot, but you should have a preponderance of cabbage. Vary the vegetables to use the best of the season. This is the type of soup that cooks used to preserve in huge glass canning jars to eat throughout the winter. Serve this soup piping hot with stacks of saltines to crumble in it. Crackers in soup make instant dumplings.

MAKES 2 QUARTS

1. Melt the butter in a large, heavy pot over medium-high heat. Add the onion and celery and a pinch of salt and cook, stirring often, until softened, about 8 minutes. Stir in the dried herbs, allspice, cloves, and paprika and cook, stirring constantly, for 1 minute. Stir in the wine and cook for 1 minute, stirring up any bits from the bottom of the pot. Stir in the stock, vegetable juice, and cola. Stir in the salt, tomatoes, cabbage, potato, and chopped vegetables.

2. Bring just to a boil, reduce the heat, and simmer, partially covered, until all of the vegetables are tender, 30 to 40 minutes. Stir in the hot sauce, pepper, parsley, and vinegar. Check the seasoning. Serve hot.

MAKE-AHEAD NOTE: This soup can be made up to 4 days ahead. It's usually best the second day. Cool, cover, and refrigerate. If the soup seems a little dull or flat when reheated, add more salt. If it still needs a boost, add a touch more vinegar, only enough to brighten the soup without making it taste vinegary.

# Creamy Slaw with Boiled Dressing

½ cup Boiled Dressing (recipe follows)

½ teaspoon kosher salt

¼ teaspoon ground black pepper

¼ teaspoon celery seed

1 tablespoon sugar

1 tablespoon distilled white vinegar or cider vinegar

4 cups finely grated green and/or purple cabbage

¼ cup peeled and finely grated carrot

2 tablespoons finely grated onion

There are as many styles of slaw in the South as there are types of barbecue. Some of those differences are due to habit, heritage, or personal preference. But other times the differences are due to the purpose of the slaw, such as whether it is a side dish or a topping on a sandwich. Where I live in North Carolina, we usually put slaw on our hot dogs and sometimes on our hamburgers and barbecue sandwiches. This is my sandwich slaw: finely chopped, creamy, and slightly sweet. It's also great on a plate, particularly with fried fish and hushpuppies.

Boiled dressing is an old-fashioned cooked sauce similar to homemade mayonnaise. Slaw made with boiled dressing rarely gets watery, even after a few days in the refrigerator. The vegetables should be finely grated. A box grater is best, but you can use a food processor. Working in batches, fill the bowl of the processor fitted with the metal blade no more than half full. Pulse the machine so that the vegetables bounce around as they are chopped; otherwise, the pieces on the bottom will get pulverized while the pieces on top never move.

MAKES 4 TO 6 SERVINGS

1. Whisk together the Boiled Dressing, salt, pepper, celery seed, sugar, and vinegar in a large bowl. Taste the mixture to make sure it has the right balance of sugar and vinegar, leaning toward the sweet side. Let sit for 10 minutes to give the sugar time to dissolve.

2. Add the cabbage, carrot, and onion and stir well. It will seem dry at first, but keep stirring until the cabbage releases some of its own moisture. Check for salt and serve soon, or cover and refrigerate until ready to serve. Stir well before serving.

VARIATION: You can replace the Boiled Dressing with mayonnaise. To combat watery slaw when using mayonnaise, toss the cabbage with 1 tablespoon of salt in a colander and let sit at room temperature for 1 hour, pressing out the moisture with your hands every 20 minutes. The slaw will probably not need additional salt.

## Boiled Dressing

2 tablespoons instant or all-purpose flour

1 tablespoon dry mustard

1 tablespoon sugar

1 teaspoon kosher salt

⅛ teaspoon ground white pepper

½ cup cold water

2 large egg yolks

3 tablespoons distilled white vinegar

3 tablespoons butter, cut into small cubes and chilled

3 tablespoons heavy cream

Time was that many southern cooks bound their salads and slaws with boiled dressing, a creamy, tangy sauce that keeps in the fridge for days and can be used in place of mayonnaise. Any community cookbook printed before the mid-1970s includes at least one recipe for boiled dressing because it was the ingenious solution for cooks who could not afford the expensive vegetable or olive oils needed for homemade mayonnaise. Although we now take it for granted, mayonnaise was once so exotic that Eudora Welty wrote of its coming to Jackson, Mississippi.

Even though boiled dressing isn't really boiled, it was once commonly made in a double boiler. I suspect this "boiler" method gave the sauce its name. Many old recipes called for making delicate, egg-based sauces and custards in a double boiler because the thin metal pots most cooks used could not protect the food from the direct heat of the stove. These days, if you use a heavy pan over low heat you probably won't need a double boiler, particularly if you use a true saucepan (*saucier*) with a rounded bottom and curved sides. Compared to a pan with a flat bottom and straight sides, the *saucier*'s curved shape makes it easier to stir evenly and eliminates corners where food can collect, lump, and burn.

MAKES ABOUT 1 ½ CUPS

1. Sift the flour, mustard, sugar, salt, and white pepper into a small, heavy saucepan. Whisking constantly, add the cold water in a slow, steady stream, whisking until smooth. Whisk in the yolks and vinegar.

2. Cook over medium-low heat, stirring constantly with a heat-proof spatula, until the sauce is thick enough to coat the spatula, about 3 minutes. The sauce can thicken abruptly, so watch it carefully and stir well around the edge of the pan.

3. Remove the pan from the heat and whisk in the butter until it melts. Whisk in the cream.

4. Transfer the sauce into a small glass bowl or jar, let cool to room temperature, then cover and refrigerate until chilled. Store covered and refrigerated for up to 1 week.

## Skillet Cabbage

3 thick bacon slices, cut crosswise into ¼-inch strips (about 3 ounces)

1 small green cabbage, quartered, cored, and shredded (about 8 cups)

3 tablespoons cider vinegar, preferably organic unfiltered cider vinegar

1 teaspoon sugar, or to taste

1 teaspoon kosher salt, or to taste

½ teaspoon ground black pepper, or to taste

This is "fried" cabbage. It's not actually fried, but it is cooked with bacon in a skillet. Many traditional southern dishes that hail from a skillet are called fried, even when minimal fat is used. This tender cabbage is somewhere between warm slaw and fully cooked cabbage. It showcases the delicate, slightly sweet flavor of well-cooked cabbage. Cabbage that emits a strong odor usually is very old or has been boiled beyond recognition; the odor is not caused by an inherent flaw in the vegetable.

For sentimental reasons and because it's flat-out delicious, I sometimes add about 1 cup of chicken stock and another spoonful of sugar to the recipe, cover the skillet, and simmer the cabbage until it's soft and yields sweet, peppery sopping juices for cornbread. Because it's the way my grandmother fixed her cabbage, it's a taste of home that never fails to soothe me.

MAKES 4 TO 6 SERVINGS

1. Cook the bacon in a large, heavy skillet (preferably cast-iron) over medium-high heat until crisp, about 10 minutes. Transfer with a slotted spoon to paper towels to drain.

2. Reduce the heat to medium. Add the cabbage and a pinch of salt to the skillet and toss with tongs until lightly coated with fat. (The cabbage should be only about 1 inch deep in the skillet. If your skillet is too small, cook the cabbage in two batches. Add a little oil or more drippings to the pan if needed for the second batch.) Cover the skillet and cook, stirring often, until the cabbage is tender, about 8 minutes. Transfer into a large serving bowl.

3. Pour the vinegar into the skillet and bring to a simmer, scraping up the browned glaze from the bottom of the pan. Pour over the cabbage and toss to coat. Season with sugar, salt, and plenty of pepper. Sprinkle with the reserved bacon and serve warm.

WHAT ELSE WORKS? You can use all red cabbage or half red and half green. If you use both, cook them separately or the red cabbage will stain the lighter cabbage.

## Cider-Braised Cabbage with Apples and Pecans

2 tablespoons
vegetable oil

2 tablespoons butter

1 large onion,
halved lengthwise
and thinly sliced

½ cup apple cider
(regular or hard cider)

1 medium red
cabbage, quartered,
cored, and shredded
(about 12 cups)

2 large, crisp apples,
peeled, cored, and
thinly sliced

1 tablespoon sugar

2 teaspoons kosher
salt, or to taste

1 teaspoon ground black
pepper, or to taste

2 tablespoons
sherry vinegar

½ cup pecan halves

In this recipe, the pleasant sweetness of apples and cider complement fresh cabbage. The cabbage is cooked only until it is barely tender, before it gets slick. You can use red wine in place of the cider.

Served with confit duck leg or pan-roasted quail, this humble dish becomes gourmet fare. For a warm, filling entrée salad, add shredded roast chicken or browned slices of apple-chicken sausage and crumble blue cheese over the top.

A fresh cabbage is sweet and mild. Although nearly every recipe calls for cutting out the core of a cabbage, the core can be the best part of a freshly picked cabbage. It used to be a real treat for a child to receive the whittled-out core, offered like a prize of stick candy.

MAKES 8 SERVINGS

1. Heat the oil and butter in a large, heavy saucepan over medium heat. Add the onion and cook, stirring often, until softened and slightly browned, about 10 minutes. Stir in the cider, scraping up the browned bits from the bottom of the pan.

2. Stir in the cabbage, apples, sugar, salt, and pepper. Cover the pan and cook, stirring occasionally, until the cabbage is barely tender, 15 to 20 minutes.

3. Uncover, stir in the vinegar and cook, stirring, until the liquid cooks away.

4. Season with more salt and pepper, if needed. Top with the pecans and serve warm.

WHAT ELSE WORKS? You can use a ripe, firm pear in place of the apple. You can also cook a thinly sliced fennel bulb along with the onion.

# Brussels Sprouts Hash with Bacon and Chestnuts

1 pound small Brussels sprouts

3 thick bacon slices, cut crosswise into ¼-inch strips (about 3 ounces)

¼ to ½ cup chicken stock

1 tablespoon sugar

1 cup cooked, peeled, and chopped chestnuts

Kosher salt and ground black pepper, to taste

It's sad when people confuse bad cooking with a bad vegetable, the common plight of beleaguered and berated Brussels sprouts. Too many of these little cabbages are boiled into gruesomeness. They deserve better. A quick sauté or roast, away from water, is what they need.

I don't believe in tricking people into eating vegetables they do not like, but I'm not above altering the usual appearance of Brussels sprouts to throw the naysayers off their game. I thinly shred the sprouts into wispy disks that cook quickly. For special occasions, I will painstakingly snap loose the individual leaves of each sprout. The tiny leaves look impressive (and no one can guess what they are), but it's slow going.

MAKES 4 TO 6 SERVINGS

1. Trim the ends of the sprouts and remove any blemished outer leaves. Shred the sprouts with a knife or with the shredding disc of a food processor.

2. Cook the bacon in a large, heavy skillet over medium-high heat until crispy. Transfer with a slotted spoon to paper towels to drain.

3. Add the sprouts to the skillet and stir to coat with the bacon drippings. Pour in ¼ cup of the stock, cover, and cook, stirring often, until the sprouts are barely tender, about 10 minutes. (Only about 3 minutes for sprouts separated into individual leaves.) Add more stock if they start to cook dry. Do not let the sprouts get soggy or turn drab.

4. Stir in the sugar, chestnuts, and bacon. Season with salt and a generous amount of pepper. Serve warm.

VARIATION: For tasty skillet-roasted Brussels sprouts, cut them in half, toss with enough bacon drippings or olive oil to coat, then arrange cut-side down in a cast-iron skillet. Cover and cook undisturbed until they are nearly tender, about 5 minutes. Uncover, increase the heat to high, and cook until the cut side is caramelized, about 3 minutes. Season with salt and pepper and toss well. Serve hot.

TIPS AND TECHNIQUES

It's fine to use vacuum-sealed jars or packages of cooked and peeled chestnuts in this recipe, but if you want to roast your own, here's how. Use a sharp knife to cut an X through the skin of the flat side of each chestnut. Arrange them cut-side up on a rimmed baking sheet and roast in a 400°F oven until the nutmeats are tender and the skins start to crack open, about 20 minutes. Cover with a clean towel or aluminum foil, set aside until cool enough to handle, and then peel while warm.

## Peanut and Wasabi Slaw

¼ cup flavorful
peanut oil

2 tablespoons
toasted sesame oil

2 tablespoons
rice vinegar or
rice wine vinegar

1 tablespoon packed
light brown sugar

1 tablespoon
peanut butter

1 teaspoon soy sauce

1 teaspoon wasabi paste
or sriracha chile sauce,
or to taste (optional)

1 small napa, savoy,
or red cabbage
(about 1 pound)

½ cup thinly sliced
scallions cut on the
diagonal (white and
tender green parts)

½ cup cilantro leaves

1 cup roasted,
salted peanuts

½ cup wasabi peas
(optional)

Kosher salt, to taste

This is a great recipe for cabbages other than the traditional heads, such as napa or savoy. Actually any recipe that calls for raw or quickly cooked cabbage can be made with members of the extended cabbage clan, so long as they are fresh and tender.

You can make the slaw spicy by adding a little wasabi paste or chile sauce, such as sriracha. You can also garnish the top with wasabi peas in addition to the peanuts. Crunchy green wasabi peas are a wickedly pungent snack that will sharply remind you of the shape and location of your sinuses, but some people really like that.

Although this recipe does have a slight Asian bent, peanut slaw is a traditional southern recipe, particularly in the heart of peanut country. Most of those recipes mix peanut butter into mayonnaise. This recipe gets most of its peanut flavor from peanut oil, so be sure to buy flavorful oil meant to be used as a condiment, not the bland oil used for deep-frying turkeys. The best peanut oil is often organic and is usually found in Asian markets or in a well-stocked grocery store near other nut oils.

MAKES 6 SERVINGS

1. Whisk together the peanut oil, sesame oil, vinegar, brown sugar, peanut butter, and soy sauce in a large bowl until smooth. Whisk in the wasabi paste, if using.

2. Use a vegetable peeler, sharp knife, or vegetable slicer to cut the cabbage as thinly as possible into long, thin strands or ribbons (avoiding the core) to measure about 6 cups. Add the cabbage, scallions, and cilantro to the bowl of dressing and toss well with tongs. It will seem as though there isn't enough dressing, but there is, so keep tossing.

3. Stir in the peanuts and wasabi peas, if using. Taste the slaw and add a pinch of salt, if needed. Serve lightly chilled or at room temperature. If you plan to eat the slaw over several days, add the peanuts and wasabi peas just before serving so they'll stay crunchy.

## Sautéed Baby Bok Choy

2 garlic cloves,
thinly sliced

1 large shallot,
finely chopped

2 tablespoons rice
vinegar or rice
wine vinegar

¼ cup mirin or
cream sherry

1 tablespoon
toasted sesame oil

2 tablespoons
sesame seeds

Pinch of crushed
red pepper flakes

2 teaspoons
vegetable oil

8 baby bok choy, halved
lengthwise or cut
crosswise into 1-inch
pieces (about 1 ¼
pounds)

Bok choy, Chinese cabbage, and other similar Asian greens and cruciferous vegetables are common in some southern gardens and most farmers' markets these
days. Whereas head cabbage is a fall crop, these cabbage cousins are among the
first things to show up in the spring. Early in the season, CSA farm boxes are often filled with baby bok choy, much to the puzzlement of people who haven't
enjoyed them before, the phenomenon I call the Baby Bok Choy Conundrum.
Young, tender bok choy can be eaten raw in salads or slaw, but they are best
when lightly sautéed or stir-fried with a little seasoning. If you come across an
unfamiliar Asian vegetable, let its flavor and texture suggest how to use it. Most
are similar to cabbage, broccoli, or leafy cooking greens. If the new vegetable
reminds you of cabbage, try it in a cabbage recipe. If it's more like broccoli, treat
it like broccoli, and so on.

Although Asian ingredients do not always have to be used in Asian recipes,
that's a logical approach, even in the southern kitchen. Soy sauce, rice vinegar, sesame oil, and other basic Asian condiments are standard pantry fare for
most cooks everywhere these days. Plus, there is a long history of using sesame
seeds and sesame products in traditional southern cooking, particularly in the
Lowcountry, where the seeds still go by their African name of benne. Around
1800, there was an effort to grow huge quantities of benne seeds as a source of
cold-pressed cooking oil. The plan never took off, but many people grew smaller
quantities of the seeds to use in home kitchens.

MAKES 4 TO 6 SERVINGS

1. Whisk together the garlic, shallot, vinegar, mirin, sesame oil, sesame seeds,
and red pepper flakes in a small bowl.

2. Heat the vegetable oil in a large, heavy skillet over high heat. Add the bok choy
and stir to coat. Cook, tossing with tongs, until the bok choy leaves start to
wilt, about 1 minute. Add the garlic mixture and continue cooking and tossing until the leaves are wilted and the stems are crisp-tender, about 2 minutes
more. Serve hot.

WHAT ELSE WORKS? You can use regular bok choy, napa cabbage, Chinese
cabbage, tatsoi, mizuna, mustard greens, watercress, arugula, or other spicy
greens in place of some or all of the baby bok choy.

## Scalloped Cabbage

Vegetable oil spray

4 tablespoons (½ stick) butter, divided

1 large onion, chopped

1 bell pepper, cored and chopped

1 medium green cabbage, quartered, cored, and thinly shredded (about 12 cups)

2 tablespoons chicken stock or water

5 tablespoons instant or all-purpose flour

1 ½ cups milk

⅔ cup grated mild cheddar or Monterey Jack cheese

1 teaspoon kosher salt

½ teaspoon ground black pepper

¼ teaspoon freshly grated nutmeg

2 cups fresh bread crumbs (page 389)

2 tablespoons butter, melted

Scalloping vegetables is a classic southern technique that cooks once did by rote, never measuring or glancing at a recipe. The vegetable, cabbage in this case, is mixed with mild cream sauce and topped with buttered crumbs. Old recipes call for boiling the cabbage, which does it no favors and can leave it waterlogged, bland, and sometimes smelly. A fresh cabbage contains enough moisture to release its own cooking liquid, so my update to the classic is to lightly sauté the cabbage until barely tender, so that it retains its identifiable flavor—in a good way.

MAKES 8 SERVINGS

1. Preheat the oven to 350°F. Mist the inside of a 9 × 13-inch baking dish with the spray.

2. Heat 1 tablespoon of the butter in a large skillet over medium-high heat. Stir in the onion and bell pepper and a pinch of salt and cook, stirring often, until softened, about 8 minutes. Stir in the cabbage and stock. Cook, stirring often, until the cabbage is crisp-tender, about 10 minutes. Remove the skillet from the heat.

3. Heat the remaining 3 tablespoons of butter in a large saucepan over low heat. Whisk in the flour and cook, whisking constantly, for 2 minutes; do not let the flour brown. Slowly whisk in the milk, whisking until the mixture is smooth. Cook, stirring slowly and constantly with a heat-proof spatula, until the sauce is thick enough to coat the back of the spatula. Remove from the heat and stir in the cheese. Season with the salt, pepper, and nutmeg. Pour over the cabbage and mix well. Scrape into the prepared baking dish.

4. Toss the bread crumbs with the melted butter in a small bowl and sprinkle over the cabbage mixture. Bake until the crumbs are browned and the cabbage is bubbly around the edges, about 35 minutes. The dish will be like hot lava straight from the oven, so let it sit for at least 10 minutes before serving. Serve warm.

# Unrolled Stuffed Cabbage Rolls

**OVEN-BRAISED CABBAGE**

- 2 teaspoons vegetable oil
- 1 small green cabbage (about 2 pounds)
- ¼ cup chicken stock or water
- 1 teaspoon kosher salt
- ½ teaspoon ground black pepper

**SWEET AND SOUR MEAT AND TOMATO SAUCE**

- 1 tablespoon vegetable oil
- 1 medium onion, chopped
- 1 pound ground round or meatloaf mix
- 1 (28-ounce) can crushed tomatoes
- 3 tablespoons raisins
- 3 tablespoons packed light brown sugar
- 1 teaspoon sour salt or 3 tablespoons lemon juice
- 6 cups hot cooked white rice, for serving

Stuffed cabbage rolls are delicious, but they are a pain to make. All of the traditional components—tender cabbage, sweet-and-sour tomato sauce, ground meat, and rice—are here, but they are cooked separately and served together, instead of tediously assembling rolls. The cabbage is braised in the oven and served in wedges, so those curious conical cabbages are ideal, although regular round cabbage is fine.

A friend taught me to use sour salt in the sauce. Sour salt is powdered citric acid that adds bright tang to food, not actually a type of salt. It is found in the kosher section of well-stocked grocery stores and in most Middle Eastern markets. Lemon juice is a good substitute.

MAKES 6 SERVINGS

1. Preheat the oven to 325°F. Oil a 9 × 13-inch glass or ceramic baking dish.

2. For the cabbage: Remove any tough, ragged, or unruly outer cabbage leaves. Cut the cabbage in half lengthwise. Cut each half into 3 equal wedges, leaving a sliver of core attached to each wedge to hold it together. Arrange the wedges in a single layer in the baking dish. They must be in a single layer, so tuck them in tightly if necessary. Pour the stock over the wedges and sprinkle with the salt and pepper. Cover the dish tightly with aluminum foil and bake until the cabbage is tender but the wedges are not falling apart, about 1 hour.

3. For the sauce: Heat the oil in a large skillet over medium-high heat. Stir in the onion and a pinch of salt and cook, stirring often, until softened, about 5 minutes. Add the meat and cook until no longer pink, stirring often to break it up into small pieces. Add the tomatoes, raisins, brown sugar, and sour salt. Reduce the heat, cover, and simmer until the sauce is thick, about 1 hour, or until the cabbage is done. Taste the sauce and adjust the seasoning to make sure there is a good balance of sweet and sour.

4. To serve, spoon rice onto serving plates. Top with a wedge of cabbage and ladle the sauce over all. Serve hot.

MAKE-AHEAD NOTE: The sauce can be made a day ahead. Cool, cover, and refrigerate and then reheat before serving. Cook the cabbage just before serving because it does not reheat well.

# CARROTS

**The first carrots appeared in the New World** along with the first colonists. Carrots were valued as medicine and as elemental seasoning in other dishes. When old cookbooks said to season the base of a savory dish, it was assumed that the cook would know that meant some combination of carrots and onions. Young carrots were used to add sweetness to pies and puddings, as were parsnips. Some mothers used small sweet carrots as pacifiers and teethers for their babies. Southerners did not develop a fondness for the tops of carrots the way they did with turnips and beets, but they are sometimes included among the many greens in the Lenten dish Gumbo z'Herbes.

One of the many advantages of eating local food is the opportunity to find regional varieties of vegetables rarely seen in commercial grocery stores. A walk down most produce aisles would suggest that all carrots must be uniformly long and pointy or whittled down into little stubs. Not so. Carrots are diverse; some varieties stay pencil-thin and others turn out short and stout. Beyond the familiar orange, carrots can be white, yellow, and magenta. A well-grown carrot is bursting with intense sweet, earthy carrot flavor that is enjoyable raw or cooked. ■

## Roasted Carrots

2 pounds whole baby carrots with their greens

2 tablespoons extra-virgin olive oil

1 teaspoon coarse or kosher salt

½ teaspoon ground black pepper

This is my favorite way to cook whole baby carrots. I mean truly young carrots that are only a few inches long and quite slender. These carrots, which sometimes come in bunches of mixed colors, are exceptionally tender, juicy, and sweet. These shapely carrots are too pretty to cut, so roast them whole. However, if you want to roast larger carrots, cut them lengthwise into halves or quarters, or on the diagonal into ½-inch-thick slices. The attached greens should look lively and fresh. Harvested root vegetables draw moisture from their greens, so if the greens are wilted, the edible roots are well past fresh.

The so-called baby carrots sold in bags at the grocery are not immature carrots; they are large carrots that have been whittled down to that uniform size, so they do not have the same sweet and focused flavor as real baby carrots.

MAKES 4 TO 6 SERVINGS

1. Position a rack in the lower third of the oven and preheat to 425°F.
2. Thoroughly scrub and dry the carrots. (Peel only if necessary.) Trim off all but ½ inch of the greens, or remove them completely if you prefer. Arrange the carrots in a single layer on a foil-lined rimmed baking sheet. Drizzle with the oil and roll back and forth to coat.
3. Roast until the carrots are tender when pierced with a knife, 20 to 40 minutes, depending on the size and freshness of the carrots.
4. Remove from the oven and season generously with the salt and pepper. Serve warm or at room temperature.

VARIATION: Drizzle the hot carrots with a little honey and finely chopped fresh rosemary, in addition to the salt and pepper, as soon as they come out of the oven.

WHAT ELSE WORKS? You can add parsnips cut lengthwise into strips that are the same size as the carrots.

# Skillet Carrots with Bright Spices

4 large carrots, peeled (about 8 ounces)

½ teaspoon ground cumin

½ teaspoon ground cinnamon

¼ teaspoon paprika

1 tablespoon extra-virgin olive oil

½ teaspoon kosher salt

⅛ teaspoon ground Grains of Paradise or black pepper

2 teaspoons fresh lemon juice

2 tablespoons chopped flat-leaf parsley

The bright, bold spices in this simple dish balance the natural sweetness of fresh carrots. Served warm, the carrots are a great side dish at dinner. Served at room temperature, they are more like a salad or pickled vegetable and go well with sandwiches.

MAKES 4 TO 6 SERVINGS

1. Cut the carrots into long diagonal slices that are ¼-inch thick. If the slices are very wide, cut them in half lengthwise.
2. Stir together the cumin, cinnamon, and paprika in a small bowl.
3. Heat the oil in a large skillet (preferably cast-iron) over high heat until shimmering hot. Add the carrots and stir to coat with the oil. Cook, stirring often, until crisp-tender and lightly browned along the edges, about 5 minutes.
4. Remove the skillet from the heat, sprinkle the cumin mixture over the carrots, and stir quickly to lightly coat the carrots. Immediately pour onto a serving plate so that the spices won't burn in the hot pan. Season with the salt and Grains of Paradise. Sprinkle with the lemon juice and parsley. Serve hot, warm, or at room temperature.

VARIATION: You can vary this recipe by playing up either its salty side or its sweet side. To go with the salty, garnish the carrots with a few finely chopped oil-cured black olives. To go with the sweet, serve them with juicy orange sections and perhaps a drizzle of pomegranate molasses.

## Savory Carrot and Cheese Soufflé

2 pounds small carrots, peeled and coarsely chopped

½ cup freshly grated Gruyère cheese

¼ cup pecans

2 large eggs, at room temperature

1 tablespoon unsalted butter, at room temperature

½ teaspoon ground white pepper

This is not an official soufflé but an example of the traditional southern practice of using the word "soufflé" to describe certain baked vegetable dishes that contain eggs. This type of soufflé is very similar to the vegetable *sformato* I enjoyed in Italy.

This savory dish has layers of subtle flavors that are a wonderful accompaniment to roasted meats, from turkey to beef. The nutty flavor of Gruyère is always a good choice for this dish, but if you adore blue cheese, try it. I suggest a mild domestic blue or Gorgonzola dolce.

Unlike real soufflés, this dish tastes better when given time to cool a little after it comes out of the oven. When the soufflé is too hot, you can't taste all the subtle flavors (not to mention that the molten cheese will burn the roof of your mouth).

MAKES 6 SERVINGS

1. Preheat the oven to 350°F. Generously butter a shallow 1 ½-quart glass or ceramic baking dish.

2. Bring a medium saucepan of water to a boil. Add ½ teaspoon kosher salt per cup of water. Add the carrots, reduce the heat, and simmer until just tender, about 15 minutes. Drain the carrots and set aside to steam dry and cool a little.

3. Combine the Gruyère and pecans in the bowl of a food processor fitted with the metal blade and pulse until coarsely chopped. Add the carrots and pulse until chopped. With the machine running, add the eggs one at a time and process until smooth. Add the butter and pulse to mix. Season with the white pepper. The purée shouldn't need salt, but taste to make sure.

4. Scrape the purée into the prepared dish and bake until the top is lightly browned, about 30 minutes. Let cool for at least 10 minutes before serving warm.

WHAT ELSE WORKS? You can use roasted sweet potato or winter squash purée in place of the carrots. The purée must have the texture of canned pumpkin, so drain it in a mesh sieve if necessary. See the directions for making purée on page 326 or 368.

## Carrot Snack Cake with Cream Cheese Buttercream

CAKE

- 1 cup all-purpose flour
- 1 teaspoon baking powder
- 1 teaspoon baking soda
- 1 teaspoon ground cinnamon
- ½ teaspoon ground ginger
- ½ teaspoon fine sea salt
- ½ cup vegetable oil
- ¼ cup well-shaken buttermilk
- ½ teaspoon pure vanilla extract
- 2 large eggs, at room temperature
- ½ cup granulated sugar
- ½ cup packed light brown sugar
- 2 cups coarsely shredded carrots
- ½ cup pecan pieces (about 2 ounces)
- 1 cup peeled and finely grated golden beets or additional carrots

FROSTING

- 6 ounces cream cheese, at room temperature
- 4 tablespoons (½ stick) unsalted butter, at room temperature
- 1 teaspoon pure vanilla extract
- 2 cups sifted confectioners' sugar

This is not a huge, rich, layer cake. Instead, this is a single layer of spice cake, studded with carrots and nuts and capped with incredibly creamy frosting. It's a reasonable size that can be finished in a day or two without needing to fend off the too-much-cake sugar-shock blues.

The frosting is a cross between traditional cream cheese frosting and buttercream, which makes it soft and fluffy. It spreads on easily without tearing up the cake. If you should happen to have any leftover frosting after you've put all you want on the cake, use it on bagels.

If you're up for a little experimentation, try using yellow beets in place of some of the carrots. After all, some beets are sweet enough to be used as a source of sugar.

MAKES 8 SERVINGS

1. For the cake: Preheat the oven to 350°F. Grease and flour a 9-inch round cake pan.

2. Whisk together the flour, baking powder, baking soda, cinnamon, ginger, and salt in a medium bowl. Whisk together the oil, buttermilk, and vanilla in a small bowl.

3. Beat the eggs, granulated sugar, and brown sugar until light and fluffy in a large bowl with an electric mixer set to high speed, about 5 minutes. Beat in the oil mixture. Add the flour mixture and beat only until it disappears into the batter. Use a rubber spatula to fold in the carrots, pecans, and beets.

4. Bake until a tester inserted into the center of the cake comes out clean, the top springs back when lightly pressed in the center, and the sides begin to pull away from the pan, 30 to 35 minutes. Cool the cake in the pan on a wire rack for 30 minutes and then turn out onto the rack to cool to room temperature before frosting.

5. For the frosting: Beat the cream cheese, butter, and vanilla until smooth and creamy in a medium bowl with an electric mixer. Add the confectioners' sugar, ½ cup at a time, beating until smooth after each addition.

6. Spread the frosting over the top of the cooled cake, leaving the sides bare.

# Gingered Root Vegetable Soup

4 tablespoons
(½ stick) butter

1 large onion, chopped

¼ cup peeled and
very finely chopped
fresh ginger

2 medium carrots,
peeled and chopped
(about 3 cups)

2 medium sweet
potatoes, peeled and
chopped (about 3 cups)

2 medium parsnips,
peeled and chopped
(about 2 cups)

1 apple, peeled,
cored, and chopped
(about 1 cup)

4 to 5 cups chicken or
vegetable stock,
divided

1 teaspoon kosher salt,
plus more to taste

½ teaspoon ground
black pepper, plus
more to taste

½ cup half-and-half

¼ cup pure maple syrup

2 teaspoons chopped
fresh thyme

Crème fraîche
(page 388 or store-
bought) and root
vegetable chips,
for garnish

This warm, lush soup is like autumn in a bowl. Earthy root vegetables are enhanced by the spark of fresh ginger and a sweet splash of pure maple syrup. A dollop of crème fraîche and a handful of those jewel-toned root vegetable chips finish each serving with a flourish. Crème fraîche — thick cultured cream that is less tangy and more velvety than sour cream — is available in the cheese department of specialty stores and many grocery stores, or you can make your own using the recipe on page 388.

Most of the flavor of fresh ginger is in its juice, so look for pieces that are plump and unblemished. Old ginger gets quite dry and fibrous, so when grated it looks and tastes like broom straw in the soup.

MAKES 8 SERVINGS

1. Melt the butter in a large, heavy pot over medium heat. Add the onion and a pinch of salt and cook, stirring often, until softened, about 8 minutes. Add the ginger and cook for 1 minute. Add the carrots, sweet potatoes, parsnips, and apple, 4 cups of the stock, and the salt and pepper. Increase the heat to high and bring just to a boil. Reduce the heat to medium-low, partially cover the pot, and simmer until the vegetables are tender, about 15 minutes.

2. Purée in a blender (working in batches to not fill the blender more than half full) and return it to the pot or purée the soup directly in the pot with an immersion blender. Stir in the half-and-half, maple syrup, and thyme. The soup should be very thick, but if it's more like a purée than a soup, add more stock.

3. Season with salt and pepper. Serve warm, garnished with crème fraîche and chips.

WHAT ELSE WORKS? You can use cubes of winter squash or sugar pumpkin in place of some or all of the sweet potatoes.

MAKE-AHEAD NOTE: You can make the soup up to 2 days ahead. Cool, cover, and refrigerate. Check the seasoning when you gently reheat the soup.

# Braised Corned Beef and Carrots
## with Whiskey and Marmalade Glaze

**BRAISED
CORNED BEEF**

1 corned beef brisket,
drained and rinsed
(about 3 pounds)

2 bay leaves

2 teaspoons black
peppercorns

4 whole allspice

2 whole cloves

12 large carrots, peeled
and halved or
quartered lengthwise

Kosher salt and ground
black pepper, to taste

**WHISKEY AND
MARMALADE GLAZE**

1 cup sweet orange
marmalade

½ cup whiskey
or bourbon

⅛ teaspoon
ground nutmeg

1 tablespoon
whole-grain
Dijon mustard

There's a lot of Celtic ancestral blood running through the Blue Ridge Mountains where I grew up, which might explain why I felt so at home with the wonderful food I enjoyed during my trips to Ireland. Each time I serve this great dish, I see people going back to the platter in search of more carrots. It's true, the carrots are the best part, but it would be a shame to throw away all that meat, so you might as well eat it, too.

MAKES 8 SERVINGS

1. Preheat the oven to 300°F.

2. Place the corned beef in a large Dutch oven with a tight-fitting lid and cover with cold water. Add the bay leaves, peppercorns, allspice, and cloves. Bring to a boil uncovered, then skim off and discard any foam that rises to the surface. Cover the pot and transfer to the oven. Braise the meat until very tender, about 4 hours.

3. Meanwhile, make the glaze: Combine the marmalade, whiskey, and nutmeg in a small saucepan. Bring to a simmer over medium-high heat and reduce to 1 cup, stirring often. Remove the pan from the heat and stir in the mustard.

4. Increase the oven temperature to 425°F. Line a large rimmed baking sheet with nonstick aluminum foil or with regular foil misted with vegetable oil spray. Drain the beef and pat it dry. Scrape off the visible fat and place the meat in the center of the prepared baking sheet.

5. Arrange the carrots around the beef and sprinkle them with salt and pepper. Spoon the glaze over the meat and carrots.

6. Roast until the carrots are tender and the beef is warmed through, about 35 minutes. Serve hot.

## Carrot and Tropical Fruit Salad

2 tablespoons mayonnaise

2 tablespoons sour cream

1 tablespoon sugar

¼ teaspoon kosher salt

1 pound carrots, peeled

½ cup flaked coconut

½ cup finely diced fresh pineapple or drained, crushed pineapple

¼ cup finely chopped dried mango or golden raisins

This is what I make instead of the usual carrot and raisin salad. Any variety of carrot works so long as it is a very tender, sweet, and juicy one, but I'm partial to white carrots. This recipe is very popular with children, probably because it's a little sweet. When served with a few crisp gingersnaps on the side, you could pass this off as a light dessert.

Coconut has long been popular in southern cooking, especially near the coast, where coconuts first entered the South through the deep ports of Charleston and Savannah. Hard, sturdy coconuts traveled well and were slow to spoil, so they could make their way inland and spread throughout the South in the days before trains, trucks, and refrigeration.

MAKES 4 TO 6 SERVINGS

1. Whisk together the mayonnaise, sour cream, sugar, and salt in a large bowl and set aside.
2. Coarsely grate the carrots with a box grater or in a food processor fitted with the coarse shredding disc and add them to the mayonnaise mixture. Add the coconut, pineapple, and dried mango and stir to coat.
3. Cover and refrigerate for at least 1 hour. Stir well before serving.

## Vegetable Stew over Almond Couscous

### STEW

4 tablespoons vegetable oil, divided

2 red and/or yellow bell peppers, cored and cut into 1-inch pieces (about 2 cups)

2 small zucchini, trimmed and cut into 1-inch pieces (about 2 cups)

Kosher salt, to taste

1 medium carrot, peeled and cut into 1-inch pieces (about 1 cup)

2 medium sweet potatoes, peeled and cut into 1-inch pieces (about 3 cups)

(continued on next page)

This flavorful, colorful, delightful stew is worth all the steps. It's inspired by tagine, a traditional dish from North Africa in which vegetables (and often meat) are simmered in spicy broth and served over couscous. This stew is a great recipe to make during the transitional season of early autumn, when the summer produce is still available and the fall produce has started to come in. The recipe is contemporary, but the art of generously seasoning fresh produce with aromatic spices is not new to the southern kitchen.

Three things will make this recipe a winner. First, keep the pieces of vegetable large so that it really is a stew and not a soup. Second, be sure to cook the vegetables in batches as described, so that each ingredient gets its appropriate cooking time. That can't happen if everything is dumped into the pot at once. Third, make sure your spices are fresh, potent, and aromatic. A dried spice that has no aroma has no flavor, so the only thing it adds to your dish is dust.

A traditional garnish for this type of stew is a fiery condiment called harissa, but any spicy condiment such as an Indian-style tomato chutney or Tomato Jam (page 354) is fine.

MAKES 8 SERVINGS

3 small parsnips, peeled and cut into 1-inch pieces (about 2 cups)

1 large yellow onion, halved lengthwise and cut into thin strips (about 3 cups)

1 teaspoon ground turmeric

1 tablespoon garam masala

1 teaspoon ground cinnamon

¼ teaspoon cayenne pepper

½ teaspoon ground black pepper

1 cup chicken or vegetable stock

1 (14 ½-ounce) can whole tomatoes

2 (14 ½-ounce) cans chickpeas, drained

½ cup currants, raisins, or chopped dried apricots

North African harissa, Indian-style tomato chutney, or Tomato Jam (page 354), for garnish

## ALMOND COUSCOUS

3 cups chicken or vegetable stock

1 tablespoon extra-virgin olive oil

1 teaspoon kosher salt

1 ½ cups uncooked couscous

½ cup slivered almonds, toasted

1. For the stew: Heat 1 tablespoon of the oil in a large pot or Dutch oven over medium heat. Stir in the peppers and zucchini and a pinch of salt. Cover and cook until crisp-tender, about 8 minutes, stirring often. Transfer into a large bowl.

2. Heat another 1 tablespoon of the oil in the pot. Stir in the carrot, sweet potatoes, and parsnips and a pinch of salt. Cover and cook until crisp-tender, about 12 minutes, stirring often. Add to the bowl.

3. Heat the remaining 2 tablespoons of oil in the pot. Stir in the onion and a pinch of salt. Cover and cook until softened, about 8 minutes, stirring often. Stir in the turmeric, garam masala, cinnamon, cayenne, and black pepper and cook until the spices release their fragrance, about 1 minute, stirring constantly. Do not let them scorch. Stir in the stock.

4. Return the cooked vegetables to the pot and stir in the tomatoes, chickpeas, and currants. Break up the tomatoes with the spoon. Simmer until the vegetables are tender, about 15 minutes. The broth should be generously spiced and richly flavored, so check the seasoning. Keep the stew warm over low heat.

5. For the couscous: Bring the stock, oil, and salt to a boil in a large saucepan. Stir in the couscous. Remove the pan from the heat, cover, and set aside until the couscous absorbs all of the liquid, 7 to 10 minutes. Fluff with a fork and stir in the almonds.

6. To serve, spoon the warm stew over the warm couscous, garnishing with a spoonful of harissa.

MAKE-AHEAD NOTE: You can make the stew up to 2 days ahead. Reheat gently and check the seasoning before serving.

# CAULIFLOWER

"Cauliflower," wrote Mark Twain, "is nothing but cabbage with a college education." Cauliflower is indeed a cultivated member of the cabbage family and was being planted in the American colonies by the 1600s. Each group of immigrants that brought along cauliflower, mainly the English, the Sicilians, and some Asians, took its own approach to handling cauliflower's noncommittal flavor, from taming it down even further with cream and eggs to punching it up with bold spices. Even now, southern cooks rarely rave about any intrinsic tastiness in naked cauliflower, but they do appreciate its willingness to play well with other ingredients. Beyond basic steaming, cooks are discovering the mellow, nuanced flavor of cauliflower cooked in other ways, particularly roasted.

Most cauliflowers grow in large heads of thick white clusters, shielded from too much sunlight by broad, deeply ribbed leaves. However, some new varieties produce small heads with astonishing, vibrant colors, such as orange, canary yellow, deep purple, and bright green. Mild Romanesca cauliflower, sometimes called broccoli Romanesco or summer cauliflower, is particularly striking, with its lime green florets rising up in pointed, spiraling pyramids and cones. ■

## Spice-Roasted Cauliflower Florets

2 teaspoons sugar

½ teaspoon kosher salt

¼ teaspoon ground black pepper

½ teaspoon curry powder, preferably red sambahr-style

½ teaspoon ground cinnamon

¼ teaspoon ground ginger

Pinch of cayenne pepper

4 cups 2-inch cauliflower florets (about 1 pound)

2 tablespoons butter, melted

2 tablespoons extra-virgin olive oil

The crispness of freshly picked cauliflower makes it a good candidate for roasting. In this recipe, florets are lightly dusted in bright spices before they go into the oven. The result is an interesting dish that can be used as a side dish or snazzy appetizer, particularly when served with Tomato Jam (page 354) or Coconut-Cilantro Pesto (page 190).

MAKES 4 TO 6 SERVINGS

1. Preheat the oven to 450°F.

2. Mix the sugar, salt, pepper, curry powder, cinnamon, ginger, and cayenne in a small bowl.

3. Place the cauliflower in a large bowl. Drizzle with the butter and oil and toss to coat. Sprinkle the spices evenly over the cauliflower and toss to coat.

4. Spread in a single layer on a foil-lined rimmed baking sheet. Roast, stirring every 5 minutes, until the florets are crisp-tender and browned on the edges, about 25 minutes. Serve warm or at room temperature.

## Layered Overnight Salad

3 cups bite-sized crunchy romaine or iceberg lettuce pieces

2 cups fresh or thawed tiny green peas

1 small red onion, halved lengthwise and thinly sliced

3 cups small cauliflower florets

1 large red bell pepper, chopped

1 cup diced cooked bacon

1 to 2 cups mayonnaise

¼ to ½ cup sugar, to taste

2 cups coarsely grated cheddar cheese

People either grew up with this salad or have never heard of it. The mayonnaise, sugar, and bacon meld into an incredible dressing that lightly coats the vegetables without making them soggy. Because the recipe makes a ton and the salad holds well for a few days, it is great for potlucks, family reunions, or dinner on the grounds. Be sure to assemble the salad in a pretty glass bowl; it's too pretty to hide.

This is a great place to use colored cauliflower, from golden to purple.

MAKES 8 SERVINGS

1. Layer the lettuce, peas, onion, cauliflower, bell pepper, and bacon in a large, deep serving bowl.

2. Spread the mayonnaise evenly over the top. (The amount varies, depending on the diameter of the bowl.) Sprinkle the sugar evenly over the mayonnaise. (Don't omit the sugar or substitute artificial sweetener. Real granulated sugar is integral to the salad, but you can adjust the amount to taste.) Sprinkle the cheese over the top.

3. Cover and refrigerate overnight. Just before serving, stir well to coat the vegetables with the dressing.

## Savory Mashed Cauliflower

1 small cauliflower, cored and chopped (about 2 pounds)

4 garlic cloves

1½ cups chicken stock

2 tablespoons butter, at room temperature

1 cup sour cream

½ cup grated cheddar cheese

½ cup grated Parmesan cheese

2 teaspoons kosher salt, or to taste

1 teaspoon ground black pepper, or to taste

I love creamy, buttery foods, so perhaps that's why I'm a sucker for this recipe. It is reminiscent of mashed potatoes but lighter and more appropriate for warm weather. We usually think of cauliflower's crunch, but the smooth texture of this recipe seems to bring out the best of a cauliflower's flavor. You might never again settle for plain steamed florets.

MAKES 6 TO 8 SERVINGS

1. Bring the cauliflower, garlic, and stock to a simmer in a large saucepan over medium-high heat. Cook until the cauliflower is very tender, about 15 minutes.

2. Working in batches, use a slotted spoon to transfer the cauliflower and garlic into the bowl of a food processor fitted with the metal blade. Do not fill the bowl more than half full. Process to the consistency of soft mashed potatoes. Add a splash of the cooking liquid, if needed. (For coarser texture, simply mash the cauliflower with a hand-held potato masher or a fork.) Transfer the purée into a large bowl. Fold in the butter, sour cream, cheddar, and Parmesan. Season with the salt and pepper. Serve hot.

WHAT ELSE WORKS? You can replace some or all the cauliflower with broccoli or broccoli Romanesco.

## Caramelized Cauliflower Slices with Pine Nuts, Capers, and Raisins

3 tablespoons golden raisins

1 large cauliflower, trimmed of leaves

2 tablespoons extra-virgin olive oil, divided

Kosher salt and ground black pepper, to taste

2 tablespoons butter

¼ cup fresh bread crumbs (page 389)

¼ cup pine nuts

2 teaspoons finely chopped garlic

(continued on next page)

Sometimes a vegetable tastes new and different simply because it's cut in an unexpected way. Here, the cauliflower is cut into thick slices, which not only look intriguing, but have plenty of surface area to capture the natural sweetness that comes from caramelizing vegetables. The dish is finished with a simple topping that adds loads of Mediterranean flavor. This is hearty enough to serve as a meatless entrée.

MAKES 6 TO 8 SERVINGS

1. Preheat the oven to 350°F. Lightly oil a 9 × 13-inch baking dish.

2. Place the raisins in a small bowl, cover with hot tap water, and set aside to let the raisins plump up.

3. Cut the cauliflower from top to bottom into quarters. Cut each quarter crosswise into ½-inch-thick slices. Heat 2 teaspoons of the oil in a large skillet (preferably cast-iron) over medium-high heat. Add enough cauliflower slices to cover the bottom of the skillet and cook until lightly browned and caramelized on both sides. Arrange the slices, overlapping slightly, in the prepared dish. Repeat with the rest of the cauliflower, adding more oil as needed. Season with salt and pepper. Place in the oven to roast until tender, about 15 minutes.

1 tablespoon
    capers, drained

1 tablespoon white
    wine vinegar

1 tablespoon finely
    chopped flat-leaf
    parsley

8 tablespoons
    (1 stick) butter

2 cups chopped onion

1 cup chopped leeks (white
    and tender green parts)

1 cup diced celery
    root (celeriac)

½ cup instant or all-
    purpose flour

4 cups chicken stock

6 cups coarsely
    chopped cauliflower
    (about 1 ½ pounds)

1 tart apple, peeled,
    cored, and chopped

1 teaspoon kosher salt,
    plus more to taste

1 cup apple cider

½ cup half-and-half or
    whole milk

1 teaspoon chopped
    fresh thyme

3 ounces crumbled
    blue cheese

1 teaspoon whole pink
    peppercorns or coarsely
    ground Grains of
    Paradise, for garnish

④ Meanwhile, heat the butter in the skillet over medium-high heat. Add the bread crumbs, pine nuts, and garlic and stir to coat. Cook, stirring often, until the crumbs are toasted, about 5 minutes. Transfer into a medium bowl. Drain the raisins and add to the bread crumb mixture. Stir in the capers, vinegar, and parsley and season with salt and pepper. Sprinkle over the cauliflower and serve hot.

VARIATION: The recipe also works with those miniature heads of colorful cauliflower. If the heads are no larger than a baseball, leave them whole; otherwise, cut them in half lengthwise. Skip the browning step and simply roast until tender.

## Cauliflower, Apple, and Blue Cheese Soup

The flavor of this soup is subtle, making a great background for a little blue cheese. Milder blue cheese keeps the flavor in check and doesn't give the soup a gray tinge, so choose one that isn't too old and has minimal blue veining. Cambozola, a Brie-style cheese with only a single thin strand of blue in the center, is a good choice.

A sprinkling of pink peppercorns adds color and crunch. Pink peppercorns are not really peppercorns; they are the bud of a member of the rose family, so they have a fruity, floral quality. Another choice is Grains of Paradise, a dried spice that tastes like a blend of coriander, black pepper, and nutmeg.

When served in demitasse cups, this soup is a lovely warm appetizer.

MAKES ABOUT 2 QUARTS

① Melt the butter in a large, heavy saucepan or small soup pot over medium heat. Add the onion, leeks, and celery root and a generous pinch of salt. Cook, stirring often, until the vegetables soften but do not brown, about 8 minutes.

② Add the flour and cook, stirring constantly, for 2 minutes. Gradually whisk in the stock and stir until smooth. Add the cauliflower, apple, and salt. Bring the soup to a boil, reduce the heat, cover partially, and simmer until the cauliflower is tender, about 20 minutes. Stir in the cider and the half-and-half.

③ Purée in a blender (working in batches to not fill the blender more than half full) and return it to the pot or purée the soup directly in the pot with an immersion blender. Bring to a simmer, add the thyme and cheese, and stir until the cheese melts. Season with salt. Serve warm, garnished with a few pink peppercorns.

MAKE-AHEAD NOTE: The soup can be partially made up to 1 day ahead. Store covered and refrigerated. Do not add the cheese until you reheat the soup.

# CHERRIES

**Some food historians write that the French and the English** introduced more than twenty varieties of cherries to the American colonies during the 1700s. As schoolchildren, we were certainly taught to believe that George Washington's family had at least one tree, at least for a time.

In the southern colonies, the growing season for cherries was brief and the fruit was highly perishable, so fresh cherries were not as valuable to early southerners as the brandy, wine, and ratafia made from them. The limited supply of fresh cherries was most valuable in medicine, often used as a flavoring to mask bitter potions. Even now, cherry remains a favorite flavoring for cough drops, and cherry-esque red is the most popular "flavor" for Kool-Aid and other very sweet drinks.

Cherries are stubbornly seasonal, giving us months of eager anticipation. During the fleeting season, cherry lovers clamor for the plump, juicy orbs, eager to gobble up as many of the sweet ones as they can hold and using the rest—even the sour ones—in tempting recipes. Cherries have a cheerfulness about them. ■

# Pan-Roasted Duck Breasts with Cherries

CHERRIES

1 ½ cups large sweet cherries, pitted (about 8 ounces)

2 teaspoons extra-virgin olive oil

1 tablespoon ruby port wine or Madeira

2 teaspoons balsamic vinegar, preferably cherry balsamic

½ teaspoon finely chopped fresh rosemary

½ teaspoon kosher salt

¼ teaspoon ground black pepper

DUCK

2 duck breasts (each about 1 pound; see note)

1 teaspoon kosher salt

½ teaspoon ground black pepper

This is my favorite way to cook duck breasts. I start them in a cold cast-iron skillet so that the delicious fat has time to melt before the skin sears. The result is wonderfully browned and crisp skin, tender meat, and lots of flavorful rendered fat to use in other recipes.

The warm, soft cherries are part sauce, part side dish, and very easy. I pit the cherries, but some people skip that step. They figure that you ought to know that a whole cherry contains a pit, just like you know that a whole apple contains seeds. These cherries also go well with venison, game birds, salmon, and blue cheese.

For a great menu, serve this with Glazed Baby Turnips and Apples (page 363) and Mashed Root Vegetables (page 360).

MAKES 2 TO 4 SERVINGS

1. Preheat the oven to 400°F.

2. Put the cherries in a small ovenproof skillet or baking dish, drizzle with the oil, and roll them around to coat.

3. Trim away the fat around the edges of the duck breasts so that it does not hang over the sides of the meat. Score the skin in a crosshatch pattern, making diagonal cuts at ½-inch intervals just through the skin and fat but not into the meat. Sprinkle both sides with the salt and pepper. Place the breasts, skin-side down, in a large cast-iron skillet. (Do not preheat the skillet.) Place on the stove and cook undisturbed over medium heat until the skin is very crisp and browned and much of the fat is rendered, about 15 minutes. When well seared, the duck will release easily from the skillet with no tugging. Carefully pour off the fat into a glass jar with a tight-fitting lid to store for another use. Turn the breasts over.

4. Put both the cherries and the duck into the oven. Roast the duck until it is done to your liking, about 10 minutes for medium-rare. (If you cut into the center of a breast, it should be deep pink, but not raw. An instant-read thermometer inserted into the center of the breast should register 130°F.) Roast about 3 minutes longer if you prefer your duck medium. Transfer the breasts to a cutting board and let rest for 5 minutes before cutting into thin slices.

5. Roast the cherries until they are soft, about 13 minutes. Stir in the port, vinegar, and rosemary. Season with the salt and pepper. Stir in any accumulated duck jus.

6. Serve the sliced duck warm, topped with the roasted cherries.

NOTE: This recipe calls for large duck breasts, such as magret. You can also use 4 smaller breasts, such as pekin or wild duck, but reduce the roasting time by about 5 minutes.

## Fresh Cherry Compote with Cream Cheese Pound Cake

1 cup cherry or red currant jelly

2 tablespoons fresh lemon juice

3 cups fresh sweet or sour cherries, pitted

2 teaspoons chopped fresh thyme, preferably lemon thyme

1 tablespoon kirsch or cassis (optional)

This easy compote is fantastic on the moist Cream Cheese Pound Cake, but it's also good on ice cream or with cheese. Any variety of cherry will do, but larger cherries usually look better because they remain intact after pitting. The thyme complements the cherries and makes the compote interesting. You can also use other herbs, such as lemon balm, lemon verbena, or rose geranium.

MAKES ABOUT 3 CUPS

1. Melt the jelly in a medium saucepan over low heat. Stir in the lemon juice, cherries, thyme, and kirsch, if using.
2. Serve slightly warm or cover and refrigerate until chilled.

## Cream Cheese Pound Cake

1 ½ cups (3 sticks) unsalted butter, at room temperature

8 ounces cream cheese, at room temperature (not reduced fat or fat-free)

3 cups sugar

6 large eggs, at room temperature

3 cups cake flour, sifted

1 teaspoon pure vanilla extract

½ teaspoon ground mace or 1 teaspoon almond extract

This is my favorite pound cake—it's dense, moist, simple, and old-fashioned. Southern bakers take special pride in flawless homemade pound cake, although we eaters are surprisingly tolerant of a less-than-perfect cake that just didn't turn out this time. Sometimes pound cakes develop a little doughy ribbon of dense cake that runs through the center. We call this the sad streak, and some people consider this a failure. But some people think it's the best part of the cake and root for it to happen.

I add ground mace because my grandmother loved mace in this cake. Not everyone at home liked mace, so she would scrape half the batter into one side of the pan and then stir the mace into the other half before adding it to the pan. She marked the mace side with a single drop of red food coloring swirled through the batter with a toothpick. I was nearly grown before I learned that not everyone did this.

This cake freezes well. Wrap individual slices in plastic wrap and then put the wrapped slices in a large freezer bag to store frozen for up to three months. Suddenly remembering that you have cake in the freezer can be the best thing that happens all day.

MAKES 12 SERVINGS

1. Position one rack in the bottom and another in the middle of the oven. Place a large baking pan of water on the lower rack. Preheat the oven to 325°F. Thoroughly grease and flour a 10-inch light metal tube pan. (A dark metal, nonstick, or heavy Bundt pan will make the crust too dark and thick and will alter the baking time.)

2. Beat the butter and cream cheese until smooth and creamy in a large bowl with an electric mixer set to medium speed, about 2 minutes. With the mixer running, slowly add the sugar. Increase the mixer speed to high and continue beating until the mixture is light and fluffy, about 5 minutes. Scrape down the sides of the bowl with a rubber spatula. Add the eggs one at a time, beating well after each addition. Add the flour to the egg mixture in three additions, beating at low speed only until it disappears into the batter each time. Mix in the vanilla and the mace. Stir the batter with the rubber spatula to make sure all the ingredients are stirred up from the bottom. Scrape the batter into the prepared pan.

3. Bake on the middle rack until a tester inserted into the center of the cake comes out clean, 1 hour 30 minutes to 1 hour 45 minutes.

4. Cool the cake in the pan on a wire cooling rack for 20 minutes. Turn out the cake and set it face up on the rack. Cover with a clean tea towel and let cool to room temperature before cutting. Store covered at room temperature. An old-fashioned domed cake plate or cake tin is ideal.

## Smoked Turkey and Cherry Salad in Melon Rings

⅓ cup mayonnaise

⅓ cup sour cream

3 tablespoons finely grated fresh ginger

2 tablespoons floral honey, such as acacia or tupelo

2 teaspoons white wine vinegar or rice vinegar

1 ¼ teaspoons poppy seeds

2 cups cubed smoked turkey

1 cup cherries, pitted and halved or quartered

2 tablespoons thinly sliced scallions (white and tender green parts)

¼ cup thinly sliced celery

¼ cup chopped pecans

Kosher salt, to taste

1 large ripe but firm melon, such as cantaloupe or honeydew

I was once served something in melon rings at a friend's bridal shower. I've lost touch with the bride, but I've kept up with the idea of melon rings. The rings make the salad very pretty, but you can also spoon it into lettuce cups or tuck it into croissants for sandwiches. For a retro touch, serve this salad with Captain's wafers, preferably in individual cellophane packets. (Why are crackers in those little packets always the best?)

MAKES 4 SERVINGS

1. Whisk together the mayonnaise, sour cream, ginger, honey, vinegar, and poppy seeds in a large bowl. Stir in the turkey, cherries, scallions, celery, and pecans. Season with salt. Cover and refrigerate until chilled, at least 2 hours and up to overnight.

2. Cut the melon crosswise into ¾-inch rings. Peel the rings and discard the seeds. You should be able to get 4 rings of similar size from the widest part of the melon. Place a ring on each serving plate. Spoon the salad into the rings and serve lightly chilled.

WHAT ELSE WORKS? You can replace the cherries with grapes, blueberries, or melon balls carved from the pieces left after cutting the rings.

# Black Cherry Hand Pies

CREAM CHEESE
PASTRY

3 cups all-purpose flour

¼ teaspoon baking soda

1 teaspoon baking powder

½ teaspoon fine sea salt

2 teaspoons finely
grated lemon zest

8 tablespoons (1 stick)
unsalted butter,
at room temperature

1 ¼ cups granulated sugar

1 large egg

3 ounces cream cheese,
at room temperature

2 tablespoons well-
shaken buttermilk
or heavy cream

1 teaspoon pure
vanilla extract

1 large egg yolk

2 tablespoons ice water

2 tablespoons coarse
sanding sugar, raw
sugar, or additional
granulated sugar

CHERRY FILLING

2 ½ cups black cherries,
pitted (about 1 pound)

½ cup granulated sugar

1 tablespoon cornstarch

1 teaspoon fresh
lemon juice

½ teaspoon pure
vanilla extract

½ teaspoon rose
water (optional)

There is a long southern tradition of hand pies, usually fried pies with dried peach or dried apple filling. This recipe is similar but uses fresh fruit baked inside a sugar cookie crust. When I can get them, I use those tiny, fragile black cherries. They are a pain to pit but worth it.

My grandparents had an enormous black cherry tree. When the cherries came in, the branches were covered in berries and birds. The tree grew up against one of the outbuildings, so we could climb on the flat metal roof and walk around to pick cherries without having to use a ladder. We picked gallons each year, a fraction of what the scavenging birds ate.

MAKES 8 HAND PIES

① For the pastry: Whisk together the flour, baking soda, baking powder, salt, and lemon zest in a medium bowl. Beat the butter until smooth in a large bowl with an electric mixer. With the mixer running on high speed, slowly add the granulated sugar and continue beating until the mixture is light and fluffy, about 5 minutes. Beat in the egg. Beat in the cream cheese, buttermilk, and vanilla. With the mixer running on low speed, slowly add the flour mixture and beat until the dough is smooth and forms large clumps. Pour the dough onto a piece of plastic wrap, gather into a ball, flatten to a disk, wrap tightly, and refrigerate for at least 1 hour and up to overnight.

② For the filling: Stir together the cherries, granulated sugar, cornstarch, and lemon juice in a medium saucepan. Set aside at room temperature for 30 minutes. Cook over medium heat, stirring gently to avoid crushing the cherries, until the mixture boils and thickens to the consistency of preserves, about 4 minutes. Remove from the heat and stir in the vanilla and rose water, if using. Cool completely, cover, and refrigerate until chilled, at least 1 hour and up to 1 day ahead.

③ To assemble the pies, divide the pastry into 8 equal pieces and roll each into a ball. Working with one at a time, place a ball of pastry on a lightly floured surface and use a floured rolling pin to roll it into a 5-inch round that is about ⅛-inch thick. (You can use a large cookie cutter or small plate as a template.) Transfer the pastry rounds to a rimmed baking sheet lined with parchment paper or a silicone baking mat.

④ Make an egg wash by whisking together the egg yolk and ice water in a small bowl. Spoon 2 tablespoons of the filling into the center of each round. Moisten the edge of the pastry with a little egg wash, fold over to make a semicircle, press the edges together, and crimp closed with a fork. When all of the pies are ready, lightly brush the tops with egg wash, and sprinkle with the sanding sugar. Cover with plastic wrap and refrigerate for 30 minutes. (The pastry will have gotten warm and soft when handled, so this firms it up again.)

5. Preheat the oven to 375°F. Bake until golden brown, about 25 minutes. Cool to room temperature on a wire rack.

WHAT ELSE WORKS? You can use other fresh cherries in place of the black cherries.

## Ground Cherry Pie

The ground cherry is not a cherry at all. It's a member of the gooseberry family. Like gooseberries and tomatillos, the round fruit grows inside a papery husk that dries and splits open as the fruit ripens. They are called ground cherries because the fruit often falls from the low, lanky bushes onto the ground when ripe. They are also sometimes called husk cherries. The fruit is small, usually not much larger than a marble, and is a bright yellow that darkens to gold as it ripens. Their flavor is unlike anything else and is often described as a blend of strawberry, pineapple, and yellow tomato.

Ground cherries are not common in much of the South because they prefer cooler climates, but they flourished in the Blue Ridge where I grew up, growing wild and lush in some places. Some people transplanted a few clumps near the edges of their gardens, but the plants have a tendency to take hold and spread like weeds. My family used them in preserves because their high pectin content made thick, luscious jam. But our favorite was a ground cherry pie, a simple, old-fashioned fruit pie.

Don't fret if there is a gap between the top crust and the fruit when you slice this pie. This sometimes happens when a pie is baked at high heat because the crust sets before the juicy fruit in the filling cooks down.

MAKES 8 SERVINGS

3 tablespoons quick-cooking (instant) tapioca

2 tablespoons cornstarch

1 cup plus 1 tablespoon sugar

½ teaspoon ground cinnamon

¼ teaspoon kosher salt

5 cups husked ground cherries

1 tablespoon fresh lemon juice

1 teaspoon pure vanilla extract

Pastry for double-crust 9-inch pie (page 396 or store-bought)

2 tablespoons unsalted butter, cut into ½-inch cubes and chilled

2 tablespoons whole milk, for brushing

1. Whisk together the tapioca and cornstarch, 1 cup of the sugar, and the cinnamon and salt in a large bowl. Add the ground cherries, lemon juice, and vanilla. Toss to coat and set aside for 30 minutes.

2. Meanwhile, position a rack in the center of the oven. Place a rimmed baking sheet on the rack and preheat the oven to 425°F. (The hot baking sheet will help brown the bottom of the pie because the pastry is not baked before it is filled.)

③ To make the pie shell, use a lightly floured rolling pin to roll half of the pastry into an 11-inch round on a lightly floured piece of waxed paper or parchment paper. Fit it into a 9-inch pie plate, cover with plastic wrap, and refrigerate for at least 30 minutes. (See page 398 for tips on rolling pastry.)

④ To make the pastry top, use a lightly floured rolling pin to roll the other half of the pastry into an 11-inch round on a lightly floured piece of waxed paper or parchment paper. Slide it onto a baking sheet, cover with plastic wrap, and refrigerate until needed.

⑤ Stir the fruit mixture and pour it into the pie shell. It will be very full, but the fruit cooks down considerably. Dot the fruit with the cubes of butter. Cover the filling with the pastry top. Lightly press the edges of the pastry together and trim off any excess to leave a ½-inch overhang. Fold under the edge to be even with the rim of the pie plate and crimp to seal. Cut a few slits on top to allow steam to escape. Brush the pastry with milk and sprinkle with the remaining 1 tablespoon of sugar.

⑥ Place the pie on the baking sheet and bake for 30 minutes. Reduce the oven temperature to 375°F and continue baking until the crust is browned and any escaped juices are thick and bubbling, 50 to 60 minutes more. If the edges of the crust start browning too quickly, lay a flat sheet of aluminum foil over the pie. Take the pie off the baking sheet and place on a wire rack to cool to room temperature before cutting.

WHAT ELSE WORKS? You can use sour cherries in place of the ground cherries.

# CHILE PEPPERS

**The words "chile" and "pepper" are often used interchangeably,** but they are not the same thing. Chiles are capsicums, a New World plant native to the Americas. True peppercorns come from plants native to Asia. The confusion started when Columbus and other explorers in search of spices misidentified chiles and called them pepper, and the name stuck.

Some chiles are hot and some are not. (In this book, the hot ones are called chile peppers and the mild ones are called sweet peppers.) Hot chiles contain varying levels of a colorless, odorless, and fiery compound known as capsaicin. Describing the heat of a chile is extremely difficult because no two people experience it the same way. Some people can seemingly eat the hottest chile peppers and barely break a sweat, while others won't let a hot pepper get within ten feet of them. The only way to know a chile is to taste it, but in general, red chiles are hotter than green or yellow chiles and small chiles are hotter than large ones.

Because most of the heat is held in their seeds and inner ribs, whole chiles release less capsaicin than chopped chiles. Wear gloves or wash your hands well after cutting hot chiles. The reaction to exposure to capsaicin can range from barely noticeable to blistering burns. Hot chile peppers can irritate all mucous membranes. (*All* membranes. Head to tail. Without exception. Be careful.)

A little heat is nearly as popular as sweet is to the southern palate. Many cooks can't resist slipping a pepper pod or a generous pinch of cayenne into the pot. In many homes, diners, and 'cue shacks, a bottle of hot sauce or pepper vinegar can be as important as the salt and pepper shakers. ■

# Chicken and White Bean Chili

4 tablespoons
(½ stick) butter

2 cups chopped onion

1 cup cored and diced
poblano chile or
other green chile

¼ cup instant flour or
all-purpose flour

2 cups chicken stock

2 cups whole milk

1 tablespoon green
Tabasco sauce,
or to taste

1 tablespoon chili
powder

2 teaspoons ground
cumin

2 teaspoons dried
marjoram or
Mexican oregano

3 cups home-cooked
or canned white beans,
drained and rinsed

3 cups diced
grilled chicken

Kosher salt and ground
black pepper, to taste

1 ½ cups grated Monterey
Jack, Pepper Jack, or
Mexican blend cheese

1 teaspoon cornstarch

Sour cream and lime
wedges, for garnish

This is a creamy, decadent soup that is a nice change from regular chili. Grilled chicken is best, but meat pulled from a whole smoked or rotisserie chicken also works. As with any dish that calls for fresh chiles, you can control the heat by selecting the chile you like most, from pungent to puny. I like to use poblanos for subtle, family-friendly heat.

When compiling this section of the book, I was choosing between this recipe and another recipe that uses poblanos. That very day, I happened to run into one of my daughter's former teachers who had tasted this chili years ago. Out of the blue, he said that if I didn't put this recipe in my book, he'd never forgive me. Issue settled.

MAKES ABOUT 2 QUARTS

1. Heat the butter in a large, heavy pot over medium-high heat. Add the onion and chiles and a pinch of salt. Cook, stirring often, until softened, about 8 minutes. Sprinkle in the flour and cook, stirring, for 2 minutes. Whisk in the stock and milk. Cook, stirring slowly, until the mixture thickens slightly, about 5 minutes.

2. Stir in the Tabasco, chili powder, cumin, marjoram, beans, and chicken. Simmer, stirring occasionally, for 20 minutes. Season with salt and pepper. Toss together the cheese and cornstarch in a small bowl, add to the soup, and stir until melted. (If you plan to reheat leftovers more than once, omit the cornstarch and use the cheese as a garnish instead of melting it into the soup.) Serve warm, garnished with sour cream and lime.

## Hot Pepper Vinegar

5 to 10 small hot red or green chile peppers, such as cayenne or serrano

8 whole peppercorns

1 to 2 whole, peeled garlic cloves (optional)

1 ½ cups distilled white vinegar

¼ teaspoon kosher or pickling salt

Bottles of pepper vinegar adorn tables in many homes and meat-and-three eateries across the South, just as certain as the salt and pepper shakers. Practically a requirement on cooked greens, pepper vinegar can liven up all sorts of things.

MAKES 1 PINT

1. Have ready a 1-pint bottle that has been sterilized in boiling water or run through the dishwasher on the hottest cycle. The bottle should have a sterilized tight-fitting lid. The bottle and lid do not have to stay hot, but they must stay sterile.
2. Pierce the chiles in several places with a hat pin or toothpick. Push the chiles and peppercorns into the prepared bottle. Add the garlic, if using.
3. Bring the vinegar and salt to a boil in a medium saucepan and then slowly pour through a funnel into the bottle. Wipe the rim, close the bottle, and let sit undisturbed until cooled to room temperature. If the peppers are not fully submerged, heat a little more vinegar and top off the bottle. Cover and set aside for at least 7 days before using. Hot pepper vinegar keeps at room temperature for weeks.

## Sassy Pepper Jam

1 pound red bell or other sweet red peppers

2 ounces jalapeño, serrano, cayenne, or other hot chile peppers, or to taste

½ cup white distilled vinegar

½ teaspoon kosher salt

¼ cup fresh lemon juice

1 (1.75-ounce) box premium fruit pectin, such as Sure-Jell

1 ¼ cups sugar

This sweet-hot concoction is a cousin of the beloved southern classic condiment known as pepper jelly. I call this jam instead of jelly because it is full of soft, cooked bits of the peppers and chiles, whereas jelly is clear or only flecked with peppers. Sweetened pepper jams, jellies, and relishes are popular in the South because they bring together two favorite tastes: sugar and heat. The type of chile will determine the level of heat, from harmless to hiccupping hot. You can also affect the heat by decreasing or increasing the number of chiles, but keep in mind that the sugar subdues their heat.

Like pepper jelly, this jam is delicious spooned over a block of cream cheese or log of goat cheese. It's also darn good on Okra Fritters (page 199), Corn Cakes (page 106), and Crispy Zucchini and Potato Skillet Cakes (page 376). I find pepper jam, peanut butter, and bacon sandwiches irresistible. For a new taste adventure, try it over vanilla, caramel, or chocolate ice cream.

MAKES ABOUT 3 CUPS

1. Have ready one 1-quart jar or three half-pint jars that have been sterilized in boiling water or run through the dishwasher on the hottest cycle. The jars should have sterilized tight-fitting lids. The jars and lids do not have to stay hot, but they must stay sterile.

2. Core and coarsely chop the sweet peppers and place them in the bowl of a food processor fitted with the metal blade. Trim the stems from the chile peppers. (To reduce their heat, cut them in half lengthwise and trim away their seeds and inner ribs.) Coarsely chop the chiles and add to the processor. Pulse until the peppers are finely chopped, but not puréed.

3. Transfer the chopped peppers into a medium saucepan. Stir in the vinegar, salt, and lemon juice. Bring to a boil, reduce the heat, and simmer, stirring occasionally, for 10 minutes. Stir in the pectin. Increase the heat and bring the mixture to a full rolling boil, stirring constantly. Quickly add the sugar, return to a rolling boil, and cook for exactly 1 minute, stirring constantly. Remove the pan from the heat and carefully ladle the jam through a wide-mouth funnel into the prepared jar. Let the jam cool to room temperature, cover, and refrigerate for up to 3 months.

## Hominy and Pork in Green Chile Sauce

1 pound tomatillos, husked, rinsed, and patted dry

2 tablespoons vegetable oil

2 pounds boneless pork shoulder (Boston butt), cut into 2-inch chunks

2 teaspoons kosher salt

¾ teaspoon ground black pepper

1 large onion, finely chopped

2 Anaheim or poblano chiles, cored and chopped

1 or 2 jalapeño, serrano, or other small chiles, cored and finely chopped

1 large green bell pepper, cored and chopped

4 garlic cloves, chopped

1 tablespoon dried oregano, preferably Mexican

(continued on next page)

In this recipe, hominy and pork shoulder are bathed in a piquant green chile and tomatillo sauce and topped with crumbly cheese, crunchy pumpkin seeds, and peppery radishes. This thick, hearty stew can be served in bowls or spooned into tortillas to make soft tacos. It should be made a day ahead and is worth the wait.

Hominy is dried corn kernels from which the hull and germ have been removed, either mechanically or chemically by soaking the corn in slaked lime or lye. It was one of the first food gifts the Native Americans gave to the colonists. Whole kernel hominy is sold wet or dry. Wet hominy comes in cans and is ready to eat. Dried hominy must be soaked and reconstituted. In some places, hominy is known as *posole*. (And in some places, grits are called hominy, but that's a whole other story.)

A pork shoulder is also called a Boston butt. This is not due to some physical anomaly in the pig. People say that it got that name in New England during the Revolutionary War when some pork cuts were packed into casks or barrels known as butts for storage and shipment. Pork shoulder has wonderful flavor but it's fatty. All that fat keeps the dish moist as it cooks but can be too much to eat. However, if you refrigerate the cooled stew overnight, the fat will rise to the top and solidify, making it easy to scrape off and discard before reheating for serving. Thus you have the benefit of including the fat during cooking but can then let go of those calories afterward.

An enameled cast-iron Dutch oven is perfect for this recipe because it gives the incomparable high-heat sear to the meat that comes only from cast iron. Unlike plain cast iron, the enameled coating makes it a good choice for simmering acidic ingredients for a long time. If you don't have a Dutch oven, a small, heavy soup pot will work.

2 teaspoons
ground cumin

2 tablespoons instant
or all-purpose flour

2 cups chicken or pork
stock

2 cups canned hominy,
drained and rinsed

¼ cup fresh lime juice

1 cup *queso fresco*
(about 4 ounces)

1 cup toasted,
salted *pepitas*
(pumpkin seeds)

½ cup thinly sliced
radishes

(1) Preheat the broiler. Place the tomatillos on a rimmed baking sheet and broil, turning with tongs as needed, until charred in spots on all sides. Transfer into a small bowl and mash coarsely with a fork.

(2) Heat the oil in an enameled cast-iron Dutch oven over medium-high heat. Season the pork with the salt and pepper. Working in batches to avoid crowding the food into the pan, sear the meat until deeply browned on all sides. Transfer into a bowl.

(3) Add the onion, Anaheims, jalapeño, and bell pepper to the pot and stir to coat in the pork drippings. Cook, stirring often, until softened, about 8 minutes. Stir in the garlic, oregano, cumin, and flour. Cook, stirring, for 2 minutes. Reduce the heat if the mixture starts to scorch. Stir in the stock and scrape up the browned bits from the bottom of the pot.

(4) Return the pork and any accumulated juices to the pot. Stir in the hominy and tomatillos. Bring to a boil, reduce the heat, and simmer gently until the meat is tender enough to shred with a fork, about 1 ½ hours. Check the seasoning and add more salt if needed.

(5) Cool to room temperature, cover, and refrigerate overnight. Discard the fat that solidifies on top before reheating the stew.

(6) Just before serving, stir in the lime juice. Serve hot, topped with *queso fresco*, *pepitas*, and radishes.

MAKE-AHEAD NOTE: This stew must be made at least 1 day ahead.

## Shrimp Salad and Charred Jalapeño BLTs

4 jalapeños

1 tablespoon vegetable oil

1 pound medium (21 to 25 count) Succulent Brined Shrimp (recipe follows)

½ cup high-quality mayonnaise

2 tablespoons chopped fresh basil

2 tablespoons fresh lemon juice

½ teaspoon ground black pepper

8 large slices toasted sourdough bread or 4 crusty sub rolls, split open

8 thick slices crisp bacon

4 large, crunchy lettuce leaves

8 thick slices juicy, vine-ripened tomato

I've seen many things done to a classic BLT and some of them were just plain silly, but adding shrimp is a great idea, as is a touch of heat from roasted and lightly charred jalapeños. You can reduce the heat by using milder chiles, such as poblano or Anaheim, or skip the heat by using roasted sweet red peppers.

Tomato sandwiches have a cult following in the South, so some people will not be able to resist sneaking in a quick tomato sandwich while getting these BLTS ready. I believe that you should eat a tomato sandwich bent over the sink in a celebration of dripping glory.

MAKES 4 SERVINGS

① Heat a large cast-iron skillet over high heat. Add the jalapeños and cook, turning with tongs, until the skins wrinkle and are charred in spots. Place in a small bowl, cover, and let sit until cool enough to handle. The steam will finish cooking them. Rub off the skins (it's okay if a few bits stick to the chiles). Cut off the stems and split the chiles open into flat pieces. To reduce the heat, scrape away the seeds and inner ribs with the tip of a knife or a spoon.

② Heat the oil in the skillet over medium-high heat. Add the shrimp and cook, stirring, only until they are opaque, about 2 minutes. Cut the shrimp into bite-sized pieces and transfer into a medium bowl. Stir in the mayonnaise, basil, lemon juice, and pepper. Taste for salt, but the shrimp are probably well seasoned from the brine.

③ To assemble the sandwiches, divide the shrimp mixture among 4 slices of the bread. Top with the jalapeño, bacon, lettuce, and tomato. Close the sandwiches with the remaining 4 slices of bread and serve soon.

## Succulent Brined Shrimp

¼ cup kosher salt

¼ cup sugar

1 cup water

2 cups ice

1 pound shelled and deveined shrimp (thawed if frozen)

If you saw the shrimp boat pull up with your own eyes, you can skip the brining. Otherwise, the brine restores some of that ocean freshness, particularly when using frozen shrimp. They don't call it the briny deep for nothing.

MAKES 1 POUND

① Combine the salt, sugar, and water in a large bowl, stirring until the solids dissolve. Add the ice. Immerse the shrimp in the brine and refrigerate for 20 minutes, but no longer or the shrimp will be too salty.

② Drain the shrimp, rinse them thoroughly under cold water, and pat dry with paper towels. Cook at once.

. . . . . . . . . . . . . . . . . . . . . . . . . . . . . . . . . . . . . . . . . . . . . . . . . . .

Salsa might not be traditional throughout the entire South, but these days many southern cooks consider it to be a staple. Although there are as many types of salsa as there are types of homemade soup, these are my favorite versions of the basics. You can customize the heat to your personal preference by changing the type or amount of chile. Removing the ribs and seeds will reduce the heat of any chile.

## Red Tomato Salsa

It might seem odd to use both fresh and cooked tomatoes in salsa, but each brings different characteristics to the dish.

MAKES ABOUT 2 CUPS

3 garlic cloves, chopped

2 jalapeño or other small chiles, stemmed and coarsely chopped

1 cup seeded and diced tomato

¼ cup finely chopped white onion

1 ½ cups smoked tomatoes (page 358) or canned fire-roasted tomatoes

Juice of 1 lime (about 3 tablespoons)

2 tablespoons lightly packed chopped cilantro leaves

1 teaspoon kosher salt

1 teaspoon sugar

1. Combine all of the ingredients in the bowl of a food processor fitted with the metal blade and pulse until coarsely chopped.

2. Serve at room temperature or lightly chilled. Stir well and check the seasoning before serving.

## Green Tomatillo Salsa

1 pound fresh tomatillos, husked, rinsed, and dried

1 cup lightly packed cilantro leaves

1 jalapeño, serrano, or other small chile, stemmed and coarsely chopped

½ cup finely chopped white onion

2 garlic cloves, chopped

1 tablespoon vegetable oil

1 teaspoon kosher salt, or to taste

The tart, astringent flavor of tomatillos is essential to green salsa, but they are better cooked than raw. In this recipe, the salsa is briefly cooked, which thickens the salsa and takes care of the tomatillos.

MAKES ABOUT 2 CUPS

1. Purée the tomatillos, cilantro, chile, onion, and garlic in a blender or the bowl of a food processor fitted with the metal blade. Heat the oil until shimmering hot in a large saucepan over high heat. Carefully pour in the purée; it will vigorously bubble and hiss at first.

2. Reduce the heat and simmer until reduced to 2 cups, about 10 minutes. Season with the salt.

3. Transfer into a medium bowl or glass jar and cool to room temperature. Serve at room temperature or lightly chilled. Stir well and check the seasoning before serving.

## Black Bean, Corn, and Pepper Tart with Chunky Tomatillo Guacamole

### SPICY CORNMEAL PASTRY

1 cup all-purpose flour

¼ cup stone-ground cornmeal

1 teaspoon ground cumin

1 teaspoon ground chipotle chili powder

1 teaspoon paprika

½ teaspoon kosher salt

4 tablespoons (½ stick) butter, cut into small cubes and chilled

4 tablespoons vegetable shortening, chilled

2 to 3 tablespoons ice water

(continued on next page)

This colorful, flavorful entrée pleases vegetarians and omnivores alike. The spicy, crunchy pastry is perhaps the best part of this tart. It comes together quickly and easily in a food processor (or bowl) and can be pressed into the tart pan with no rolling. This recipe is best made as a tart because the filling doesn't get too thick, which it would if baked as pie. The crust can be made up to one day ahead, so this is a great dish for after-work dinners or casual entertaining.

MAKES 6 TO 8 SERVINGS

1. For the pastry: Mix the flour, cornmeal, cumin, chili powder, paprika, and salt together in a large bowl or in the bowl of a food processor fitted with the metal blade or pastry blade. Cut (or pulse) in the butter and shortening until the mixture looks like sand and clumps together when pressed lightly. Sprinkle 2 tablespoons of the ice water over the flour mixture. Use a fork (or pulse) to mix the ingredients together. If the dry ingredients are not mixing in, sprinkle in another tablespoon of ice water. Mix with the fork (or pulse) until the mixture begins to form large clumps. Pour the clumps onto a sheet of plastic wrap and gently form into a disk. Wrap the disk in the plastic wrap and let rest in the refrigerator for at least 30 minutes and up to 1 day.

2 tablespoons
vegetable oil

1 medium onion,
diced (about 1 cup)

1 red or yellow bell
pepper, cored and
diced (about 1 cup)

1 to 2 jalapeños, finely
chopped

1 cup fresh or thawed
corn kernels (about
2 ears of corn)

2 cups home-cooked or
canned black beans,
drained and rinsed

1 ½ cups grated Monterey
Jack, Pepper Jack,
or Mexican blend
cheese, divided

Kosher salt and ground
black pepper, to taste

Chunky Tomatillo
Guacamole, for serv-
ing (recipe follows)

Lime wedges and sour
cream, for garnish

2. Heat the oven to 350°F. Press the pastry evenly into a 10-inch tart pan with a removable bottom, making sure that it isn't too thick or sloped in the corners. (You can make an even corner by pressing the pastry with the edge of a straight-sided metal measuring cup.) Line the pastry with parchment paper and fill it with uncooked beans, uncooked rice, or pie weights. Bake the crust for 10 minutes. Carefully remove the weights and parchment and continue baking until the crust is firm and looks dry, 8 to 10 minutes more. Cool to room temperature on a wire rack.

3. For the filling: Preheat the oven to 350°F.

4. Heat the oil in a large skillet over medium-high heat. Add the onion and a pinch of salt and cook, stirring often, until it begins to soften, about 5 minutes. Add the bell pepper, jalapeño, and corn and cook, stirring often, until the vegetables soften, about 5 minutes. Remove the mixture from the heat and stir in the beans and 1 cup of the cheese. Season with salt and black pepper. Use a slotted spoon to spread the vegetable mixture into the crust, leaving behind any accumulated liquid. Scatter the remaining ½ cup of cheese over the top.

5. Bake the tart in the middle of the oven until hot and the cheese has melted, about 20 minutes. Let rest at room temperature for 10 minutes before cutting into wedges. Serve with Chunky Tomatillo Guacamole, lime wedges, and sour cream.

MAKE-AHEAD NOTE: You can bake the crust up to 1 day ahead. Cool to room temperature on a wire rack and then store covered at room temperature.

## Chunky Tomatillo Guacamole

½ teaspoon cumin seed

1 to 4 fresh serrano or other green chiles

8 ounces fresh tomatillos, husked, rinsed, and dried

½ cup finely chopped red onion

¼ cup finely chopped cilantro

Juice of 1 lime (about 3 tablespoons)

1 teaspoon kosher salt, or to taste

½ teaspoon ground black pepper, or to taste

1 pound ripe but firm Hass avocados

This is guacamole of substance, chunky and full of bright flavor. If you have leftovers, you can deter the darkening on the surface by pressing a piece of plastic wrap directly onto the surface, under the lid of the storage container. The darkening is the result of exposure to air, so the less air that reaches the surface, the better.

In addition to topping the Black Bean, Corn, and Pepper Tart, this guacamole is fantastic with corn chips, especially alongside the Zesty Black-Eyed Pea Salsa on page 131.

MAKES ABOUT 3 CUPS

1. Heat a heavy skillet (preferably cast-iron) over medium-high heat. Add the cumin seed and cook, gently shaking the skillet, until fragrant, about 3 minutes. Pour into a large bowl and set aside to cool.

2. Add the chiles to the skillet and cook, turning as needed, until blistered and lightly charred on all sides, about 3 minutes. Transfer to a plate and set aside until cool enough to handle.

3. Add the tomatillos to the skillet and cook, turning as needed, until blistered and lightly charred on all sides, about 10 minutes. Set aside until cool enough to handle. Working over the bowl with the cumin seeds, peel away the charred skin, letting the flesh and juice drop into the bowl. Use a pastry blender or a fork to coarsely mash the tomatillos.

4. Use the tip of a knife to scrape the charred skins from the chiles. Split the chiles down one long side and discard the stem. Scrape out and discard the seeds, or leave them in for an extra punch. Finely chop the chiles and add to the tomatillos. Add the onion, cilantro, lime juice, salt, and pepper and mix well.

5. Halve, pit, and peel the avocados. Cut them into bite-sized chunks and add to the tomatillo mixture. Stir gently until the guacamole is well mixed but still chunky. Taste and adjust the seasoning. Serve at room temperature.

## Spice-Rubbed Pork Tenderloins
## with Fresh Pineapple Salsa

2 ½ pounds whole
pork tenderloins

¼ cup light brown sugar

1 teaspoon ground
cumin

1 teaspoon ground
chili powder

1 teaspoon smoked
paprika (*pimentón*)

1 teaspoon kosher salt

½ teaspoon pepper

Fresh Pineapple Salsa
(recipe follows)

I've been teaching this recipe in cooking classes for nearly fifteen years. It is quick, easy, and very good, just the thing to keep in your go-to file of reliable recipes. The pork is quite straightforward if you remember that you cannot cook lean pork indefinitely. If you trust an instant-read thermometer, you'll have juicy pork. When done, the meat might be ever-so-slightly rosy in the center, but the juices will have no traces of pink.

You can make extra brown sugar and spice rub to keep on hand for a few weeks. Store in an airtight container at room temperature. You can substitute your favorite packaged pork rub or barbecue rub.

MAKES 4 TO 6 SERVINGS

1. Preheat the oven to 425°F. Line a rimmed baking sheet with aluminum foil.

2. Rinse the tenderloins and pat them dry with paper towels. Use kitchen shears or a sharp paring knife to trim away any loose fat or large pieces of silver skin from the tenderloins. Combine the brown sugar, cumin, chili powder, smoked paprika, salt, and pepper in a small bowl. Rub the sugar mixture over the tenderloins and shake off any excess. Place the coated tenderloins on the prepared baking sheet. Turn under the small pointy ends of the tenderloins to make the thickness of the meat fairly uniform.

3. Roast the pork until it reaches an internal temperature of 150°F on an instant-read thermometer inserted into the center of the thickest part of the meat, 20 to 25 minutes.

4. Transfer the meat to a cutting board and let stand for 5 minutes before slicing. The temperature will continue to rise as it rests. Slice the meat and serve warm or at room temperature with the Fresh Pineapple Salsa.

# Fresh Pineapple Salsa

3 cups fresh
   pineapple chunks

2 tablespoons finely
   diced red onion

1 red bell pepper,
   cored and diced

1 to 2 jalapeño or other small
   chiles, seeded and
   finely chopped

Zest of 1 lime

¼ cup fresh lime juice
   (about 2 limes)

¼ cup chopped
   cilantro leaves
   and tender stems

½ cup pineapple, peach,
   or apricot preserves

¼ teaspoon kosher
   salt, or to taste

Sweet peppers, chile peppers, and pineapple are the stars of this colorful salsa. You can customize the heat by adjusting the type and number of hot chiles to your liking. The pineapple should be fresh because canned pineapple is too wet and often tastes tinny. The preserves make the salsa thick and glossy, but you can reduce the amount if you prefer a less-sweet salsa.

Choose pretty green limes for zest, but choose pale, creamy limes for juice. Limes lighten in color as they ripen, so an underripe bright green lime has less juice than a pale lime.

This salsa is perfect with the pork, but it's also good with grilled chicken, fish, and shrimp. It's lovely with sweet potatoes in many forms, such as a dip for sweet potato chips or as a garnish for roasted sweet potatoes (page 326).

MAKES ABOUT 3 CUPS

1. Place the pineapple, onion, bell pepper, jalapeño, lime zest, lime juice, and cilantro in the bowl of a food processor fitted with the metal blade. Pulse only until the ingredients are chopped coarsely; leave plenty of texture.

2. Transfer into a medium bowl and stir in the preserves. Season with the salt and serve at room temperature or lightly chilled.

WHAT ELSE WORKS? You can use peaches or mango instead of the pineapple.

MAKE-AHEAD NOTE: You can make the salsa up to 1 day ahead. Store covered and refrigerated. Do not add the cilantro until just before serving because the acidity of the other ingredients will chemically cook it, leaving it drab and soggy, as though small pieces of wet newspaper were stirred into the salsa.

# CORN

**Corn is the giant of the southern garden,** not only in size but also in importance. No other crop is more versatile or more important to the traditional southern diet. Traditionally, every inch of a cornstalk had its uses, from the grains to the cobs to the stalks to the shucks. Corn, both fresh and dried, was our grain, cereal, vegetable, flour, and fodder and the basis of our best liquors—bourbon and moonshine.

Corn is native to the New World and was probably first cultivated more than 7,000 years ago as a domesticated version of a wild grass. It was so integral to the diets of some Native Americans that they considered it holy. Many of us still agree.

Farmers and gardeners immediately saw the value of corn over wheat. Unlike wheat, corn can be grown as a field crop or as a garden item in small plots, minimizing the amount of land that had to be cleared, which was no small thing. Acre for acre, corn has a much higher yield than wheat and requires less manpower. Corn has a short growing cycle, produces throughout the growing season, and can handle heat and direct sunshine. All of this made it possible for families and small farms to raise decent amounts of corn. It could be used and sold fresh, dried, preserved, or processed into other products, which made it versatile as food and as a commodity. It's little wonder that corn was the largest single crop grown in the antebellum South.

Corn continues to be integral and iconic to the southern diet. Imagine our tables and our recipes with no sweet corn, gritted corn, dried corn, cornmeal, hominy, or grits. For corn, we remain purely grateful. ■

## Southwestern Vegetables

3 tablespoons butter

2 cups corn kernels
(from about 4 ears)

2 cups diced
summer squash

2 cups diced zucchini

1 to 1 ½ cups salsa

Kosher salt and ground
black pepper, to taste

2 tablespoons chopped
cilantro, for garnish

This dish is incredibly quick, easy, and tasty. The melted butter and salsa make a wonderful sauce that lightly coats and perks up the vegetables. Use your favorite salsa to make the dish as spicy as you like. This is a little like revved-up *maque choux*, the classic Louisiana recipe for smothered corn.

MAKES 4 TO 6 SERVINGS

1. Melt the butter in a large skillet over medium-high heat. Add the corn, squash, and zucchini and a pinch of salt and cook, stirring often, until the vegetables are tender, about 6 minutes.

2. Stir in enough salsa to coat the vegetables. Cook until hot and bubbly, about 2 minutes. Season with salt and pepper. Garnish with the cilantro and serve hot.

WHAT ELSE WORKS? You can vary the proportions of squash and zucchini or replace some of it with diced mirliton.

8 tablespoons (1 stick)
butter, at room
temperature

1 tablespoon finely
chopped sun-dried
tomatoes in oil,
well drained

1 tablespoon finely
chopped scallions

1 teaspoon dried basil

HERB AND SHALLOT

8 tablespoons (1 stick)
butter, at room
temperature

2 tablespoons
finely chopped
flat-leaf parsley

2 tablespoons finely
chopped fresh basil

1 tablespoon finely
chopped shallot

1 teaspoon finely
chopped garlic

MUSTARD SEED AND
CRACKED PEPPER

8 tablespoons (1 stick)
butter, at room
temperature

1 teaspoon finely
chopped garlic

1 tablespoon
whole-grain mustard

½ teaspoon dry mustard

½ teaspoon freshly
cracked black pepper

# Sweet Corn on the Cob with Gobs of Butter

If there's a rule for fresh corn on the cob, it is to eat it as soon as possible after it's picked. I know a man who said that his mama didn't even send him out to pick corn until the water was boiling on the stove. Out came the corn, on went the butter and salt—eight minutes flat from stalk to plate. Mark Twain is said to have remarked that the best way to eat corn would be to set up a kettle right in the field. It is true that sweet corn loses up to 25 percent of its sugars in the first twenty-four hours after it's picked.

For many years, most people boiled their corn because they were eating starchy, chewy field corn that needed aggressive cooking. In contrast, delicate fresh sweet corn needs minimal cooking that barely crosses the line between raw and cooked.

I most often steam ears of corn in the microwave. Here's how. Remove all of the tough outer husks, leaving only the thin, moist, pale green, inner husk that covers the kernels. The inner husk holds in the moisture and creates a little steam as the corn cooks. Break off or cut away the tip of the cob if it is immature or blemished. (If your corn is already naked, wrap each ear in a lightly dampened white paper towel.) Arrange the ears in a single layer in the microwave and cook for 3 minutes on high power and then let them rest in the microwave until they are cool enough to handle, about 3 minutes more. Peel away the husks and brush off the silks with the damp paper towel.

Another option is to roast the partially husked ears in a preheated 400°F oven, rotating the ears a quarter turn every 5 minutes, until tender when gently squeezed, about 20 minutes. The ears can also be grilled, as described on page 105.

8 tablespoons (1 stick) butter, at room temperature

1 teaspoon ground ancho chile powder

2 teaspoons finely grated lime zest

1 tablespoon fresh lime juice

Pinch of cayenne pepper

SHALLOT, LEMON, AND THYME

8 tablespoons (1 stick) butter, at room temperature

1 tablespoon finely chopped shallot

2 teaspoons finely grated lemon zest

1 tablespoon fresh lemon juice

2 teaspoons chopped fresh thyme

CHIVE

8 tablespoons (1 stick) butter, at room temperature

2 tablespoons finely chopped chives

¼ teaspoon paprika

## BUTTER, BUT BETTER

Once you've cooked the corn to your liking—through steaming, roasting, grilling, or boiling—it's time for seasoning. As a kid, I thought the best part of eating corn on the cob was getting to use those corn holders stabbed into the ends of the cobs, like little handlebars to steer the corn through butter.

You can't go wrong with butter and salt. However, butter can be even better when jazzed up with herbs and spices. Beyond corn, these flavored compound butters can be used to season other vegetables, rice, potatoes, grits, and bread. The butters can also be used to finish simple pan sauces or rubbed under the skin of chickens before they are roasted.

## Compound Butter

The ingredients in a compound butter can vary, but the method is always the same. Blend the ingredients in a small bowl. Spoon the butter into a log the size of a stick of butter down the center of a piece of plastic wrap. Tightly roll up the butter in the plastic and twist the ends closed like a Tootsie Roll. The taut plastic will smooth the surface of the butter and make the log nice and round. Chill until firm.

These butter logs can be refrigerated for up to three days or tucked into freezer bags and frozen up to three months, so you can make plenty while you're at it and stash the extras in the freezer.

EACH RECIPE MAKES 8 SERVINGS

8 tablespoons (1 stick)
butter, at room
temperature

2 teaspoons finely
chopped chipotles
in adobo sauce

Finely grated zest
of 1 orange

2 tablespoons pure
maple syrup

BROWN SUGAR,
CHILE, AND
CINNAMON

8 tablespoons (1 stick)
butter, at room
temperature

2 teaspoons light or
dark brown sugar

1 teaspoon ground
ancho or chipotle chile

1 teaspoon ground
cinnamon

GARLIC AND LEMON

8 tablespoons (1 stick)
butter, at room
temperature

2 tablespoons chopped
flat-leaf parsley

1 tablespoon finely
chopped shallot

1 teaspoon finely
chopped garlic

2 teaspoons grated
lemon zest

1 teaspoon kosher salt

¼ teaspoon black pepper

## TIPS AND TECHNIQUES

"Room temperature butter" means butter that is between 65°F and 70°F, which is quite cool compared to most kitchens in summer. A quick test to determine whether a stick of butter is soft enough to use is to gently bend the stick. If it bends without breaking, it's perfect. If it's a squishy mess, it's usable, so long as it has not begun to melt along the edges. Melted butter does not work properly in a recipe that calls for room temperature butter because the liquid whey has begun to separate from the butter solids, even if it re-solidifies. If you soften the butter in the microwave, use the lowest power setting in 30-second intervals to avoid melting the butter.

## Stirred Corn and Seared Sea Scallops with Lime Sauce

8 ears freshly shucked sweet corn, silks wiped away with a damp towel

2 tablespoons butter, divided

1 to 4 tablespoons half-and-half or whole milk, if needed

Kosher salt and ground black pepper, to taste

This is the best creamed corn in the world, thick and velvety with concentrated corn flavor. It is thickened not with flour but with the starchy milk released by the corn as it slowly cooks. Therefore, it must be done with corn so fresh and juicy that the kernels pop open and squirt out their milk when poked. This process takes a few minutes of mindful stirring, but the finished dish looks like risotto, with tender grains of corn held together by thick, creamy sauce.

MAKES 4 TO 6 SERVINGS

1. Cut the top half of the kernels off the cobs into a large bowl. Use the back of the knife or a spoon to scrape the remaining kernels and the milky corn liquid into the bowl. Run your hands down the cobs to squeeze out any remaining milk.

2. Heat 1 tablespoon of the butter in a large cast-iron skillet over medium-high heat. Add the corn and its liquid to the skillet. Add a pinch of salt. Bring to a boil, stirring to keep the corn from sticking. Reduce the heat and cook at a bare simmer, stirring continuously, until the corn is very tender and thick, about 10 minutes. If the corn gets dry before it thickens, stir in a little half-and-half.

3. Remove the skillet from the heat and stir in the remaining 1 tablespoon of butter. Season with salt and pepper and serve hot.

## Seared Sea Scallops with Lime Sauce

16 large dry-pack sea scallops, cleaned

1 teaspoon kosher salt, or to taste

½ teaspoon ground black pepper, or to taste

¼ cup instant or all-purpose flour

2 tablespoons vegetable oil

8 tablespoons (1 stick) butter cut into cubes, at room temperature

1 teaspoon finely grated lime zest

¼ cup fresh lime juice

To transform the simple splendor of Stirred Corn into an entrée, top it with succulent scallops bathed in buttery lime sauce. Be sure to use dry-pack scallops that will sear instead of steaming in the hot pan. Fresh sea scallops should look creamy white or even slightly pink. Bright white or soggy scallops might have been soaked in preservatives or other liquids, which dilute their flavor.

Make the corn first and keep it warm over low heat, stirring occasionally. Stir in another splash of half-and-half if the corn gets too thick.

MAKES 4 TO 6 SERVINGS

1. Pat the scallops dry with paper towels. Season both sides with the salt and pepper and lightly dust with the flour. Set aside in a single layer on a plate to dry a little while the oil gets hot.

2. Heat the oil in a large nonstick skillet or well-seasoned cast-iron skillet over medium-high heat. Working in batches if necessary, add the scallops to the skillet, leaving about a 1-inch space between them so that they will brown instead of steam. Cook the scallops undisturbed until the edges are well browned, about 2 minutes.

③ Meanwhile, spoon the hot Stirred Corn onto serving plates.

④ Turn the scallops over with tongs and cook just until browned on the bottom and opaque in the center, about 2 minutes more, then place them on top of the corn. The scallops will continue to cook and firm up as they rest.

⑤ Melt the butter in the skillet, scrapping up any browned glaze from the bottom of the pan. Stir in the lime zest and lime juice. Pour over the scallops and serve immediately. Scallops will not wait.

## Crabby Rice

This is southern fried rice, a skillet full of good ingredients quickly sautéed together to make an impressive one-pan meal. This is easy enough for weeknights and nice enough for guests.

Chilled rice works best, so it's an excellent use of leftover rice. If you start with freshly cooked rice, spread it in a thin layer on a baking sheet so that it will cool quickly without lumping together into a mass. Crumble the rice into loose grains before adding it to the skillet.

As with crab cakes or any crab-centric dish, the quality of crab makes a difference. You don't have to spring for jumbo-lump here, but avoid finely minced, watery, canned crab that will make a mess of the dish.

MAKES 6 SERVINGS

① Heat the butter and oil in a large skillet over medium-high heat. Add the onion and a pinch of salt and cook, stirring often, until softened, about 5 minutes. Add the Old Bay Seasoning and mix well.

② Stir in the tomatoes, rice, and corn and cook, stirring often, until the corn is tender, about 3 minutes.

③ Stir in the crabmeat and heat through, about 1 minute. Season with the salt and pepper. Sprinkle with the lemon juice and scallions and serve hot.

2 tablespoons butter

1 tablespoon extra-virgin olive oil

1 medium onion, finely chopped (about 1 ½ cups)

1 tablespoon Old Bay Seasoning

1 ½ cups finely diced fresh or canned tomatoes with their juices

3 cups cooked and cooled long-grain rice

2 cups corn kernels (from about 4 ears)

14 to 16 ounces jumbo-lump or lump crabmeat, picked over for bits of shell

1 teaspoon kosher salt, or to taste

½ teaspoon ground black pepper, or to taste

1 tablespoon fresh lemon juice

2 scallions, thinly sliced (white and tender green parts)

## Grilled Corn and Potato Salad

2 tablespoons mayonnaise

2 tablespoons sour cream

2 tablespoons fresh lime juice

1 teaspoon kosher salt

1 teaspoon ground ancho chile or chili powder

½ teaspoon smoked paprika (*pimentón*), plus more for sprinkling

⅛ teaspoon cayenne pepper

1 pound small, waxy potatoes (such as Red Bliss or creamers), halved or quartered

2 tablespoons vegetable oil

4 to 6 ears freshly shucked corn, silks wiped away with a damp towel

¼ cup chopped scallions (white and tender green parts)

2 tablespoons finely chopped flat-leaf parsley

¼ cup freshly grated *queso Cotija* or Parmesan cheese

I love grilled corn on the cob served Mexican street-food style, where the hot ears are coated in mayonnaise and sprinkled with grated cheese and ground chilies. And I love to use grilled potatoes in a salad. This recipe brings those flavors together. To turn this tasty side dish into a main dish, add grilled chicken or shrimp. It can also be served inside hollowed-out fresh tomatoes, roasted sweet peppers, or large roasted green chiles.

I've heard too many ardent debates on how to grill corn to believe that people will ever agree, but I grill my corn after it's been shucked. I want the corn to come in direct contact with the heat, so that the kernels get toasted, caramelized, and a little charred in spots.

It's difficult to successfully cook hard, dense chunks of raw vegetables completely on the grill. By the time the interior is softened, the outside is ruined. I partially cook the potatoes in boiling, salted water and then finish them in a grill basket on the grill. The potatoes turn out tender on the inside and nicely crisped and smoky on the outside.

MAKES 6 TO 8 SERVINGS

1. Preheat the grill to medium high.

2. Whisk together the mayonnaise, sour cream, lime juice, salt, ground chile, smoked paprika, and cayenne in a large bowl.

3. Place the potatoes in a large saucepan and cover with cold water. Add ½ teaspoon kosher salt per cup of water. Bring to a boil, reduce the heat, and simmer until the potatoes are barely tender, about 8 minutes. Don't cook them too long or they'll get too mushy to grill. Drain the potatoes well, transfer into a large bowl, and let steam dry for 2 minutes. Drizzle the oil over the potatoes and toss to coat. Grill the potatoes in a mesh grill basket until nicely browned and cooked through, about 8 minutes.

4. Place the ears of corn directly on the grill grate. Cook the ears, turning them with tongs as needed, until most of the kernels are browned and a few are lightly charred, about 12 minutes. Set the corn aside until cool enough to handle.

5. Pour the hot potatoes into the bowl with the mayonnaise mixture and stir gently to coat. Cut the kernels from the cobs and add to the potato mixture. Stir in the scallions, parsley, and cheese. Check the seasoning.

6. Sprinkle with more smoked paprika and serve warm or at room temperature.

# Corn Cakes

3 to 4 ears freshly shucked sweet corn, silks wiped away with a damp towel

¼ cup fine stone-ground cornmeal

¼ cup all-purpose flour

1 teaspoon baking powder

½ teaspoon baking soda

½ teaspoon kosher salt

1 large egg

⅓ cup well-shaken buttermilk

1 tablespoon butter, plus more as needed

1 tablespoon vegetable oil, plus more as needed

Call them corn cakes or corn fritters or skillet cakes, these are a classic way for southerners to enjoy corn. There are many styles, ranging from crusty deep-fried balls (like hushpuppies) to little round disks (like blini). These are little cakes of kernels held together with a bit of batter. This type of cake is called a corn oyster in some old southern cookbooks because of the resemblance to fried oysters.

Quite good eaten straight out of the skillet as soon as they are made, if you have the discipline to wait until you have a full plate, they are good any time of day. For breakfast, drizzle them with honey, sorghum, or maple syrup. For an appetizer, top them with sour cream and salsa or crème fraîche and smoked fish. Or top them with Sassy Pepper Jam (page 88) or shredded chicken that's been tossed with Blackberry Barbecue Sauce (page 39). For dinner, just put them on a plate and pick up a fork.

MAKES ABOUT 12 CAKES

1. Preheat the oven to 200°F. Set a wire rack inside a large rimmed baking sheet and place near the stove.

2. Grate the corn on the large holes of a grater set inside a shallow bowl to collect the kernels and their milky liquid, to measure 1 ½ cups. (You can also cut the whole kernels off the cobs with a knife and milk the cobs with a small spoon.)

3. Whisk together the cornmeal, flour, baking powder, baking soda, and salt in a large bowl. Whisk the egg in a medium bowl until the white and yolk are blended, then whisk in the buttermilk and stir in the corn. Pour the corn mixture into the flour mixture and stir with a rubber spatula only until the dry ingredients are incorporated into the batter. The batter will be a little lumpy, like pancake batter.

4. Heat the butter and oil in a large, heavy skillet (preferably cast-iron) over medium-high heat. Working in batches, drop the batter into the pan by heaping tablespoonsful. (The first cake should sizzle when it hits the pan; if not, let the pan get a little hotter before adding more batter. Cook no more than 4 to 6 fritters, not touching, at a time.) Cook until golden brown, about 2 minutes per side. Unless someone is standing there with plate in hand, transfer the cooked cakes to the wire rack and place in the oven to stay warm until all are cooked, or up to 30 minutes. Repeat with the remaining batter, adding more butter and oil to the pan in equal measure as needed. Serve the cakes warm.

TIPS AND TECHNIQUES

When pan-frying, the oil should be hot enough for the food to sizzle when it touches the oil but not so hot that the oil smokes or the food scorches. You can test the oil by dropping in a pinch of flour; it should sizzle instantly and brown slowly without the oil popping or smoking. Do not add too much food to the pan at once or the temperature of the oil will drop rapidly and the food will languish and get greasy while the oil heats up again. The oil tends to get hotter with each batch, so adjust the heat as needed to keep it at the right temperature. Between batches, skim the oil and discard any bits of food floating around before they have a chance to burn.

## Corn Pudding Cornbread

A search through any collection of southern cookbooks reveals countless ways to make cornbread. A few of the older books, particularly those written during the 1930s, include recipes for custard cornbread, a fluffy cake with a layer of creamy custard running through in the middle. Although the original recipes are great, I decided to try adding corn kernels to the batter to make it more like corn pudding. The texture also reminds me of spoon bread, but this is much easier to make. Like both corn pudding and spoon bread, this is a spoonable side dish, not a sliceable cornbread.

MAKES 8 SERVINGS

2 ears freshly shucked sweet corn, silks wiped away with a damp towel

1 tablespoon butter, at room temperature

¾ cup all-purpose flour

¾ cup finely ground cornmeal

1 teaspoon baking powder

½ teaspoon baking soda

2 large eggs

3 tablespoons butter, melted and slightly cooled

¼ cup sugar

1 ½ teaspoons fine sea salt

2 cups whole milk

6 teaspoons distilled white vinegar

1 cup heavy cream

1. Grate the corn into a small bowl on the large holes of a grater, or cut the top half of the kernels off the cobs into a large bowl and then use the back of the knife or a spoon to scrape the remaining kernels and the milky corn liquid into the bowl. Run your hands down the cobs to squeeze out any remaining milk. You should have 1 cup of grated corn and liquid.

2. Use the room temperature butter to generously grease the inside of a thin, light metal 8-inch square baking pan. (Skillets or heavy dark metal pans interfere with the baking magic that creates the silky custard interior.)

3. Whisk together the flour, cornmeal, baking powder, and baking soda in a medium bowl.

4. Whisk the eggs in a large bowl until the whites and yolks are blended, then whisk in the melted butter. Whisk in the sugar, salt, milk, and vinegar. Whisking constantly, slowly add the flour mixture and whisk until smooth. Fold in the corn with a rubber spatula.

5. Pour the batter into the prepared pan. Slowly pour the cream into the center of the batter; do not stir. Bake until the cornbread is lightly browned on top, about 50 minutes. The bread will be set and firm around the edges, but a 2-inch circle in the center should quiver slightly when the pan is gently shaken, just like when baking other custards or a cheesecake. Serve warm. This does not reheat well.

It's a good idea to let melted butter cool a little before adding it to a batter that contains eggs so that the heat will not curdle the eggs. However, don't let it sit so long that it solidifies on top because it will no longer function properly in recipes that call for melted butter.

## Sweet Corn Custard Ice Cream

4 ears freshly shucked sweet corn, silks wiped away with a damp towel

2 cups whipping cream

2 cups whole milk

1 vanilla bean

¾ cup sugar

6 large egg yolks

People are either intrigued or quite skeptical when I describe this ice cream. But when you consider that most modern varieties of sweet corn are extremely sweet and juicy, it makes sense that they would work in custard ice cream.

Sweet corn ice cream is best when served as part of other desserts. My favorite is to serve it on top of warm berry cobblers and pies, particularly blueberry and blackberry creations, such as Dewberry Roll (page 40) or Jumble Berry Breakfast Crisp (page 46). It's also fun to use in a caramel corn sundae, made by topping scoops of ice cream with caramel sauce and a sprinkling of caramel corn or honey-roasted peanuts. For adults, I like to use Bourbon-Pecan Caramel Sauce (page 335).

MAKES ABOUT 1 ½ QUARTS

1. Cut the kernels from the cobs into a medium saucepan. Use the back of the knife or a small spoon to scrape the milky liquid from the cobs into the pan. There should be at least 2 cups of kernels and scrapings. Keep the cobs. Stir in the cream and milk. Cut the vanilla bean in half lengthwise and use the tip of the knife to scrape out the small, sticky seeds from inside the bean. Add the seeds to the pan and set the pod aside. Cook the mixture over medium heat until the milk is scalded, which means that there will be a few wisps of steam rising from the milk and a few small bubbles around the edge.

2. Remove the mixture from the heat and purée in a blender, working in batches so as not to fill the blender more than half full at a time. Pour the purée into a large bowl and add the cobs and vanilla bean pod so that they can release their flavor into the mixture as it steeps. Set the mixture aside to steep for 1 hour at room temperature, then discard the cobs and vanilla bean pod. Pour the mixture through a fine mesh strainer into a large saucepan, pressing on the solids to remove all the liquid.

3. Bring the mixture back to a simmer over medium heat. Meanwhile, whisk together the sugar and yolks in a small bowl until smooth. Whisking constantly, slowly pour 1 cup of the warm liquid into the yolks to temper them. Whisk the yolk mixture into the corn mixture and cook, stirring constantly with a heatproof spatula, until the custard thickens enough to coat the back of the spatula, about 10 minutes. Pour the mixture through a fine-mesh sieve into a large

glass or metal bowl. Let the custard cool to room temperature, then press a piece of plastic wrap directly onto the surface and refrigerate until very cold (under 40°F), at least 4 hours, then mix well.

4. Churn the ice cream in a small electric ice cream freezer according to the manufacturer's instructions. The ice cream will be soft, like a thick milk shake. To freeze hard enough to scoop, transfer into an airtight container, press plastic wrap directly onto the surface, and freeze until firm.

# CUCUMBERS

**Along with melons and squashes,** cucumbers are members of the gourd family. By the seventeenth century, cucumbers were grown in much of the South, but more often in Native American gardens than in colonial kitchen gardens. Native Americans, who were experts at growing gourds, are credited with spreading cucumbers up the Atlantic coast. English colonists used cucumbers for little more than animal fodder, even referring to them as "cow-cumbers" in some records. It wasn't until subsequent waves of immigrants and creative cooks came along that cucumbers found their way into most southern kitchens, where they were usually cooked or pickled. Cold, crunchy, refreshing raw cucumbers are a relatively recent treat.

As the case with homegrown tomatoes, home gardens and small farms have been the guardians of cucumber diversity, battling the assumption that all cucumbers are green and cylindrical. A quick glance at a seed catalog or a walk through a farmers' market reveals cucumbers in a range of colors, sizes, and shapes. ■

## Cucumber and Cottage Cheese Salad in Tomato Shells

4 large tomatoes (about 10 ounces each) or 36 cocktail tomatoes

1 ½ cups cottage cheese

3 tablespoons mayonnaise

2 teaspoons cider vinegar or white wine vinegar

1 tablespoon finely chopped chives

2 tablespoons finely chopped scallions (white and tender green parts)

¼ cup finely diced red bell pepper

1 cup seeded and finely diced cucumber

Coarse or kosher salt and ground black pepper, to taste

My grandmother ate cucumbers with cottage cheese every day that there was a cucumber to pick from the garden. She saved all those dozens (hundreds?) of plastic cottage cheese containers and used them to store everything from leftovers to loose buttons. Finding things in her refrigerator required opening many identical containers to see what was in them. The upside was that I sometimes came across something better than what I went in for.

If you use bite-sized tomatoes, this is a great summertime hors d'oeuvre. If hollowing out tomato shells is too tedious, spoon the cottage cheese mixture over sliced tomatoes. If you have any large-crystal garnishing salt, such as Maldon or fleur de sel, sprinkle some over the tops just before serving.

MAKES 3 CUPS

1. For the tomato shells, use a serrated knife to carefully cut a sliver off the tops of the tomatoes and then use a melon baller or sharp spoon to scoop out the centers, leaving hollow shells. Sprinkle the insides with salt and turn them upside down on paper towels to drain for 15 minutes.

2. Stir together the cottage cheese, mayonnaise, vinegar, chives, scallions, bell pepper, and cucumber. Season with salt and pepper. Spoon the cottage cheese filling into the tomatoes, mounding it up a little on top. Sprinkle with salt and pepper and serve soon.

MAKE-AHEAD NOTE: You can make the filling up to 2 days ahead. Store covered and refrigerated. Drain off any liquid that rises to the top and stir well before serving.

## Cucumber, Dill, and Yogurt Dip and More

4 cups peeled, seeded, and coarsely grated cucumbers (about 1 ½ pounds)

1 tablespoon kosher salt

2 cups plain Greek yogurt (see note)

1 cup sour cream

2 tablespoons white wine vinegar

2 tablespoons fresh lemon juice

2 tablespoons extra-virgin olive oil

1 tablespoon finely chopped garlic

2 tablespoons finely chopped fresh dill

½ teaspoon ground black pepper

In Greek communities this is called tzatziki. It is useful stuff. It makes a great dip for pita crisps, pita bread wedges, or thick potato chips. It makes a light yet creamy sauce for poached, roasted, or grilled salmon or other fish, or for chicken kabobs. When mixed with cooked and cooled potatoes, it makes quick potato salad. When thinned with a little buttermilk, it makes great salad dressing. When thinned with a little more buttermilk, it makes fantastic cold cucumber soup.

Seedless cucumbers, such as Armenian, English, and Persian varieties, work best in this recipe. Other varieties will do so long as they have not grown so large that they are spongy and bitter.

MAKES ABOUT 4 CUPS

1. Toss the grated cucumbers with the salt and place in a fine mesh sieve set over a large bowl. Refrigerate for 4 hours and discard the accumulated liquid. (There will be as much as 2 cups of liquid, which shows the importance of draining the cucumbers. Imagine how watery the dip would be with all that liquid in it.)

2. Place the drained cucumbers in a bowl and stir in the remaining ingredients. Refrigerate for at least 1 hour to let the flavors develop. Stir before serving lightly chilled.

NOTE: Greek yogurt is available in most grocery stores, but you can substitute 4 cups of drained regular plain yogurt. To drain, spoon the yogurt into a large fine mesh sieve lined with a double thickness of white paper towels or overlapping paper coffee filters set over a large bowl. Press a piece of plastic wrap directly onto the surface of the yogurt to keep it from drying out and refrigerate for at least 8 hours. Discard the accumulated liquid.

# Summer Farro Salad

1 ½ cups uncooked farro

6 tablespoons garlic-infused olive oil, divided (see note)

2 tablespoons sherry vinegar or red wine vinegar

1 cup shelled fresh fava beans

2 cups cored, seeded, and finely chopped ripe tomatoes

1 cup peeled seedless cucumber, halved lengthwise and thinly sliced

½ cup brine-cured, pitted black olives

Kosher salt and ground black pepper, to taste

½ cup lightly packed basil leaves, cut crosswise into thin ribbons

Farro, a grain related to spelt and wheat, is one of the world's oldest foods. It is often used in creamy soups, but it works well in salads, such as this light yet filling combination of grain and crunchy vegetables. Most farro is imported from Italy, but an heirloom variety is being grown in the United States and sold through Anson Mills, protector and champion of heirloom grains (ansonmills.com). You can substitute cooked pearl barley or long-grain rice for the farro.

Fava beans are being rediscovered in southern gardens after a long absence. There are records of them being grown in the earliest southern gardens after they were imported by Spanish explorers.

This salad travels well and is served at room temperature, so it's great for picnics, patio dining, and tailgating. I like to serve it with cheese and cured meats such as salami, soppressata, and pepperoni. Plus wine, of course.

MAKES 4 TO 6 SERVINGS

1. Put the farro in a large bowl and cover with cold water. Cover and let soak at least 2 hours and up to overnight. Drain and transfer into a large saucepan. Cover with fresh water to a depth of 1 inch and add ½ teaspoon kosher salt per cup of water. Bring to a boil, reduce the heat, cover the pan, and simmer until tender, about 30 minutes. Do not let the farro get mushy. (The longer the grain soaked, the less time it will take to cook.) Drain in a colander, rinse quickly with cool water, and transfer into a large bowl.

2. Toss the warm farro with 3 tablespoons of the oil and the vinegar and set aside to cool to room temperature, stirring occasionally.

3. Fill a medium bowl with ice water. Bring a small saucepan of water to a boil. Add ½ teaspoon kosher salt per cup of water. Add the fava beans and cook for 2 minutes. Immediately transfer into the ice water to stop the cooking and set the color. Drain well and pat dry. If the favas are large and the skin is tough or loose, peel it off and discard, leaving only the tender, bright green inner beans.

4. Stir the favas, tomatoes, cucumber, and olives and the remaining 3 tablespoons of oil into the farro. Season generously with salt and pepper, plus additional vinegar, if needed. Just before serving, stir in the basil.

NOTE: If you don't have a bottle of garlic-infused olive oil on hand, stir together 6 large garlic cloves and ½ cup extra-virgin olive oil in a small saucepan. Warm over low heat until the garlic releases its aroma and turns pale golden, about 15 minutes. Discard the garlic. Use the oil at once and do not store the leftovers.

WHAT ELSE WORKS? You can use shelled and blanched fresh soybeans (edamame) or lightly cooked butter beans or field peas in place of the blanched fava beans.

# Chilled Cucumber Soup

2 cups 1-inch cubes crustless Italian or French bread

2 cups cold water

4 cups peeled, seeded, and diced cucumbers (about 1 pound)

3 cups seedless green grapes (about 12 ounces)

2 garlic cloves, chopped

¾ cup blanched almonds, preferably Marcona, toasted and finely chopped, plus more for garnish

3 tablespoons verjus or sherry vinegar (see note)

½ cup extra-virgin olive oil

1 teaspoon kosher salt

½ teaspoon ground black pepper

1 teaspoon green Tabasco sauce, or to taste

¼ cup quartered green grapes, for garnish

Cold soup is controversial. Some people cannot imagine enduring the withering heat and humidity of southern summers without it; others think the purpose of soup is to warm them up on cold winter nights. I did not grow up with chilled soup. Our soup was cold only when we dawdled when called to the table and had to live with the consequences.

The secret ingredient in this soup is green grapes. No one will be able to guess what's giving the soup its subtle, fruity sweetness. This is a good first course or light meal, but for an intriguing appetizer, I serve this in chilled shot glasses, garnished with whole green grapes threaded onto picks.

MAKES 2 QUARTS

1. Put the bread cubes in a medium bowl, pour the water over them, and set aside for 5 minutes. Squeeze the bread dry and place in a large bowl.

2. Stir in the cucumbers, grapes, garlic, and almonds. Working in batches, purée the vegetable mixture in a blender, adding enough of the verjus and oil to each batch to keep it moving. Don't rush this step; it might take more than 1 minute for the mixture to get completely smooth.

3. Pour the purée into a fine mesh sieve set over a large bowl. Press the purée through the sieve with a rubber spatula. Discard any solids. Season the soup with the salt, pepper, and Tabasco.

4. Cover and refrigerate overnight. Before serving, whisk the soup and adjust the seasoning. Serve chilled, garnished with almonds and grapes.

NOTE: Verjus (verjuice) means "green juice" and is the pressed juice of unripe grapes. Verjus has a fruity, sweet-tart flavor that is milder than vinegar. It's good in vinaigrettes or drizzled over food in place of fresh lemon juice. It's sold in bottles in gourmet stores, natural food stores, and online.

# Smoked Trout Salad in Cucumber Cups

4 ounces cream cheese, at room temperature

2 tablespoons heavy cream

2 tablespoons finely chopped red onion

1 teaspoon finely grated lemon zest

2 teaspoons fresh lemon juice

2 teaspoons finely chopped fresh dill

1 ½ teaspoons prepared horseradish

1 cup skinned and crumbled hot-smoked trout (about 4 ounces)

Kosher salt and freshly ground black pepper, to taste

1 long or 2 medium seedless cucumbers, preferably about 2 inches in diameter

24 tiny dill sprigs, for garnish

There are two parts to this recipe, and each can be used separately. The first part is the shallow cucumber cups that hold the salad, used instead of a cracker or crostini. You can fill the cups with other things, such as herbed cream cheese or chicken salad. It is easiest to make cups from seedless cucumbers that are about 2 inches in diameter. If your cucumbers are too narrow to make good cups, cut them into 2-inch lengths, cut each piece in half lengthwise, and then hollow them out so that they resemble little boats.

The second part of this recipe is the terrific trout salad. It's made with hot-smoked trout, which is fully cooked and meaty. You can substitute hot-smoked salmon or leftover grilled salmon.

To turn this appetizer into a plated salad, arrange thinly sliced cucumbers on serving plates and serve a small scoop of salad on top.

MAKES 24 CUCUMBER CUPS AND ABOUT 1 ½ CUPS OF SALAD

1. For the trout salad, stir together the cream cheese, cream, onion, lemon zest, lemon juice, dill, and horseradish in a small bowl. Use a rubber spatula to gently fold in the trout. Season with salt, if needed, and pepper. Use at once or cover and refrigerate for up to 2 days.

2. For the cucumber cups, taste a little of the cucumber skin; if it's tough or bitter, peel it off. Otherwise, leave the cucumbers plain or score them lengthwise with a fork to make a pretty edge. Cut the cucumbers crosswise into ¾-inch-thick slices. You should have about 24 slices in all. Use a small spoon or melon baller to gently scoop out about half of the center of each cucumber slice, just enough to make an indentation to hold the trout salad.

3. Place about 1 tablespoon of salad in each cucumber cup, pressing it lightly to make it stay on the cucumber. Garnish each with a small sprig of dill and serve soon or refrigerate for up to 6 hours covered with a damp paper towel and wrapped loosely in plastic wrap.

WHAT ELSE WORKS? You can spoon the salad into individual Belgian endive leaves. You can also serve this as a plated salad, using thinly sliced tart apples or thinly sliced chilled roasted beets in place of the sliced cucumber or a combination of the two. Dip the apples in lemon juice or lemon-lime soda to reduce browning.

## Cucumbers and Onions

1 pound small, slender cucumbers, peeled if necessary and cut into ¼-inch-thick slices

1 medium onion, halved lengthwise and cut into thin strips

1 ½ cups unseasoned rice vinegar or 1 cup distilled white vinegar diluted with ½ cup water

¼ cup sugar

2 teaspoons pickling spices (see note)

1 teaspoon pickling salt or kosher salt

½ teaspoon ground black pepper

Many southern families put out a dish of these sweet and tangy quick pickles with every meal during the summer. The vegetables keep for days in the refrigerator, and you can reuse the brine for weeks. I store mine in a 1-quart canning jar. Cucumbers and onions are used as both a side dish and a relish. They are great on sandwiches or in summer salads, such as potato salad and coleslaw. I think they are integral to vegetable plates.

Small cucumbers work best, so pickling cucumbers are a natural choice, but Persian, Armenian, or other slender varieties also work. Avoid large cucumbers with wet, seedy interiors.

MAKES ABOUT 4 CUPS

1. Place the cucumbers and onion in a large glass bowl or quart jar.
2. Combine the vinegar, sugar, picking spices, salt, and pepper in a saucepan. Bring to a simmer over medium-high heat and cook, stirring frequently, until the sugar dissolves. Pour the vinegar mixture over the cucumbers and onions.
3. Let cool to room temperature. Cover and refrigerate until well chilled before serving, at least 4 hours and preferably overnight. The vegetables keep in the refrigerator for up to 1 week. The brine can be reused multiple times so long as it stays refrigerated.

NOTE: Pickling spice is a mixture of spices that includes whole cloves, whole allspice, whole mustard seed, and bits of bay leaf. It's sold in small jars on the spice rack at the grocery store.

WHAT ELSE WORKS? You can use onions alone. Red onions or peeled pearl onions are stunning.

Roasted Roma Tart

Herbed Summer Squash and Pasta Salad with Crispy Chicken Thighs

Roasted Fingerling Potato Salad
with Lemon-Basil Vinaigrette

Southern Skillet Greens Bruschetta and
Smoked Tomato Soup with Herbed Beans

Savory Smoked Ham, Spinach, and Cheese Bread
Pudding with Smoky Roasted Red Pepper Sauce

Chilled Honeydew Soup with Coconut-Cilantro Pesto and
Watermelon and Tomato Salad with Fresh Herbs

Salmon and Roasted Beet Salad
with Creamy Herb Dressing

Sweet Corn on the Cob with Gobs of Butter

# EGGPLANT

**An eggplant is an oversized berry.** Like tomatoes, potatoes, and tobacco, it is in the nightshade family. It has grown in the South since the eighteenth century, but most colonists used eggplant only as a garden ornament, if that, because they believed that nightshades caused madness. Some of the earliest specimens were small, oval, and white, just like a hen's egg, so the name was fitting and came to be used for all varieties.

Italian American cooks popularized the purple globe eggplant, nearly overshadowing all other types. These days, however, southern gardens produce Asian and Persian eggplants in addition to the Mediterranean varieties. These eggplants come in myriad shapes and sizes, from as small as a pea to pound-plus whoppers, both round and long. Their solid, striped, and variegated skins can be white, green, red, orange, pink, purple, or lavender. People who extol eggplant claim there's a thousand ways to cook them. It's true that versatile eggplant is amenable to many cooking techniques, which is good news since eggplant should never be served raw. ■

## Eggplant Caponata

Extra-virgin olive oil or vegetable oil for pan-frying

1 pound eggplant, trimmed and cut into 1-inch cubes

2 red Italian frying peppers or other sweet peppers, cored and cut into 1-inch pieces

2 large yellow onions, diced

3 medium tomatoes, cored, seeded, and diced

1 cup pitted green olives

½ cup raisins

3 tablespoons drained capers

2 tablespoons brown sugar

2 tablespoons red wine vinegar

1 teaspoon kosher salt, or to taste

Italian immigrants spread their love for eggplant throughout the South. This dish has roots in Sicily and the Middle East. Sicilian immigrants have had significant culinary influence in New Orleans and other areas of the South. It is an example of their talent for mixing flavors, aromas, colors, and textures into an amazing dish. Although there are many variations, caponata always contains eggplant, tomatoes, and onions cooked in olive oil and seasoned with vinegar. This version features the sweetness of ripe peppers and the salty tang of olives and capers. Even though the vegetables are pan-fried, this dish is not heavy or greasy. The finished dish includes less oil than most salad dressings. (See page 106 for tips on pan-frying.)

Caponata has many uses: relish, salad, side dish, pasta sauce, and bruschetta topping. It can be served warm or at room temperature, which is great during the summer. It's best made at least one day ahead.

MAKES 6 TO 8 SERVINGS

1. Set a wire rack inside a large rimmed baking sheet. Cover the rack with a few layers of paper towels and place near the stove to use for draining the cooked vegetables.

2. Pour the oil into a large skillet to a depth of ½ inch and heat over medium-high heat until shimmering hot.

3. Pat the eggplant cubes as dry as possible. Working in batches, add a single layer of the eggplant to the skillet and cook until tender and browned on all sides, 7 to 9 minutes per batch. Transfer with a slotted spoon to the paper towels to drain. Replenish the oil as needed.

4. Add the peppers to the skillet and cook, stirring often, until tender and slightly browned, about 5 minutes. Transfer with a slotted spoon to the paper towels to drain.

5. Add the onions to the skillet and cook, stirring often, until tender and golden, about 8 minutes. Transfer with a slotted spoon to the paper towels to drain.

6. Stir together the tomatoes, olives, raisins, capers, brown sugar, and vinegar in a large saucepan. Bring to a simmer over medium heat. Stir in the eggplant, peppers, and onions. Season with the salt. Cover and cook over low heat, stirring occasionally, until the vegetables are tender and the sauce thickens, about 20 minutes. Add a little water if the mixture gets dry before the vegetables are done.

7. Remove the pan from the heat and let the vegetables cool to room temperature. For best flavor, cool, cover, and refrigerate overnight. Check the seasoning and add more salt, sugar, or vinegar if needed to balance the flavors. Return to room temperature or gently warm before serving.

# Grilled Eggplant Parmesan

6 tablespoons extra-virgin olive oil, divided

3 cups Simmered Tomato Sauce (page 353) or bottled tomato-basil pasta sauce

½ cup coarsely chopped fresh basil

¾ cup finely grated Parmesan cheese, divided (about 2 ounces)

2 cups fresh bread crumbs (page 389)

2 garlic cloves, finely chopped

2 tablespoons chopped flat-leaf parsley

2 pounds small to medium eggplants

1 teaspoon kosher salt

½ teaspoon ground black pepper

2 cups grated whole-milk mozzarella or Italian blend (*quattro formaggio*) cheese

This recipe is less heavy and oily than traditional fried and baked eggplant Parmesan. Smoky, tender grilled eggplant is layered with tomato sauce and a little cheese and sprinkled with garlicky crumbs.

Many old recipes call for peeling, salting, and draining eggplant. The idea was to draw out excess liquid and bitterness, which is a good strategy when all you have are enormous, thick-skinned, seedy globe eggplants. Beyond that, some culinary scientists point out that salting collapses the air pockets in the spongy flesh, resulting in eggplant that is less prone to soak up oil when fried. However, if you are using young, small, tender eggplants in this grilled recipe, you can skip the peeling and salting.

This recipe is written for outdoor grilling, but you can also cook the vegetables indoors on a ridged grill pan or an electric countertop grill, although the flavor is not the same.

MAKES 4 TO 6 SERVINGS

1. Heat 2 tablespoons of the oil in a large, heavy saucepan over medium-high heat until shimmering hot. Carefully add the tomato sauce. It will sizzle and bubble vigorously. Cook, stirring, until the sauce thickens slightly, about 2 minutes. Stir in the basil and ¼ cup of the Parmesan. Keep warm over very low heat.

2. Heat 2 tablespoons of the oil in a large, heavy skillet over medium-high heat. Add the bread crumbs and garlic and stir to coat. Cook, stirring often, until the crumbs are golden brown and crispy, about 8 minutes. Remove from the heat, stir in the parsley and the remaining ½ cup of Parmesan.

3. Preheat a gas grill or charcoal grill for direct cooking over medium heat. For a gas grill, preheat the burners on high, covered, for 10 minutes and then reduce the heat to medium. For a charcoal grill, open the vents in the bottom of the grill and light the charcoal. (Natural hardwood charcoal is best.) When the coals are covered in gray ash (about 15 minutes after lighting), spread them into an even layer. When you can hold your hand 5 inches above the grate for 5 seconds, the heat is medium.

4. While the grill preheats, cut off and discard the ends of the eggplants. Cut the eggplants into ½-inch-thick slices. (Cut round eggplants crosswise into rounds and slender ones lengthwise into strips.) Lightly brush the eggplant slices with the remaining 2 tablespoons of oil and sprinkle with the salt and pepper.

5. When the grill is hot, clean the grate with a stiff wire brush and then oil it generously with vegetable oil to prevent sticking. Use tongs to arrange the eggplant slices on the grate in a single layer. Grill, turning occasionally, until the eggplant begins to soften and is lightly charred in spots, about 4 minutes. Brush it with more oil if it starts to look dry. Transfer the cooked eggplant into a large bowl and cover to hold in the steam. The steam should finish cooking

the eggplant; if it doesn't, arrange the slices in a single layer on a baking sheet and roast in a 400°F oven until tender, about 5 minutes.

6. Arrange one-third of the eggplant slices in the bottom of a shallow baking dish or gratin dish. Sprinkle with one-third of the mozzarella and drizzle with one-third of the warm tomato sauce. Make two more layers in the same way. Sprinkle the bread crumb mixture over the top.

7. Place the dish on the cool edge of the grill (or in a 400°F oven) until the cheese starts to melt, about 10 minutes. Serve hot.

VARIATION: You can assemble individual servings by stacking the ingredients. This works best with large balls of fresh mozzarella and globe eggplants of similar diameter. Layer thin slices of mozzarella between the hot rounds of eggplant as soon as they come off the grill, either on a platter or on individual serving plates. Top the stacks with warm pasta sauce and the crumbs. You can also insert large pieces of other grilled vegetables, such as sweet peppers, zucchini, sliced onions, or portobello mushrooms.

## Eggplant and Rice Dressing

What some people call stuffing southerners often call dressing. The distinction is that stuffing must be actually stuffed into something, a bird, for instance, whereas dressing is baked in a dish. To add to the confusion, in some parts of the Deep South, particularly Louisiana, the word "dressing" is also used to describe certain rice dishes that are cooked in a pot on top of the stove. This is one of those dressings. It's a fixture on many holiday menus, and although it's billed as a side dish, it's hearty enough to be served as an entrée. Many people think this dressing tastes best made a day ahead and reheated.

The recipe calls for hot, freshly cooked rice, so get it going before starting the rest of the recipe.

MAKES 8 SERVINGS

1. Heat the oil in a large, heavy pot over medium heat. Add the beef and pork and cook, stirring often, until the meat is no longer pink, about 15 minutes.

2. Stir in the onion, celery, bell pepper, and garlic. Cook, stirring often, until the vegetables begin to soften, about 5 minutes. Stir in the eggplant, stock, salt, and pepper. Cover the pot and simmer, stirring occasionally, until the eggplant is very soft and tender, about 30 minutes. Coarsely mash the eggplant with a fork or the back of a spoon. Stir in the hot cooked rice, thyme, and parsley. Season with more salt and plenty of hot sauce and serve warm.

1 tablespoon vegetable oil

12 ounces lean ground beef

12 ounces lean ground pork

1 large yellow onion, chopped (about 2 cups)

2 celery stalks, chopped (about ½ cup)

1 medium green bell pepper, cored and chopped (about ½ cup)

3 garlic cloves, chopped

6 cups peeled bite-sized eggplant cubes

1 cup chicken stock or water

1 teaspoon kosher salt, plus more to taste

½ teaspoon ground black pepper, or to taste

(continued on next page)

3 cups hot, freshly cooked long-grain rice

1 teaspoon chopped fresh thyme

2 tablespoons chopped flat-leaf parsley

½ teaspoon hot sauce, or to taste

MAKE-AHEAD NOTE: This can be made 1 day ahead. Cool, cover, and refrigerate. Check the seasoning when you reheat the dressing.

## Charred Eggplant Dip

1 large or 2 medium globe eggplants (about 2 pounds total)

4 garlic cloves, chopped

¼ cup well-stirred tahini

¼ cup fresh lemon juice

½ teaspoon ground cumin

Kosher salt, ground black pepper, and cayenne pepper, to taste

½ cup extra-virgin olive oil

2 tablespoons finely chopped flat-leaf parsley

Charring eggplant on a grill gives it a smoky flavor and makes the pulp very silky. This dip is similar to Middle Eastern baba ghanoush, so it's good with pita wedges or crunchy pita chips. For that matter, it's a good sauce for grilled kabobs.

Because they yield lots of pulp and are easy to peel, common purple globe eggplants work well here, even when they have gotten a little larger than is good for other recipes. When grilled, the eggplants collapse to about half their original size, like a birthday balloon the day after the party.

You can also roast the eggplant on a baking sheet in a 400°F oven, but it won't have the same smoky allure.

MAKES ABOUT 3 CUPS

1. Preheat a grill to high temperature. Prick the eggplant several times with a fork to let steam escape as it cooks. Grill the eggplant, turning with tongs as needed, until the skin blackens and the inside collapses and softens, about 15 minutes, depending on the size of the eggplant. Transfer into a large bowl, cover tightly with plastic wrap, and set aside until cool enough to handle. Peel the eggplant. Discard the skin and any juices that collect in the bowl because they are usually bitter.

2. Place the eggplant pulp in the bowl of a food processor. Add the garlic, tahini, lemon juice, and cumin and process until smooth. Transfer into a serving bowl and season with salt, pepper, and cayenne. Drizzle the oil over the top and sprinkle with the parsley. Serve at room temperature. Store covered and refrigerated for up to 3 days.

# FIELD PEAS

**There are dozens of varieties** and nearly as many names for this family of legumes, including field peas, cow peas, stock peas, crowder peas, shell peas, and southern peas. Field peas is the most common moniker because for generations they were grown in the crop fields rather than in kitchen gardens. Heat- and drought-tolerant field peas were intercropped in the rice fields and cornfields, where they added valuable nitrogen back into the soil. Field peas were usually so plentiful that there was no need to plant them in the kitchen garden, which was the space reserved for vegetables and fruits grown for the family table, such as the eponymous garden peas.

Field peas were brought by enslaved Africans from West and North Africa to the West Indies as early as 1674. Without the Africans' expertise in growing rice with the peas, the profitable rice industry that spread across the sea islands of Georgia and South Carolina would never have been possible. Hoppin' John, one of the most iconic and enduring dishes of the South, is a vestige of the humble practice of eating rice and field peas, first eaten by African slaves in an effort to replicate dishes from home. It's easier to uproot people than it is to expunge their beloved foodways. Considering their dire beginnings, it's hard to imagine why field peas came to be associated with good luck, but they are traditionally eaten on New Year's Day in the South for this purpose. The peas are said to represent coins, just as leafy collards represent folding money.

Hundreds of varieties of field peas once grew across the South. Many are now lost to time. Others are regional favorites rarely seen elsewhere. The individual varieties of field peas have fabulous, idiosyncratic names that give hints of their origin and appearance, such as black-eyed, purple hull, lady, cream, zipper, ripper, rattlesnake, rouge et noir, clay, bird, cornfield, wash day, whip-poor-will, white acre, turkey craw, calico crowder, Sea Island red, and the like. Some noble bean historians are working hard today to find and restore the remaining old varieties before they become extinct.

Nearly all field peas are shelled out of their pods before they are cooked. The notable exceptions are yard beans and snaps. Yard beans are a variety that grows preposterously long, although perhaps not quite a yard long, but never develops full-size peas that can be shelled out. Snaps are immature field pea pods that are picked while they are still tender enough to eat. The slender pods are broken and cooked like snap beans.

Despite the availability of shelling machines, many people prefer peas shelled by hand. When done in groups, hand shelling can be social, giving people a chance to visit and tell stories while they sit and shell. When done alone, hand shelling is the handiwork of philosophers, because you can't do much other than sit and think when you're shelling pods. ■

# Basic Cooked Field Peas

3 cups freshly
shelled field peas

1 onion, cut in half with
a little of the root left
attached to hold the
pieces together

2 bay leaves

4 short thyme sprigs

2 dried hot chile peppers
or 1 teaspoon hot
sauce

1 teaspoon kosher salt,
plus more to taste

1 ham hock, 1 smoked
turkey wing, a 2-inch
square of slab bacon,
or 3 thick slices
of bacon

4 cups chicken stock

Most field peas are traditionally cooked in homemade smoked pork stock rather than plain water. This recipe speeds up the process by starting with chicken stock boosted with a ham hock, a smoked turkey wing, or a little bacon. To keep the peas meatless, cook them in Smoked Vegetable Stock (page 181).

Field peas have a wide range of cooking times, depending on their size and freshness. To get an idea of what to expect, taste a raw pea. If it's small, tender, and juicy, it will cook more quickly than a larger, denser pea that fights back a little.

You should get 3 cups (1 pound) of shelled peas from 3 pounds of pods.

MAKES 4 SERVINGS

1. Rinse the peas thoroughly in several changes of water to remove any bits of hull and stickiness. When the water runs clear, transfer the peas into a large saucepan and add the onion, bay leaves, thyme, chiles, salt, meat, and stock. The peas should be covered by at least 1 inch of liquid, so add cold water if needed. Bring to a boil, skim off the foam, reduce the heat, and simmer gently until the peas are tender, 15 to 45 minutes, depending on their size and freshness. The peas should stay submerged, so add water as needed. Taste a pea and add more salt if needed.

2. Remove the pan from the heat, cover, and set the peas aside for at least 30 minutes to give them time to absorb the salt. Discard the onion, bay leaves, thyme sprigs, and chiles. You can pull the meat from the hock or wing and stir it into the peas, if you want to serve it, or discard it. Discard the bacon if you used it.

3. Reheat the peas if you are serving them now. Otherwise, let them cool, then cover and refrigerate. Store the peas in their cooking liquid; it keeps them moist and is delicious.

# Lady Pea and Mixed Heirloom Tomato Salad

3 cups shelled lady
peas or other
delicate field peas

4 tablespoons extra-
virgin olive oil, divided

Kosher salt and
ground black pepper

¾ cup high-quality
mayonnaise

2 teaspoons finely
grated lemon zest

2 tablespoons fresh
lemon juice

1 large garlic clove,
finely chopped

2 cups ripe cherry
or other miniature
tomatoes, left whole
or halved, depending
on size

2 tablespoons finely
chopped sweet
onion or shallot

1 tablespoon
sherry vinegar

1 tablespoon
finely chopped
flat-leaf parsley

2 to 3 large heirloom
tomatoes, cored,
peeled if necessary,
and cut into a total
of 12 slices

12 large basil leaves

I love to use tiny, delicate, creamy white lady peas in this salad, for they are the empress of all field peas and my favorite by far. Unlike most field peas, lady peas stay light in color and delicate in constitution when cooked. These peas need very light seasoning and do not yield rich potlikker, making them more like garden peas in that respect.

Be sure to use a colorful assortment of tomatoes in this pretty salad, preferably local heirloom varieties that have exceptional flavor. On a warm summer night, this salad might be all you need for supper.

MAKES 6 SERVINGS

1. Bring a large saucepan of water to a boil. Add ½ teaspoon kosher salt per cup of water. Stir in the peas, reduce the heat, and simmer until just tender, about 15 minutes. Skim off any foam. Drain, transfer into a large bowl, and stir in 2 tablespoons of the oil. Season with salt and pepper, cover, and refrigerate until chilled.

2. Whisk together the mayonnaise, lemon zest, lemon juice, and garlic in a small bowl. Cover and refrigerate until chilled.

3. Stir the cherry tomatoes into the field peas. Stir in the onion, vinegar, and parsley and the remaining 2 tablespoons of oil. Season generously with salt and pepper.

4. To serve, divide the tomato slices among the serving plates and tuck the basil leaves around them. Spoon the tomato and pea mixture over the slices. Top each serving with a generous spoonful of the mayonnaise mixture. Serve at once.

MAKE-AHEAD NOTE: The peas can be cooked up to 1 day ahead; store covered and refrigerated. The mayonnaise mixture can be made up to 1 day ahead; store covered and refrigerated.

## Crunchy Fried Field Peas

2 cups shelled field peas

Vegetable oil,
for frying

1 teaspoon coarse salt
or kosher salt

½ teaspoon smoked
paprika (*pimentón*),
or to taste

I tasted a version of these at Blackberry Farm, a gracious place known for thinking of creative ways to serve traditional southern ingredients. The chefs served crunchy fried field peas in tiny cast-iron skillets with cocktails, like very inventive bar nuts. I don't have their recipe, but these come pretty close. The salty, smoky peas are a delicious bar snack, but they're also great sprinkled over salads or a platter of sliced tomatoes.

Smoked paprika is made from peppers that have been smoked over hardwood. The aroma is exotic and the flavor is intense. It's a great way to add smokiness to foods without adding meat, heat, or artificial flavoring.

MAKES 6 TO 8 SERVINGS

1. Fill a large bowl with ice water. Bring a large saucepan of water to a boil. Add ½ teaspoon kosher salt per cup of water. Add the peas and cook until crisp-tender, about 3 minutes. Use a slotted spoon or strainer to transfer them into the ice water to cool. Drain and pat completely dry.

2. Fill a large, deep skillet or heavy saucepan with oil to a depth of 2 inches. Heat the oil over medium-high heat to 325°F on a deep-fry thermometer. When hot, a pinch of flour sprinkled into the oil should sizzle immediately and slowly brown without popping.

3. Working in batches to not overfill the pan, carefully add some peas to the hot oil. The peas should be able to float freely in the oil. Fry until the peas are crisp, about 3 minutes. Transfer with a slotted spoon or strainer to paper towels to drain. Sprinkle the hot peas with the salt and smoked paprika and toss to coat. Serve the peas warm or at room temperature. Store any leftovers at room temperature in an airtight container.

## Field Pea and Greens Soup with Black Pepper Cornbread Croutons

6 thick bacon slices, cut crosswise into ¼-inch strips (about 6 ounces)

1 tablespoon extra-virgin olive oil, if needed

1 ¼ cups chopped onion

¾ cup chopped celery

¾ cup chopped carrots

4 garlic cloves, finely chopped

1 small bay leaf

2 teaspoons chopped fresh thyme, divided

2 teaspoons chopped fresh rosemary, divided

5 cups chicken stock or one of the smoked stocks (page 180)

2 ½ cups shelled field peas or peas and snaps

1 teaspoon kosher salt

3 cups lightly packed stemmed and thinly shredded leafy greens, such as spinach, chard, kale, escarole, or very young collards

1 tablespoon Hot Pepper Vinegar (page 88) or cider vinegar

Black Pepper Cornbread Croutons, for serving (recipe follows)

Some traditional field pea recipes and greens recipes describe the nearly lost art of simmering cornmeal dumplings in the rich potlikker, nestled on top of the cooked vegetables. Those dumplings were tasty, dense, and filling, which was the whole point. They were one way that a resourceful cook could make a little food go a little farther when there were many bellies to fill. This recipe honors that humble tradition by serving this satisfying soup with a few peppery croutons made from leftover cornbread.

MAKES ABOUT 2 QUARTS

1 Cook the bacon in a large soup pot or Dutch oven over medium heat, stirring often, until browned and crisp, about 10 minutes. Transfer with a slotted spoon to paper towels to drain. The bacon drippings make the soup heartier and meatier, but you can pour them off and use the oil instead, if you wish.

2 Stir in the onion, celery, and carrots and a pinch of salt. Cook, stirring often, until softened, about 8 minutes. Stir in the garlic and bay leaf, 1 teaspoon of the thyme, and 1 teaspoon of the rosemary and cook, stirring, for 1 minute. Add the stock, peas, and salt. Bring to a boil, reduce the heat, and simmer until the peas are tender, about 25 minutes. Stir in the greens and the remaining 1 teaspoon of thyme and rosemary. Cook, stirring often, until tender, about 5 minutes.

3 Remove the bay leaf. Stir in the bacon and vinegar and check the seasoning. Serve hot, topped with a few Black Pepper Cornbread Croutons.

WHAT ELSE WORKS? You can replace the field peas with fresh shell beans or sliced potatoes; adjust the cooking time accordingly. When time is tight, replace the field peas with a drained can or two of cannellini beans.

MAKE-AHEAD NOTE: The soup can be made up to 1 day ahead. Cool, cover, and refrigerate. Do not add the bacon until time to serve. Check the seasoning because the soup will likely need more salt and vinegar.

## Black Pepper Cornbread Croutons

Vegetable oil spray

3 cups 1-inch corn-
bread cubes

4 tablespoons (½ stick)
butter, melted

1 teaspoon coarsely
cracked black pepper

½ teaspoon coarse salt
or kosher salt

For this recipe, the cornbread needs to be a little stale so that it won't fall apart when cut into cubes, so leftover cornbread works best. (If you buy the cornbread, be sure it doesn't contain sugar.) These croutons are also good in other soups and in salads, such as Tomato and Bread Salad (page 346). By the way, in old southern recipes of English descent, these would be called *sippets* instead of the French *croutons*.

MAKES 3 CUPS

① Preheat the oven to 375°F. Mist a rimmed baking sheet with the spray.

② Spread the cornbread in an even layer on the prepared sheet and toast until firm and just beginning to color on the edges, about 15 minutes, stirring occasionally.

③ Meanwhile, stir together the melted butter, pepper, and salt. Drizzle over the bread cubes and toss lightly to coat. Continue baking until the croutons are crispy and golden brown on the edges, about 15 minutes longer, stirring occasionally. Pour onto a cutting board or large plate to cool.

MAKE-AHEAD NOTE: You can make the croutons up to 2 days ahead. Cool and store at room temperature in an airtight container.

## Hoppin' John Risotto with Collard Pesto

4 to 5 cups chicken stock

12 ounces mild or hot
bulk breakfast sausage

1 cup chopped onion

½ cup chopped
red bell pepper

½ cup chopped celery

1 ½ cups Carolina Gold
or Arborio rice

½ cup dry white wine

1 ½ cups cooked and
drained black-eyed
peas or other field
peas (page 124)

(continued on
next page)

Hoppin' John is an iconic dish that is mostly misunderstood outside of the South. First, it's not as ubiquitous as it seems. Many southerners have never eaten one bite. I didn't taste it until after I finished college.

Second, Hoppin' John is not always made with black-eyed peas. That assumption seems to be the result of black-eyed peas becoming the most common variety of peas, which gives them wider availability. That doesn't mean that black-eyed peas are the best or the only choice for Hoppin' John. Too many black-eyed peas have suffered the same fate as the commercially successful red delicious apples that usurped superior local apples: there are a lot of them out there, but most don't taste like much. The moral of this lesson is to use the best field pea specimen that grows where you live.

Finally, there are as many versions of Hoppin' John (and its decrepit kin, such as Limpin' Susan, Limpin' Kate, and Skippin' Jinny) as there are cooks. Reflective of my love of applying Italian techniques to traditional southern ingredients, I cook mine like risotto, creating a large pot of creamy rice and peas studded with sausage. To continue the theme, I top each serving with a heaping spoonful of Collard Pesto.

1 tablespoon butter

2 tablespoons finely chopped flat-leaf parsley

¼ cup finely grated Parmesan cheese, plus more for serving

Kosher salt and ground black pepper, to taste

Collard Pesto, for serving (recipe follows)

Risotto recipes call for short-grain rice (such as Arborio or Carnaroli) because it releases lots of starch, which makes the risotto creamy. In this southern risotto, I prefer to use Carolina Gold rice, an heirloom variety of Lowcountry rice. Depending on how it is cooked, Carolina Gold can turn out fluffy like long-grain rice or creamy like short-grain rice. The flavor and aroma are exceptional. You can order it from ansonmills.com. From them you can also order Sea Island red peas, the original peas used in Hoppin' John.

MAKES 8 SERVINGS

1. Bring the stock just to a simmer in a medium saucepan and keep warm over low heat.

2. Cook the sausage in a large skillet or wide saucepan over medium heat until cooked through, about 10 minutes, breaking it up with the side of a spoon. Transfer with a slotted spoon to paper towels to drain. Pour off all but 2 tablespoons of the fat. (If you happen to have particularly lean sausage, add olive oil to make up the difference.)

3. Heat the fat over medium-high heat. Stir in the onion, bell pepper, and celery and a pinch of salt. Cook, stirring often, until softened, about 8 minutes. Add the rice and stir to coat each grain in the fat. Cook, stirring slowly and constantly, until the outside of each grain is shiny and translucent with a tiny white dot in the center, about 2 minutes. Stir in the wine and cook until it evaporates.

4. Reduce the heat to medium, add 1 cup of the warm stock and cook, stirring slowly and steadily, until the rice absorbs the liquid. Continue adding stock ½ cup at a time, stirring all the while and letting the rice nearly absorb the stock before adding more. When done, the rice should be tender, yet a little firm in the center of each grain (like pasta al dente). The rice should be suspended in thick, creamy sauce. You might not need all of the stock. The entire process should take about 25 minutes.

5. Remove the risotto from the heat and stir in the peas, sausage, butter, parsley, and cheese. Check the seasoning, but the sausage probably contains all the salt and pepper the risotto needs. Serve at once, topped with a sprinkling of cheese and a spoonful of Collard Pesto.

## Collard Pesto

10 ounces small,
tender collards

2 large garlic cloves

2 tablespoons
chopped green
olives or capers

2 tablespoons chopped
oil-packed sun-
dried tomatoes

¼ cup chopped pecans,
lightly toasted

¼ cup grated Par-
mesan cheese

1 teaspoon Hot Pepper
Vinegar (page 88)
or sherry vinegar

6 tablespoons extra-
virgin olive oil

½ teaspoon kosher salt

¼ teaspoon ground
black pepper

Pinch of cayenne
pepper or crushed
red pepper flakes

Although we often think of pesto as made only from basil, it comes in many forms, such as this delicious, bright green version made from collards. It's perfect with the risotto, but it can be served in any way you'd serve traditional basil pesto. Collard pesto holds its color for days.

MAKES 1 ½ CUPS

1  Strip the collard leaves off the stems. Discard the stems. Stack the leaves and roll them up into a cylinder and then cut the cylinder crosswise into thin strips. You should have about 5 cups of lightly packed collards. Bring a large saucepan of water to a boil. Add ½ teaspoon kosher salt per cup of water. Add the collards and cook until tender, 10 to 15 minutes. Meanwhile, place the garlic in a slotted spoon and lower it into the boiling water for 30 seconds to poach away some of the pungent raw garlic taste. Set the garlic aside. Drain the collards in a colander and rinse under cold running water until cool. Drain well and transfer into the bowl of a food processor fitted with the metal blade.

2  Add the garlic, olives, tomatoes, pecans, cheese, and vinegar and pulse until the mixture is finely chopped. With the machine running, add the oil in a slow, steady stream until the pesto is smooth and thick. Season with the salt, pepper, and cayenne. Serve at room temperature.

MAKE-AHEAD NOTE: You can make the pesto up to 3 days ahead. Store covered and refrigerated. Return to room temperature for serving.

## Hoppin' John Risotto Cakes

2 cups Hoppin'
John Risotto

¼ cup instant or
all-purpose flour

1 tablespoon butter,
plus more as needed

1 tablespoon extra-
virgin olive oil, plus
more as needed

Collard Pesto,
for serving

Any Junior League cookbook from the South will include at least one recipe for black-eyed pea cakes, ranging from little ones served as hors d'oeuvres to big ones served as bean burgers. I cook my Hoppin' John like Italian risotto, so I might as well make my pea cakes like Italian risotto cakes. Making these cakes is a good way to use up any leftover risotto. The cakes should be quite crispy on the outside and creamy on the inside. The warm cakes are delicious topped with any leftover Collard Pesto.

MAKES 6 CAKES

1  Spread the risotto in a shallow dish, cover, and refrigerate until well chilled, at least 4 hours. Divide the risotto into 6 equal portions. Rinse your hands in cold water and shape each portion into a cake about 3 inches in diameter and ¾-inch thick. Place in a single layer on a plate or baking sheet, cover, and refrigerate for at least 1 hour and up to 8 hours.

② Lightly coat the cakes with flour, tapping off the excess.

③ Heat the butter and oil in a large well-seasoned cast-iron or nonstick skillet over medium-high heat until the butter stops foaming. Add the cakes and cook, turning once, until both sides are crisp and golden brown and the rice is hot in the center, about 3 minutes on each side. Depending on the size of your skillet, you might have to cook the cakes in batches, so add more butter and oil as needed. Serve the cakes warm, topped with the pesto.

## Zesty Black-Eyed Pea Salsa

This recipe pops up under a variety of names, such as pickled peas, Texas caviar, pea dip, pea relish, and pea salad. I call this colorful and crunchy dish a salsa because it has a little kick from jalapeños and vinegar. It is good with tortilla chips, although in Texas it's often served with old-fashioned saltines.

This is the only way I can get my husband to enjoy black-eyed peas on New Year's Day, for luck. Otherwise he takes two plain peas (two because the custom calls for eating peas, plural), tosses them in his mouth, throws back his head, and washes them down with a cold brew, like he's swallowing bitter pills to ward off something worse.

If you are making this when fresh tomatoes are available, use fresh instead of canned. This is not the case on New Year's Day.

MAKES 2 CUPS

2 cups fresh black-eyed peas

¼ cup sherry vinegar or red wine vinegar

¼ cup vegetable oil

½ teaspoon Worcestershire sauce

¼ teaspoon hot sauce

1 teaspoon kosher salt

½ teaspoon ground black pepper

½ teaspoon ground cumin

½ cup canned fire-roasted diced tomatoes, drained

½ cup cored and diced red bell pepper

¼ cup finely chopped onion

½ cup corn kernels

1 to 2 pickled or fresh jalapeños, finely chopped

2 tablespoons chopped fresh or canned mild green chiles

¼ cup finely chopped flat-leaf parsley

① Place the peas in a large saucepan. Add cold water to cover the peas by 2 inches. Add a pinch of kosher salt and bring to a boil. Skim off the foam, reduce the heat, and simmer until tender, about 25 minutes. Drain and transfer into a medium bowl. Stir in the vinegar, oil, Worcestershire, hot sauce, salt, pepper, and cumin and let the beans cool to room temperature, stirring occasionally.

② Stir in the tomatoes, bell pepper, onion, corn, jalapeños, green chiles, and parsley. Cover and refrigerate until well chilled, at least 4 hours and preferably overnight. Just before serving, stir well and check the seasoning.

WHAT ELSE WORKS? You can use other field peas of similar size and texture as black-eyed peas.

MAKE-AHEAD NOTE: The salsa can be made up to 2 days ahead, but don't add the parsley until just before serving. Store covered and refrigerated. Stir well and check the seasoning before serving.

# FIGS

**When the Spanish set out for the New World** in the 1500s, they brought along figs and established them as a staple crop in their early coastal settlements. Other immigrant groups did the same, and figs quickly worked their way northward and inland, passing through the Lowcountry and arriving in the Carolinas and Virginia. An entry in Thomas Jefferson's garden book mentions a row of figs growing alongside pomegranates. It's tempting to say that everything that eventually flourished in the southern kitchen garden got its start at Monticello or at least passed through there. The story isn't that simple or clear-cut, though that garden did feature over 250 varieties of 89 species of fruits and vegetables. Moreover, Jefferson had the means and the passion to keep meticulous notes and records. Most home gardeners and small-scale farmers were more concerned with getting things to grow than in journaling their efforts.

Hardy fig trees can flourish under tough conditions, but weather can critically affect the yield of fruit from year to year. Luscious, fully ripe figs are as delicate as damp tissue and cannot withstand shipping or storage. So, despite their popularity and the repeated efforts of horticulturists, figs have never been a viable commercial crop in the South. The upside is that luxurious figs, with droplets of sweet syrup peeking through their ripe skins, are always available close to home, where they grow. ■

# Ocracoke Fig Cake with Buttermilk Sherbet

2 cups all-purpose flour

1 teaspoon ground nutmeg

1 teaspoon ground allspice

1 teaspoon ground cinnamon

1 teaspoon fine sea salt

3 large eggs, at room temperature

1 ½ cups sugar

1 cup vegetable oil

½ cup well-shaken buttermilk

1 teaspoon baking soda

1 tablespoon hot water

1 teaspoon pure vanilla extract

1 cup Easy Fig Preserves (recipe follows)

1 cup chopped walnuts

Buttermilk Sherbet, for serving (recipe follows)

GLAZE

1 cup sugar

1 tablespoon cornstarch

½ teaspoon baking soda

½ cup well-shaken buttermilk

4 tablespoons (½ stick) unsalted butter

1 tablespoon light corn syrup

1 teaspoon pure vanilla extract

This cake is a signature recipe from Ocracoke Island in the Outer Banks of North Carolina. It's dark and spicy, like many traditional southern cakes in areas where there was relatively easy access to spices shipped in from elsewhere. The delicious, thick glaze tastes like homemade candy and keeps the cake moist for days. The cake is leavened with baking soda dissolved in hot water, a technique that predates commercial baking powder.

Although the cake doesn't need it, I can't resist serving it with Buttermilk Sherbet. The tang of the sherbet balances the sweetness of the cake. Plus, you can't go wrong with cake and ice cream.

MAKES 12 SERVINGS

1. For the cake: Preheat the oven to 350°F. Grease and lightly flour a 10-inch, light metal tube pan, tapping out any excess flour. (A dark metal, nonstick, or heavy Bundt pan will make the crust too dark and thick and will alter the baking time.)

2. Sift together the flour, nutmeg, allspice, cinnamon, and salt into a large bowl.

3. Beat the eggs until foamy in a large bowl with an electric mixer. With the mixer running, slowly add the sugar, beating until the mixture is thick and pale, about 3 minutes. Slowly add the oil, beating until well mixed. Beat in half of the flour mixture, then the buttermilk, and then the remaining flour mixture, beating each time only until the batter is smooth.

4. In a small bowl, stir together the baking soda and water until the soda dissolves. With the mixer set to low speed, beat the soda mixture, vanilla, preserves, and walnuts into the batter. Scrape down the sides of the bowl and stir well with a rubber spatula.

5. Pour the batter into the prepared pan. Bake until a tester inserted into the center of the cake comes out clean, about 1 hour. Set the cake in the pan on a wire rack for 15 minutes, run a thin knife around the edge of the cake, and then turn it out on the rack to cool to room temperature before glazing.

6. For the glaze: Stir together the sugar, cornstarch, baking soda, buttermilk, butter, and corn syrup in a large saucepan. Bring the mixture to a boil over medium-high heat and cook, stirring constantly, for about 10 minutes, until the glaze is thick and opaque. Remove the glaze from the heat, stir in the vanilla, and let cool to room temperature; it will continue to thicken as it cools. Drizzle the cooled glaze over the cooled cake.

7. To serve, cut the cake into wedges and serve with a small scoop of Buttermilk Sherbet.

A toothpick makes a great cake tester, but when a cake is tall use a thin skewer or dry strand of uncooked spaghetti. Cooks once used a clean broom straw, but most of us no longer have one handy.

## Easy Fig Preserves

2 pounds ripe figs, stemmed and cut into ½-inch pieces

1 ½ cups sugar

6 tablespoons fresh lemon juice

½ cup water

Fig preserves are perhaps the easiest of all homemade preserves. When made in small batches and stored in glass jars with tight-fitting lids, they keep in the refrigerator for months. Preserves are a good way to use figs that are too split, soft, and ripe to eat out of hand. The color of the preserves can range from light golden to dark purple, depending on the type of fig.

This recipe makes more than is needed for the Ocracoke Fig Cake. Enjoy the leftovers on a gooey, stretchy grilled cheese sandwich. The preserves are also inexplicably good on thin slices of toasted cornbread with crispy fried chicken livers.

MAKES ABOUT 2 CUPS

(1) Have ready one 1-pint jar or two half-pint jars that have been sterilized in boiling water or run through the dishwasher on the hottest cycle. The jars should have sterilized tight-fitting lids. The jars and lids do not have to stay hot, but they must stay sterile.

(2) Stir together the figs, sugar, lemon juice, and water in a medium nonreactive saucepan. Bring to a boil, stirring until the sugar dissolves. Reduce the heat and simmer, stirring occasionally, until the figs collapse into a soft, thick stew, about 30 minutes. The preserves should fall off the spoon in thick, heavy drops.

(3) Spoon the preserves into the prepared jars. Close the jars and set them where they will not be disturbed until the preserves cool to room temperature, preferably overnight. Store in the refrigerator for up to 3 months.

TIPS AND TECHNIQUES

Even when you don't seal jars in a water bath or pressure canner, the jars and lids must be scrupulously clean and sterilized. Wash them in hot, soapy water and then sterilize them in boiling water, or run them through your dishwasher on the hottest cycle. The jars and lids do not have to stay hot, but they must stay sterile. You can use glass jars repeatedly, but I suggest replacing any lids that are bent or nicked. You can also use jars that rely on rubber gaskets for sealing. The gaskets work as long as they are pliable.

## Buttermilk Sherbet

1 ½ cups sugar

½ cup fresh lemon juice

4 cups well-shaken buttermilk

I love buttermilk, so of course I love this sherbet. It's tangy and refreshing, and it makes a great accompaniment to sweet cakes that contain buttermilk. It's also great on its own, especially on a hot summer night when anything heavier would smother you. Needless to say, only fresh liquid buttermilk will do, preferably from a local dairy.

MAKES ABOUT 1 ½ QUARTS

1. Stir together the sugar, lemon juice, and buttermilk in a large glass or metal bowl until the sugar dissolves. Cover and refrigerate until the mixture is very cold (under 40°F), at least 4 hours, then stir well.

2. Churn the sherbet in a small electric ice cream freezer according to the manufacturer's instructions. The sherbet will be soft, like a thick milk shake. To freeze hard enough to scoop, transfer into an airtight container, press plastic wrap directly onto the surface, and freeze until firm.

## Warm Figs and Cheese in Crisp Ham

12 fresh, firm figs

¼ cup soft, fresh goat cheese (chèvre) (about 2 ounces)

6 paper-thin slices country ham, prosciutto, or speck, cut in half lengthwise to make a total of 12 long strips

2 to 3 tablespoons honey

½ teaspoon cracked or coarsely ground black pepper

These bundles of sweet fruit, creamy cheese, and salty ham are irresistible. I've served them for breakfast, for hors d'oeuvres, and for dessert. I've also plunked them onto arugula salad ever-so-lightly dressed with balsamic vinaigrette.

When I can find a store that will shave a real country ham into long, paper-thin slices, I use it. But the sad truth is that it's usually easier to find prosciutto or speck than it is to find artisanal country ham.

Some figs are so fragile when ripe that they collapse when you look at them. For best results in this recipe, use figs that are ripe but still firm enough to withstand a little handling.

MAKES 4 TO 6 SERVINGS

1. Preheat the oven to 400°F.

2. Trim off the fig stems. Using a small sharp knife or kitchen scissors, cut the top of each fig into quarters, stopping before the fig comes apart at the bottom. Gently pry open the fig, like opening the petals on a tulip, to make a little cup.

3. Tuck a scant teaspoon of cheese inside of each fig. Wrap the fig in a slice of ham and press lightly to make it adhere. Stand the figs upright on a baking sheet. (If the figs refuse to stand up, set them in a mini muffin tin.)

4. Roast the figs until the ham becomes crisp around the edges, about 10 minutes.

5. Transfer the figs to serving plates, drizzle with the honey, and sprinkle with the pepper. Serve warm.

VARIATION: You can wrap wedges of peeled peaches, pears, or Fuyu persimmons in the ham and serve the cheese on the side. Feel free to use different types of cheese, such as blue cheese or Brie.

## Fresh Fig and Mascarpone Ice Cream with Walnuts in Port Syrup

1 ½ pounds very ripe figs, stemmed and cut into ½-inch pieces

¾ cup sugar

Finely grated zest of 1 lemon

6 tablespoons fresh lemon juice

1 tablespoon light corn syrup

¼ cup mascarpone

Walnuts in Port Syrup, for serving (recipe follows)

This is sultry, sexy, sensuous ice cream. Certain versions of the Garden of Eden story say that it was a fig, not an apple, that led to Eve's eviction from paradise. It might have been this ice cream.

This recipe was the result of a hopeful experiment one summer afternoon. I wanted a quick and easy ice cream base that didn't require cooked eggs. Plain heavy cream made the ice cream too hard, so I replaced it with a little bit of mascarpone, just enough to hold the fruit together without masking its flavor. It will look as though there is not enough dairy in the unfrozen base, but mascarpone tastes fatty when it freezes and a little goes a long way. With nothing to hide behind (not even a fig leaf), the fruit must be perfectly ripe and full of flavor.

The ice cream is wonderful as is, but usually I top each serving with a spoonful of the Walnuts in Port Syrup because the flavors are so good together.

MAKES ABOUT 1 QUART

1. Stir together the figs, sugar, lemon zest, and lemon juice in a medium saucepan. Cook over medium heat, stirring constantly, only until the sugar dissolves. Remove from the heat and add the corn syrup and mascarpone, stirring gently until smooth. Transfer into a large glass or metal bowl, cover, and refrigerate until the mixture is very cold (under 40°F), at least 4 hours, then stir well.

2. Churn the ice cream in a small electric ice cream freezer according to the manufacturer's instructions. The ice cream will be soft, like a thick milk shake, but it's good that way. To freeze hard enough to scoop, transfer into an airtight container, press plastic wrap directly onto the surface, and freeze until firm. Let sit at room temperature for 5 minutes before serving.

## Walnuts in Port Syrup

¾ cup ruby port

¾ cup sugar

2 cups walnut halves, lightly toasted and cooled

These walnuts are inspired by the southern tradition of glazing nuts to serve as a garnish or snack. These are a little syrupy, like a grown-up version of the wet walnuts used on banana splits and sundaes. They are delicious with the Fresh Fig and Mascarpone Ice Cream, but they are also wonderful spooned over cheese, particularly blue cheese.

MAKES 2 CUPS

1 Stir together the port and sugar in a large skillet over medium heat, stirring until the sugar dissolves. Cook, stirring occasionally, until the mixture thickens to the consistency of pancake syrup, about 4 minutes.

2 Remove the skillet from the heat and stir in the walnuts. Cool for at least 5 minutes, stirring occasionally. Serve slightly warm or at room temperature.

MAKE-AHEAD NOTE: You can make this up to 1 month ahead. Store covered and refrigerated. Return to room temperature or reheat gently before serving.

## Bacon-and-Herb-Crusted Pork Loin with Fig and Red Wine Sauce

1 boneless pork loin roast (3 ½ to 4 pounds)

2 to 3 tablespoons Tuscan Herbed Salt (recipe follows)

4 ounces thinly sliced unsmoked bacon or pancetta

Fig and Red Wine Sauce (recipe follows)

This is my favorite way to roast a pork loin. The bacon holds in moisture and gets very crispy and lightly charred as it roasts. A thin layer of Tuscan Herbed Salt works like a dry cure that makes the outside of the meat strong and salty but keeps the inside of the meat sweet and juicy. The contrast and cooperation among the flavors and textures is fantastic. Use very thin bacon, preferably unsmoked, to wrap the roast. It might be easier to find pancetta, which is Italian bacon that comes in round slices instead of long strips.

The secret to a good pork loin roast is to not overcook it. Many of us were raised with pork that was cooked for hours. (My grandmother believed we were only one pink pork chop away from lockjaw.) Of course, pork should be cooked until safe to eat, but modern pork is very lean and cannot withstand excessive cooking. Pastured heirloom pork is very special and does not deserve ruinous cooking. Test for doneness with an instant-read thermometer and trust it. Done is done, even if the pork is still a little pink in the center.

MAKES 8 SERVINGS

1. Depending on where you buy the pork loin, it might be a single piece of meat or it might be two pieces tied together with kitchen twine. If it's two pieces, cut them apart and discard the strings. Rinse the meat and pat dry with paper towels. Rub the rounded top of the meat (the fatty side) lightly and evenly with Tuscan Herbed Salt. Cover the top of the meat with the bacon, overlapping the edges a little and tucking the ends under the meat if necessary. Tie the bacon in place with kitchen twine every 1 to 2 inches to hold firmly in place. Trim off the loose ends of the strings close to the knots.

2. Wrap the meat in plastic wrap and refrigerate for at least 4 hours and preferably overnight. Let the meat rest at room temperature for 30 minutes before roasting.

3. Preheat the oven to 400°F. Discard the plastic wrap. Place the meat on a wire rack set inside a large rimmed baking sheet. Roast until an instant-read thermometer inserted into the center of the pork registers 150°F, 1 hour to 1 hour 15 minutes. Transfer the roast to a carving board and let rest for 15 minutes before carving. The internal temperature will rise to about 155°F as it rests.

4. Remove the strings, carve the roast into serving portions, and serve warm with the Fig and Red Wine Sauce.

## Tuscan Herbed Salt

2 tablespoons coarse sea salt or kosher salt

2 teaspoons whole black peppercorns

3 tablespoons lightly packed chopped fresh sage

3 tablespoons chopped fresh rosemary

This seasoned salt is great on nearly any cut of pork, from loin to tenderloin to chops. It's also great sprinkled on roasted vegetables, particularly winter squash, sweet potatoes, and carrots.

It is vital to use fresh herbs in this salt. Make sure the herbs are completely dry before adding them to the grinder so that the mixture doesn't turn into wet paste.

MAKES ABOUT ½ CUP

Place all of the ingredients in a spice grinder or small food processor and pulse until finely chopped and well mixed. Use the salt right away or store in an airtight container up to 1 month.

TIPS AND TECHNIQUES

The herbs will leave a sticky green residue on the blades of the spice grinder. To remove it, fill the grinder half full of uncooked rice. Grind the rice until it is pulverized, then pour it out. The rice should have polished away the residue, but if it was particularly sticky, repeat. Wipe away any rice dust with a dry towel.

# Fig and Red Wine Sauce

2 cups dry red wine

1 cup veal or
chicken stock

¼ cup red wine vinegar

1 cup sugar

12 ounces fresh figs,
stemmed and
quartered

1 tablespoon chopped
fresh rosemary

This sauce has deeper flavor and better body when it is made with veal stock. Almost no one outside of the restaurant world makes homemade veal stock because you have to cook down the bones from a small herd to get a few cups of the precious stuff. I use veal stock concentrate that is reconstituted with water. The concentrate is available at well-stocked grocery stores and gourmet markets.

In addition to the Bacon-and-Herb-Crusted Pork Loin, this sauce is delicious with other cuts of pork, quail, and other game birds. You can use this sauce in place of the roasted cherries in the Pan-Seared Duck Breasts on page 79.

MAKES ABOUT 3 CUPS

1. Bring the wine, stock, vinegar, and sugar to a boil in a large saucepan over medium-high heat, stirring until the sugar dissolves. Boil until the mixture reduces to 2 cups, stirring occasionally.

2. Stir in the figs, reduce the heat, and simmer gently until softened, about 15 minutes. Remove from the heat, stir in the rosemary, and set aside to cool to room temperature. Rewarm gently before serving.

MAKE-AHEAD NOTE: The sauce can be made up to 3 days ahead. Store covered and refrigerated. Rewarm gently before serving.

# GARDEN PEAS

**Little round peas have numerous names:** green peas, sweet peas, spring peas, English peas, *petits pois*, and garden peas. Each name tells part of their story. They are green, the good ones are sweet, they come up in the spring, many varieties hailed from England and France, and at one time they were grown in kitchen gardens (in contrast to field peas, which were usually grown among crops in the field). Humans have grown peas for more than 10,000 years, making them one of the earliest cultivated crops, but it wasn't until about the sixteenth century that growers developed peas that could be eaten fresh instead of dried.

Peas likely came ashore in the New World with the earliest English and French explorers and spread along with the colonies. Thomas Jefferson has a nearly mythical association with garden peas. He's reported to have cataloged at least fifty varieties and grown at least thirty. Records indicate that he competed with fellow growers as to who could serve the first bowl of peas each spring, sometimes letting other people believe they had won, just to keep the game interesting. Over time, southern gardens came to include snow peas and sugar snaps as well.

Garden peas are tastiest when picked, shelled, and eaten in quick sequence. No spring vegetable is more delightful when fresh, and few are more disappointing when not. Their sugars decline precipitously the moment they are picked, and no recipe can replace that natural sweetness. Truly fresh and tender peas cook quickly. If they aren't tender soon, continued cooking will never make them so. Many garden pea aficionados eat them right out in the garden, avoiding all risk of delay or deleterious cooking. Carpe peas. ■

# Pea, Radish, and Pea Shoot Salad

3 tablespoons finely
chopped shallot

2 teaspoons
white wine vinegar

½ teaspoon kosher salt,
plus more to taste

2 tablespoons sour
cream or mayonnaise

¼ cup extra-virgin
olive oil

½ teaspoon ground black
pepper, or to taste

2 cups sugar snap peas
or snow peas, ends
snapped to remove
stems and strings

1 cup freshly shelled
garden peas

1 cup trimmed and
thinly sliced radishes

3 cups lightly packed
pea shoots

½ cup ricotta salata
or farmer cheese cut
into ¼-inch cubes
or crumbled *brebis*

Peas and radishes are among the first things to pop up in the spring garden. What grows together usually goes together, so I combined the two in this refreshing salad. The sharp bite of a spring radish is a great contrast to the sweet peas. Not all radishes are red; some are purple, some are pink, and some are white. Thin rounds of the aptly named watermelon radish look just like tiny slices of fresh melon, so they're gorgeous on a plate.

I like to serve this on a bed of garden pea or sugar snap pea shoots, those curling, clinging tendrils from the top of the plants. Pea shoots are often pruned to encourage the development of pea pods; instead of discarding them, eat them. When harvested early in the season, they are tender and taste just like the peas themselves. The shoots can be used raw or quickly cooked. Pea shoots are also good mixed in with spring salad greens. To make pea shoot pesto to serve with warm, freshly cooked new potatoes, use blanched pea shoots in place of the basil in the Classic Basil Pesto recipe (page 281).

You should get about 1 cup of shelled garden peas from 1 pound of pods.

MAKES 4 TO 6 SERVINGS

1. Whisk together the shallot, vinegar, and salt in a medium bowl and set aside for at least 5 minutes. Whisk in the sour cream and oil. Season with the pepper.

2. Fill a large bowl with ice water. Bring a large saucepan of water to a boil. Add ½ teaspoon kosher salt per cup of water. Add the sugar snaps and garden peas and cook for 1 minute, then use a slotted spoon or strainer to transfer them into the ice water to stop the cooking and set their color. Drain the peas, pat dry, and transfer into a medium bowl. Add the radishes and dressing and stir gently to coat. Season with salt and pepper.

3. Cut the pea shoots into bite-sized lengths and arrange on a serving platter. Spoon the pea and radish mixture over the shoots, scatter the cheese over the top, and serve.

## Sweet Peas with Spring Onions and Lettuce

2 cups freshly shelled garden peas

2 tablespoons butter, divided

¼ cup thinly sliced spring onions

¼ cup chicken stock or water

1 teaspoon sugar

½ teaspoon kosher salt

¼ teaspoon ground black pepper

1 cup finely shredded tender leaf lettuce

Old southern cookbooks often mention cooking sweet garden peas with leaf lettuce, another example of combining ingredients that appear in the garden at the same time. The dish was often called *petits pois*, a nod to the French tradition behind the recipe. Some versions called for covering the peas with lettuce while they cooked, like a little leafy lid, which was stirred into the peas before serving. In this version, the lettuce is shredded and only lightly wilted, so it stays pretty.

MAKES 4 TO 6 SERVINGS

(1) Bring a medium saucepan of water to a boil. Add ½ teaspoon kosher salt per cup of water. Add the peas and cook until crisp-tender, from 3 to 8 minutes, depending on the size and freshness of the peas. Transfer into a colander and rinse under cold running water until cool. Drain and set aside.

(2) Melt 1 tablespoon of the butter in a large saucepan over medium-high heat. Add the onions and a pinch of salt; cook, stirring often, until softened, about 8 minutes. Add the stock and simmer until the liquid reduces by half.

(3) Stir in the peas and the remaining 1 tablespoon of butter and heat through. Season with the sugar, salt, and pepper.

(4) Add the lettuce, stir just until it wilts, and serve at once.

## Chilled Garden Pea and Mint Soup

2 tablespoons butter

1 cup chopped spring onions or chopped baby leeks (white and tender green parts)

3 cups chicken stock

4 cups freshly shelled garden peas

½ cup half-and-half

¾ cup lightly packed mint leaves

1 teaspoon kosher salt

1 teaspoon sugar

½ teaspoon ground black pepper

Sour cream, for garnish

I created this soup to be served warm. The next day I pulled the leftovers out of the refrigerator to reheat. I licked a little chilled soup off the spoon. What an improvement! The chilly overnight rest mingled the flavors. The flavor of the peas really came through, and the mint was a hint rather than a punch. The soup held its lovely emerald green color. Voilà, a chilled soup was born.

MAKES 4 SERVINGS

(1) Melt the butter over medium heat in a large saucepan. Stir in the onions and a pinch of salt and cook, stirring occasionally, until softened, about 5 minutes. Add the stock and bring to a simmer. Add the peas and cook until tender, about 8 minutes. Stir in the half-and-half, mint, salt, sugar, and pepper.

(2) Purée in a blender (working in batches to not fill the blender more than half full) and return to the pot, or purée the soup directly in the pot with an immersion blender. Cool to room temperature, cover, and refrigerate until well chilled, at least 4 hours and preferably overnight. Stir well, check the seasoning, and serve chilled. Garnish with a spoonful of sour cream.

## Peas, Tuna, and Noodles in Creamy Cheese Sauce

Vegetable oil spray

2 tablespoons butter

1 small onion, finely chopped (about 1 cup)

1 cup regular or reduced-fat sour cream

¾ cup whole or 2 percent milk

1 ½ cups grated Asiago or Italian blend cheese

1 teaspoon kosher salt, plus more to taste

½ teaspoon ground black pepper, plus more to taste

2 cups freshly shelled garden peas

8 ounces wide egg noodles

2 (6-ounce) cans albacore tuna, drained

3 tablespoons chopped pimento, drained

1 cup fresh bread crumbs (page 389)

¼ cup coarsely grated Parmesan cheese

1 tablespoon extra-virgin olive oil

This one-dish meal is my updated version of classic tuna casserole. Instead of a can of cream of something, a quick and easy cheese sauce pulls the ingredients together. The result is an attractive, baked pasta dish instead of a gloppy casserole. You can make a number of variations from this basic recipe by changing the vegetable, the protein, and/or the cheese. Try chopped broccoli instead of peas, cooked chicken instead of the tuna, or mild cheddar instead of Asiago.

MAKES 6 SERVINGS

1. Preheat the oven to 400°F. Mist a 2 ½-quart baking dish with the spray.

2. Melt the butter in a large saucepan over medium heat. Add the onion and a pinch of salt and stir to coat. Cover and cook, stirring often, until softened, about 5 minutes. Stir in the sour cream, milk, cheese, salt, and pepper and cook, stirring, until the cheese melts and the sauce is smooth. Remove from the heat.

3. Fill a large bowl with ice water. Bring a large pot of water to a boil. Add ½ teaspoon kosher salt per cup of water. Add the peas and cook until barely tender, 3 to 8 minutes, depending on the size and freshness of the peas. Use a slotted spoon or strainer to transfer the peas into the ice water to stop the cooking and set the bright green color. Drain well.

4. Add the noodles to the boiling water and cook according to package directions, but stop 2 minutes short of the suggested cooking time. Drain well in a colander and stir into the cheese sauce. Stir in the peas, tuna, and pimento. Season with additional salt and pepper. Scrape the mixture into the prepared baking dish.

5. Stir together the bread crumbs and Parmesan in a small bowl. Drizzle with the oil and toss to coat. Scatter the crumb mixture evenly over the noodle mixture. Bake until the topping is browned, about 20 minutes. Let sit for 5 minutes before serving hot.

## Flash-Cooked Sugar Snaps

1 pound sugar snaps, ends snapped to remove stems and strings

1 tablespoon butter

1 tablespoon extra-virgin olive oil

¼ cup tiny mint leaves or coarsely chopped large leaves

½ teaspoon kosher salt

¼ teaspoon ground black pepper

It's fun to eat sugar snaps and snow peas straight from the vine, when they are assuredly fresh, sweet, and earthy. Any cooking should be quick and strategic to protect that freshness. If you have freshly picked pods that you don't plan to eat for a day or two, go ahead with the first step in the recipe. Fresh green vegetables often retain better color and flavor when blanched and shocked than when refrigerated raw.

Once I came across some dried-up pea pods that had slipped into the dark recesses of the fridge. They weren't moldy, just desiccated, like a flower pressed between the pages of a heavy book. Out of curiosity, I fried them for a few seconds in a little bit of very hot oil. They puffed back up instantly. Sprinkled with salt, they were delicious, like pea pod french fries. You just never know what will happen when you play with your food.

MAKES 4 SERVINGS

1. Fill a large bowl with ice water. Bring a large saucepan of water to a boil. Add ½ teaspoon kosher salt per cup of water. Add the sugar snaps and cook for 1 minute. Use a slotted spoon or strainer to immediately transfer into the ice water to stop the cooking and set the bright green color. Drain and pat dry. Proceed with the recipe, or wrap the peas in paper towels, place in an open zip-top bag, and refrigerate.

2. Heat the butter and oil in a large skillet over medium-high heat. Add the peas and cook, stirring constantly, until crisp-tender, about 3 minutes. Remove from the heat, stir in the mint, season with the salt and pepper, and serve warm.

VARIATION: Season the peas with 1 teaspoon toasted sesame oil and 1 teaspoon toasted sesame seeds or black sesame seeds.

WHAT ELSE WORKS? You can replace some or all of the sugar snaps with snow peas or pea shoots. You can replace the mint with other fresh herbs, such as chives, dill, chervil, or tarragon.

# Peas and Parmesan Dip

2 cups freshly shelled garden peas

½ cup chicken stock or water

1 garlic clove

1 teaspoon finely grated lemon zest

1 tablespoon lemon-infused olive oil, plus more for drizzling

½ cup lightly packed freshly grated Parmesan cheese, divided

½ teaspoon kosher salt

½ teaspoon ground black pepper

1 tablespoon fresh lemon juice

It's a dip for potato chips. It's a topping for crostini. It's a side dish to serve with garlicky lamb or glazed ham. In any guise, it's a tasty bowl of bright green goodness. The dish needs a little lemon juice, but don't add it until right before serving because the acidity quickly dulls the brilliant green color.

Citrus-infused olive oil is a great way to add bright flavor to dishes that already call for oil. The most common varieties are lemon, orange, lime, and pink grapefruit. For the best flavor, look for brands in which the fruit is crushed along with the olives.

MAKES ABOUT 2 CUPS

1. Combine the peas and stock in a small saucepan and cook over medium heat until the peas are barely tender, 3 to 5 minutes, depending on freshness and size. Use a slotted spoon to transfer the peas into the bowl of a food processor fitted with the metal blade and pulse to crush the peas, adding a little of the cooking liquid if needed to get them moving.

2. Add the garlic, lemon zest, and oil and 6 tablespoons of the cheese and pulse until the mixture is fairly smooth but not puréed. The mixture should be thick enough to eat with a fork. Add a little more cooking liquid or oil if needed. Season with the salt and pepper. Transfer into a serving bowl.

3. Just before serving, stir in the lemon juice. Sprinkle with the remaining 2 tablespoons of cheese and a final drizzle of oil. Serve at room temperature.

VARIATION: Spoon the mixture into an oven-proof serving dish and stick under the broiler until the cheese is melted and lightly browned in spots. If serving as a crostini topping, spread the crostini with a little ricotta cheese or quark before spooning on the pea mixture; the sweetness of the cheese is delicious with the citrusy peas.

WHAT ELSE WORKS? You can use blanched asparagus, shelled edamame, or shelled fava beans in place of the peas. When using favas, cook the shelled beans in a small saucepan of boiling salted water until just tender, about 3 minutes. Drain in a colander and rinse under cold running water. Peel the hull from each bean, leaving only the bright green inner beans.

## Rice and Peas

3 tablespoons
butter, divided

1 medium yellow onion,
finely chopped

1 ½ cups Carolina Gold
or Arborio rice

3 cups chicken stock

1 teaspoon kosher salt

1 small thyme sprig

1 bay leaf

2 cups freshly
shelled green peas

3 spring onions, thinly
sliced (about ½ cup)

1 tablespoon
finely chopped
flat-leaf parsley

1 tablespoon finely
chopped chives

½ cup freshly
grated Parmigiano-
Reggiano cheese

I love rice with peas, even simple leftovers stirred together in a bowl and sprinkled with cheese. This is a dish where that's done deliberately and deliciously. In Italy, it's called *risi bisi*, but it couldn't be more southern at heart. The South, after all, is a place where rice is daily fare for many families. This is a lovely dish for spring.

The recipe calls for Carolina Gold rice, an heirloom variety that dates back to when rice was a major cash crop in the Lowcountry area around Charleston. (Many of the first rice farmers were Italians, incidentally, which might explain why a Gullah version of this dish is called reesy peesy.) Carolina Gold rice is magnificent. Depending on how it's cooked, it can produce fluffy, individual grains or the creamy, sticky grains appropriate for risotto. Since the texture of *risi bisi* is somewhere between brothy perloo and creamy risotto, Carolina Gold is ideal. It's available in some stores and online through Anson Mills, purveyors of exceptional handmade mill goods from heirloom and organic grains. See ansonmills.com.

MAKES 8 SERVINGS

(1) Melt 1 tablespoon of the butter in a medium saucepan over medium heat. Add the onion and cook until softened, about 8 minutes. Add the rice, stock, salt, thyme sprig, and bay leaf and bring to a simmer. Cover the pan tightly and cook until the rice is al dente and has absorbed most of the liquid, about 20 minutes. The rice should be a little soupy. Remove from the heat and set aside, still covered.

(2) Bring a small saucepan of water to a boil. Add ½ teaspoon kosher salt per cup of water. Add the peas and cook until just tender, 1 to 5 minutes, depending on their size and freshness. Drain the peas.

(3) Melt the remaining 2 tablespoons of butter in a medium skillet over low heat. Cook the spring onions until softened, about 6 minutes.

(4) Uncover the rice and discard the thyme sprig and bay leaf. Gently stir in the peas, spring onions, parsley, chives, and cheese. Serve warm.

WHAT ELSE WORKS? You can use delicate field peas in place of the green peas.

# GARLIC

**Since the first head of southern-grown garlic was pulled,** people have both praised and condemned garlic for its distinctive flavor and aroma and its reputation as a potent aphrodisiac, appetite stimulant, tonic, and talisman. Every time it was dismissed as food of the poor and the crass (who couldn't escape the evidence of their eating it), garlic worked its way back up. Now we grow it in our gardens and welcome it into our kitchens, but it took a while. We also still use it for its purported (and fairly well-documented) healthful properties. The best old wives' tales, like the best gossip, revolve around a bit of truth.

It seems counterintuitive, but the smaller the pieces of raw garlic, the stronger the flavor. Finely chopped garlic is strongest, whole cloves are the subtlest, and sliced garlic is in between. Be sure to remove any green sprouts from garlic cloves because they can taste bitter. Plump heads of fully formed garlic cloves are the most familiar, but the immature heads known as green garlic are delicious and useful as well. Garlic scapes, the green stalks that poke up through the ground as the garlic grows, can be eaten if harvested while they are still tender and pliant. Roasting garlic is a bit like alchemy, transforming the pungent cloves into soft, buttery, golden goodness. ■

## Roasted Garlic Mayonnaise

¼ cup roasted garlic pulp (recipe follows)

1 cup high-quality mayonnaise

1 teaspoon onion powder

Finely grated zest and juice of 1 lemon (about ¼ cup)

¼ teaspoon kosher salt

½ teaspoon sugar

There are always two jars of mayonnaise in my refrigerator: a jar of Duke's and this one. Sometimes there is also a jar of homemade mayonnaise (page 317), but that is for special occasions.

This mayonnaise is much more than a sandwich spread. It's a wonderful finishing sauce for vegetables and grilled meats, particularly fish and shellfish. It's a great dip for raw vegetables and potato chips. It's great with anything fried, from potatoes to okra to oysters. When thinned with olive oil, it's a great salad dressing or faux aioli.

You need this stuff.

MAKES ABOUT 1 ¼ CUPS

1. Place the roasted garlic in a small bowl and mash with a fork until smooth. Stir in the mayonnaise, onion powder, lemon zest, lemon juice, salt, and sugar. Taste the mayonnaise to make sure the flavors are balanced.

2. Serve soon or cover and refrigerate for up to 1 week. For best flavor, serve at room temperature.

## Roasted Garlic

½ cup whole garlic cloves (2 to 3 heads)

1 to 2 tablespoons extra-virgin olive oil or vegetable oil

Roasted garlic tastes subtle, buttery, and a little sweet, the opposite of raw garlic. It's tame enough to spread on bread and it's a great addition to many recipes. Unlike nearly every other recipe for roasted garlic, I separate the heads of garlic into individual cloves before they go into the oven. I think it's less messy and there is less waste.

MAKES ABOUT ¼ CUP OF ROASTED PULP

1. Preheat the oven to 350°F.

2. Use a paring knife to cut off the hard stem end of each clove of garlic. Arrange the cloves in a single layer on a large piece of aluminum foil. Drizzle with only enough oil to barely moisten the cloves and toss to coat. Excess oil will pond up under the garlic and burn the bottoms of the cloves. Fold up the foil into a flat pouch and place directly on the oven rack.

3. Roast until the garlic is pale golden and soft when squeezed, about 30 minutes. Do not let the cloves of garlic get hard or darken on the bottom. Open the pouch and let the cloves cool enough to handle. Gently squeeze each clove so that the soft pulp can slide out of the trimmed end. Use at once or cover and refrigerate for up to 3 days.

WHAT ELSE WORKS? You can roast whole peeled cloves of garlic the same way.

# Garlic and Parmigiano-Reggiano Broth

1 cup whole
garlic cloves

10 cups chicken or
vegetable stock

2 pieces Parmigiano-
Reggiano cheese rind
(about 3 ounces)

¾ cup lightly packed
flat-leaf parsley
leaves and stems

1 bay leaf

15 large sage leaves

2 large thyme sprigs

4 whole cloves

4 whole allspice

2 teaspoons kosher salt

1 teaspoon ground
black pepper

3 tablespoons extra-
virgin olive oil

Freshly grated or
shaved Parmigiano-
Reggiano cheese,
for serving

This broth is so richly flavored that it can be served as soup. It also makes fantastic, beyond-the-ordinary golden stock that can be used in other recipes. It freezes well, so you can make extra while you're at it.

Parmigiano-Reggiano is the finest quality Parmesan cheese, the real deal imported from the Parma region of Italy. It's expensive, but the flavor is incomparable. The cheese rinds are too hard to eat, so they often go to waste. In this recipe, the hard rinds act as a meatless soup bone, releasing flavor into the simmering broth. If you buy wedges of cheese, you can save up your own rinds. You might as well use them because you paid the same dear price for the hard rind as you paid for the rest of the wedge. To get several rinds at once, return to where you bought the cheese because stores that grate their own cheese usually save the rinds to sell or give away.

MAKES 2 QUARTS

1. Peel the garlic cloves. (If you lightly crush each clove with the side of a heavy knife, the papery skins come loose easily.) Cut the cloves in half and discard any green sprouts because they will make the broth bitter. Coarsely chop the garlic and transfer into a large soup pot. Add the stock, cheese rinds, parsley, bay leaf, sage, thyme sprigs, cloves, allspice, salt, and pepper. Bring just to a boil over high heat, reduce the heat, and gently simmer until the liquid reduces to 8 cups. Do not let the broth return to a boil or it will become cloudy and bitter. Taste the broth; it should be flavorful enough to serve as soup. If not, continue simmering until the broth reduces further and concentrates the flavors.

2. Strain the broth through a mesh sieve and discard the solids. (Some find the softened cheese rinds to be delicious. It's chewy, like beeswax.) Stir in the oil.

3. If serving the broth as soup, season with salt and pepper and top with more cheese. If using as stock in other recipes, add no more seasoning. Cool, cover, and refrigerate for up to 3 days or freeze in airtight containers for up to 3 months.

VARIATION: To bulk up this broth into a more substantial soup, stir in some cooked pasta, rice, or lightly cooked vegetables. I love to poach an egg in a portion of the broth and serve them together in a warm bowl. Another egg option is to pour 2 beaten eggs into the barely simmering broth and stir with a fork until wispy strands appear. In Italy, they call this stracciatella, a word that means little rags, which is exactly what the eggs look like after they cook in the broth.

# Garlic Custards

Vegetable oil spray

2 teaspoons unsalted butter

1 tablespoon chopped garlic

1 ½ cups half-and-half

¾ teaspoon kosher salt

Pinch of ground white pepper

2 large eggs

3 large egg yolks

Wedge of Parmigiano-Reggiano cheese, for serving

Chive blossoms or chopped chives, for garnish

To make an elegant first course, slip one of these garlic custards into a serving of warm Garlic and Parmigiano-Reggiano Broth. The custards are also delicious served atop a simple salad or as a side dish.

MAKES 4 SERVINGS

1. Preheat the oven to 325°F. Mist the insides of four 6-ounce ramekins with the spray. The custards will cook in a hot water bath, so place the ramekins inside a baking dish and set aside. (A hot water bath, sometimes called a *bain-marie*, is the preferred method for cooking custard. The hot water helps the custard cook evenly and come out creamy.)

2. Melt the butter in a small saucepan over low heat. Add the garlic and cook, stirring often, until softened and fragrant, about 1 minute. Stir in the half-and-half, salt, and white pepper, increase the heat to medium, and bring just to a simmer. Remove from the heat, cover, and set aside to steep for 30 minutes. Strain into a small bowl.

3. Whisk together the eggs and yolks in a large bowl until the whites and yolks are blended. Add the warm half-and-half mixture to the yolk mixture, pouring in a slow, steady stream and whisking constantly.

4. Divide the egg mixture among the prepared ramekins. Pour enough very hot tap water into the baking dish to come halfway up the sides of the ramekins. Bake in the center of the oven for 15 minutes. Carefully rotate the baking dish 180 degrees and bake until the custards are nearly set and slightly jiggly in the center, about 15 minutes more. Remove the ramekins from the water and transfer to a rack to cool for 5 minutes.

5. Working with one custard at a time, run a thin knife around the inside edge of the ramekin to loosen the custard. Place a soup bowl over the ramekin and invert the custard into the bowl. Ladle warm soup around the warm custards and serve immediately, topped with Parmigiano-Reggiano curls shaved from the wedge with a vegetable peeler and a few chive blossoms.

# Green Garlic and Potato Gratin

2 tablespoons butter, at room temperature

6 ounces green garlic shoots

1 cup whole milk

1 cup heavy cream

½ teaspoon whole black peppercorns

4 flat-leaf parsley sprigs

2 small thyme sprigs

1 small marjoram sprig

1 bay leaf

2 pounds starchy potatoes (such as russets)

1 tablespoon extra-virgin olive oil

2 teaspoons kosher salt

¾ teaspoon ground black pepper

2 tablespoons finely chopped chives or garlic chives, divided

1 ½ cups freshly grated Gruyère cheese, divided

½ cup freshly grated Parmesan cheese

Green garlic is young, immature garlic that has not yet formed cloves. It looks like a slender leek, although when you cut right above the root end you can see the outline of the burgeoning cloves. As with a leek, the leafy end of the shoots is not as tender as the bulb end, but in this recipe both parts can be used. The tougher leaves are part of the seasoning in the herb-infused cream, and the tender ends are chopped and layered with the potatoes. Green garlic is milder than mature garlic, but it's unmistakably garlic. (See page 245 for tips on making a potato gratin.)

MAKES 8 SERVINGS

1. Preheat the oven to 375°F. Spread the butter on the bottom and sides of a 2-quart gratin dish or shallow baking dish.

2. Trim off and discard the root ends and any yellowed or withered leaves from the garlic shoots. Roughly chop the green tops and combine them in a medium saucepan with the milk, cream, peppercorns, parsley sprigs, thyme sprigs, marjoram sprig, and bay leaf. Bring just to a simmer over medium-low heat and cook for 5 minutes. Remove from the heat, cover, and set aside to steep for 30 minutes. Strain though a sieve, discard the solids, and return the liquid to the pan.

3. Working with one potato at a time, peel the potatoes, cut them into even slices that are no more than ⅛-inch thick, and stir them into the milk mixture. A vegetable slicer is ideal, although the slicing can be done with a sharp knife. To make the process easier and safer when using a knife, cut a thin slice off one of the long sides of the potato so that it sits flat and does not wobble on the cutting board. Bring the potatoes just to a simmer over medium-high heat, then remove the pan from the heat.

4. Finely chop the tender white parts of the shoots. Heat the oil in a small skillet over medium-high heat. Add the chopped shoots and cook, stirring often, until softened, about 5 minutes. If the garlic starts to stick, add a few drops of water. Remove the skillet from the heat and set aside.

5. Use a slotted spoon to transfer one-third of the potatoes into the prepared dish, spreading them evenly. Sprinkle with the salt and pepper, 2 teaspoons of chives, 2 tablespoons of the cooked garlic, and ½ cup of the Gruyère. Make two more layers the same way. Pour the infused milk mixture evenly over the top, pushing the potatoes down into the liquid. Sprinkle with the Parmesan.

6. Bake until the potatoes are tender and the top is golden and bubbling, about 20 minutes. If the top starts to brown too quickly, lay a flat sheet of aluminum foil over the dish. Let the gratin rest at room temperature for at least 10 minutes before serving warm.

WHAT ELSE WORKS? You can replace some or all of the green garlic with spring onions, ramps, baby leeks, or scallions.

# Garlic-Crusted Halibut on Roasted Garlic Scapes and Asparagus

### GARLIC SCAPES AND ASPARAGUS

- 6 garlic scapes
- 16 asparagus spears
- 1 tablespoon lemon-infused olive oil or extra-virgin olive oil

Kosher salt and ground black pepper, to taste

### HALIBUT

- 1 cup fresh bread crumbs (page 389)
- 1 tablespoon extra-virgin olive oil
- 1 teaspoon finely chopped garlic
- 4 skinless halibut fillets (each about 6 ounces and 1 ½ inches thick)
- ½ teaspoon kosher salt
- ¼ teaspoon ground black pepper

Fresh Herb and Caper Sauce (recipe follows) or Romesco Sauce (page 320), for serving

Scapes are those graceful tendrils that rise up from the center of a fall-planted garlic bulb for a few days each spring. The bright green spiraling stems swirl up toward the sky and wave in the breeze, as though they were taking a look around the garden to see what changed since last year. Gardeners often remove the scapes to concentrate the plant's energy in the bulbs growing underground. Many people throw them away, but they're good to eat. Their garlic flavor is very mild and subtle. The entire scape is edible, although sometimes the little bumps from the growing flower bud can be tough and need to be trimmed out.

Whenever I want to cook something that I've never had before, I consider what the new thing resembles. Scapes look like long asparagus spears and show up in the garden at the same time, so I often cook them like asparagus. In this recipe, I cook them together.

The roasted scapes and asparagus serve as a bed for halibut, a delicate, meaty white fish that is in season at the same time as the vegetables. There's garlic in the crumb crust, which echoes the flavor of the scapes. If there's no time to make the halibut, it's fine to serve the vegetables alone. It's also fine to roast the scapes all by themselves.

To finish the dish in a wash of green, use the Fresh Herb and Caper Sauce. To add a flourish of red instead, use Romesco Sauce (page 320).

MAKES 4 SERVINGS

1. For the scapes and asparagus: Preheat the oven to 400°F. Line a rimmed baking sheet with aluminum foil.
2. Pinch the little flower bud bump in each scape. If it's too hard to squeeze then it is too tough to eat, so trim it out. Cut the scapes into 1-inch lengths. Snap off and discard the tough asparagus ends. Place the scapes and asparagus on the prepared pan, drizzle with the oil, season with salt and pepper, toss to coat, and spread them out into a single layer.
3. For the halibut: Toss together the bread crumbs, oil, and garlic in a small skillet. Cook over medium-high heat, stirring often, until the crumbs are golden brown. Remove the skillet from the heat.

④ Sprinkle both sides of the fillets with the salt and pepper and place on the bed of scapes and asparagus. Roast for 10 minutes. Top the fillets with the bread crumb mixture and continue roasting until the vegetables are tender when pierced with the tip of a knife and the fish is opaque, about 8 minutes longer. To test the fish for doneness, slide a small paring knife into the center of a fillet (the knife is parallel to the baking sheet), count to 3 and slowly pull out the knife. If the blade feels warm, the fish is done.

⑤ Serve hot, topped with a generous spoonful of sauce.

WHAT ELSE WORKS? You can replace some or all of the garlic scapes with pencil-thin scallions or baby leeks.

## Fresh Herb and Caper Sauce

2 cups coarsely chopped flat-leaf parsley

1 cup lightly packed, coarsely chopped fresh basil

1 tablespoon coarsely chopped fresh mint

4 garlic cloves, chopped

2 heaping tablespoons capers

Zest and juice of 1 lemon (about ¼ cup)

⅔ cup extra-virgin olive oil

Kosher salt and ground black pepper

This bright, pungent sauce has a shocking green color and smells like a walk through an herb garden on a warm summer day. It's delicious on nearly any kind of roasted, grilled, or poached mild fish. It's also good on cooked summer vegetables that need a boost of color and herbal flavor.

MAKES ABOUT 1 ½ CUPS

Combine the parsley, basil, and mint in a large bowl. Add the garlic, capers, lemon zest, and lemon juice. Whisk in the oil. Season the sauce with salt and pepper. Serve at room temperature.

# GRAPES

**Grapes have always grown in North America,** home to more varieties of wild grapes than any other place on earth. Topping the list of the South's native grapes are muscadines and scuppernongs. The oldest grapevine in America is a sweet white scuppernong that grows on the northern end of Roanoke Island in the Outer Banks of North Carolina. This Mother Vine is at least 400 years old and continues to bear fruit annually. It was likely cultivated by the local Croatan Indians. Early explorers that came across this vine wrote of its imposing size and profusion of fruit.

Colonists enjoyed eating the native grapes but considered them unsuitable for wine making. Early efforts to grow Old World wine grapes failed because the vines always succumbed to New World diseases. The solution was to graft the wine grapes onto hearty native stock that had already developed natural resistance and immunity. A few table grapes are also successfully cultivated in the South. And the wild grapes still run wild. ■

# Muscadine Streusel Pie

½ cup all-purpose flour, divided

½ cup old-fashioned rolled oats or quick oats

½ cup packed light brown sugar

4 tablespoons (½ stick) unsalted butter, cut into small cubes and chilled

4 cups fresh muscadine grapes

¾ cup granulated sugar

1 tablespoon quick-cooking (instant) tapioca

1 tablespoon fresh lemon juice

¼ teaspoon kosher salt

1 (9-inch) pie shell (page 396 or store-bought)

Muscadine grapes are native to the southeastern United States, where they thrive in the heat and humidity. Some are dark purple and some are light bronze. I call the dark ones muscadines and the light ones scuppernongs, although other people have more complicated criteria for identifying what is what. You can use the light scuppernongs, but the pie is prettiest made with the dark muscadines.

The pulp and juice of these grapes is sweet and fragrant, unlike no other grape and superior to most. Alas, they are full of seeds and the skins are tough. Children who grow up eating these grapes learn early the art of pulling them off the vine, crushing them in their mouths to capture the pulp, then spitting out the seeds and tough skins, either tactfully out into the yard or vigorously toward their siblings.

Most recipes using muscadines call for slipping the grapes out of their skins, cooking the pulp to remove the seeds, and adding the skins back in. The skins soften when cooked and add both color and perfume to the filling. Trust me, this task is completely worth it. This is one of the finest southern pies there is. I made one for my neighbor, who grew up eating muscadines. He didn't bother with a plate; he just grabbed a fork and tucked in, eating straight out of the dish.

MAKES 8 SERVINGS

1. Preheat the oven to 425°F. Place a rimmed baking sheet in the oven to heat at the same time. (The hot baking sheet will help the crust get done on the bottom.)

2. Make the streusel topping by mixing ¼ cup of the flour and the oats, brown sugar, and butter in a medium bowl. Use your fingertips to work in the butter until it is in pieces the size of small peas. Squeeze together a few marble-sized lumps of streusel, but leave the rest crumbly. Cover and refrigerate.

3. Remove the skins from the grapes by gently squeezing them over a medium saucepan. If the grapes are fully ripe, the pulp will easily slide out of the stem end. If they are stubborn, use a sharp paring knife to make a shallow cut on the stem end. Coarsely chop the skins and set them aside in a large bowl.

4. Cook the pulp over medium heat until the seeds come loose, about 5 minutes. Force the pulp through a food mill or a mesh sieve into the bowl with the skins. Discard the seeds. Stir in the remaining ¼ cup of flour and the granulated sugar, tapioca, lemon juice, and salt. Pour the filling into the pie shell. Sprinkle the streusel over the filling.

5. Place the pie on the hot baking sheet and bake for 10 minutes. Reduce the oven temperature to 350°F and continue baking until the topping is golden brown and the filling bubbles around the edges, about 30 minutes more. Cool to room temperature on a wire rack before serving.

## Roasted Grapes and Sausages

1 ½   pounds black
      seedless grapes

1   small red onion,
    halved lengthwise
    and cut into thin strips

3   tablespoons extra-
    virgin olive oil

8   links of sweet or hot
    Italian pork sausage
    (about 4 ounces each)

¼   cup balsamic vinegar
    Kosher salt and ground
    black pepper, to taste

I discovered this dish in the rolling Umbrian hills of Italy, an area that, like the South, is known for legendary pork dishes. The first bite brought back memories of those slow cookers filled with tiny smoked sausages in grape jelly sauce that have graced many southern party tables for decades. But this is so much better.

I've tried all sorts of sausages in this recipe and learned that short links of coarsely ground fresh sausage in natural casings work best. Loose bulk sausage breaks apart and floats around. Firm smoked sausage such as kielbasa or little smokies get flinty dry and suspiciously stained with the inky grape juice.

I use seedless black grapes for their size and flavor and because they are easy to eat. In Italy, the grapes were full of seeds because Italians assume that people expect whole grapes to contain seeds. Around here, if you go with seedy grapes, warn people before they do dental damage. No matter the type of grape, leave them whole. Cut grapes won't work.

MAKES 4 TO 6 SERVINGS

1. Preheat the oven to 450°F.
2. Place the grapes and onion in a large cast-iron skillet or small roasting pan, drizzle with the oil, and toss to coat. Nestle the sausages down into the grapes, but do not bury them. Roast for 15 minutes. Turn the sausages over and continue roasting until they are browned and the casings are crispy in spots, about 15 minutes more. Before serving, pierce the sausages to make sure the juices run clear.
3. Pour the vinegar over the top and season with salt and pepper. Serve hot.

VARIATION: You can also roast the grapes without the sausages. They make a great accompaniment for roasted game birds or a wonderful garnish for a cheese or antipasti platter. Roasted seedless grapes are delicious stirred into relish or chutney in place of raisins. To roast only the grapes, simply toss individual grapes or small clusters with a tiny bit of olive oil, spread onto a parchment-lined rimmed baking sheet, and sprinkle with salt and pepper. Roast at 450°F until their skins are shriveled and slightly crisp but the grapes are still juicy inside, about 15 minutes. Serve warm or at room temperature. You can also grill-roast the grapes over coals that are covered in gray ash, which makes them both sweet and smoky.

# Fresh Grape Cake with Luscious Lemon Sauce

1 ½ cups all-purpose flour

1 teaspoon baking powder

¼ teaspoon baking soda

1 teaspoon kosher salt

¾ cup plus 2 tablespoons sugar, divided

8 tablespoons (1 stick) unsalted butter, at room temperature, divided

3 tablespoons extra-virgin olive oil

2 large eggs, at room temperature

1 teaspoon finely grated lemon zest

1 teaspoon finely grated orange zest

1 teaspoon pure vanilla extract

1 cup orange muscat wine or other citrusy white dessert wine

1 ½ cups red seedless grapes

Luscious Lemon Sauce, for serving (recipe follows)

This cake surprises everyone who eats it. The whole red grapes stay intact as the cake bakes, but they soften into juicy orbs. There is plenty of sunny citrus flavor from the zest and the wine. Although there is a thin sweet crust of sugar on top, the cake isn't very sweet overall, which makes it a light dessert or indulgent breakfast.

I don't usually mention the olive oil to people who have never tasted this cake because it makes them suspicious of the whole thing. The trick is to use a light, floral olive oil instead of one of those peppery bruisers. Grapeseed oil will also work, as will vegetable oil, although it's not nearly so interesting.

MAKES 8 SERVINGS

1. Preheat the oven to 400°F. Brush the inside of a 10-inch springform pan with olive oil. Line the bottom of the pan with a round of parchment paper and then brush the parchment with olive oil.

2. Whisk together the flour, baking powder, baking soda, and salt in a medium bowl.

3. Whisk together ¾ cup of the sugar, 6 tablespoons of the butter, and the oil in a large bowl until smooth. Whisk in the eggs until smooth. Whisk in the lemon zest, orange zest, and vanilla. Add the flour mixture in thirds, alternating with half of the wine, whisking the batter after each addition just until it is smooth.

4. Spread the batter into the prepared pan. Sprinkle the grapes over the top of the batter. (The grapes will sink as the cake bakes.)

5. Bake until the top is just set, about 20 minutes. Dot the top of the cake with the remaining 2 tablespoons of butter, and sprinkle with the remaining 2 tablespoons of sugar. Continue baking until the top of the cake is golden and a tester inserted into the center comes out clean, about 20 minutes more. Cool the cake in the pan on a wire rack for 20 minutes. Release the pan sides, remove the cake, and gently peel away the parchment paper from the bottom.

6. Serve the cake slightly warm or at room temperature topped with a generous spoonful of Luscious Lemon Sauce.

## Luscious Lemon Sauce

1 cup lemon curd (page 43 or store-bought)

1 cup crème fraîche (page 388 or store-bought)

2 tablespoons cassis (optional)

This is one of those deceptively simple recipes that adds up to far more than the sum of the parts. The sauce tastes like a slowly cooked custard but comes together in about two minutes. It keeps up to a week and is good on all sorts of things, from cake to fresh fruit.

If using purchased lemon curd, use high-quality curd that is pale yellow, buttery, and creamy. Avoid the neon-hued, artificially flavored brands sold near the peanut butter and jelly.

MAKES ABOUT 2 CUPS

1. Whisk together the lemon curd and crème fraîche in a medium bowl until smooth and well combined. Whisk in the cassis, if using.
2. Serve soon or store covered and refrigerated for up to a week.

## Brie Tartlets with Fresh Grape Relish

½ cup thinly sliced seedless red grapes or whole champagne grapes

1 tablespoon finely chopped scallions (white and tender green parts)

2 teaspoons high-quality balsamic vinegar

1 ½ teaspoons very finely chopped fresh rosemary

¼ teaspoon kosher salt

¼ teaspoon ground black pepper

24 (1 ½-inch) baked pastry shells

3 ounces high-quality Brie or other similar cheese, rind removed

¼ cup coarsely chopped walnuts, lightly toasted

This is a new, creative, and attractive way to serve cheese and fruit. The grapes can be quartered for the relish, but they are lovely cut crosswise into paper-thin rounds that look like tiny pieces of stained glass in ruby frames. The downy white rind on Brie and other similar cheeses is natural and edible, but it doesn't taste or look very good, so I usually trim it away with a vegetable peeler. This is easiest when the cheese is first pulled from the fridge and is still firm. If the cheese is already soft, just pull out small pieces from the interior with your fingertips or a small spoon and drop them into the shells.

When time is tight, skip assembling the tartlets and simply spoon the relish over a wedge or wheel of Brie, Camembert, or other similar cheese and serve with crackers or bread.

MAKES 24 TARTLETS

1. Preheat the oven to 300°F.
2. To make the relish, stir together the grapes, scallions, vinegar, rosemary, salt, and pepper in a small bowl.
3. Arrange the pastry shells on a baking sheet. Place 1 teaspoon of the cheese and ½ teaspoon of the walnuts in each shell. Bake only until the cheese begins to melt, about 5 minutes; do not overbake.
4. Top each tartlet with about ½ teaspoon of the relish. Serve soon. They taste best slightly warm but are fine at room temperature.

MAKE-AHEAD NOTE: You can make the grape relish up to 1 day ahead. Store the relish covered and refrigerated. You can fill the pastry shells with walnuts and cheese up to 6 hours ahead. Store covered and refrigerated.

# Sautéed Chard with Grapes and Almonds

1 ¼  pounds chard

1  tablespoon butter

¼  cup slivered almonds

2  tablespoons extra-virgin olive oil

½  cup finely chopped onion

¾  cup seedless grapes, cut in half

2  garlic cloves, thinly sliced

½  teaspoon kosher salt

¼  teaspoon ground black pepper

Pinch of crushed red pepper flakes

This pretty and tasty dish shows how quickly fresh greens can be ready to serve. The grapes add subtle sweetness and the almonds add crunch. When chard is young and fresh, the stems are edible and delicious. Any type of chard will do, but the bright stems of red chard or rainbow chard add color to the dish.

MAKES 4 SERVINGS

1   Trim away the tough ends of the chard stems. Cut the tender stems into ½-inch pieces and set aside. Stack the leaves, roll into a cylinder, and cut crosswise into ½-inch ribbons.

2   Heat the butter in a large skillet over medium heat. Add the almonds and cook, stirring frequently, until golden, about 4 minutes. Transfer into a small bowl.

3   Heat the oil in the skillet over medium heat. Add the onion and chard stems and a pinch of salt. Cook, stirring often, until tender, about 8 minutes. Add the grapes and garlic and cook, stirring constantly, until the grapes begin to wrinkle and soften, about 2 minutes.

4   Add the chard in handfuls, tossing with tongs and adding more as the leaves collapse. When all of it has been added, cover and cook, tossing occasionally, only until wilted and barely heated through, about 3 minutes. Season with the salt, pepper, and red pepper flakes. Use tongs or a slotted spoon to transfer to a serving platter, leaving behind any liquid.

5   Scatter the almonds over the top and serve warm.

WHAT ELSE WORKS? You can use other quick-cooking leafy greens, such as spinach or escarole, in place of some or all of the chard.

# GREENS

**They rarely get any press other than around New Year's Day.** They rarely hold court in the center of the plate. They get few (if any) pages in cookbooks, not even many southern ones, old or new. And yet there is no vegetable more southern than greens. There is perhaps no southern food more maligned and misunderstood, not even okra and grits.

Southerners, starting with the Native Americans, have always eaten greens. Even in places where greens flourished in gardens, people headed out to look for wild greens growing along creek banks and in meadows. Wild greens were often available weeks before even the earliest spring garden greens, at a time when bodies and palates were aching for something fresh and verdant after months of winter food. In hard times, wild greens were survival food when there would be no greens from a garden. They say that pioneer women figured out which greens were edible by watching the milk cow graze. If something didn't kill Ole Bossy, it probably wouldn't kill the family either.

One type of traditional cooked southern greens are the ones simmered until they are soft, sultry, and swimming in the rich cooking liquid known as potlikker. Greens and potlikker have social implications. Although nearly everyone ate them, they were often associated with poverty and dismissed as food of the lower class. Perhaps the most well-known long-cooked green is collards, but not all southerners were raised on collards. For generations it was possible to make an educated guess about where a southerner grew up by knowing which green his family favored. People in the Upland South ate turnip and mustard greens. People in the Deep or Coastal South ate collards. Collards came to the South from Africa, as did the practice of cooking greens like stew and drinking the cooking liquid. A map that shows the traditional preferences for a particular green might reveal social, cultural, and culinary history with undercurrents of socioeconomic and racial boundaries far more clearly than the Mason-Dixon Line ever did.

Many southern gardens and most farmers' markets now offer greens from all over the world that can be prepared in countless ways that reflect all our ethnicities. We no longer have a greens line; instead, we have a million fine lines that cannot be drawn with such broad strokes. ■

Here we're talking salad greens, mostly lettuces, meant to be eaten uncooked. Most salad greens are leafy (individual leaves or loose-leaf heads) or grow in compact heads with an inner core. When I make a salad, I let the type of dressing guide my selection of the greens. To illustrate that concept, here are three classic salad dressings matched with the appropriate type of salad green. The first recipe is for basic vinaigrette meant for leafy green salads. The second recipe is for a hot bacon dressing that is also used on leafy greens, but the dressing wilts some of the leaves, walking the thin line between raw and cooked. The third recipe is for a thick, creamy dressing that must go on chunky, crispy, firm, dense head lettuce with an inner core, such as iceberg and romaine.

## Leafy Salad Greens with Basic Vinaigrette

Most lettuces and salad greens are light and leafy. They are picked one leaf at a time or come in loose heads. There are no hard and fast rules for leafy salads, but there are a couple of commonsense suggestions.

First, the greens should be dry before they are dressed. Excess water dilutes the dressing and turns the greens into a slimy mess that resembles the stuff stuck on the bottom of a lawn mower after running over wet grass. A good salad spinner is very useful. The leaves must spin freely, so don't overfill the basket. Spin, pour off the water, fluff the leaves, and spin again. You can also pat the greens dry with paper towels or a clean kitchen towel. Put large amounts of greens into a clean cotton or linen pillowcase reserved solely for this purpose and then go outside and spin them over your head, like a centrifuge. Your neighbors might talk, but your greens will be nice and dry.

Second, dress the salad with a light hand. Perfectly dressed greens will glisten but still feel light. Never add so much vinaigrette that it ponds up in the bottom of the bowl. Different greens require different amounts of dressing, so never dump all of the dressing in at once, even when following a recipe. Give the greens plenty of room in a large bowl so that you can toss as you slowly add vinaigrette. Don't dress a salad until shortly before it's served.

# Basic Vinaigrette

1 tablespoon finely chopped shallot

¼ cup red wine vinegar

½ teaspoon kosher salt, plus more to taste

1 teaspoon Dijon mustard

¾ cup extra-virgin olive oil

Ground black pepper

Most salad dressings are vinaigrettes, which means that they are based on oil and vinegar. A recipe for vinaigrette is really more of a template. Once you know how to make basic vinaigrette, you can make an infinite variety of vinaigrettes by simply changing the type of oil, vinegar, or mustard or by adding fresh or dried herbs. You can replace some or all of the vinegar with fresh citrus juice or other acidic foods, such as finely chopped tomato. (If the dressing contains citrus juice instead of vinegar it's a citronette, but few people use that term.)

Making vinaigrette is a balancing act. Too much vinegar will grab the back of your throat and make you cough. Too much oil will coat your mouth so that you can't taste anything, like an olive oil gargle. That being said, the proportion of vinegar and oil is a personal preference, so taste as you go. Strong salad can stand up to the sharpness of a little more vinegar, and delicate ingredients need less. To make sure the vinaigrette has the right balance of oil and acid, taste it with a bite of the lettuce or the main salad ingredient. Always be willing to make adjustments to suit your own palate. If it suits you, it's right, no matter what a recipe says.

MAKES 1 CUP

(1) Place the shallot, vinegar, and salt in a medium bowl and set aside for 5 minutes. This mellows the shallot and dissolves the salt. Whisk in the mustard. While whisking vigorously, add the oil in a slow, steady stream. Season with pepper and more salt, if needed.

(2) Use soon or transfer into a glass jar with a tight-fitting lid and refrigerate for up to 1 week. Return to room temperature, shake vigorously, and check the seasoning before serving.

TIPS AND TECHNIQUES

Leafy greens can be quite dirty or sandy, particularly if they were harvested on a rainy day, so wash them well. If there is dirt clinging to the greens, they should be washed before they are cut; otherwise, they can be washed after they are cut. Fill the sink or a large bowl with cool water. Lower the leaves into the water, gently swish them with your hands to loosen the grit, then let them sit for a bit so that the dirt can fall to the bottom of the sink. Lift the leaves out of the water and drain well in a colander or spread them out on paper towels or a clean towel.

If you are making salad or cooking the greens in only a small amount of fat and liquid, drain them well and pat them dry. If you are adding the greens to a large amount of liquid, it's fine to leave a little water clinging to the leaves.

## Killed ("Kilt") Lettuce

12 cups freshly picked
baby leaf lettuce

4 spring onions,
trimmed and
thinly sliced

4 thick bacon slices,
cut crosswise into
½-inch pieces
(about 4 ounces)

¼ cup cider vinegar

2 teaspoons sugar

1 teaspoon kosher salt

½ teaspoon ground
black pepper

This was my favorite thing my grandmother made each spring, mostly because we got to enjoy it for only those few fleeting days when the first tender leaves of lettuce poked up out of the ground. When the lettuce started to get big, there was no more kilt lettuce for that year. We had a full year to remember how good it was and to look forward to having it again the next spring. Kilt Lettuce ought to be served with Soupy Taters (page 253).

There are other salads with hot bacon dressing all over the South, but kilt lettuce is a Blue Ridge Mountains thing. My grandmother used garden lettuce, but I've heard of people using wild greens—such as branch lettuce and cresses—as well. I can imagine how delicious those greens must have tasted to people who had just endured a winter of dried and salted foods with barely a speck of fresh vegetables. It must have been a tonic to the body, mind, and palate.

MAKES 4 TO 6 SERVINGS

1. Dry the lettuce thoroughly. (See page 162 for tips.) Place the lettuce and onions in a large heatproof serving bowl and set aside.

2. Cook the bacon in a large skillet (preferably cast-iron) over medium heat, stirring often, until it renders its fat and is very crispy, about 15 minutes. Transfer with a slotted spoon to paper towels to drain, leaving the drippings in the skillet.

3. Add the vinegar, sugar, salt, and pepper to the drippings and stir until the sugar dissolves. Cook until the mixture is shimmering hot and then carefully pour it over the lettuce and onions, tossing with tongs to coat and lightly wilt the greens. Sprinkle the bacon over the top and serve immediately—this won't keep.

## Crisp Iceberg Wedges with Blue Cheese Dressing

DRESSING

¼ cup mayonnaise

¼ cup sour cream

1 tablespoon fresh lemon juice

1 tablespoon finely chopped fresh chives

2 tablespoons well-shaken buttermilk

4 ounces blue cheese, crumbled (about 1 cup)

Kosher salt and ground black pepper, or to taste

SALAD

1 large head iceberg or other crisp head lettuce, chilled

4 thick bacon slices, cooked crisp and crumbled (optional)

Cracked black pepper

This is why iceberg deserves a little respect. A wedge of chilled, crisp iceberg can hold rich, thick, creamy dressing, such as homemade blue cheese dressing. Lesser, leafier greens would give way like pond ice in spring. To blue cheese connoisseurs, this dressing is food of the gods. Be sure to use high-quality blue cheese, preferably a domestic farmstead one such as Clemson, Maytag, or Point Reyes.

In some southern steak houses and barbecue joints, it's a tradition to eat blue cheese dressing on saltines. The servers will bring a dish of dressing, a basket of crackers, and a pitcher of iced tea to the table first thing, without the guests having to order it.

MAKES 4 TO 6 SERVINGS

① For the dressing: Stir together the mayonnaise, sour cream, lemon juice, chives, and buttermilk in a medium bowl. Fold in the cheese. Season with salt and pepper. Cover and refrigerate for at least 30 minutes and up to overnight to give the flavors time to meld. Return to room temperature for serving.

② For the salad: Core the lettuce and cut into 4 or 6 wedges. Divide the wedges among serving plates and top each generously with the dressing, an equal portion of bacon, if using, and a big pinch of cracked pepper. Serve soon.

## QUICK-COOKING GREENS

Most cooked greens fall into the quick-cooking category. These greens taste better cooked than raw, but they do not need lengthy cooking to bring out their flavor and make them tender. Most recipes for quick-cooked greens call for cooking in a little fat or a little liquid. These greens can be served alone or used in other recipes.

The good news is that nearly all of the greens in this category are interchangeable, which means that if you know how to cook one, you pretty much know how to cook all of them. It also means that if you have your heart set on using a recipe and the featured green isn't available, you can substitute a similar green and get great results. For example, you can take all your spinach recipes and use chard instead, and you have a new set of recipes.

Common greens that are good candidates for quick cooking include spinach, leafy Asian greens, chard, escarole, arugula, and young or small leaves of sturdier greens such as kale, collards, mustard greens, and turnip greens. Sometimes these greens are mixed and sold as braising greens. To determine whether a particular green is a good candidate for quick cooking, nibble on a leaf. If the leaf and center rib are chewable, it's fine. If the leaf is leathery and the stem is tough and stringy, it will require longer cooking.

The quick-cooking category is usually the place for what I like to call The Weeds, wild greens that were once commonly harvested in the earliest days of spring, when bodies and palates ached for fresh greens after a long winter of dried, salted, and preserved food. The Weeds include dock, nettles, cresses, lamb's-quarters, sorrel (sour grass), poke, purslane, creasy greens, and dandelions. You can still find these greens in the wild, but many can also be grown in the garden.

The small leaves of cooking greens can be left whole, but most greens need to be torn or cut into bite-sized pieces. Check the stems and cut them off if they are tougher than the leaves. The stems of chard, young beets, and young turnips are usually tender enough to cook if they are thinly sliced. To cut the leaves, make a stack of about 12 leaves, with the larger leaves on the bottom. Starting with a long side, roll the stack into a cylinder and cut the cylinder crosswise into ½-inch-wide strips.

## Grilled Radicchio

1 large radicchio, preferably radicchio Treviso

2 tablespoons vegetable oil or extra-virgin olive oil

Kosher salt and ground black pepper, to taste

Freshly shaved Parmesan or Pecorino cheese, for serving

¼ cup pine nuts or chopped walnuts, toasted

1 tablespoon balsamic vinegar

Grilled lettuce sounds like a joke, but it's not. Head lettuces and leafy greens with an inner core to hold them together can weather a quick trip to the grill (or a turn in a hot cast-iron grill pan or skillet). The quick cooking softens and lightly chars the tips of the leaves, but the centers remain firm and cool. It's a wonderful contrast of textures.

MAKES 4 SERVINGS

1. Discard any bruised leaves and quarter the radicchio lengthwise, using the core to keep the pieces intact. Submerge the wedges in ice water for 1 hour, using a small plate to keep them submerged. The water will perk up the leaves and rinse away any hidden grit.

2. Preheat a grill, grill pan, or skillet over medium-high heat. Shake the water off the radicchio and brush the cut sides with oil, letting a little run between the leaves. Sprinkle the cut sides with salt and pepper.

3. Place the wedges cut-side down on the grill grate and cook, turning gently with tongs, until the outer leaves are browned and a little charred along the edges but the inner leaves are still firm and cool, 3 to 5 minutes. Top with the cheese and nuts, drizzle with the vinegar, and serve warm.

VARIATION: You can move the wedges of radicchio to a cool corner of the grill and let them cook, turning with tongs as needed, until wilted and warmed through, about 25 minutes in all.

WHAT ELSE WORKS? You can also grill Belgian endive, romaine, and other similar vegetables with an inner core. Grilling is also a good technique for baby bok choy or other similar Asian vegetables. Season the Asian varieties with soy sauce, toasted sesame oil, and sesame seeds instead of cheese, nuts, and balsamic.

## Beginner Greens

1 ½ to 2 pounds tender greens

1 tablespoon butter

1 tablespoon extra-virgin olive oil

1 medium onion, finely diced

1 apple, peeled if necessary, cored and coarsely grated

½ teaspoon kosher salt, plus more to taste

½ teaspoon ground black pepper, plus more to taste

½ to ¾ cup chicken or vegetable stock or apple cider, divided

I call these beginner greens for two reasons:

1. This is a great, easy recipe for anyone who has never cooked greens.
2. This is a great, tasty recipe for anyone who has never eaten greens.

The sweetness of the apple and slowly cooked onion tempers any bitterness or sharpness in the greens. Any type of quick-cooking green will do, such as spinach or chard or small tender leaves of kale, mustard, beets, turnips, or mixed braising greens.

Don't be alarmed by the amount of raw greens; they cook down considerably, making a molehill out of a mountain.

MAKES 4 SERVINGS

1. Wash and dry the greens. Discard the large stems and any tough inner ribs. Thinly slice the leaves.
2. Heat the butter and oil in a large skillet over medium-high heat. When the butter foams, add the onion and a pinch of salt and cook, stirring frequently, until the onion softens and turns golden, about 10 minutes. Stir in the apple and cook, stirring often, until crisp-tender, about 3 minutes.
3. Add the greens one handful at a time and stir to coat with the butter and oil. Let each addition cook down a little before adding the next. Cook, tossing the greens constantly with tongs, just until they wilt, 1 to 3 minutes, depending on the size and type of the greens.
4. Add the salt, pepper, and ½ cup of the stock. Cover the pan and simmer until tender, 1 to 5 minutes. Add a splash of the remaining stock if the greens get dry. Check the seasoning and serve warm.

WHAT ELSE WORKS? You can use a chopped ripe tomato instead of the apple.

# Mediterranean Skillet Greens

½ cup golden raisins

½ cup extra-virgin olive oil

12 garlic cloves, peeled and smashed

½ cup pine nuts

2 ½ pounds quick-cooking greens, tough stems removed and leaves thinly sliced

2 tablespoons sherry vinegar or red wine vinegar

Kosher salt and ground black pepper, to taste

Quick-cooking greens such as these are common in Italy and Spain. The seasoning is a balancing act between a splash of vinegar and a handful of plump, sweet raisins. The pine nuts add crunch and texture, things often lacking in braised greens. You can use other nuts in place of the pine nuts. Likewise, you can use other dried fruits (such as dried cherries or chopped apricots) in place of the raisins. You can add a pinch of crushed red pepper flakes if you like a little heat. Like many Mediterranean vegetable dishes, this is good warm or at room temperature.

MAKES 6 SERVINGS

1. Place the raisins in a small bowl and cover with hot tap water. Set aside until the raisins plump, at least 15 minutes. Drain well.

2. Heat the oil in a large skillet over medium heat. Add the garlic and pine nuts and cook, stirring often, until the nuts are golden brown, 5 minutes. Add the greens in large handfuls, stirring until they wilt before adding more. Continue to cook, tossing the greens with tongs until they are tender, but do not let them get slick. If the greens get dry before they get tender, add a splash of water. Stir in the raisins. Pour the vinegar over the greens and season with salt and pepper.

3. Serve warm or at room temperature.

WHAT ELSE WORKS? You can use almost any type of quick-cooking leafy green in this dish. If you prefer milder greens, use spinach or chard. If you like more assertive tastes, try mixed braising greens, baby collards, baby mustard greens, baby turnip greens, kale, or blanched broccoli raab.

## Southern Skillet Greens

1 ½ pounds quick-cooking greens, tough stems removed and leaves thinly sliced

2 thick bacon slices, cut crosswise into ¼-inch strips (about 2 ounces)

1 tablespoon extra-virgin olive oil, if needed

1 small onion, thinly sliced (about 1 cup)

1 garlic clove, finely chopped

2 teaspoons granulated sugar or firmly packed light brown sugar

1 small dried hot chile or ¼ teaspoon crushed red pepper flakes

Kosher salt and ground black pepper, to taste

Hot Pepper Vinegar, for serving (page 88)

These are fully southern in spirit and flavor, but they are on the opposite end of the continuum from soft greens swimming in potlikker. These greens remain toothsome with a texture similar to slaw, so they often appeal to people who do not like slick greens. The greens are blanched and shocked to keep their colors vibrant. I often blanch the greens as soon as they are picked, then stash them in the refrigerator so they're ready for a quick finish in the skillet at supper time up to three days later.

Although they are great served alone, these greens are glorious spooned onto a cushion of piping hot grits (page 392). For households that serve nearly everything over rice, that'll do too.

These are my favorite greens to use in Beans and Greens Bruschetta (page 279).

MAKES 4 SERVINGS

1. Fill a large bowl with ice water. Bring a large saucepan of water to a boil. Add ½ teaspoon kosher salt per cup of water. Add the greens and cook until wilted, about 2 minutes. Use a slotted spoon or strainer to immediately transfer into the ice water to stop the cooking and set the color. Drain well and squeeze out as much water as possible. Use soon or cover and refrigerate for up to 3 days.

2. Cook the bacon in a large skillet over medium heat until it renders its fat and is crispy, stirring often, about 10 minutes. If the bacon does not render at least 2 tablespoons of fat, stir in the oil. Stir in the onion and cook, stirring often, until softened, about 10 minutes. Stir in the garlic, sugar, and chile and cook, stirring, until the garlic is fragrant, about 1 minute. (The whole chile will give mild heat and can be discarded before serving. Crushed flakes are a commitment to heat, but the amount can be adjusted to taste.)

3. Add the greens and cook, tossing with tongs, until glossy and warmed through, 3 to 4 minutes. Season with salt and pepper and serve warm with Hot Pepper Vinegar on the side.

# Creamed Spinach

2 pounds spinach, preferably baby spinach

6 tablespoons butter, divided

3 tablespoons finely chopped onion

1 tablespoon finely chopped garlic

6 tablespoons instant or all-purpose flour

3 cups half-and-half or whole milk

¼ teaspoon freshly grated nutmeg

½ cup finely grated Parmesan or other hard grating cheese

1 teaspoon kosher salt, or to taste

½ teaspoon ground black pepper, or to taste

This is classic comfort food, often served as the token green vegetable in venerable, wood-paneled steak houses. Creamed spinach is so very good and so very decadent. If the spinach stems are very tender, you can chop them up and add them to the leaves, but tough stems will turn into twigs.

Despite the name of the recipe, using cream in creamed spinach is simply too much and weighs down the dish. I prefer half-and-half or whole milk. On the other hand, skim milk is puny, meager, and inadequate.

MAKES 6 SERVINGS

1. Fill a large bowl with ice water. Bring a large saucepan of water to a boil. Add ½ teaspoon kosher salt per cup of water. Working in batches, place the spinach in a large strainer and lower it into the boiling water until it wilts, about 3 seconds. Quickly transfer the spinach into the ice water to stop the cooking and set the bright green color. Remove the spinach and squeeze it as dry as possible. Coarsely chop the spinach.

2. Melt 4 tablespoons of the butter in a medium saucepan over medium heat until it begins to foam. Stir in the onion and garlic and cook, stirring continuously, for 1 minute. Sprinkle the flour over the onion mixture and cook, stirring continuously, until the flour mixture is smooth and golden, about 3 minutes.

3. Whisking constantly, add the half-and-half in a slow, steady stream. Cook the mixture, stirring continuously with a wooden spoon until the sauce comes to a boil and thickens enough to coat the back of the spoon. Reduce the heat and continue to cook the sauce until it is the consistency of soft pudding. Stir in the nutmeg.

4. Stir in the spinach and cook over low heat until the spinach is warm and the sauce is gently bubbling, about 5 minutes. Stir in the remaining 2 tablespoons of butter and the cheese. Season with the salt and pepper. Serve very soon.

MAKE-AHEAD NOTE: You can make the recipe through Step 3 up to 1 day ahead. As soon as the sauce thickens, gently press plastic wrap directly onto the surface to prevent the sauce from forming a skin. Cool to room temperature and then refrigerate. Gently reheat the sauce before continuing. Store the spinach separately, covered and refrigerated.

## Creamed Spinach Baked Eggs

1 recipe Creamed
Spinach (page 171),
warmed

6 large eggs, at room
temperature

Hot sauce

1 teaspoon kosher salt

½ teaspoon ground
black pepper

6 tablespoons half-
and-half or cream

2 tablespoons butter,
cut into a total of
6 pieces

Creamed spinach is its own good thing, but sometimes I can't resist using it as a nest for baked eggs, a wonderful way to prepare eggs for a group without needing to cook for each person one at a time. For best results, bring the eggs to room temperature before cracking them into the spinach. Cold eggs require longer baking and the whites will turn rubbery.

MAKES 6 SERVINGS

1. Position a rack in the upper third of the oven and preheat the oven to 350°F.
2. Set six 6- or 8-ounce ramekins on a rimmed baking sheet. Divide the warm Creamed Spinach among the ramekins. Use the back of a spoon to make a little hollow in the center of the spinach and crack an egg into each hollow.
3. Sprinkle each egg with a dash of hot sauce and a little salt and pepper. Spoon 1 tablespoon of half-and-half on top of each egg and dot with a piece of butter.
4. Bake the eggs until the whites are firm and the yolks are as set as you like, 8 to 12 minutes. The yolks will continue to firm up after they come out of the oven, so serve them very soon.

## Greek Shrimp with Spinach, Feta, and Orzo

7 tablespoons extra-
virgin olive oil, divided

12 ounces uncooked
orzo pasta

4 cups lightly packed
baby spinach or
stemmed and
shredded chard

1½ cups crumbled feta
cheese, divided

½ cup grated Parm-
esan cheese

2 pounds extra-large
(21 to 25 count) shrimp,
peeled and deveined
(thawed if frozen)

(continued on
next page)

This recipe combines convenience foods (canned tomatoes, dried pasta, and frozen peeled shrimp) with fresh greens and transforms them into a special weeknight meal that is snazzy enough for casual entertaining.

Be sure to use very large shrimp that won't shrivel into rubbery knots as they cook. I am a fan of U.S. wild shrimp, even if they've been frozen. Unless you have access to truly fresh shrimp, shrimp that were frozen as soon as they were caught can often have superior flavor and texture to so-called fresh shrimp that have been in transit for a few days. The trick is to not thaw them until just before you cook them, so there is no time for them to decline. Thaw the shrimp under cool running water.

When there is no time to make the entire dish, you can make a stellar quick side dish from the spinach and orzo alone. The heat of the drained, freshly cooked orzo is all it takes to gently cook the spinach. Season with olive oil, cheese, salt, and pepper and you're done. It's fine to use other very small pasta shapes, such as risi, pastina, or stelline.

4 garlic cloves,
peeled and chopped

1 (28-ounce) can
crushed tomatoes

¼ cup dry white wine

2 teaspoons dried
Mediterranean
oregano

½ teaspoon crushed
red pepper flakes

½ cup chopped flat-
leaf parsley

1 teaspoon kosher salt

½ teaspoon ground
black pepper

MAKES 6 TO 8 SERVINGS

1. Preheat the oven to 400°F. Brush a glass or ceramic 9 × 13-inch baking dish with 1 tablespoon of the oil.

2. Cook the orzo according to package directions. Drain well in a colander and return to the same pot. Stir in 3 tablespoons of the oil, the spinach, ½ cup of the feta cheese, and the Parmesan. Spread the orzo mixture in the bottom of the prepared baking dish and cover with foil to keep warm.

3. Heat 1 tablespoon of the oil in a large skillet over medium-high heat. Add the shrimp and cook only until they start to turn opaque, about 1 minute. The shrimp will finish cooking in the oven. Arrange the shrimp over the orzo.

4. Heat the remaining 2 tablespoons of oil in the skillet. Add the garlic and cook until you can smell the aroma, about 30 seconds. Stir in the tomatoes, wine, oregano, and red pepper flakes. Simmer uncovered, stirring occasionally, until the mixture reduces to the consistency of pasta sauce, about 5 minutes. Stir in the parsley. Season with the salt and pepper. Spoon the sauce over the shrimp and orzo.

5. Bake until the shrimp are opaque, about 10 minutes. Sprinkle with the remaining 1 cup of feta cheese and serve hot.

## Savory Smoked Ham, Spinach, and Cheese Bread Pudding

8 cups lightly packed
small, tender spinach
(about 1 pound)

1 cup whole milk

4 cups 1-inch cubes
crustless day-old
Italian or French bread

¾ cup cream

3 large eggs

2 garlic cloves,
finely chopped

1 teaspoon kosher salt

½ teaspoon pepper

½ teaspoon freshly
ground nutmeg

2 tablespoons
chopped fresh sage

(continued on
next page)

This is my take on a breakfast or brunch casserole, a bread and egg custard dish that can be assembled the night before and popped in the oven the next morning. I like to serve it with the Skillet-Roasted Cherry Tomatoes (page 347), but if tomatoes are out of season, you can serve the pudding in a pool of Smoky Roasted Red Pepper Sauce (page 382) or gently warmed marinara sauce.

If you are serving a crowd, this is easily doubled to bake in a 9 × 13-inch baking dish that yields 12 to 16 servings.

MAKES 6 TO 8 SERVINGS

1. Fill a large bowl with ice water. Bring a large saucepan of water to a boil. Add ½ teaspoon kosher salt per cup of water. Working in batches, place the spinach in a large strainer and lower it into the boiling water until it wilts, about 3 seconds. Quickly transfer the spinach into the ice water to stop the cooking and set the bright green color. Drain the spinach and squeeze it as dry as possible. Coarsely chop the spinach.

2. Combine the milk and bread cubes in a large bowl and let stand until the bread absorbs the milk, about 10 minutes.

3. Whisk together the cream, eggs, garlic, salt, pepper, nutmeg, sage, and thyme in a medium bowl.

1 tablespoon chopped
fresh thyme

2 cups diced smoked
ham (about 8 ounces)

¾ cup soft, fresh goat
cheese (chèvre)

½ cup grated Asiago
cheese, divided

¾ cup grated Parm-
esan cheese

(4) Spread half of the bread mixture in a lightly greased 2 ½-quart baking dish. Layer on the ham, the spinach, the goat cheese, and ¼ cup of the Asiago. Top with the remaining bread mixture. Slowly pour the cream mixture evenly over the top and sprinkle with the remaining ¼ cup Asiago and the Parmesan. Cover the dish with plastic wrap and refrigerate for at least 4 hours and prefer-ably overnight.

(5) Preheat the oven to 350°F. Bake the pudding uncovered until it is firm in the center and brown around the edges, 50 to 60 minutes. Let sit for 10 minutes before serving.

## Broccoli Raab and Salami Calzones

Broccoli raab, also known as rapini, is a member of the turnip family. Some peo-ple delight in broccoli raab's full, aggressive flavor, but blanching tempers the bitter note to a more pleasing level and allows other ingredients to have their say. You can blanch the raab and store it in the refrigerator for up to two days before baking the calzone. Even with the blanching, this is a quick dish if you use store-bought pizza dough.

MAKES 4 SERVINGS

1 pound broccoli raab,
tough stems removed

1 large egg

⅔ cup whole-milk
or part-skim
ricotta cheese

1 cup grated mozzarella
or Italian blend cheese

2 tablespoons grated
Parmesan or other
hard grating cheese

2 ounces finely chopped
salami, pepperoni,
or soppressata

½ teaspoon kosher salt

½ teaspoon ground
black pepper

¼ teaspoon freshly
grated nutmeg

1 pound pizza dough,
thawed if frozen

Instant flour or
all-purpose flour,
for rolling

Extra-virgin olive
oil, for brushing

1 cup warm marinara
sauce, for serving

(1) Preheat the oven to 450°F.

(2) Bring a large saucepan of water to a boil. Add ½ teaspoon kosher salt per cup of water. Add the raab and cook until barely tender, about 3 minutes. Drain in a colander and rinse under cold running water until cool enough to handle. Pick up the raab in small handfuls, squeeze out as much liquid as possible, and coarsely chop.

(3) Whisk the egg in a large bowl until the white and yolk are blended. Add the raab, ricotta, mozzarella, Parmesan, meat, salt, pepper, and nutmeg and mix well.

(4) Divide the dough into 4 equal pieces. Working with one piece at a time, use a rolling pin to roll the dough into a 6-inch round on a lightly floured surface. Spoon one-fourth of the broccoli raab mixture into the center. Fold the dough over to enclose the filling and make a half-moon or rectangle. Press the edges together, turning under and pinching tightly closed. Place the calzones on a baking sheet or pizza stone. Brush the tops lightly with oil.

(5) Bake until the calzones are puffed and browned, about 20 minutes. Let rest on the baking sheet for 5 minutes before serving warm with the marinara sauce.

WHAT ELSE WORKS? You can replace the raab with spinach, chard, brocco-lini, or broccoli. You can replace the salami with other cooked, chopped meats. To make this meatless, replace the salami with sautéed mushrooms.

# Pasta with Escarole and Sausage

1 pound sweet Italian sausage, casings removed

1 medium onion, halved lengthwise and cut into thin strips

3 garlic cloves, finely chopped

½ cup dry white wine

1 (28-ounce) can whole peeled tomatoes

1 pound escarole, tough stems removed and cut into 1-inch ribbons

½ cup cream

¼ cup chopped flat-leaf parsley

Kosher salt and ground black pepper, to taste

8 ounces penne pasta

1 cup freshly grated Parmesan or other hard grating cheese, plus more for sprinkling

Crushed red pepper flakes, for serving

This is great comfort food on a cold night. You can change the dish's personality by changing the green. Choices range from little leafies, such as spinach or arugula, to heartier greens with a little bite, such as mustard greens or broccoli raab. Keep in mind that if you choose a green that is more leathery than leafy, you'll need to blanch it in boiling salted water until nearly tender and then drain it very well before adding it to the skillet.

MAKES 4 TO 6 SERVINGS

1. Cook the sausage in a large, heavy skillet over medium-high heat until cooked through, about 7 minutes, breaking it into bite-sized pieces with the side of a spoon. Drain all but 2 tablespoons of the fat from the skillet. If you happen to have very lean sausage, make up the difference with olive oil. Add the onion and garlic and cook, stirring often, until softened, about 8 minutes.

2. Add the wine, tomatoes, and escarole. Reduce the heat and simmer for 10 minutes, crushing the tomatoes with the side of the spoon. Add the cream and parsley. Season with salt and pepper and keep warm while the pasta cooks. Be sure the sauce does not boil after the cream is added.

3. Cook the pasta according to the package directions, stopping 2 minutes short of the recommended cooking time. Drain the pasta well, stir into the sauce, and simmer until the pasta is al dente. Stir in the cheese. Serve hot, sprinkled with additional cheese and a few pepper flakes.

VARIATION: You can replace the cooked pasta with 4 cups of cooked white beans or other shell beans. You can replace the sweet Italian sausage with sliced smoked sausage browned in 2 tablespoons olive oil.

WHAT ELSE WORKS? You can replace some or all of the escarole with another blanched sturdy green, such as kale or mustard. You could also use a leafy green that does not need to be blanched, such as spinach or arugula.

### TIPS AND TECHNIQUES

Cook with a wine you would be willing to drink, although that doesn't have to mean expensive. When a recipe calls for red wine, I avoid those that are very tannic. I try to match the level of fruitiness and sweetness (if any) to the recipe. When a recipe calls for white wine, I often turn to an unoaked American Sauvignon Blanc because I think it is food friendly and will enhance nearly any dish. If you need only a little wine for a recipe and don't want to open a bottle, stock up on the small picnic bottles of wine that hold about 1 cup each. Another option is to use dry vermouth, which keeps well in the pantry. Never use so-called cooking wine.

## Spring Greens Soup

3 cups lightly packed baby spinach

4 cups lightly packed watercress, arugula, dandelion greens, and/or nettles

1 cup lightly packed sorrel

3 tablespoons butter

1 cup chopped leeks, scallions, or spring onions (white and tender green parts)

4 cups chicken stock

1 teaspoon kosher salt, plus more to taste

8 ounces starchy potatoes, peeled and diced (such as russets)

1 cup heavy cream

¼ teaspoon ground white pepper

3 large egg yolks (optional)

This soup should be made with the bright, peppery, upstart greens of spring that wake up the palate, the kind that people once picked wild along the creek banks and in the fields. You can change the proportion of the greens, but try to include sorrel because it adds a tang that no other green can provide. (Sorrel is also called sour grass.) The greens are quickly blanched and shocked to set their color, so this soup is the color of liquid emeralds. The soup is thickened and enriched with egg yolks, but you can reduce the number or omit them for a lighter soup.

MAKES 6 SERVINGS

1. Fill a large bowl with ice water. Bring a large saucepan of water to a boil. Add ½ teaspoon kosher salt per cup of water. Place all the greens in a strainer and lower into the water for 1 minute. Transfer into the ice water to stop the cooking and set the color. Drain the greens, squeeze dry, coarsely chop, and set aside. There will now be only a paltry handful of greens, which is the way of cooked greens.

2. Melt the butter in a large saucepan over medium heat. Add the leeks and a pinch of salt and cook, stirring often, until softened, about 10 minutes. Do not let them brown.

3. Stir in the stock, salt, and potatoes. Bring to a boil, reduce the heat, and simmer until the potatoes are very tender and starting to fall apart, about 25 minutes. Stir in the greens.

4. Purée in a blender (working in batches to not fill the blender more than half full) and return to the pot, or purée the soup directly in the pot with an immersion blender. Be patient; it takes a while to purée cooked greens.

5. Bring the soup to a gentle simmer and stir in the cream. Season with salt and the white pepper.

6. If you are adding the yolks, whisk them in a medium bowl until smooth. While whisking constantly, slowly pour in a ladleful of hot soup to temper the yolks. Stir the yolks into the soup and heat through. Do not let the soup boil or the yolks might curdle. Serve warm.

## Oysters Rockefeller Soup

By adding freshly shucked oysters with their liquor to the warm Spring Greens Soup, you are making a simple oyster stew reminiscent of legendary Oysters Rockefeller, the baked oyster dish created at Antoine's Restaurant in New Orleans.

Oysters are clearly coastal food, but I strongly associate them with my granddaddy, who was born in 1911 and always lived in the Blue Ridge Mountains. He described the wonder of getting fresh oysters, coconuts, and oranges at Christmastime when he was a child. The oysters came packed in barrels of ice, hauled up from the coast. There were many flavors in mountain food, but none tasted of the ocean, so a freshly shucked oyster must have been an exotic experience. Throughout his life, he wanted oysters for Christmas.

To make Oysters Rockefeller Soup, prepare Spring Greens Soup through Step 5 and omit the yolks. When a few wisps of steam rise from the soup, stir in 1 pint of freshly shucked oysters and their liquor. Cook the oysters only until they plump in the center and their edges begin to curl like Elvis's lip, 1 to 5 minutes, depending on the size of the oysters. Season with a splash of Herbsaint or other anise-flavored liqueur and serve at once, with oyster crackers or saltines.

## LONG-COOKING GREENS

These are the legendary southern greens, simmered until they are the texture of crushed velvet, often in the exquisitely seasoned liquid known as potlikker. Only sturdy greens can hold up and flourish during long cooking. Likewise, only long cooking is appropriate for leathery greens that scoff at steaming and sautéing. Undercooked tough greens are inedible and should be left to ruminants that get more than one crack at chewing them. And, of course, long cooking is ruinous to tender, delicate greens. The art of cooking greens is matching the right green with the right cooking technique. It's exactly the same thought process and rationale behind braising tougher cuts of meat versus searing a tender steak.

I think that many people who love greens might love the potlikker even more. Those people are emotional and consecrated about potlikker. Rifts, tiffs, and full-bore hostilities can emerge over how to consume it. Is it served with the greens? Is it served separately like soup in a bowl or like tea in a porcelain cup? Is it sopped or sipped? Is the requisite cornbread dipped or crumbled into it? Yes.

# Melted Tuscan Kale

4 ounces pancetta or unsmoked bacon, chopped

1 cup very finely chopped onion

½ cup very finely chopped carrot

3 garlic cloves, chopped

3 to 4 cups chicken stock or one of the smoked stocks (page 180)

2 to 2 ½ pounds Tuscan kale, tough stems and ribs removed and shredded

1 teaspoon kosher salt

½ teaspoon ground black pepper

¼ teaspoon crushed red pepper flakes

There is a time and a place for crisp-tender vegetables. This is not it.

The kale is simmered until it is fully tender and bathed in concentrated broth that tastes like good vegetable soup. The kale is very moist but not submerged in potlikker. Although you can make this recipe with any sturdy green (mustard, turnip, collards), my favorite is kale, particularly Tuscan kale, which is also known as Lacinto kale, black kale, black cabbage, *cavolo nero*, or dinosaur kale. Tuscan kale is hearty and full flavored but rather mild, particularly when cooked with naturally sweet onions and carrots cut so finely that they nearly disappear into the sauce. You can omit the meat and cook the vegetables in ¼ cup of flavorful extra-virgin olive oil.

Both traditional Italian cooking and traditional southern cooking celebrate the depth of flavor that comes from slowly cooking sturdy vegetables, a technique that coaxes flavor from the pot through gentle persuasion, adroit handling, and persistent effort. In fact, I learned this recipe in an Umbrian farmhouse on a chilly late October evening. With the guidance of a local Italian chef, my cohorts and I cooked our supper on an open hearth. We simmered these greens in a pot hanging from a hook. We made plump links of fresh wild boar sausage and then roasted them in a cast-iron skillet nestled into the coals. Last, we formed a big, flat cake of bread that was remarkably like an oversized southern biscuit and baked it directly on the hearthstone. When it was time to eat, each of us ravenous diners tore off and split open a hunk of that crusty bread, tucked in a sizzling, juicy, garlicky link of sausage, and piled on the greens. We'd been laughing and carrying on as we worked, but when we took the first bites, the room went still. It was the best meal of my life that my grandmother did not cook.

MAKES 6 SERVINGS

1. Cook the pancetta in a large, heavy pot over medium heat until it renders its fat and the meat is crispy, about 15 minutes. Transfer the pancetta with a slotted spoon to a paper towel to drain, leaving the drippings in the pan.

2. Add the onion, carrot, and garlic and a pinch of salt. Cover and cook, stirring often, until the vegetables are completely soft but not browned, about 10 minutes.

3. Add the stock, kale, salt, pepper, and red pepper flakes and stir well. Bring to a boil, reduce the heat, cover the pot, and simmer until the kale is very tender, about 45 minutes.

4. Remove the lid, increase the heat to high and boil until the liquid reduces so that the kale is no longer floating, but still very moist, about 15 minutes. Stir in the reserved pancetta and check the seasoning. Serve hot.

# Potlikker Greens

2 to 2 ½ pounds collards or similar sturdy greens, washed and drained

4 tablespoons bacon fat, chicken fat, or extra-virgin olive oil

1 large onion, thinly sliced or finely diced (about 2 cups)

8 cups Smoked Pork Stock, Smoked Poultry Stock, or Smoked Vegetable Stock (recipes follow)

1 tablespoon cider vinegar

1 teaspoon kosher salt

½ teaspoon ground black pepper

1 dried hot pepper pod or generous pinch of crushed red pepper flakes (optional)

2 tablespoons sugar, cane syrup, or sorghum (optional)

Hot Pepper Vinegar (page 88), or hot sauce, for serving

To make top-notch potlikker greens, three things are crucial: the greens must be sturdy, the cooking liquid must be richly flavored and smoky, and the cooking must be low and slow. Beyond that, there are choices. The most popular candidate for potlikker greens is collards, particularly the ones picked after a heavy frost, when huge beads of impossibly cold dew collect on the surface and shine like diamonds. People say the frost sweetens the collards. It's true; the cold converts some of the starches to sugars and makes them more digestible. Other good choices for long cooking are large-leafed or slightly mature mustard greens, turnip greens, and kale. The leaves should be pliable and smell sweet with no yellowing or wilting.

Some people add heat to their greens with pepper pods, crushed red pepper flakes, ground cayenne, hot pepper vinegar, or some combination of these things. Some people sweeten their greens with a little (or a lot of) sugar, cane syrup, or sorghum. Go with what you know, or feel free to experiment.

Potlikker greens should be served with Real Skillet Cornbread (page 391).

MAKES 6 SERVINGS

1. Remove and discard the stems and tough part of the inner ribs of the greens by cutting them out with a knife or by stripping the leaves off the stems by hand. Working in batches, cut the leaves into manageable pieces. Stack a few leaves, with the largest ones on the bottom. Starting on a long side, roll the stack into a cylinder. Cut the cylinder crosswise into 1-inch strips. If the leaves are huge, stack the leaves and cut them into 1-inch wide strips (like slicing a roast) and then cut the stack of strips crosswise into 2-inch pieces, to create rectangles. To remove the inevitable hidden grit, swish the greens in a sink or large bowl of cool water, then let them sit in the water for a few minutes so that the grit can fall to the bottom of the sink. Lift the greens out of the water and let them drain, but you don't need to dry them.

2. Heat the fat in a large pot over medium heat. Add the onion and cook, stirring often, until softened, about 8 minutes.

3. Stir in the stock, greens, vinegar, salt, and pepper. Add the hot pepper and/ or sugar, if using. Bring to a boil, reduce the heat, and simmer gently until the greens are tender, at least 45 minutes, or longer if you want them even softer. They should be like velvet.

4. Remove the pot from the heat and let sit, covered, for 1 hour. Taste the potlikker and adjust the seasoning as needed. Reheat over medium heat and serve warm, doused with a little vinegar or hot sauce.

MAKE-AHEAD NOTE: Greens and potlikker are almost always better when made at least 1 day ahead. They seem to improve with age. Check the seasoning each time you reheat.

## SMOKED STOCKS

. . . . . . . . . . . . . . . . . . . . . . . . . . . . . . . . . . . . . . . . . . . . . . . . . . . . . .

Traditional potlikker starts with smoked pork stock made from hocks, bones, side meat, or bacon. Nothing else tastes like smoked pork, but if you choose not to use pork, you need to use another stock that delivers similar smokiness and depth of flavor. My first alternate choice is Smoked Poultry Stock made with smoked turkey wings simmered in chicken stock. You can also use Smoked Vegetable Stock. Meatless smoked stock is a challenge, but doable when generously seasoned with smoked paprika and smoked salt. The paprika and salt actually spend time in the smokehouse, so they'll bring that critical flavor and aroma to the pot. I also add these seasonings to my Smoked Pork Stock and Smoked Poultry Stock when the meat isn't as flavorful as I'd hoped.

These stocks can be used in other recipes as well, not just when making potlikker.

## Smoked Pork Stock

MAKES 2 QUARTS

1 pound smoked pork pieces, with or without bones (such as ham hocks, ham bones, pork shoulder, or very smoky bacon)

3 carrots, peeled and roughly chopped

2 celery stalks, roughly chopped

1 medium onion, quartered

1 bay leaf

4 large thyme sprigs

12 cups cold water

(1) Combine the pork, carrots, celery, onion, bay leaf, thyme sprigs, and water in a large stockpot. Bring to a boil, reduce the heat, partially cover the pot, and simmer until the liquid reduces to 8 cups and develops strong smoked pork flavor, about 3 hours.

(2) Strain the stock through a fine-mesh sieve into a large bowl. The stock can be used immediately, but for best results, let it cool to room temperature and then cover and refrigerate until chilled. Just before using or freezing, remove and discard the solidified fat from the stock. The stock can be refrigerated for up to 1 week or frozen in airtight containers for up to 6 months.

## Smoked Poultry Stock

MAKES 2 QUARTS

2 pounds smoked turkey wings and/or legs

3 carrots, peeled and roughly chopped

2 celery stalks, roughly chopped

1 medium onion, quartered

1 bay leaf

4 large thyme sprigs

12 cups chicken stock, preferably home-made (page 400)

(1) Combine the wings, carrots, celery, onion, bay leaf, thyme sprigs, and stock in a large stockpot. Bring to a boil, reduce the heat, partially cover the pot, and simmer until the liquid reduces to 8 cups, about 3 hours.

(2) Strain the stock through a fine-mesh sieve into a large bowl. The stock can be used immediately, but for best results, let it cool to room temperature and then cover and refrigerate until chilled. Just before using or freezing, remove the solidified fat from the stock. Discard the fat or save it to use in other recipes, such as in place of bacon drippings. The stock can be refrigerated for up to 1 week or frozen in airtight containers for up to 6 months.

## Smoked Vegetable Stock

MAKES 2 QUARTS

2 pieces Parmigiano-Reggiano cheese rind (about 3 ounces)

1½ cups smoked tomatoes (page 358) or canned fire-roasted crushed tomatoes

10 cups vegetable stock, preferably homemade (page 401)

1 teaspoon smoked paprika (*pimentón*), or to taste

1 teaspoon smoked salt, or to taste (see note)

(1) Combine the cheese rinds, tomatoes, and stock in a large stockpot. Bring to a boil, reduce the heat, partially cover the pot, and simmer until the liquid reduces to 8 cups, about 1 hour. Discard the rinds (or nibble on them).

(2) Season the stock with smoked paprika and smoked salt.

(3) Strain the stock through a fine-mesh sieve into a large bowl. The stock can be used immediately, but for best results, let it cool to room temperature and then cover and refrigerate until chilled. The stock can be refrigerated for up to 1 week or frozen in airtight containers for up to 6 months.

NOTE: Smoked salt is kosher or sea salt that has been smoked over wood. It is a good seasoning choice for meatless versions of recipes that are traditionally cooked with smoked meat. It's sold in well-stocked grocery stores, gourmet stores, and online. Be sure to buy real smoked salt, not artificially flavored salt.

# Creamed Collard and Country Ham
## Pot Pie with Cornmeal Pastry

4 thick bacon slices, cut crosswise into ¼-inch strips (about 4 ounces)

2 large onions, thinly sliced (about 3 cups)

4 cups chicken stock or one of the smoked stocks (page 180)

1 teaspoon kosher salt, plus more to taste

1 teaspoon sugar

½ teaspoon ground black pepper, plus more to taste

1 small red pepper pod, a pinch of crushed red pepper flakes, or a pinch of cayenne pepper

3 pounds collards, stems and tough ribs removed, leaves cut into thin ribbons

1 cup half-and-half

4 ounces chopped country ham

4 garlic cloves, coarsely chopped

3 tablespoons cornstarch

(continued on next page)

This is a triumvirate (and triumph) of southern traditional ingredients: greens, pig, and corn. The greens are cooked with ham, then thickened like creamed spinach and topped with cornmeal pastry. It looks like pot pie or savory cobbler, but this dish is rooted in the old custom of simmering cornmeal dumplings in potlikker. Dumplings were humble extenders, making a little bit go a little bit farther.

I love salty country ham in this dish, but you can substitute cooked sausage or spicy tasso. You can also use turkey bacon and poultry sausage if you prefer to not use pork.

MAKES 12 SERVINGS

(1) For the filling: Cook the bacon in a large, heavy pot over medium heat, stirring often, until it renders its fat and is crispy, about 15 minutes. Transfer with a slotted spoon to paper towels to drain, leaving the drippings in the pot.

(2) Add the onions and a pinch of salt to the pot. Stir to coat with the drippings and cook, stirring often, until softened, about 8 minutes. Stir in the stock, salt, sugar, black pepper, and red pepper and bring to a simmer. Add the collards a big handful at a time, stirring until they wilt before adding more. Reduce the heat to low, cover the pot, and simmer until tender, 30 to 45 minutes. Discard the pepper pod.

(3) Meanwhile, stir together the half-and-half, ham, and garlic in a small saucepan. Bring to a simmer over medium heat, then remove the pan from the heat, cover, and set aside to steep. When the collards are done, stir in the half-and-half mixture.

(4) Place the cornstarch in a small bowl and whisk in enough cold water to make a smooth paste and then pour into the collards. Bring to a low boil and cook, stirring constantly, until the liquid thickens to the consistency of thin gravy. Stir in the reserved bacon. Season with salt and pepper. Keep the collards warm over low heat, stirring occasionally.

(5) For the pastry: Preheat the oven to 375°F.

(6) Whisk together the flour, cornmeal, baking powder, and salt in a large bowl. Use a pastry blender or your fingertips to work in the butter until the pieces are no larger than grains of rice. If you press a little against your thumb, it should cling like a small leaf. Slowly add the half-and-half and stir with a fork until the dough comes together. Pour the pastry onto a lightly floured surface and knead gently only until smooth and no longer sticky, 4 or 5 turns. Roll or pat the pastry into a rectangle that is about ⅓-inch thick. Use a sharp knife or pastry wheel to cut the pastry into long strips about 1 ½-inches wide.

1 cup all-purpose flour

½ cup coarse stone-ground yellow cornmeal

2 ½ teaspoons baking powder

½ teaspoon kosher salt

4 tablespoons (½ stick) butter or lard, cut into small cubes and chilled

¾ cup half-and-half

Instant flour or additional cornmeal, for rolling

2 tablespoons butter, melted

½ teaspoon coarse salt or additional kosher salt

½ teaspoon coarsely ground black pepper

⑦ Spoon the warm collard filling into a 9 × 13-inch baking dish. Arrange the strips of pastry over the filling, leaving only about ⅛ inch of space between the strips. Trim the ends of the pastry as needed to make them fit. You might have a little left over. Lightly brush the pastry with the melted butter and sprinkle with the coarse salt and pepper.

⑧ Bake until the pastry is golden brown and the collards are bubbling, 30 to 35 minutes. Let the cobbler sit for 15 minutes before serving hot.

# JERUSALEM ARTICHOKES

**This is a good vegetable with a misleading name.** Jerusalem artichokes are neither from Jerusalem nor artichokes. These tubers are actually a member of the sunflower family, and their name is probably a derivative of *girasole*, the Italian word for sunflower, and *girasol*, a Spanish word that means "follow the sun." The association with sunflowers explains why they are sometimes marketed as sunchokes. In southern Louisiana they are known as tompinambours. By any name, they are intrepid growers that come back and flourish annually, to the point that some gardeners might wonder whether the towering plants will take over the garden.

A native of North America, Jerusalem artichokes were eaten by Native Americans, who both cultivated them and harvested the ones that grew wild along the eastern seaboard. Jerusalem artichokes were taken back to the Old World in the early 1600s by explorers who suspected they would be a hit back home. They were. Even now, Jerusalem artichokes are more popular in most of Europe than they are in the United States, although there are pockets of great devotion in communities across the South. Aficionados praise this vegetable's sweet, nutty crunch when raw and its earthy, silky smoothness when cooked. ■

# Jerusalem Artichoke Soup with Wild Mushrooms and Hazelnuts

**SOUP**

1 tablespoon white distilled or cider vinegar

1 ½ pounds well-scrubbed Jerusalem artichokes

2 tablespoons butter

1 cup chopped leeks (white and tender green parts), shallots, or sweet onion

½ cup chopped celery or celery root

3 ½ to 4 cups chicken, duck, or light-colored vegetable stock

1 teaspoon kosher salt

8 ounces russet potatoes, peeled and cut into 1-inch chunks (about 1 ½ cups)

1 small bay leaf

2 teaspoons chopped fresh thyme

¾ cup half-and-half

1 tablespoon Madeira, tawny port, or dry sherry

½ teaspoon ground black pepper

(continued on next page)

This is a sophisticated soup that is still homey and comforting. It's an ideal soup for cool autumn evenings. The sautéed wild mushroom and hazelnut mixture spooned into each portion echoes the earthy, yet slightly sweet and nutty flavor of the Jerusalem artichokes. It also provides a contrast in textures to the smooth, creamy soup and makes this beige soup a little prettier. Most so-called wild mushrooms are cultivated exotic varieties, not actually wild. Shiitakes are usually a safe bet, but take advantage of more interesting mushrooms if you have them. White button mushrooms are too anemic to do the job in this recipe. If you have any leftover mushroom mixture, spoon it onto cheese toasts made with blue cheese or a creamy washed-rind cheese such as Tallegio or Grayson by Meadow Creek Dairy in Galax, Virginia.

MAKES ABOUT 2 QUARTS

1. For the soup: Fill a medium bowl with cool water and add the vinegar. (This acidulated water keeps the artichokes from oxidizing and darkening when cut.) Peel the artichokes only if the skins are blemished and cut them into thin slices, dropping them into the water as you go.

2. Melt the butter in a large saucepan or small soup pot over medium heat. When the butter stops foaming, stir in the leeks and celery and a pinch of salt. Cook, stirring often, until the vegetables are soft, about 8 minutes. Stir in 3 ½ cups of the stock and the salt and potatoes.

3. Drain and quickly rinse the artichokes, then add them to the pot. Add the bay leaf and thyme. Bring to a boil, reduce the heat, and simmer partially covered until the artichokes and potatoes are very soft, about 30 minutes. Discard the bay leaf. Purée in a blender (working in batches to not fill the blender more than half full) and return to the pot, or purée the soup directly in the pot with an immersion blender. Stir in the half-and-half and Madeira. The soup should be very thick but not pasty, so add the rest of the stock or another splash of half-and-half if needed. Season with the pepper and more salt, if needed. Keep the soup warm over low heat, stirring occasionally.

2 tablespoons butter

8 ounces wild mush-
rooms, stemmed and
cut into ¼-inch slices

¼ cup peeled and
finely diced Jeru-
salem artichokes

¼ cup shelled, skinned,
and coarsely chopped
hazelnuts

2 tablespoons Madeira,
tawny port, or dry
sherry

¼ teaspoon freshly
grated nutmeg

1 teaspoon chopped
fresh thyme

1 tablespoon
finely chopped
flat-leaf parsley

Kosher salt and
ground black pepper

Porcini oil or hazelnut
oil, for drizzling
(optional)

④ For the mushrooms: Melt the butter in a large skillet over medium-high heat. When the butter stops foaming, add the mushrooms, making sure they are in a single layer in the skillet; cook them in batches if necessary. Stir the mushrooms briskly to coat them with butter. Sauté, stirring or shaking the skillet occasionally, until the mushrooms are browned and barely tender, about 4 minutes. Add the artichokes and hazelnuts and cook, stirring, for 1 minute. Add the Madeira and cook, stirring, until the liquid cooks away. Remove the skillet from the heat and stir in the nutmeg, thyme, and parsley. Season with a tiny bit of salt and pepper.

⑤ To serve, ladle the soup into serving bowls. (Shallow soup plates work well.) Spoon a portion of the mushroom mixture into the center of each serving. Drizzle a few drops of oil around the edge of the soup, if using, and serve straightaway.

WHAT ELSE WORKS? You can use roasted or steamed chestnuts in place of the hazelnuts, although they will not be as crunchy.

# Jerusalem Artichoke and Celery Root Rémoulade

1 pound well-scrubbed Jerusalem artichokes

2 tablespoons fresh lemon juice

1 pound celery root (celeriac), peeled

½ teaspoon kosher salt

Pinch of sugar

¼ cup mayonnaise, preferably homemade (page 317)

2 tablespoons Dijon mustard, preferably whole-grain

3 tablespoons finely chopped flat-leaf parsley

1 tablespoon finely chopped cornichons (optional)

1 tablespoon drained capers (optional)

Rémoulade can refer to a sauce, a salad, or a way to serve cold shrimp. In this recipe, it's a slawlike salad like you'd find in a little side-street bistro in France or Switzerland. Even though it contains a bit of mayonnaise, rémoulade seems to clean the palate, so it's often served before or alongside rich, fatty foods such as beef short ribs or cheese fondue.

The most common rémoulade salad is made with celery root alone, but the nutty crunch of the Jerusalem artichokes fits right in. These preternaturally knobby and gnarly vegetables have an affinity for one another. The bumpy, irregular surface of the Jerusalem artichokes can be maddening to peel. I suggest first cutting off all those little bumps to create smoother sides and then starting to peel. There is precious little flesh to be lost in all those nodules, certainly not enough to warrant the time it would take to pare them.

MAKES 6 SERVINGS

1. Peel the artichokes and cut them into very thin julienne strips (like matchsticks) on a vegetable slicer or grate them in a food processor using the coarsest shredding disc. (If the vegetables are finely grated, they will turn mushy.) As soon as they are cut, place them in a large bowl and toss with the lemon juice so that they will not oxidize and darken. Cut the celery root the same way and add it to the bowl. Add the salt and sugar and toss well.

2. Whisk together the mayonnaise, mustard, and parsley in a small bowl. Add the cornichons and capers, if using. Pour the mayonnaise mixture over the vegetables and stir well to coat.

3. Cover and refrigerate until chilled, at least 1 hour. Stir well and check the seasoning before serving lightly chilled or at room temperature.

# Pickled Jerusalem Artichoke Relish

2 ½ cups cider
vinegar, divided

2 ½ pounds fresh
Jerusalem artichokes,
scrubbed and trimmed
of blemishes

1 cup sugar

1 ½ teaspoons kosher salt

½ teaspoon ground
black pepper

1 tablespoon ground
turmeric

2 teaspoons dry mustard

1 teaspoon celery seed

2 ½ teaspoons yellow
mustard seed

1 teaspoon
coriander seed

1 large red onion,
thinly sliced or
coarsely chopped

2 large red bell peppers,
thinly sliced or
coarsely chopped

I contend that this is among the finest of the South's many fine relishes. It has a cult following in some communities, particularly around the holidays, when jars of relish are presented as gifts of great value, not unlike gold, frankincense, and myrrh. Recipients sometimes hide and hoard jars of this sweet, tangy, crunchy relish as a bulwark against bland winter food, yet nothing compares to the sneaky pleasure of eating it straight out of the jar while home alone or hiding out in the car so you won't get caught and have to feel guilty about not sharing.

For the best texture, leave the pieces of artichoke, onion, and pepper fairly large and nubby, either diced or thinly sliced. Finely grated vegetables are too mushy and detract from the relish's distinctive crunch.

The artichokes are not peeled, so they must be thoroughly cleaned. They are notorious for harboring sand and dirt in their bumpy, irregular skins. Wash them repeatedly and check them carefully. I know people who actually put them into mesh laundry bags used for lingerie and run them through the rinse cycle in their washing machines. Whatever works.

MAKES 4 PINTS

1. Have ready four 1-pint jars or two 1-quart jars that have been sterilized in boiling water or run through the dishwasher on the hottest cycle. The jars should have sterilized tight-fitting lids. The jars and lids don't have to stay hot, but they must stay sterile.

2. Fill a large bowl with cold water and stir in ½ cup of the vinegar. (This acidulated water will keep the artichokes from darkening after they are cut.) Coarsely chop or thinly slice the artichokes by hand or in a food processor fitted with the french-fry cut or slicing disc. Immediately transfer the cut artichokes into the bowl of vinegar water and set aside.

3. Bring the remaining 2 cups of vinegar and the sugar, salt, pepper, turmeric, dry mustard, celery seed, mustard seed, and coriander seed to a boil in a very large pot over medium-high heat, stirring to dissolve the sugar. Add the onion and peppers. Drain the artichokes and add them to the pot. Stir well and return to a boil. Cook until the vegetables are crisp-tender, 5 to 10 minutes, stirring occasionally. Remove the pot from the heat.

4. Pack the relish into the prepared jars. Close the jars and set aside to cool to room temperature. Store in the refrigerator for up to 3 months.

# MELONS

**Melons go all the way back to the beginning in the South.** These fruits are technically vegetables, related to other trailing, vine-bound gourds such as squash and cucumbers. Melons were one of the first foods cultivated by the Native Americans, and most of the melons that have flourished in the South were native or developed from native rootstock. Melons were probably the first crop manipulated through crossbreeding to enhance flavor and aroma.

Two of the most popular southern melons have a bit of a story. First, the netted melon that we call a cantaloupe is usually a muskmelon, but we've called them by the wrong name so long that it seems fixed by now. Although many varieties nearly faded into obscurity because of the popularity of commercial cantaloupes, a bounty of melons in assorted shapes and sizes are now returning to our gardens and tables.

The other storied melon is the watermelon, which is strongly associated with the South even though it didn't originate here. Native to Central Africa, watermelons grew so successfully in the South that they were more often a field crop than a kitchen garden planting. Perhaps watermelons are so beloved in the South because almost nothing tastes better on a scorching day than a chilled melon. Even before refrigeration, the underside of a ripe watermelon felt cooler than the air around it and promised refreshment. Mark Twain said it best in *Pudd'nhead Wilson*: "[The watermelon] is chief of the world's luxuries, king by the grace of God over all the fruit of the earth. When one has tasted it, he knows what the angels eat. It was not a Southern watermelon that Eve took; we know it because she repented." ■

# Chilled Honeydew Soup with Coconut-Cilantro Pesto

## SOUP

6 cups honeydew melon chunks

½ cup well-stirred canned coconut milk (regular or lite)

2 tablespoons light, floral honey (such as acacia, tupelo, or orange blossom), or to taste

¼ cup fresh lime juice

¼ teaspoon kosher salt

## PESTO

6 tablespoons fresh lemon juice

4 teaspoons sugar

2 tablespoons peeled and finely grated fresh ginger

2 teaspoons chopped garlic

1 teaspoon finely chopped serrano chile, or to taste

2 tablespoons dried unsweetened coconut or sweetened flaked coconut

¼ teaspoon kosher salt

2 cups firmly packed, coarsely chopped cilantro leaves

The pale green color and enticing floral aroma of perfectly ripe honeydew is ideal for this soup, although any melon fragrant enough to perfume your kitchen will work. Since the soup is puréed, a dead-ripe melon that is too ripe to eat out of hand works well.

The soup is good, but the refreshing Coconut-Cilantro Pesto puts it over the top. The use of coconut has a long history in southern recipes. Because of our extensive coastline dotted with deep ports, we've long received exotic fruits and vegetables shipped in from tropical climes. This pesto recipe has roots in India, where it would be called chutney. I call it pesto because that is what it looks like and because the word "chutney" means something quite different to most Americans.

I once stirred some of this pesto into cooled rice to make an impromptu rice salad with a few chunks of fresh pineapple and mango thrown in for good measure.

This soup is wonderful served with Watermelon and Tomato Salad with Fresh Herbs (page 192).

MAKES 4 SERVINGS

1. For the soup: Purée the melon in a blender. Add the coconut milk, honey, lime juice, and salt. Pour into a bowl or large jar, cover, and refrigerate until chilled, at least 2 hours.

2. For the pesto: Place (in the order listed) the lemon juice, sugar, ginger, garlic, chile, coconut, and salt and 1 cup of the cilantro in a blender and blend just until ground; do not liquefy. Add the rest of the cilantro and blend just until the cilantro is incorporated and the pesto is a thick paste. Scrape into a bowl or glass jar, cover, and refrigerate for up to 2 days.

3. Serve the soup cold, topped with a generous spoonful of Coconut-Cilantro Pesto.

WHAT ELSE WORKS? You can use fresh spearmint in place of some of the cilantro.

# Melon Tabbouleh

½ cup fine or medium bulgur (cracked wheat)

2 tablespoons extra-virgin olive oil

2 tablespoons fresh lemon juice

1 garlic clove, finely chopped

¾ teaspoon ground cinnamon

½ teaspoon ground cumin

1 cup sugar snaps (about 4 ounces)

1 ½ cups small melon cubes

¼ cup thinly sliced scallions (white and tender green parts)

½ cup finely chopped flat-leaf parsley

Kosher salt and ground black pepper, to taste

Tabbouleh is a brightly flavored salad made with cracked wheat, vegetables, and herbs. Most recipes call for fresh tomatoes, but this version features melon instead. Any of the netted melons will work, particularly the old varieties that are a little less sweet and truer to their gourd and cucumber cousins. Good ole cantaloupe is fine, too.

Tabbouleh originated in Lebanon. It is an example of an ethnic dish that found its place on southern tables in some communities. Waves of Lebanese families poured into the South, particularly into Mississippi and Louisiana, around the turn of the last century. Many Lebanese became the grocers and restaurateurs in their towns. Immigrating families often continued to prepare familiar dishes from their old country, sometimes adapting them to include new ingredients and serving them alongside the dishes they discovered in their new country. Southern food has always included multicultural fare, so a beloved local or regional specialty with ethnic roots can be authentically southern even when it isn't universally southern.

MAKES 4 TO 6 SERVINGS

1. Put the bulgur in a large bowl and cover with boiling water. Cover the bowl tightly with plastic wrap and let sit until the bulgur is plump and tender, about 30 minutes. Drain in a mesh strainer, pressing with the back of a wooden spoon to squeeze out as much water as possible. Pour the bulgur back into the bowl. Stir in the oil, lemon juice, garlic, cinnamon, and cumin and let sit until the bulgur cools to room temperature, stirring occasionally.

2. Fill a large bowl with ice water. Bring a small saucepan of water to a boil. Add ½ teaspoon kosher salt per cup of water. Add the sugar snaps and cook until crisp-tender, about 2 minutes. Use a slotted spoon to immediately transfer into the ice water to stop the cooking and set the color. When cool, drain, pat dry, and cut on the diagonal into ¼-inch strips. It's okay if a few whole peas roll out. Add the sugar snaps and any escaped peas to the bulgur mixture.

3. Stir in the melon, scallions, and parsley. Season with salt and pepper. Cover and let sit at room temperature for 1 hour before serving.

WHAT ELSE WORKS? You can use peaches or tomatoes in place of the melon. You can use blanched garden peas or snow peas in place of the sugar snaps.

## Melon Granita with Port Wine

6 tablespoons water

4 to 6 tablespoons sugar

1 small Charantais or other sweet, fragrant melon, cut into chunks (about 4 cups)

1 tablespoon fresh lemon juice

1 tablespoon light corn syrup

Pinch of kosher salt

Ruby port wine, for serving

There are several old southern recipes that dress cantaloupe and other similar melons with port wine, a practice that traces back to England. In this recipe, that flavor pairing comes forward and lands in a thoroughly modern icy granita topped with a drizzle of the wine. It's like a very sophisticated snow cone with syrup. To serve this to children, leave off the port and perhaps use a splash of grape juice instead. For best results, use a fully ripe and delectable Charantais melon or another sweet melon with a heavenly fragrance.

MAKES 1 QUART

1 Bring the water and sugar to a boil in a small saucepan, stirring to dissolve the sugar. Adjust the sugar according to the sweetness of the melon and personal preference. (Keep in mind that freezing subdues sweetness, so make the base a little sweeter than you want the finished granita to be.) Cool the sugar syrup to room temperature.

2 Put the melon in the bowl of a food processor fitted with the metal blade. Add the sugar syrup, lemon juice, corn syrup, and salt. Process until smooth. Pour the purée into a shallow container and freeze until the edges are slushy, about 30 minutes. Stir with a fork every 30 minutes, until the base has frozen into a mass of fluffy ice shards, about 1 ½ hours total.

3 When ready to serve, you can control the size of the ice crystals. For big snow-cone crystals, rake up the frozen base with a fork. For smooth crystals that are more like sorbet, quickly buzz the frozen base in a food processor. Serve at once, drizzled with a little port, about 2 teaspoons per serving.

## Watermelon and Tomato Salad with Fresh Herbs

4 cups bite-sized watermelon cubes (drained of any standing juice)

2 cups seeded and diced tomatoes

½ small Vidalia or other sweet onion, halved lengthwise and cut into thin strips (about ½ cup)

(continued on next page)

Perhaps the best recipe for ripe watermelon is no recipe at all. Simply slice and dig in. However, watermelon is also a great ingredient in a summer salad. This dish unites three summertime favorites: icy cold melon, vine-ripened tomatoes, and fresh herbs.

Ricotta salata starts as the same soft, mild cheese that is often used in lasagna or manicotti, but the cheese maker presses and molds the cheese until it is firm enough to slice. The flavor is still mild, but concentrated and a little salty. It remains firm in moist salads such as this. Look for it in the cheese department of well-stocked grocery stores. You can substitute well-drained feta cheese, but it will be considerably more salty.

¾ cup ricotta salata
cheese cut into
very small cubes

3 tablespoons extra-
virgin olive oil

2 tablespoons fresh
lime juice

2 tablespoons
chopped fresh mint

2 tablespoons chopped
flat-leaf parsley

2 tablespoons
chopped fresh basil

1 teaspoon kosher salt

½ teaspoon black pepper

1 teaspoon sugar

Leftover salad does not keep well because the vegetables get watery and the herbs get soggy. Pour any leftovers into a blender and purée into watermelon gazpacho. Chill it thoroughly and check the seasoning before serving.

MAKES 4 TO 6 SERVINGS

(1) Gently stir together the watermelon, tomato, onion, cheese, oil, and lime juice in a large bowl. Cover and refrigerate until chilled, at least 1 hour. (Normally tomatoes are not good when chilled, but it works here.)

(2) Add the mint, parsley, basil, salt, pepper, and sugar and serve right away.

WHAT ELSE WORKS? You can use cubes of fresh pineapple or peaches in place of the watermelon, particularly those little hard green peaches that never seem to ripen.

1½ cups cucumber
cubes, peeled and
seeded if necessary

1½ cups seeded
watermelon cubes

1½ cups melon cubes

1½ cups fresh pine-
apple cubes

6 tablespoons
fresh lime juice

1 teaspoon ground
ancho chile or chili
powder, or to taste

Coarse or kosher
salt, to taste

## Street Salad with Chile and Lime

In my town, we have a large community of immigrants from Mexico and Central America, and the local street food scene is better as a result. A few years ago, I was wandering through a local outdoor festival and came across a vendor selling paper cones of this juicy, refreshing salad. I love to see what cooks with backgrounds that are different from mine do with our local ingredients. The mingling of old and new ensures that southern cuisine will continue to evolve and endure.

The recipe is very flexible, so mix and match the components that appeal to you. Although it is easier to serve as a salad when you cut the ingredients into cubes, the traditional style is to cut the ingredients into spears to eat with your fingers. Squeeze lime wedges over the fruit and sprinkle with the ground chile and salt, like putting ketchup and salt on fries.

When selecting limes for juice, keep in mind that the paler the lime, the more juice inside. Save those bright green limes for zest.

MAKES 4 TO 6 SERVINGS

(1) Mix the cucumber, watermelon, melon, and pineapple cubes in a large bowl. Cover and refrigerate until well chilled.

(2) Just before serving, pour the lime juice over the fruit, sprinkle with the ground chile and salt, and toss to coat. Serve chilled.

# OKRA

**Okra is defended and defamed with equal passion.** Although certain recipes and meals are incomplete without okra, its inclusion is incomprehensible to people who just don't like it or just won't give it a try.

Originally from Africa, okra wound up in gardens and kitchens not only in the American South but in temperate zones around the world. Many of the South's iconic dishes would never have been created without the kitchen wisdom of the African cooks who knew and grew okra.

A common use of okra is to thicken gumbo (although even a cursory look at gumbo recipes reveals that that's not a given), but southerners cook okra pods in nearly every way imaginable, except for the ones they pickle. Although they aren't as popular as the pods, okra leaves and flower buds are also edible. In a few high-concept restaurants, okra seeds are served under the guise of okra "caviar."

Okra plants belong to the mallow family. One look at okra blossoms confirms their botanical relation to flowering hibiscus and hollyhocks. An old southern anecdote tells that some gardeners planted extra okra and hollyhocks near outhouses because the plants would tower over the surrounding vegetation, marking the spot and preventing anyone from having to ask the indelicate question of where the facilities were located. Instead of saying they were going to "powder their noses," ladies could excuse themselves by saying they were going to look at the blossoms. ■

## Skillet Okra

1 pound whole small okra pods, stem ends trimmed to within ¼ inch of the pod

3 tablespoons extra-virgin olive oil

Kosher salt and ground black pepper, to taste

This is the fastest and easiest way I know to cook okra, pure and simple. There are no issues with stringiness because the pods are cooked whole. There's nothing to interfere with the flavor of the vegetable. There's no deep-frying that could kick up a dust of stereotypes about southerners frying everything. The okra is cooked in olive oil instead of bacon drippings. This is okra as free of discord as it is going to get.

Okra has a natural mucilaginous nature that has been described in words that range from delicate to disgusting. Let's call it goo. To avoid releasing the goo, don't cut into the pod when trimming the stem. That pulls the plug, so to speak. Funny how some people cringe at the notion of okra goo but turn right around and suck down raw oysters.

MAKES 4 TO 6 SERVINGS

1. The okra must be very dry, so pat it dry if necessary. Heat the oil in a large, heavy skillet (preferably cast-iron) over high heat until shimmering hot. Add the okra and cook, gently shaking the skillet to roll it around to cook evenly, until the pods are browned on all sides, about 5 minutes. The okra might hiss and pop a little.

2. Remove the skillet from the heat, cover, and let sit for 5 minutes. Season with salt and pepper and serve straightaway.

## Okra Tempura with Comeback Sauce or Pickled Okra Rémoulade

Southerners have perfected the art of deep-frying, but so have the Japanese, as evidenced by their light hand with tempura. In this recipe, classic fried okra becomes light and airy by trading the traditional cornmeal dredge for tempura batter. Either rice flour or cornstarch will help the batter cling to the okra, but using rice flour keeps that whole southern rice and okra thing alive. You can find rice flour in Asian markets and some grocery stores, but you can make your own by pulverizing uncooked white rice in a spice grinder or small food processor.

In addition to being a great side dish, this okra makes an interesting appetizer when served with a creamy dipping sauce, such as the Comeback Sauce or Pickled Okra Rémoulade.

For an outrageous companion to the okra and a fine thing in its own right, try tempura bacon. Cook 2-inch lengths of sliced bacon in a skillet over medium heat until they are lightly browned but still pliable, then drain well and pat dry. Dip the bacon in the same batter used for the okra and fry until the pieces are golden and crisp, about 6 minutes. Better count on several pieces per person.

1 pound okra pods, stem ends trimmed to within ¼ inch of the pod

½ cup fine rice flour or cornstarch

Vegetable oil, for frying

1 cup all-purpose flour

1 teaspoon kosher salt, plus more for sprinkling

1 large egg

1 ¼ cups sparkling water or club soda, chilled

¾ cup ice water

1. The okra must be very dry, so pat it dry if necessary. Short, slender okra pods can be left whole. Larger pods should be cut so that the okra will get done during the quick frying. You can cut the pods crosswise into ¾-inch rounds to make little okra balls that will look like beignets, or lengthwise into thin strips that will look like french fries. Lightly and evenly coat the okra in the rice flour, shaking off the excess. Set aside in a single layer.

2. Pour oil to a depth of 2 inches in a large, deep skillet (preferably cast-iron). Heat over medium-high heat to 350°F on a deep-fry thermometer. If you do not have a thermometer, test the temperature by dropping a pinch of flour into the hot oil. It should sizzle immediately and slowly start to brown without popping or spitting. Set a large wire rack inside a rimmed baking sheet, cover the rack with paper towels, and set near the stove to use for draining the okra.

3. While the oil is heating, whisk together the all-purpose flour and salt in a medium bowl. In a small bowl, whisk the egg until the white and yolk are mixed and then whisk in the sparkling water and ice water. Pour the egg mixture into the flour mixture and whisk just until blended; the batter will be a little lumpy, like pancake batter. Use the batter immediately because the contrast between the cold batter and the hot oil makes the coating light and crisp.

4. Working in batches, dip the okra in the batter, letting the excess drip off. Gently lower the okra into the hot oil. The okra must have room to float freely, so do not overfill the skillet. Cook, rolling and turning the pieces as needed, until golden brown on all sides, 1 to 3 minutes total, depending on the size of the okra. Transfer with a slotted spoon or strainer to the paper towels to drain. The oil tends to get hotter with each batch, so adjust the heat as necessary to keep the oil at the proper temperature. Skim out any floating bits of escaped batter between batches so that they will not burn and spoil the oil.

5. Sprinkle the hot okra with salt and serve hot.

WHAT ELSE WORKS? You can use this batter to fry onion rings or strips, thinly sliced shallots, whole baby summer squash, zucchini sticks, whole snap beans, mushrooms, and asparagus spears.

## Comeback Sauce

⅔ cup mayonnaise

⅓ cup chili sauce

¼ cup vegetable oil

2 tablespoons grated or finely chopped onion

2 garlic cloves, finely chopped

1½ teaspoons paprika

2 teaspoons Worcestershire sauce

1 teaspoon hot sauce, or to taste

2 tablespoons lemon juice

½ teaspoon ground black pepper

¾ teaspoon dry mustard

¾ teaspoon kosher salt

Several establishments claim to have invented this legendary sauce, but it's pretty clear that it originated in the restaurants operated by Greek families in Jackson, Mississippi. Like many beloved regional recipes, there are numerous variations, with each cook adding a personal touch and declaring victory. Like barbecue sauce, the type of sauce that delights some people appalls others. There are nearly as many spellings for "comeback" as there as variations, but the sauce got its name because after one taste you'll be sure to come back for more.

The concoction is similar to Thousand Island dressing and tartar sauce. It can be used as a salad dressing, but it reigns supreme as a dipping sauce for pretty much anything fried. In many Delta eateries, you'll get a bowl of comeback sauce and a basket of crackers as soon as you sit down at the table.

MAKES ABOUT 2 CUPS

Whisk together all of the ingredients in a large bowl until well mixed. Cover and refrigerate until chilled. Store covered and refrigerated for up to 1 week.

## Pickled Okra Rémoulade

¾ cup mayonnaise

2 tablespoons Creole mustard

1 teaspoon finely grated lemon zest

1 tablespoon fresh lemon juice or brine from the okra

¼ cup drained, finely chopped pickled okra

3 tablespoons chopped scallions (white and tender green parts)

½ teaspoon hot sauce, or to taste

Pinch of kosher salt

The word "rémoulade" can mean more than one thing, but this is a chunky mayonnaise-based sauce used for dipping. Most sauce rémoulade recipes call for dill pickles or capers, but you can change the sauce's personality by using chopped pickled okra (or other pickles, such as bread-and-butter) instead. If your pickled okra is already peppery hot, you can tone down the seasoning.

MAKES ABOUT 1 ¼ CUPS

Whisk together the mayonnaise, mustard, lemon zest, and lemon juice in a small bowl. Use a rubber spatula to fold in the okra and scallions. Season with the hot sauce and salt. Cover and refrigerate until chilled. Store covered and refrigerated for up to 1 week.

## Oven-Toasted Okra

1 pound tender
okra pods

1 tablespoon
butter, melted

3 tablespoons extra-
virgin olive oil

1 cup plain dry
bread crumbs

¼ teaspoon paprika

½ teaspoon kosher salt,
plus more to taste

¼ teaspoon ground
black pepper

Proper, honest deep-frying can be a fine thing, yet it's not for everyone. This is another way to make okra toasty brown and lightly crisped. The crust is light, so you can still taste the okra. These delicate, crispy pieces of okra make an interesting "crouton" for a summer salad. Cornmeal is the traditional coating for fried okra, but dry bread crumbs are a better choice for this recipe because the cornmeal never loses its raw taste with this cooking method.

MAKES 4 TO 6 SERVINGS

1. Preheat the oven to 400°F.
2. Trim the stem ends of the okra to within ¼ inch of the pod. Leave very small pods whole. Cut larger pods into ½-inch rounds.
3. Stir together the butter and oil in a small bowl. Stir together the crumbs, paprika, salt, and pepper on a plate.
4. Working with a few pieces at a time, dip the okra in the butter mixture and then toss in the crumbs until they are lightly and evenly coated. Shake off the excess crumbs and arrange the okra in a single layer on a rimmed baking sheet.
5. Bake until the crust is lightly browned and the okra is tender, about 15 minutes for sliced okra and 20 minutes for whole pods. Sprinkle with a little more salt and serve hot.

# Okra Fritters

4 bacon slices, cut crosswise into ¼-inch strips (about 4 ounces)

⅔ cup finely chopped Vidalia or other sweet onion

2 ½ cups very thinly sliced okra (about 8 ounces)

1 large egg

1 cup well-shaken buttermilk

1 cup fine or medium stone-ground cornmeal

1 teaspoon sugar

¼ teaspoon cayenne pepper, or to taste

1 teaspoon kosher salt

Vegetable oil, for pan-frying

These tender little cornmeal fritters are studded with okra, onion, and bacon. They remind me of both old-fashioned cornmeal-crusted fried okra and hush-puppies. Although they are best served hot, people will nibble on any leftovers even when they cool. My daughter and I have been known to eat them stone-cold straight out of the fridge on a hot summer night. The fritters are delicious served with Tomato Jam (page 354) or a couple of fat drops of hot sauce. See page 106 for tips on pan-frying.

MAKES 24 FRITTERS, OR 6 TO 8 SERVINGS

1. Preheat the oven to 200°F. Set a wire rack inside a large rimmed baking sheet lined with aluminum foil and place in the oven.

2. Cook the bacon in a heavy skillet over medium heat, stirring occasionally, until crisp, about 10 minutes. Transfer with a slotted spoon to paper towels to drain, leaving the drippings in the skillet.

3. Add the onion and okra to the skillet and stir to coat in the drippings. Cook over medium heat, stirring, until they begin to soften, about 5 minutes. Remove from the heat, stir in the bacon, and set aside.

4. Whisk the egg and buttermilk in a medium bowl until the white and yolk are blended. Whisk in the cornmeal, sugar, cayenne, and salt until smooth. Stir in the okra mixture.

5. Wipe the skillet clean, then add oil to a depth of ¼ inch. Heat over medium-high heat until shimmering hot. Working in batches, spoon 6 rounded table-spoons of batter into the hot oil. If the first fritter does not sizzle around the edges immediately, the oil is not hot enough and the fritters will be greasy. Cook the fitters until they are firm and golden brown on the bottom, turn them over, and cook the other side, about 2 minutes per side. Adjust the temperature to keep the oil hot. Transfer the fritters to the rack in the oven to keep them warm. (The rack lets the warm air circulate around the fritters, which keeps them from getting soggy.) Use a slotted spoon to skim out any debris that's left in the oil between batches because this will eventually burn and ruin the oil. Continue with the rest of the batter. Serve the fritters hot, although they're not bad at room temperature or even lightly chilled.

WHAT ELSE WORKS? You can replace 1 cup of the okra with diced shrimp.

MAKE-AHEAD NOTE: The bacon, onion, and okra mixture can be made 1 day ahead. Store covered and refrigerated. Stir well before using.

## Shrimp, Andouille, and Okra Gumbo with Hands-Free Roux

1 tablespoon vegetable oil

12 ounces andouille sausage, cut crosswise into ¼-inch slices

½ cup Hands-Free Roux (recipe follows)

1 cup chopped onion

½ cup cored and chopped green bell pepper

½ cup thinly sliced celery

4 garlic cloves, finely chopped

2 cups chicken stock or faux shrimp stock (see note)

1 cup canned crushed tomatoes or diced tomatoes in thick purée

2 cups sliced fresh okra

1 teaspoon kosher salt, plus more to taste

½ teaspoon ground black pepper, plus more to taste

¼ teaspoon cayenne pepper, plus more to taste

2 teaspoons chopped fresh thyme

2 small bay leaves

1 pound medium (31 to 35 count) shrimp, peeled and deveined

¼ cup finely chopped flat-leaf parsley

Hot, freshly cooked long-grain white rice, sliced scallions, and a bottle of hot sauce, for serving

There are as many kinds of gumbo as there are kinds of soup. It can be dicey to discuss gumbo in certain parts of the South because people are fiercely loyal to gumbo the way it's made where they live. I come from the mountain South, and we were not gumbo people. I can't compare my gumbo to my grandmother's, so I've tried to figure it out on my own. At this point, I do not use filé because I cannot get fresh, authentic filé where I live. I use roux that is the color of milk chocolate and I add it early in the recipe instead of near the end. I use sausage and seafood. If it's nothing like the gumbo you love, no offense intended.

MAKES ABOUT 2 QUARTS

1. Heat the oil in a small Dutch oven (preferably enameled cast iron) over medium-high heat. Add the sausage and cook, stirring frequently, until browned, about 5 minutes. Use a slotted spoon to transfer the sausage into a bowl.

2. Add the roux to the pan and heat until bubbling. Stir in the onion, bell pepper, celery, and garlic and cook, stirring continuously, until the vegetables begin to soften, about 8 minutes.

3. Slowly add the stock, whisking until smooth. Bring to a boil and stir in the tomatoes, okra, salt, black pepper, cayenne, thyme, and bay leaves. Reduce the heat, cover the pot, and simmer for 20 minutes.

4. Remove the pot from the heat, stir in the sausage, shrimp, and parsley. Cover and let sit until the shrimp are opaque, about 10 minutes.

5. Discard the bay leaves and check the seasoning. Serve hot, ladled over the rice and sprinkled with scallions and hot sauce.

NOTE: You can make faux shrimp stock by enriching the chicken stock with the shrimp shells. Rinse the shells under cold running water and drain well. Toast the shells in a medium saucepan over medium-high heat, stirring constantly, until they turn pink, about 1 minute. Stir in the chicken stock and simmer for 20 minutes. Strain and discard the solids. Use the stock soon; cool, cover, and refrigerate for up to 3 days; or transfer into an airtight container to freeze for up to 3 months.

# Hands-Free Roux

1 cup vegetable oil

1 cup all-purpose flour

I was not raised in the gumbo tradition. I did not try to make roux until I was mostly grown, and I was sore afraid. I suspected that learning to make roux was like learning to speak a foreign language without an accent; if you weren't immersed before age five, you'd never do it right. I was wrong. This easy technique changed my mind. The roux bakes in the oven with minimal stirring. There's no standing over the stove stirring nonstop for upward of an hour, dodging salvos of blistering hot fat. Someone described the technique to me a few years ago during an odyssey through the Delta, and I am forever grateful. The method works like a charm every time and brings roux within the reach of any cook, even those of us who were not raised in the realm of roux.

This recipe will make more roux than you need for one batch of gumbo, but you can freeze the rest in portions in airtight containers for up to three months, ready to pull out for the next batch of gumbo.

MAKES ABOUT 1 CUP

1. Preheat the oven to 350°F.
2. Whisk together the oil and flour until smooth in a large cast-iron skillet. Bake, stirring every 15 minutes to keep it from scorching around the edge, until the roux is the desired color, from the color of peanut butter all the way to the color of rich mahogany, from 45 to 90 minutes. The darker the roux, the deeper the flavor, but the less thickening power. I usually stop mine at the color of milk chocolate.
3. Carefully transfer the roux into a bowl to cool to room temperature. If left in the hot skillet, it will continue to darken as it cools.

# Creole Potato Salad for Gumbo

2 pounds medium red potatoes, scrubbed well and cut into large, bite-sized chunks

¾ cup mayonnaise

¼ cup Creole mustard

2 tablespoons cider vinegar

1 teaspoon kosher salt

½ teaspoon ground black pepper

2 hard-cooked eggs, chopped

¼ cup thinly sliced scallions (white and tender green parts)

¼ cup finely chopped celery

¼ cup finely chopped green bell pepper

If you think there are raging debates on how to make gumbo, just ask people in Louisiana how to serve that gumbo. Some people eat it straight up. Most people ladle it over rice. But there are a few people who serve gumbo with potato salad, either under the gumbo (in place of or alongside the rice) or plopped on top. For others, the potato salad is a side item, like that little paper cup of slaw on a barbecue plate. After input from a good friend who is an expert on gumbo and NOLA foodways, I offer this recipe for a type of Creole potato salad. Do with it what you will.

MAKES 6 TO 8 SERVINGS

1. Place the potatoes in a large pot of cold water. Bring to a boil and add ½ teaspoon kosher salt per cup of water. Reduce the heat and cook at a low boil until the potatoes are tender, about 15 minutes. Drain well, transfer into a large bowl, and set aside to cool to room temperature.

2. In a small bowl, whisk together the mayonnaise, mustard, vinegar, salt, and pepper; pour over the potatoes and mix well. Crush a few of the potatoes with the spoon so that the finished texture is midway between chunky and mashed. Add the eggs, scallions, celery, and bell pepper and mix well. Check the seasoning and add more salt if needed.

# Okra in Spiced Tomatoes

¼ cup vegetable oil

1 ½ cups finely
chopped onion

1 tablespoon finely
chopped garlic

1 tablespoon peeled
and grated fresh ginger

2 teaspoons ground cumin

2 teaspoons ground
coriander

½ teaspoon whole yellow
or brown mustard seed

½ teaspoon ground
cinnamon

½ cup chicken stock
or water

2 cups peeled, seeded,
and diced fresh toma-
toes or 1 (15-ounce)
can diced tomatoes

1 tablespoon packed dark
or light brown sugar

1 ½ pounds okra pods,
small ones left whole
and large ones halved
or quartered lengthwise

1 teaspoon kosher salt

¼ teaspoon cayenne
pepper, or to taste

½ teaspoon ground
Grains of Paradise
or black pepper

3 tablespoons fresh
lemon juice

Hot, freshly cooked
rice or grits (page 392),
for serving (optional)

This recipe seasons classic southern okra and tomatoes with aromatic spices often found in Indian cuisine. Although okra is closely associated with the American South, people in India eat more okra than anyone else. They call the long, slender pods "lady fingers." Both cultures have recipes that cook okra with tomatoes, a very good idea since the acidic tomato softens the okra pods. Served over Creamy Stone-Ground Grits (page 392), this makes a great summer supper.

MAKES 6 SERVINGS

1. Heat the oil in a large skillet over medium heat. Add the onion and cook, stirring, until softened, about 8 minutes. Stir in the garlic and ginger and cook, stirring, until fragrant, about 1 minute. Stir in the cumin, coriander, mustard seed, and cinnamon and cook, stirring, for 1 minute.

2. Stir in the stock, tomatoes, and brown sugar and simmer 5 minutes, stirring occasionally. Stir in the okra and salt and simmer until the okra is tender, about 15 minutes. Do not stir for the first 10 minutes of cooking, but stir more frequently as the sauce begins to thicken.

3. Stir in the cayenne, Grains of Paradise, and lemon juice. Taste for salt. Serve hot, spooned over rice or grits, if you like.

WHAT ELSE WORKS? You can replace the okra with Romano beans or another variety of sturdy string bean.

## Succotash Sauté

3 thick bacon slices, cut crosswise into ¼-inch strips (about 3 ounces)

1 ½ cups finely chopped onion

2 garlic cloves, finely chopped

1 jalapeño or other chile, finely chopped

2 cups thinly sliced fresh okra (about 8 ounces)

3 cups chopped red tomatoes (about 1 ½ pounds)

2 cups corn kernels (about 4 ears of corn)

2 cups shelled green butter beans (from about 2 pounds pods)

3 tablespoons thinly sliced fresh basil or chives

Kosher salt and ground black pepper, to taste

It's sad when a good dish gets a bad reputation based on people's experiences with poor versions. I think that's what happened to succotash. Too many people think it is little more than canned limas and canned corn heated up together. This fresh succotash showcases the best of late summer, combining corn, butter beans, okra, tomatoes, and basil. The bacon adds tremendous flavor and crunch, but you can omit it and cook the vegetables in extra-virgin olive oil or butter instead.

MAKES 6 SERVINGS

1. Cook the bacon in a large skillet over medium-high heat, stirring often, until it renders its fat and turns very crisp, about 12 minutes. Transfer with a slotted spoon to paper towels to drain, leaving the drippings in the skillet.

2. Add the onion and a pinch of salt, stirring to scrape up the browned bits from the bottom of the skillet. Cook, stirring often, until beginning to soften, about 5 minutes. Add the garlic and jalapeño and cook until fragrant, about 1 minute.

3. Stir in the okra, tomatoes, corn, and butter beans. Reduce the heat to medium-low, cover, and cook without stirring for 10 minutes. (Letting the okra cook for a while before stirring reduces the stringiness from its juices.) Continue cooking, stirring occasionally, until the butter beans are tender, about 10 minutes more. Stir in the basil and bacon. Season generously with salt and pepper and serve hot.

VARIATION: To transform this into a delectable summer stew, add ½ to 1 cup crème fraîche (page 388 or store-bought) when you add the basil and bacon. Stir until it coats the vegetables. Served over Real Skillet Cornbread (page 321) or hot Miracle Biscuits (page 398), it's rather like upside-down vegetable pot pie.

# ONIONS

**Alliums, which include onions,** ramps, leeks, shallots, and garlic, are elemental to every cuisine, southern included. Even as one of the world's oldest and most used vegetables, onions were long considered to be poor man's fare. Perhaps their strong smell and flavor offended the sensibilities of those who could afford to season their food with something else. Onions were also blamed for inciting coarse behavior and sin, to the point that some religions prohibited their believers from eating them at all. If the goal is to make swift judgment of people based on their food choices, onions are expedient. It's not difficult to sniff out the onion eaters.

All sorts of delicious onions grow in the South, but the legendary onions are the sweet ones: Vidalia, Texas 1015, and Wadmalaw, fitting right into the southern predilection for sweet things. These onions cannot be grown anywhere other than where they are meant to be grown. For example, a Vidalia onion is a Vidalia only when grown in the sweet, low-sulfur soil of Vidalia, Georgia. The same plant will not be a proper Vidalia if planted anywhere else. This is *terroir* at its most insistent. ■

## Arugula and Roasted Pepper Salad with Warm Olive Oil

1 medium onion, halved lengthwise and cut into thin strips

1 ½ cups roasted red bell peppers cut into thin strips (page 314 or store-bought)

8 cups baby arugula, patted dry (about 10 ounces)

½ cup Kalamata olives or other ripe Mediterranean olives, pitted

¼ cup balsamic vinegar

½ cup extra-virgin olive oil

Kosher salt and ground black pepper, to taste

½ cup coarsely grated Asiago or Parmesan cheese

I'm including this salad for two reasons. First, it's really good. Although it looks Mediterranean at first glance, it's dressed with shimmering hot oil, similar to the wilted or "killed" salads common in the rural South.

Second, it provides a handy lesson in serving raw onion in a salad. Soak the sliced onions in a bowl of ice water for at least 15 minutes before serving. The cold water draws out the strong, sulfurous onion flavor and aroma, leaving milder, extremely crisp pieces. Stinky onions, the ones that leave you with tears running down your face, can turn the water milky white, so change the water until it stays clear. You can refrigerate the onions and water in a covered glass jar for up to three days, which is a great way to store leftover onion that would otherwise release fumes into the fridge.

MAKES 8 SERVINGS

(1) Place the onion slices in a small bowl and cover with ice water. Set aside for at least 15 minutes. If the thin, papery membranes between the layers of the onion come loose in the water, just pull them out and discard. Drain well and pat dry.

(2) Combine the onion, roasted peppers, arugula, and olives in a large bowl. Drizzle with the vinegar and toss to coat.

(3) Heat the oil in a small saucepan until shimmering hot. Carefully and slowly drizzle the hot oil over the salad and toss with tongs to coat and wilt some of the leaves. Be careful because it sizzles and pops!

(4) Season with salt and pepper and sprinkle with the cheese. Serve at once.

WHAT ELSE WORKS? You can replace some or all of the arugula with baby spinach.

# The Famous Marinated Cheese

1 pound firm cheese,
such as cheddar,
Havarti, and/or
Monterey Jack

½ cup extra-virgin
olive oil

¼ cup white wine
vinegar

½ cup finely chopped
scallions (white and
tender green parts)

½ cup diced pimentos,
drained

2 tablespoons
finely chopped
flat-leaf parsley

2 cloves garlic,
finely chopped

1 teaspoon sugar

1 teaspoon dried
Italian herb blend
(or equal parts dried
basil and oregano)

1 teaspoon kosher salt

½ teaspoon ground
black pepper

Triscuits, for serving

Each time I serve this cheese, guests clamor for the recipe. This is perfect party food, and it's easily doubled or tripled. The green onion and red pimento in the marinade add great color, so it's very appealing on the table. Every cook needs at least one quick and easy recipe that yields something that looks good.

Serve the cheese with crackers that are a little porous so they can soak up the delicious marinade. Woven wheat crackers (read Triscuits) are ideal. After your guests are gone and it's down to you and a few stalwart friends, soak any remaining Triscuits debris from the bottom of the box in the leftover marinade. Let it get good and soggy, then gobble it up. Use a spoon if you need to. It's the very best part.

MAKES 8 SERVINGS

① For easiest cutting, let the cheese come to room temperature, then cut into bite-sized slices that are about ¼-inch thick. If you are trying to impress your guests, start with ¼-inch-thick slabs of cheese from the deli counter, then use small, not-too-detailed cookie cutters to cut the cheese into seasonal shapes, such as fall leaves, stars, or moons. Arrange the pieces of cheese on a large rimmed platter.

② Whisk together the oil, vinegar, scallions, pimentos, parsley, garlic, sugar, herb blend, salt, and pepper in a bowl, then pour evenly over the cheese. Let the cheese sit at room temperature for at least 30 minutes before serving with Triscuits.

MAKE-AHEAD NOTE: You can mix the marinade up to 2 days ahead. Store covered and refrigerated. Return it to room temperature and stir well before using.

## Vidalia Soufflé Dip

8 ounces cream cheese, at room temperature

¼ cup mayonnaise

½ teaspoon garlic powder

1 teaspoon Worcestershire sauce

½ teaspoon hot sauce

1 ½ cups finely chopped Vidalia onions

1 ¼ cups coarsely grated Parmesan or Asiago cheese, divided

Pinch of paprika or cayenne pepper

Crackers, chips, or raw vegetables, for serving

This is fantastic stuff, bubbly and cheesy, like a warmed version of the very best cheese ball. It can be casual or elegant, depending on the presentation. The easiest thing is to set out a dish of this dip and a basket of crunchy things and let people dig in. Crackers and chips always work, or you can offer raw vegetables. To transform the dip into delicate hors d'oeuvres, spread it on thin slices of bread and bake until the bread is toasted and the dip is puffed and browned, like a tiny soufflé. This is also the best way to serve leftover dip because it does not reheat well. Never microwave this mixture.

Vidalias are the most prized, super-sweet, and juicy onion of the South. There are other sweet onions, but no other onion tastes like a Georgia-born-and-bred Vidalia. Unlike plebian onions, Vidalias are unsuitable for storing more than a few precious weeks, so people go to great lengths to make them last. The delicate onions keep best when stored without touching in a cool, dry place where air can circulate around them. I heard of one society doyenne who wrapped the onions individually in linen napkins and laid them gently in a drawer of the highboy. My favorite approach combines pure theater with practicality. Slide the onions, one at a time, into the legs of old clean pantyhose, tie a knot between each onion and hang the hose in a cool dry place. Cut the onions loose as needed. I've seen basements and rafters chock full of these Vidalia stalactites.

MAKES ABOUT 3 CUPS

1. Preheat the oven to 350°F.

2. Stir together the cream cheese, mayonnaise, garlic powder, Worcestershire, and hot sauce in a medium bowl until smooth. Fold in the onions and 1 cup of the cheese. Taste for salt, but it probably won't need any because the cheese is salty.

3. Spoon the mixture into a shallow 1-quart baking dish or 9-inch pie plate. Sprinkle the top with the remaining ¼ cup of cheese and the paprika. Bake until the dip is set in the center, lightly browned on top, and bubbling around the edges, about 35 minutes. Let sit for at least 10 minutes before serving. Serve warm with crackers, chips, or raw vegetables for dipping.

VARIATION: To make hors d'oeuvres or to serve leftover dip, spread a generous topping of baked dip (either still warm from the oven or the refrigerated leftovers) onto baguette slices or little squares or rounds of crustless white sandwich bread. Arrange on a rimmed baking sheet and bake in a 350°F oven until the bread is toasted and the topping is slightly puffed and browned, about 5 minutes for warm dip and 10 minutes for chilled dip. Serve warm.

## Chicken Smothered in Onions and Snappy Cream Gravy

4 chicken breast halves or 8 meaty thighs, preferably with skin and bones

¾ cup instant or all-purpose flour

2 teaspoons kosher salt

1 teaspoon ground black pepper

2 tablespoons extra-virgin olive oil, divided

2 tablespoons butter, divided

¼ cup brandy or white wine

2 large onions, halved lengthwise and cut into thin strips (about 3 cups)

¾ cup chicken stock, warmed

¾ cup whole milk

3 tablespoons grainy Dijon mustard

3 tablespoons crushed gingersnaps

1 tablespoon chopped fresh thyme or chives, for garnish

The traditional chicken and onion dish known as smothered chicken is a staple in many southern households. I've updated this classic by adding a little pizzazz to the creamy onion gravy. This dish begs to be served with something to sop up the gravy, such as biscuits (page 393), mashed potatoes (page 248), or mashed sweet potatoes (page 328).

Use the type of chicken that suits you. Chicken breasts or thighs with bones and skin deliver the most flavor, but even ubiquitous boneless, skinless chicken breasts come out tender and flavorful. This is also a good way to serve humble (and beloved) cube steak, those thin pieces of beef riddled with hash marks to help tenderize them—the meat and milk gravy benchmark from my childhood.

MAKES 4 SERVINGS

1. Rinse the chicken and pat dry with paper towels. Stir together the flour, salt, and pepper on a plate. Lightly and evenly coat the chicken in the flour mixture, shaking off the excess. Set aside in a single layer to dry a little while the skillet gets hot. Reserve the seasoned flour.

2. Heat 1 tablespoon of the oil and 1 tablespoon of the butter in a large, heavy (preferably cast-iron) skillet over medium-high heat. When the butter stops foaming, add the chicken skin-side down in a single layer. Leave space between the pieces of chicken so that they will brown instead of steam. Work in batches if necessary.

3. Cook the chicken undisturbed until it is richly browned on the bottom and releases easily from the skillet, about 3 minutes. Turn the chicken with tongs and brown the other side. Adjust the heat as needed to prevent any bits of flour that float into the fat from burning. Transfer the browned chicken to a clean plate and set aside.

4. Heat the remaining 1 tablespoon of oil and 1 tablespoon of butter in the skillet. Carefully add the brandy and cook, scraping up the browned bits from the bottom of the skillet. When the liquid has nearly cooked away, add the onions and a pinch of salt and stir to coat in the fat. Cook, stirring occasionally, until softened and golden brown, about 8 minutes.

5. Sprinkle 3 tablespoons of the reserved seasoned flour over the onions and stir to coat. Cook, stirring, for 2 minutes. Pour in the warm stock and cook, stirring, until the gravy begins to thicken, about 3 minutes. Stir in the milk, mustard, and gingersnaps and cook, stirring, until the gravy is thick enough to coat the back of the spoon, about 2 minutes.

6. Return the chicken to the pan, skin-side up, and cook until the juices run clear when pierced with the tip of the knife, about 5 minutes. Sprinkle with the thyme and serve hot.

# Onion Soup with Gruyère Croutons

4 tablespoons (½ stick) butter

2 ½ pounds yellow onions, halved lengthwise and cut into thin strips

8 ounces leeks, thinly sliced (white and tender green parts)

8 ounces shallots, thinly sliced

6 garlic cloves, thinly sliced

½ cup dry white wine

4 cups beef or veal stock

2 cups chicken stock

2 teaspoons whole-grain Dijon mustard

2 tablespoons Cognac or brandy

2 teaspoons kosher salt, or to taste

1 teaspoon ground black pepper, or to taste

1 tablespoon red wine vinegar

24 thin baguette slices

Extra-virgin olive oil, for brushing

1 cup coarsely grated Gruyère cheese

I am reluctant to call this recipe French onion soup, a dish with a tarnished reputation because too many versions are mediocre if not just plain bad. This one is just plain wonderful. Your kitchen will smell divine as it cooks, but resist the temptation to dip in too soon because the soup really should be made at least one day ahead. In fact, if you taste it as soon as it's made, you'll wonder what all the fuss is about. A good night's rest makes all the difference.

The trick to good onion soup is to cook the onions (and leeks and shallots) until they are fully caramelized into soft, golden sweetness. "Caramelization" is the somewhat overused term for cooking vegetables until their natural sugars are browned. Because the idea is to cook the sugars, you'd think that Vidalias or other super-sweet onions would be ideal, but they're not. Caramelization involves small amounts of controlled sticking so that a browned glaze can form on the bottom of the pan and then be stirred into the onions. Super-sweet onions contain so much juice that they can never dry out enough for that controlled glazing to occur. It's the same reason that a nonstick pot won't work; it won't let the glaze form.

Onion soup is traditionally served with a thick cap of bread and cheese fused to the side of the bowl. It's dramatic but difficult to eat. I prefer thin, crisp pieces of cheese toast, which can be dunked into the soup or floated on top. To turn this hearty soup into an even heartier meal, serve with Roast Beef Panini with Red Wine and Onion Marmalade (page 212).

MAKES ABOUT 2 QUARTS

1. Melt the butter in a large, heavy pot (not nonstick) over medium-high heat. When the butter stops foaming, add the onions, leeks, shallots, and garlic and a generous pinch of salt and stir to coat. Cover and cook, stirring often, until the vegetables soften and reduce to about half of their original volume, about 15 minutes. Uncover, reduce the heat to medium-low, and cook until the vegetables are very soft and deep golden brown, about 30 minutes, stirring occasionally to scrape up the browned glaze on the bottom of the skillet. Reduce the heat and stir more frequently if the vegetables start to scorch or get crunchy.

2. Add the wine and simmer until it cooks away, about 3 minutes. Add the beef stock, chicken stock, and mustard. Bring to a boil, reduce the heat, and simmer for 15 minutes. Add the Cognac and simmer 5 minutes. Season with the salt and pepper. Cool to room temperature, cover, and refrigerate overnight. When ready to serve, reheat over medium heat, check the seasoning, and stir in the vinegar.

③ To make the Gruyère croutons, preheat the broiler. Arrange the baguette slices in a single layer on a rimmed baking sheet and brush them lightly with oil. Broil until the bread is lightly toasted. Remove the pan from the oven and top each piece with a little mound of Gruyère. Place back under the broiler until the cheese melts.

④ Serve the hot soup with the Gruyère croutons on the side.

VARIATION: You can also use the method described in Slow Cooker Caramelized Onions (recipe follows) to cook the onions, leeks, shallots, and garlic. When done, transfer into the soup pot and pick up the recipe at Step 2.

MAKE-AHEAD NOTE: This soup tastes best made 1 day ahead. Cool, cover, and refrigerate. Check the seasoning and reheat gently before serving.

## Slow Cooker Caramelized Onions

Vegetable oil spray

8  tablespoons
   (1 stick) butter

5  pounds yellow onions,
   halved lengthwise and
   cut into thin strips

This recipe is a great reason to own a slow cooker. It sounds gimmicky, but it works as well as cooking them on top of the stove and stirring by hand. It's a watershed moment for cooks who are too time-strapped to caramelize onions the traditional way. The slow cooker will be crammed full of onions at first, but they cook down considerably. Do not skimp on the butter. It adds flavor and is an important part of the cooking process.

I like to freeze these onions in 1-cup containers, just the right amount to add to a pot roast, a skillet of gravy, or a bowl of Heavenly Mashed Potatoes (page 248).

MAKES ABOUT 4 CUPS

① Generously mist the inside of a 5- to 6-quart slow cooker with the spray. Put the butter in the bottom of the cooker and add the onions. Cover and cook on low until the onions are completely soft and deep golden brown, 8 to 10 hours. Do not remove the lid or stir during the first 2 hours, then stir as needed to keep the onions from sticking to the cooker and to help them cook evenly.

② Use at once, or cool, cover, and refrigerate for up to 3 days, or freeze in airtight containers for up to 3 months.

## Roast Beef Panini with Red Wine and Onion Marmalade

12 sandwich slices sourdough or country white bread

6 slices aged cheddar cheese

6 ounces thinly sliced high-quality roast beef

½ Granny Smith apple, cored and sliced paper thin

½ cup Red Wine and Onion Marmalade (recipe follows)

3 tablespoons butter, at room temperature

A panini is nothing but a great toasted sandwich that's pressed so that the bread is extra crisp. If you don't have a panini press or electric countertop grill, cook the sandwiches in a hot cast-iron skillet or grill pan and press them with a second skillet, bacon press, or clean brick wrapped in aluminum foil.

This decadent sandwich tastes like a steak dinner between two slices of good bread. It's the perfect thing to serve with the Onion Soup (page 210). Don't skip the apple. It adds the color and crunch of lettuce but is far more interesting.

MAKES 6 SERVINGS

1. Arrange 6 slices of the bread on a work surface and top each with a slice of cheese and equal portions of the roast beef and apple. Spoon on the marmalade and close the sandwiches with the remaining bread. Butter both sides of the sandwiches.

2. Preheat a panini press or electric countertop cooker. Place the sandwiches inside, press down, and grill until the bread is crisp and browned. Serve warm.

## Red Wine and Onion Marmalade

2 cups sugar, divided

2 cups dry fruity red wine

6 cups thinly sliced or coarsely chopped red onions

½ cup sherry vinegar

1 teaspoon finely chopped fresh rosemary

Kosher salt and coarsely ground black pepper, to taste

My husband says this needs a better name, but I haven't come up with one that is more descriptive. The tender pieces of onion are bathed in thick sweet syrup, just like marmalade. This divine concoction is great on sandwiches or spooned over ripe cheese.

MAKES ABOUT 1 CUP

1. Bring 1 cup of the sugar and the wine to a boil in a saucepan over high heat, stirring to dissolve the sugar. Add the onions, cover the pan, and cook, stirring occasionally, until beginning to soften, about 10 minutes. Drain and discard the liquid.

2. Return the onions to the pan and stir in the remaining 1 cup of sugar and the vinegar. Cook over medium heat, stirring occasionally, until the onions are completely soft and the liquid is syrupy, about 10 minutes more.

3. Stir in the rosemary and season with salt and a generous amount of pepper. Use at once, or cool, cover, and refrigerate for up to 3 weeks.

Roasted Carrots with Honey and Rosemary

Crispy Zucchini and Potato Skillet Cakes with Tomato Jam

Pasta with Roasted Winter Squash in
Browned Butter, Sage, and Hazelnut Sauce

Cucumbers and Onions, Quick Pickled Beets, Hot Pepper Vinegar,
Refrigerator Pickled Peaches with Bourbon, Quick Pickled Carrots

Chicken and Sweet Potato Stew with Sweet Potato Biscuits

Fresh Fig and Mascarpone Ice Cream with Walnuts in Port Syrup

Blackberries and Peaches in Sweet Basil Syrup with Cornmeal Pound Cake

Stirred Corn and Seared Sea Scallops with Lime Sauce

# Salt-Roasted Onions

1 (4-pound) box
food-grade rock salt

6 medium sweet or
yellow onions, papery
skins removed

Butter, sour cream,
and ground black
pepper, for serving

These delicious onions are roasted until tender and slightly charred on the edges, then split and filled with butter and sour cream, just like a baked potato. The salt makes them seasoned but not too salty. You can use Vidalia or another super-sweet variety or regular yellow onions. Small, fairly flat onions work better than large round onions. Make sure the onions are all the same size so they'll roast at the same rate.

The bed of rock salt holds the onions upright, and it also conducts heat and makes a particularly tasty roast. Plus, it looks really cool. When done, the salt keeps the onions warm until ready to serve. You can reuse the salt multiple times, so long as you discard any salt that gets wet or darkened from onion juice. The sweeter the onion, the more juice it exudes. You can find boxes of food-grade rock salt in the grocery store alongside other types of salt. It's the stuff used in old-fashioned ice cream freezers.

MAKES 6 SERVINGS

(1) Preheat the oven to 350°F.

(2) Pour salt to a depth of ½ inch in the bottom of a roasting pan just large enough to hold the onions in a single layer without their sides touching. Sit the onions upright in the salt. Pour the remaining salt around and over the onions so that only their tops peek out.

(3) Roast until a small sharp knife slips easily into the center of the onions, 1 hour to 1 hour 45 minutes, depending on the size and freshness of the onions. The exposed tops will be quite dark. Remove the pan from the oven and let sit for at least 10 minutes. (The salt can keep the onions warm for up to 1 hour.) Remove the onions from the salt and brush away any salt that clings to them. Split the onions open and season with the toppings of your choice.

WHAT ELSE WORKS? You can salt-roast potatoes the same way. Small potatoes, no more than 3 ounces each, work best. You can roast the onions and potatoes together.

# Creamed Onion Tart

1 (10-inch) tart shell (page 396 or store-bought)

3 ounces slab bacon cut into ½-inch cubes or 3 thick bacon slices, cut crosswise into ¼-inch strips

3 tablespoons butter

2 pounds yellow onions, halved lengthwise and cut unto thin strips

3 large eggs

¾ cup crème fraîche (page 388 or store-bought) or heavy cream

1 tablespoon finely chopped fresh sage

1 teaspoon chopped fresh thyme

½ teaspoon freshly grated nutmeg

1 teaspoon kosher salt

¾ teaspoon ground black pepper

Creamed onions are a classic dish, especially around the winter holidays. This is a new way to serve those familiar flavors. The creamy onions are mixed with crisp bacon and fresh herbs, then baked in a tart shell.

The tart is a lovely side dish. It's equally good warm or at room temperature, and small slices make a great appetizer or plated first course. The filling is quite rich, so I like to serve the tart alongside a simple salad made from a small handful of peppery greens (such as watercress or arugula) and tart apple cut into paper-thin slices or matchsticks very lightly dressed with Apple Cider Vinaigrette (page 15).

MAKES 8 TO 12 SERVINGS

1. Bake and cool the tart shell according to the instructions on page 398.
2. When ready to bake the tart, preheat the oven to 400°F.
3. Cook the bacon in a large skillet over medium-high heat until crisp, about 10 minutes. Transfer with a slotted spoon to paper towels to drain, leaving the drippings in the skillet.
4. Melt the butter in the skillet. Stir in the onions and a pinch of salt. Cook, stirring constantly, until the onions begin to soften, about 5 minutes. Cover the skillet and continue to cook, stirring frequently, until very soft and just beginning to color, about 10 minutes. Uncover the skillet and cook, stirring often, until the liquid evaporates. Set the skillet aside and let the onions cool to room temperature.
5. Whisk the eggs in a large bowl until the whites and yolks are blended. Whisk in the crème fraîche, sage, thyme, nutmeg, salt, and pepper. Stir in the onions and bacon.
6. Spread the filling evenly in the tart shell. Bake until the filling is set and the top is golden, about 35 minutes. Let sit at least 10 minutes before slicing and serving warm or at room temperature.

VARIATION: To make this without the bacon, replace the drippings with 1 tablespoon extra-virgin olive oil.

MAKE-AHEAD NOTE: The onions can be cooked through Step 4 up to 1 day ahead. Store covered and refrigerated. Return to room temperature before proceeding with the recipe.

Homemade pastry is best but not always possible, due to time constraints or deep-seated pastry anxiety. The packaged pastry that comes in a roll is easiest to fit into the tart pan. However, if all you have on hand is a frozen pie shell in a disposable pie pan, let it thaw at room temperature just until it begins to soften, about 15 minutes. Loosen the edge of the pastry with the tip of a small knife. Invert the disposable pan over the tart pan and let the pastry fall into the tart pan. Gently flatten the pastry and press it evenly across the bottom of the tart tin. Use your fingertips to press the crimped edge up the rim, making a flat, even edge. Bake and cool the pastry according to the directions on page 398.

# PEACHES

**Peaches, the fruit most closely associated with the South,** traveled to the New World with Spanish explorers in the fifteenth century. Native Americans cultivated peaches and planted them across the South. In addition, some peaches naturalized and grew wild to such an extent that some early botanical historians mistakenly thought peaches were native to North America.

As with other perishable fresh fruits, colonists considered peaches to be useful because they could be preserved and used through the winter. Most colonial peaches were dried or made into brandy and the pits were used to flavor other foods. When basic survival was no longer the singular concern, people allowed themselves the luxury of eating fresh peaches.

The very best peaches are those left on the tree until they are fully ripe, aromatic, and nearly ready to fall off the branch. A tree-ripened peach might have a brix value (sugar content as measured by a refractometer) as high as 18, compared to the 8 of the average commercial peach that was picked when it was rock hard and shippable. If a peach looks, smells, and feels like a green tennis ball, that's what it will taste like. A proper peach caresses all our senses with its full blush of color, sweet perfume, downy skin, dripping juice, and incomparable flavor. That's the truth of a peach. ■

This is the best way to peel peaches when you want to preserve their shape and the blush of color that appears just under their skin. Fill a large bowl with ice water. Bring a large saucepan of water to a boil. With a serrated knife, score an X just through the skin on the bottom of each peach. Working in batches, use a slotted spoon to gently lower the peaches into the boiling water. Let them simmer until the little flaps of skin around the X begin to loosen, but no longer than 1 minute so that the peaches do not begin to cook and soften. Use the slotted spoon to transfer the peaches into the ice water. When cool, strip off the peeling, using the little flaps as pull tabs to get started. The riper the peaches, the easier this will be. If the skin simply won't budge, return the peach to the boiling water for another few seconds.

## Peach Cobbler with White Cheddar Biscuit Topping

FILLING

8 cups ½-inch-thick peeled peach slices, preferably white peaches

1 ½ cups sugar

2 tablespoons cornstarch

½ teaspoon kosher salt

1 teaspoon finely grated lemon zest

2 tablespoons fresh lemon juice

½ teaspoon almond extract

3 tablespoons unsalted butter, cut into small cubes and chilled

(continued on next page)

This is my grandmother's cobbler. I cannot imagine what led her to try cheese with peaches, but we agreed that sharp white cheddar was the tastiest. The biscuits are dropped into the juicy fruit filling midway during cooking, so they simmer on the bottom and bake on the top, creating a cobber that is a little like fruit dumplings.

I don't think this cobbler needs any accompaniment, but some people will appreciate a scoop of ice cream. Vanilla always works, but try Buttermilk Sherbet (page 135) or lemon sorbet to balance the sweetness of the filling.

MAKES 12 SERVINGS

1. For the filling: Preheat the oven to 400°F. Butter a 9 × 13-inch baking dish.
2. Place the peaches in the prepared baking dish. In a small bowl, mix the sugar, cornstarch, salt, lemon zest, lemon juice, and almond extract. Sprinkle the mixture over the peaches. Dot the peaches with the cubes of butter. Bake the filling for 15 minutes. Meanwhile, make the topping.
3. For the topping: Stir together the flour and cheese in a large bowl. Stir together the melted butter and buttermilk in a small bowl. Slowly pour the buttermilk mixture into the flour mixture, stirring gently with a fork to form soft, fairly wet dough.

2 cups soft southern wheat self-rising flour

1 cup grated sharp white cheddar cheese

4 tablespoons (½ stick) unsalted butter, melted

⅔ cup well-shaken buttermilk

4. Remove the dish from the oven. Stir the filling gently to make sure all of the sugar has dissolved. Drop rounded tablespoons of dough over the filling. Return the cobbler to the oven and continue baking until the biscuits are firm and golden brown on top and the filling bubbles around the edges, about 20 minutes more. Let sit for at least 10 minutes before serving hot.

WHAT ELSE WORKS? You can replace 2 cups of the peaches with blackberries, dewberries, or raspberries.

## Refrigerator Pickled Peaches with Bourbon

In addition to making preserves or drying the fruit, early southerners had other ways to make peaches last through the winter. Some people pickled peaches in sweetened vinegar brine, and others packed peaches into jars of bourbon. This is a little of both, made in a small batch that can be stored in the refrigerator and used up quickly without the necessity of sealing the jars in a water bath.

Pickled peaches are a traditional accompaniment to baked ham, although these are plenty delicious eaten straight out of the jar all on their own. I also rather like them spooned over vanilla ice cream.

6 ripe but firm small peaches (about 2 pounds)

Zest of 1 orange, cut into ½-inch-wide strips

1 cup fresh orange juice

½ cup cider vinegar

6 tablespoon sugar

¼ teaspoon kosher salt or pickling salt

½ teaspoon whole allspice

2 small dried red peppers or a generous pinch of crushed red pepper flakes

4 whole cloves

2 small mace blades or ¼ teaspoon ground mace or nutmeg

½ split and scraped vanilla bean or 2 teaspoons vanilla bean paste or extract

¼ cup bourbon

MAKES 2 PINTS

1. Have ready two 1-pint jars that have been sterilized in boiling water or run through the dishwasher on the hottest cycle. Wide-mouth jars are easiest to use. The jars should have sterilized tight-fitting lids. The jars and lids do not have to stay hot, but they should stay sterile.

2. Peel the peaches, cut in half, and remove the pits. Pack the peaches into the prepared jars and tuck the strips of orange zest around the sides.

3. Stir together the orange juice, vinegar, sugar, salt, allspice, peppers, cloves, and mace blades in a small saucepan. Bring to a boil, reduce the heat, and simmer for 5 minutes, stirring until the sugar dissolves. Remove the pan from the heat, cover, and set aside to steep for 10 minutes. Stir in the vanilla and bourbon.

4. Ladle the hot liquid over the peaches. (A wide-mouth funnel helps.) Let the liquid trickle down around the fruit and settle before adding more. The peaches must be submerged. Close the jars and refrigerate for at least 7 days before serving. The peaches keep in the refrigerator for up to 3 months.

## Grilled Balsamic Peaches with Brown Sugar Pound Cake

4 tablespoons (½ stick) butter, melted

¼ cup raw sugar or light brown sugar

4 peaches, peeled, halved, and pitted

4 slices Brown Sugar Pound Cake (recipe follows)

1 to 2 tablespoons aged balsamic vinegar (at least 8 years old)

Grilling is a great way to serve fruit that is just shy of perfectly ripe. It should be flavorful yet firm enough to hold together and retain its texture on the grill. The goal of grilling fruit is to add flavor and warmth, not cook it through, so it will not soften very much. In this recipe, the peaches are at the center of a dessert, but they can also be a side dish when served with grilled pork or on salad greens.

Aged balsamic vinegar is a delectable finishing touch to peaches that are warm and a little smoky from the grill. The key is high-quality balsamic that has been aged at least eight years so that it is rich, thick, mellow, and well-balanced, closer to a cordial than to vinegar. Try to find an artisan-quality balsamic, such as one labeled *condimento*, if not a premium *balsamico tradizionale*. A bottle of aged balsamic is pricey, but it never goes bad and will yield many delicious servings because a little goes a long way. If you can't imagine balsamic on peaches, no matter how aged and luscious, you can top them with Bourbon-Pecan Caramel Sauce (page 335).

I think peaches cry out for good pound cake, and the Brown Sugar Pound Cake is good indeed. The caramel flavor of the cake is a great match for both the fruit and the rich balsamic.

MAKES 4 SERVINGS

1. Preheat the grill to medium. Oil the grill grate.
2. Pour the melted butter into a shallow bowl. Pour the sugar into another shallow bowl. Dip the cut side of each peach into the melted butter and then into the sugar. Arrange the peaches cut-side down on the hot grate and cook only until the bottoms are caramelized and sizzling and show grill marks, about 3 minutes. Place the pound cake slices around the edge of the grate to lightly toast, if you wish.
3. Arrange the cake and peaches on serving plates. Drizzle the peaches with the vinegar and serve warm.

VARIATION: If your fruit is too juicy or blemished to cut into clean halves or if you want to mix the peaches with other stone fruit, such as plums or apricots, you can cook it in pouches of aluminum foil. Arrange four 12-inch squares of foil on a work surface. Cut the fruit into small cubes or thin wedges and divide among the squares. Drizzle with the melted butter and sprinkle with the sugar. Fold the foil around the fruit and tightly close the edges to form flat, square pouches. Grill over medium heat until the fruit sizzles, about 10 minutes.

# Brown Sugar Pound Cake

3 cups all-purpose flour

½ teaspoon baking powder

¼ teaspoon kosher salt

1 ½ cups (3 sticks) unsalted butter, at room temperature

1 (1-pound) box dark brown sugar (about 2 ¾ packed cups)

½ cup granulated sugar

5 large eggs, at room temperature

1 cup whole milk

1 teaspoon pure vanilla extract

Although not unique to the South, pound cake seems particularly southern to me. I have a large collection of pound cake recipes, and this is one of my favorites. It's dense, moist, and sweet, with enough character to stand on its own, yet it goes well with fruit and sauces. It keeps for days and can be frozen. There will be quite a bit of cake left over after making the Grilled Balsamic Peaches. This will not be a problem.

I had an uncle who was a master of pound cake, although he never admitted that he baked at all. He pretended that his wife made them because, I suppose, he didn't think that baking cakes was manly. This is as close as I will ever come to re-creating his prize brown sugar pound cake. I wish I had thought to ask him ("her") for the recipe. He would have gladly shared it.

Some recipes are passed through the generations with generosity, like a treasured family heirloom. Other recipes are a source of swagger, secrecy, and speculation and must be pried loose from the cook. If you can coerce this type of cook to share the recipe, the real version of the recipe, you've received an inheritance. Your sorry sister might have gotten the silver, but you took The Cake.

MAKES 12 SERVINGS

1. Preheat the oven to 325°F. Grease and flour a 10-inch light metal tube pan. (A dark metal or nonstick pan makes the crust too dark and thick.)
2. Whisk together the flour, baking powder, and salt in a large bowl.
3. Beat the butter until creamy in a large bowl with an electric mixer set to high speed. Add the brown sugar ¾ cup at a time, beating at medium speed until smooth after each addition. Beat in the granulated sugar. Increase the mixer speed to high and beat until the mixture is light and fluffy, about 4 minutes.
4. Add the eggs one at a time, beating well after each addition.
5. With the mixer set to low speed, add the flour mixture in thirds, alternating with half of the milk, beating each time only until the batter is smooth. Quickly beat in the vanilla.
6. Scrape the batter into the prepared pan. Bake in the center of the oven until a tester inserted into the center comes out clean and the top springs back when lightly touched at the center, about 1 hour and 30 minutes.
7. Cool the cake in the pan on a wire rack for 30 minutes. Loosen the cake from the pan with a table knife and turn it out onto the rack to cool to room temperature before slicing.

# Ginger-Peach Icebox Cake

Vegetable oil spray

6 ounces crisp gin-
gersnaps, crushed
into crumbs

3 tablespoons butter,
melted

8 ounces cream cheese,
at room temperature

½ cup sour cream

1 pound mascarpone,
at room temperature

½ teaspoon pure
vanilla extract

⅔ cup sugar

⅓ cup heavy cream,
well chilled

½ cup finely chopped
candied ginger
(about 3 ounces)

3 medium ripe but
firm peaches

½ cup peach preserves

"Icebox" is the charming term used to describe old-fashioned, creamy desserts that are chilled instead of baked. Icebox cakes were once considered to be examples of modern sophistication in cooking and were served as posh party food. Believe me, when you taste this cake, it will feel like a party.

Ginger and peaches are a match made in heaven. The creamy filling that surrounds the peaches is studded with bits of candied ginger. For best results, look for large, moist slices or cubes of candied ginger that have the texture of gumdrops and then cut them into small pieces with a sharp paring knife or kitchen scissors. Avoid the tins and jars of baker's cut ginger chips. The chips are rock hard, and because this cake is not baked, they have no chance to soften and are quite unpleasant in the filling.

It was not unusual for old southern recipes to call for using crushed gingersnaps as an ingredient. The cookies were full of spices and kept well for long periods of time, so they were an easy way to add spice to other foods, particularly when the spices themselves were not available.

MAKES 12 SERVINGS

1  Mist the inside of a 9-inch springform pan with the spray and dust it with sugar, shaking out the excess. Toss together the cookie crumbs and melted butter in a small bowl until well mixed and then pour into the prepared pan. Press the crumbs evenly over the bottom and about ½ inch up the sides of the pan. To make sure the crumbs are not thicker around the edge than they are across the bottom of the crust, press a straight-sided metal measuring cup into the corners to even out any thick spots. Set the crust aside.

2  Whip the cream cheese, sour cream, mascarpone, and vanilla until smooth in a large bowl with an electric mixer set to high speed. (If you are using a stand mixer, use the whisk attachment.) Scrape down the sides of the bowl with a rubber spatula. With the mixer running on medium speed, slowly add the sugar. Scrape down the sides of the bowl. Add the cream and whip only until the mixture holds soft peaks, about 30 seconds. Don't overwhip the cream or the mixture will separate. Use a rubber spatula to fold in the candied ginger.

3  Carefully spoon half of the cream cheese mixture over the crust, spreading it evenly to the edges of the pan. Peel and pit one of the peaches, cut into ¼-inch-thick slices, and arrange over the filling. Do not let the slices touch the side of the pan. Spoon in the remaining filling. Gently tap the pan on the counter to eliminate any air bubbles. Cover the pan with plastic wrap and refrigerate until well chilled and firm, at least 4 hours and preferably overnight.

④ Peel and pit the remaining 2 peaches and cut them into ¼-inch-thick slices. Arrange the slices over the top of the cake. Melt the preserves in a medium saucepan over low heat, then brush or spoon over the peach slices to make them shiny and hold them in place. Cover the pan with plastic wrap and refrigerate until the preserves are set, at least 30 minutes. Remove the sides of the pan, cut the cake into slices, and serve chilled.

## Peach Iced Tea Sorbet

3 cups peeled, pitted, and chopped peaches

2 cups sweetened peach iced tea (bottled or freshly brewed)

½ cup sugar (increase to 1 cup if the tea is unsweetened)

1 tablespoon vodka, preferably sweet tea vodka

1 tablespoon light corn syrup

A frosty glass of refreshing iced tea is the inspiration for this sorbet. Iced tea flavored with peaches has nearly outpaced tea with lemon in recent years. Bottles of tasty peach tea are available in most stores, but you can also brew your own with peach tea bags. If you use bottled tea in this recipe, make sure it isn't diet. This sorbet is a good way to use peaches so dead-ripe that they cannot be eaten whole or sliced because any small brown soft spots disappear into the tea.

The vodka improves the texture of the sorbet, as does the corn syrup. Use tea-flavored vodka if you have it, although plain vodka works fine. Pouring a splash of the sweet tea vodka or bourbon over the soft sorbet makes an excellent slushy for grown-ups.

MAKES ABOUT 1 QUART

① Purée the peaches in a blender and strain through a fine-mesh sieve into a medium glass or metal bowl, pressing on the solids with a rubber spatula to remove as much liquid as possible. Discard the solids. You should have about 2 cups of purée. Add the tea, sugar, vodka, and corn syrup and stir until the sugar dissolves. Cover and refrigerate until the mixture is very cold (under 40°F), at least 4 hours, then mix well.

② Churn the sorbet in an ice cream maker according to the manufacturer's instructions. When finished, the sorbet will be thick and soft and can be served as a slushy. To make the sorbet firm enough to scoop, transfer into an airtight container, press plastic wrap directly onto the surface of the sorbet, and freeze until firm.

## Browned Butter Peach Upside-Down Cake

Upside-down cake didn't originate in the South, but we have a strong affiliation with it, likely because of our affection for and reliance on our cast-iron skillets. Upside-down cake is a real crowd pleaser, not only because it's so good but also because it evokes pleasant memories for people who haven't tasted one in years.

Most upside-down cakes are made with pineapple, but they are fantastic made with other firm fruits, such as fresh peaches. In this recipe, slices of fresh peach are nestled in a buttery brown sugar topping that is made even tastier because the butter is browned, nutty, and fragrant.

MAKES 8 SERVINGS

① For the topping: Melt the butter in a well-seasoned 10-inch cast-iron skillet over medium heat. Cook the butter until it is lightly browned and smells nutty and toasted, about 5 minutes. Immediately add the brown sugar and stir until smooth.

② Carefully arrange the peaches in concentric circles in the butter mixture. It's okay if the peaches touch, but don't pack them in—you might have a few wedges left over. Set the skillet aside.

③ For the cake: Preheat the oven to 350°F.

④ Whisk together the flour, baking powder, salt, cinnamon, and cardamom in a medium bowl.

⑤ Beat the butter until light and fluffy in a large bowl with an electric mixer set to high speed. With the mixer running, slowly add the granulated sugar. Scrape down the sides of the bowl with a rubber spatula. Add the eggs one at a time, beating well after each addition.

⑥ Beat in half of the flour mixture. Beat in the milk, vanilla, and bourbon. Add the rest of the flour mixture and beat for 2 minutes, stopping once or twice to scrape down the sides of the bowl with a rubber spatula. Pour the batter over the topping mixture in the skillet, spreading the batter evenly to the edges of the skillet.

⑦ Bake until the cake is golden brown and springs back when touched lightly in the center, 35 to 40 minutes. Cool in the skillet on a wire rack for 5 minutes.

⑧ With oven mitts, carefully turn out the warm cake onto a serving plate. (Place the plate over the skillet and then flip them over together. Be brave and confident but careful.) Gently pry loose any peaches that stuck to the skillet and put them back on the cake. Serve warm or at room temperature.

WHAT ELSE WORKS? You can use pears or apples in place of the peaches.

### TOPPING

- 6 tablespoons butter
- ¾ cup firmly packed light brown sugar
- 1 pound peaches, peeled, pitted, and cut into ⅓-inch-thick wedges

### CAKE

- 1½ cups all-purpose flour
- 2 teaspoons baking powder
- ¼ teaspoon kosher salt
- ¼ teaspoon ground cinnamon
- ¼ teaspoon ground cardamom
- 4 tablespoons (½ stick) butter, at room temperature
- ¾ cup granulated sugar
- 2 large eggs, at room temperature
- ½ cup milk
- 1 teaspoon pure vanilla extract
- 2 tablespoons bourbon or additional milk

# PEARS

**Pears have always played second fiddle to apples in the South.**
Perhaps that's because many of the first pears planted in the New World
didn't do well and either died out or produced inedible fruit. Most of the
gritty, gnarly, and sour fruit was fed to animals or used to make a fermented
pear cider known as perry. The more aromatic fruit was placed in bowls
and set around to function as air freshener, a frivolity compared to food
that actually fed people.

During the colonial era, horticulturists and pear enthusiasts worked
on developing local pears. Their efforts paid off, and by 1750 several viable
types of American pears were established, including some that grew well
in the South. Many southern pears are round and have tan skin, so they
resemble Asian pears more than European pears. Often called apple pears
or sand pears, they are both vigorous and tasty, but they have never captured the market the way other southern fruits have. Southern pears are
garden fare, destined for plates, pies, and preserves rather than commercial outlets.

A ripe, succulent pear offers pure sweetness with no trace of bitterness or acidity. Pears can be soft or crisp or slightly granular, but they are
always reliably and splendidly sweet. ◼

# Roasted Red Pepper and Pear Soup

2 tablespoons extra-virgin olive oil

1 ½ cups peeled and chopped carrots

¾ cup chopped shallots or leeks

2 garlic cloves, finely chopped

4 cups chicken stock

1 ripe pear, cored, peeled, and chopped

8 large sweet red peppers, roasted, peeled, and seeded (about 8 cups)

1 teaspoon kosher salt, plus more to taste

½ cup pear nectar

1 teaspoon smoked paprika (*pimentón*), or to taste

¼ teaspoon cayenne pepper, or to taste

Crème fraîche (page 388 or store-bought), for garnish

Beautiful and aromatic, this soup is like a bowl of fragrant liquid rubies. It's ideal for the transitional season when summer crops are slowing down and the early fall crops are ramping up. The weather is usually mixed as well, with hot days downshifting into cool evenings when a little warm soup tastes good.

Use very sweet peppers, such as bells or red Italian frying peppers. For the best flavor, roast the peppers on the grill so that they can pick up a subtle smoky flavor. If you roast the peppers indoors, you can approximate that smokiness by adding smoked paprika to the soup.

An interesting and different way to serve this soup is to serve it in a shallow soup plate and float a thin slice of Cypress Grove Humboldt Fog cheese in the center instead of the crème fraîche.

This soup is best made a day ahead.

MAKES ABOUT 2 QUARTS

1. Heat the oil in a large, heavy pot over medium heat. Add the carrots and shallots and a pinch of salt. Cook, stirring occasionally, until the vegetables begin to soften but not brown, about 8 minutes. Add the garlic and cook for 1 minute.

2. Add the stock, pear, roasted peppers, and salt. Bring the soup just to a boil. Reduce the heat and let simmer until the vegetables are tender, about 10 minutes.

3. Purée in a blender (working in batches to not fill the blender more than half full) and return to the pot, or purée the soup directly in the pot with an immersion blender. Stir in the pear nectar and season with the smoked paprika and cayenne. If the soup is too thick, thin with more nectar. Cool to room temperature, cover, and refrigerate overnight.

4. Reheat gently over medium heat, stirring often. Check the seasoning. The subtle flavors and aromas are best when the soup is not piping hot, so serve warm or at room temperature, garnished with a dollop of crème fraîche.

MAKE-AHEAD NOTE: This soup tastes best when made 1 or 2 days ahead. Let cool to room temperature, cover, and refrigerate. Check the seasoning and reheat gently before serving.

## Pear and Pomegranate Salad with Late Harvest Riesling Vinaigrette, Candied Bacon, and Spiced Pecans

2 ripe but firm pears

1 tart green crisp apple

Late Harvest Riesling Vinaigrette (recipe follows)

4 cups lightly packed baby arugula, frisée, Belgian endive, mesclun, and/or thinly sliced radicchio

Arils of 1 pomegranate (about ½ cup)

6 to 8 strips Candied Bacon, cut into bite-sized pieces (recipe follows)

½ cup crumbled blue cheese

1 cup Spiced Pecans (recipe follows)

¼ cup beet micro greens (optional)

This is a take-notice salad, one to be served as part of a special meal or perhaps as a special meal. There are several components, but they are worth the effort.

The salad gets a touch of color from pomegranate seeds, known as arils. When selecting a pomegranate, don't go by looks. A bruised and battered pomegranate is more ripe and tasty than a shiny perfect one, but it should still be plump and feel heavy for its size. Pomegranate juice stains everything it touches, so lightly score the skin with a sharp knife and then submerge the pomegranate in a bowl of water when pulling off the skin and loosening the arils from the membranes. The water will contain the spray of juices.

The recipes for the candied bacon and spiced pecans will make more than you need for the salad, but that's a good thing. It's nearly impossible to resist nibbling when they come from the oven, so making extra might be the only way to ensure there's enough left to go on the salad.

MAKES 6 TO 8 SERVINGS

1. Unless the skins are thick or blemished, don't peel the pears and apple. Core and cut into thin slices or matchsticks. Place in a bowl and toss gently with about ¼ cup of the vinaigrette to prevent browning.

2. Toss the salad greens with enough vinaigrette to moisten and spread onto a large serving platter or serving plates.

3. Arrange the pears, apple, pomegranate arils, candied bacon, blue cheese, and spiced pecans over the greens. Drizzle any remaining vinaigrette over the salad. Sprinkle with micro greens, if using, and serve straightaway.

WHAT ELSE WORKS? You can use Asian pears in place of regular pears. Try red seedless grapes or champagne grapes in place of the pomegranate. You can also use other greens, although small leafy greens work better than crisp lettuce. You can also simplify the recipe by using unglazed pecans and bacon that is not candied.

## Late Harvest Riesling Vinaigrette

¼ cup late harvest
Riesling vinegar

2 tablespoons finely
chopped shallot

½ teaspoon kosher salt,
plus more to taste

1 teaspoon
Dijon mustard

6 tablespoons grapeseed
oil or mild and fruity
extra-virgin olive oil

2 tablespoons pecan
oil or walnut oil

Ground black
pepper, to taste

This delicate vinaigrette is perfect for any green salad that includes fresh or roasted fruit. The vinegar is made from Riesling grapes that are left on the vines so long that they become slightly shriveled with concentrated sweetness. The vinegar is so tasty and mild that you could nearly sip it as an aperitif.

When making vinaigrette, I choose particular oils and vinegars according to the flavors of the salad. If a salad has a particular nut in it, I like to reinforce that flavor by including some of that nut's oil. Nut oils can be very strong, so they taste best when balanced with milder oil in a recipe. See page 266 for more tips on using nut oils.

MAKES ABOUT ¾ CUP

1. Combine the vinegar, shallot, and salt in a medium glass jar with a tight-fitting lid and let sit for 5 minutes. Add the mustard, grapeseed oil, and pecan oil. Close the jar and shake vigorously to mix well. Season with pepper and additional salt, if needed.

2. Use soon or refrigerate for up to 1 week. Return to room temperature, shake vigorously, and check the seasoning before serving.

VARIATION: Replace the late harvest Riesling vinegar with fruit vinegar, such as raspberry or pear, to make other mild, fruity vinaigrettes.

## Candied Bacon

Vegetable oil spray

1 cup packed light
brown sugar

¾ teaspoon
cayenne pepper

¼ teaspoon dry mustard

1 pound highest-quality
sliced bacon

After years of many people pretending they don't eat bacon and don't even like it, we have come clean and admitted we love the stuff. I know three people who are strictly vegetarian except for bacon on Christmas morning. Because of that devotion, some silly, gimmicky things are being done with bacon these days. This isn't silly—it's sensational pig candy that is simultaneously salty, smoky, sweet, spicy, and sticky. It's good for breakfast, salads, and all by itself. If you cut it into short lengths or triangles and put it in a bowl to serve as party food, your guests will sing your praises.

MAKES 12 TO 16 SLICES, DEPENDING ON THE THICKNESS
OF THE BACON (AT LEAST 1 SERVING)

1. Preheat the oven to 350°F. Set a wire rack inside a large rimmed baking sheet lined with aluminum foil or parchment. Mist the rack with the spray.

2. Stir together the brown sugar, cayenne, and mustard on a plate.

3. Press one side of each slice of bacon into the sugar mixture to coat. Arrange the bacon sugar-side up in a single layer on the rack. Sprinkle the tops of the

slices evenly with any remaining sugar mixture. Try not to scatter it onto the pan, where it will burn and turn black.

(4) Bake the bacon until it is crisp and the sugar is bubbling, about 15 minutes. Let the bacon cool on the rack until the glaze is firm.

## Spiced Pecans

3 tablespoons unsalted butter

2 teaspoons kosher salt

¾ teaspoon ground black pepper

¼ teaspoon cayenne pepper

½ teaspoon ground cinnamon

2 tablespoons packed light brown sugar

1 tablespoon finely chopped fresh rosemary

4 cups raw pecan halves (about 1 pound)

Spiced pecans are a southern classic. Because these are neither too sweet nor too salty, they have uses beyond being a spot-on bar snack to serve with bourbon or sparkling wine. For example, they are great on salads as a creative, crunchy alternative to croutons. They also serve as that little something that makes a cheese plate look finished. A package of these pecans makes a gracious gift from the kitchen.

Because nuts are available year-round, we can forget that they are seasonal. Tree nuts are ready to harvest in autumn, which is the original reason that they are so popular in fall and in winter holiday recipes. When nuts are freshly shelled and still plump, buttery, and moist, they are clearly superior to packaged nuts that have been stored for months.

Pecans are the most southern of tree nuts, and there will always be good-natured debate on how to pronounce the word. How a person says "pecan" depends on where that person grew up, so I try to respect those hometown differences. I say "puh-cahn," mostly because one of my elementary schoolteachers said that a "pee can" was what great-granny hid under the bed. That image made a lasting impression on me.

MAKES 4 CUPS

(1) Preheat the oven to 350°F.

(2) Melt the butter in a large saucepan over medium heat. Whisk in the salt, pepper, cayenne, cinnamon, brown sugar, and rosemary. Add the nuts and stir well until well coated with the butter mixture.

(3) Spread the pecans on a large, rimmed baking sheet and toast until fragrant, 10 to 15 minutes, stirring every 5 minutes.

(4) Pour into a serving bowl and serve warm or at room temperature.

WHAT ELSE WORKS? You can use other nuts, or a medley. If the nuts are already salted, you probably will not need to use salt in the recipe.

MAKE-AHEAD NOTE: You can store in an airtight container up to 3 days. The nuts can be reheated in a 300°F oven for 10 minutes.

# Almond Cake with Sautéed Pears and Red Wine Syrup

**RED WINE SYRUP**

3 cups fruity, off-dry red wine

1 cup granulated sugar

1 cinnamon stick, broken in half

**ALMOND CAKE**

5 tablespoons unsalted butter, at room temperature

⅓ cup grapeseed oil or mild-flavored extra-virgin olive oil

¾ cup granulated sugar

12 ounces almond paste (not marzipan), crumbled

Finely grated zest of 2 oranges

5 large eggs, at room temperature

½ cup cake flour

1 teaspoon baking powder

3 tablespoons Grand Marnier or other orange liqueur

**SAUTÉED PEARS**

4 ripe but firm pears (about 2 pounds)

6 tablespoons unsalted butter

6 tablespoons light brown sugar

½ teaspoon pure vanilla extract

This is a great dessert for entertaining because each component can be made ahead. The star of this recipe is the Red Wine Syrup. Its flavor and aroma are surprisingly complex for something so simple. The quality of the wine counts, so go for something that is soft and fruity. You might have syrup left over, but it keeps well in the refrigerator for weeks. It's delicious drizzled over poached or dried fall fruit and good cheese.

MAKES 8 TO 10 SERVINGS

1. For the syrup: Bring the wine, granulated sugar, and cinnamon stick to a boil in a large saucepan, stirring until the sugar dissolves. Boil gently until the mixture reduces by half, about 45 minutes.

2. Remove from the heat and cool to room temperature. Discard the cinnamon stick. Cover and refrigerate until chilled.

3. For the cake: Preheat the oven to 325°F. Grease and flour a 9-inch round cake pan. Line the bottom with a round of parchment paper.

4. Beat the butter, oil, and granulated sugar until light and fluffy in a large bowl with an electric mixer set to high speed, about 3 minutes. Mix in the almond paste and orange zest. Scrape down the sides of the bowl with a rubber spatula. Beat in the eggs, one at a time, mixing only until they are incorporated. Whisk together the flour and baking powder in a small bowl, then add to the batter and beat only until they disappear into the batter. Scrape the batter into the prepared pan.

5. Bake until a tester inserted into the center comes out clean, about 45 minutes. Cool the cake to room temperature in the pan on a wire rack. Turn out the cake onto a serving plate and brush with the liqueur.

6. For the pears: Peel and core the pears. Cut into ½-inch-thick slices. Melt the butter in a large skillet over medium-high heat. Stir in the brown sugar. Add the pears and sauté until barely tender and golden, about 5 minutes. Remove from the heat and stir in the vanilla.

7. To serve, cut the cake into wedges. Top each wedge with pears and a generous drizzle of the syrup.

WHAT ELSE WORKS? You can replace the pears with halved fresh figs or fresh orange sections. Do not sauté the oranges.

MAKE-AHEAD NOTE: You can store the syrup covered and refrigerated for up to 4 weeks. Return it to room temperature for serving.

## Pancetta Crisps with Chèvre and Fresh Pear

16 slices of pancetta (cut the thickness of regular bacon)

2 ripe but firm pears

3 ounces soft, fresh goat cheese (chèvre), at room temperature

2 to 3 tablespoons delicate floral honey, such as acacia or tupelo

Freshly cracked pepper, preferably a mixture of black and pink peppercorns

Pancetta is a type of rolled Italian unsmoked bacon that is cut into thin rounds that are about 3 inches in diameter. When cooked flat on a baking sheet, the pieces of pancetta turn into crisp disks, although sometimes the edges curl inward just a bit to make a shallow saucer. In this recipe, the pleasantly salty disks are stacked on rounds of sweet, juicy pear and topped with a tangy chèvre-style goat cheese. A drizzle of honey adds sweetness, and the cracked pepper is fantastic with the honey.

This is a gorgeous appetizer, but it's not finger food, so give each guest a little plate and a fork.

MAKES 16 PIECES

1. Preheat the oven to 450°F. Cover a wire rack with paper towels and set aside.

2. Arrange the pancetta in a single layer on a baking sheet lined with aluminum foil. Bake until golden, about 8 minutes. Use a spatula to transfer the pancetta to the paper towels, and let sit until firm. Use the spatula to gently transfer the pancetta crisps to a serving platter.

3. Cut off and discard the slender tops of the pears, leaving uniform, somewhat cylindrical bottom halves. Use an apple corer to core the pear bottoms. Thinly slice each cored pear bottom crosswise into 8 donut-shaped rounds, for a total of 16 rounds. Place a pancetta crisp atop each pear round. (If your pear slices fit inside the pancetta crisp, you can reverse the two.)

4. Divide the cheese evenly among the pieces, about ½ teaspoon per piece. Use your fingers or a small spoon to make them rounded and pretty on top, if you wish.

5. Drizzle each piece with about ½ teaspoon of honey and sprinkle with pepper. Serve soon. They hold nicely up to 30 minutes, but after an hour they are so soggy that they break apart when served.

WHAT ELSE WORKS? You can use rounds of Asian pears or sand pears or thin slices of firm Fuyu persimmons or fresh peaches in place of the pears. You can replace the chèvre with a similar sheep's milk cheese or a soft, ripe cheese, such as La Tur or Robiola Tre Latte.

## Savory Spiced Pear and Apple Sauce

3 pears, peeled, cored, and cut into 1-inch chunks (about 1 pound)

3 apples, peeled, cored, and cut into 1-inch chunks (about 1 pound)

¼ cup pear or apple cider

1 tablespoon brown sugar

¼ teaspoon ground cinnamon

¼ teaspoon ground ginger

¼ teaspoon ground cardamom

¼ teaspoon dry mustard

2 tablespoons butter

1 teaspoon chopped fresh thyme

Kosher salt and ground black pepper, to taste

Fruit sauce doesn't have to be sweet and slippery. This sauce showcases the natural sweetness of the fruit and remains a little chunky, so it's grown-up comfort food instead of baby food. I like to use a combination of fruit that breaks down and fruit that stays firm when cooked. The spices make the sauce taste a little like soft, subtle chutney. The sauce makes a great side dish to duck and venison and nearly any kind of ham or other cuts of pork.

MAKES 6 SERVINGS

1. Stir together the pears, apples, cider, brown sugar, cinnamon, ginger, cardamom, and mustard in a large saucepan. Bring to a simmer over medium heat, cover the pan, and cook, stirring occasionally, until the fruit is soft, about 15 minutes. If the fruit gets dry, add a bit more cider.

2. Coarsely mash the fruit directly in the pot with a hand-held potato masher or the side of a large spoon. Stir in the butter and thyme. Season with salt and pepper. Check the seasoning; the spices should be subtle but perceptible. Serve warm or at room temperature.

WHAT ELSE WORKS? You can use all pears or all apples.

# PERSIMMONS

**The only indigenous southern persimmon** is the wild persimmon, the ones the Algonquins called *pessemin*, from which we get the English word. Some old-timers called persimmon trees "possum trees," as a play on words and because possums love to eat the fruit as much as we do.

Persimmons were elemental to the diet of Native Americans, who ate them fresh, dried them whole, and ground them into a paste that was then dried like fruit leather. They also used persimmons to make bread and beer. Native Americans quickly introduced persimmons to the earliest colonists, as noted by Jamestown founder Captain John Smith, who called them "putchamins": "And now with winter approaching, the rivers became so covered with swans, geese, ducks, and cranes that we daily feasted with good bread, Virginia peas, pumpkins, and putchamins, fish, fowl, and divers sort of wild beasts as fast as we could eat them." However, a bite of an unripe persimmon is a lasting lesson. In his *Generall Historie* (1624), Captain Smith cautioned that "if it not be ripe it will draw a man's mouth awry with much torment, but when it is ripe it is as delicious as an apricok."

Wild persimmons are about the size of a golf ball. This windfall fruit drops from the trees after a hard frost or freeze. To be edible, they must be fully ripe or even post-ripe, when they are so soft that their skins barely contain the jammy pulp and so ephemeral they might collapse under a hard stare. If you can gather them up before the deer, raccoons, and possums find them, wild persimmons are one of the finest autumn fruits. Before their fall into grace, the small, dark persimmons dangle from the bare limbs like dimmed Chinese lanterns.

Nothing tastes like a wild persimmon, but it is possible to grow hybridized Hachiya and Fuyu persimmons. These Asian persimmons were introduced into the United States by Commodore Perry, who brought the rootstock home from his travels to Japan in the mid-1800s. Like wild persimmons, Hachiyas cannot be eaten until they soften and sweeten up. Fuyus, even when ripe, remain as firm and crunchy as apples and, to a wild persimmon lover's palate, utterly inferior. The moral of the story of persimmons is that good things come to those who wait. ■

To extract persimmon pulp and make purée for recipes, remove the caps and stems from the fruit. Leave wild persimmons whole and cut larger fruit into halves or quarters. Force them through a food mill or a mesh sieve, letting the smooth pulp fall into a large bowl. Discard the skins and seeds.

## Persimmon Pudding

Vegetable oil spray

¾ cup all-purpose flour

¼ cup fine stone-ground cornmeal

½ teaspoon baking soda

½ teaspoon kosher salt

¼ teaspoon ground cinnamon

¼ teaspoon ground ginger

⅛ teaspoon ground nutmeg

2 large eggs

¾ cup packed light or dark brown sugar

1 cup well-shaken buttermilk

1 cup wild persimmon purée or ¾ cup Hachiya purée plus ¼ cup apricot preserves

2 tablespoons unsalted butter, melted

Whipped cream, for serving

Persimmon pudding is a very old dessert that has countless variations. Some are firm like gingerbread cake and others are creamy spoon food. The only common denominator is persimmons, and even that isn't straightforward. Everyone agrees that the best choice is wild persimmons that are native to North America. When wild persimmons are not available, you can substitute fully ripened and squishy soft Hachiya persimmons, the variety that looks like an elongated acorn, although the flavor isn't as intense. A wild persimmon tastes like a perfect apricot with a hint of pumpkin. To mimic that flavor and perfume when I have to use Hachiya persimmons in this recipe, I add apricot preserves. Firm pieces of hard, squat Fuyu persimmons simply will not work in this recipe.

MAKES 8 SERVINGS

1. Preheat the oven to 350°F. Mist the inside of a 1 ½-quart baking dish with the spray. The pudding bakes in a water bath, so set the dish inside a baking pan.

2. Whisk together the flour, cornmeal, baking soda, salt, cinnamon, ginger, and nutmeg in a medium bowl.

3. Whisk the eggs in a large bowl until the whites and yolks are blended, then vigorously whisk in the brown sugar until it dissolves and the mixture thickens. Gently whisk in the buttermilk and persimmon purée. Add the flour mixture and stir with a rubber spatula only until the dry ingredients disappear into the batter. Stir in the melted butter.

4. Scrape the batter into the small baking dish. Pour enough very hot tap water into the baking pan to come halfway up the sides of the dish. Bake until the top is puffed and the pudding is just set, about 1 hour. A thin knife inserted about 1 inch from the center should come out moist but not wet. Remove the dish from the water bath and let sit for at least 10 minutes before serving warm or at room temperature, topped with whipped cream if you like.

# Winter Fruit Couscous Salad

1 ½ cups plain couscous (about 10 ounces)

½ cup dried cranberries

3 tablespoons fruity, mild, extra-virgin olive oil or grapeseed oil, divided

3 tablespoons chopped scallions (white and tender green parts)

1 teaspoon ground cinnamon

½ teaspoon ground cumin

⅛ teaspoon cayenne pepper

2 cups chicken or light-colored vegetable stock

½ cup apple juice concentrate

1 teaspoon kosher salt, plus more to taste

1 tart apple, cored and cubed

2 Fuyu persimmons, cored and thinly sliced

2 tablespoons chopped fresh mint

½ cup pecan pieces, lightly toasted

½ cup pomegranate arils

Fuyu persimmons are squat with a distinctive four-leaf top knot. They are meant to be eaten firm and raw, like an apple. They hold their shape when cut, which makes them a sweet and colorful addition to this simple salad. Don't try this recipe with a fully ripe wild or Hachiya persimmon, because cutting one is like trying to slice a water balloon.

The pomegranate arils add more color and fruity flavor. Pomegranates were an early feature of southern plantation gardens, although they were grown more often for ornamentation than for eating. Some mothers used dried pomegranates as baby rattles. See page 226 for tips on peeling pomegranates.

This salad makes a light, fresh Thanksgiving dish, a welcome contrast to all the heavy, creamy, rich food. I often make it as something new to serve with the turkey sandwiches, to counter my family's tendency to roll their eyes and sigh heavily when I trot out those foil-covered bowls of leftovers for the third time.

MAKES 6 TO 8 SERVINGS

① Place the couscous and dried cranberries in a large bowl.

② Heat 1 tablespoon of the oil in a small saucepan over medium heat. Stir in the scallions and a pinch of salt and cook, stirring often, until softened, about 3 minutes. Stir in the cinnamon, cumin, and cayenne. Cook, stirring, for 30 seconds. Stir in the stock, apple juice concentrate, and salt. Bring to a boil and pour over the couscous. Cover the bowl and set aside for 5 minutes. Fluff the couscous gently with a fork.

③ Stir in the remaining 2 tablespoons of oil and the apple, persimmons, mint, pecans, and pomegranate arils. Check the seasoning and add more salt, if needed.

WHAT ELSE WORKS? You can use 1 cup fresh orange sections or drained mandarin oranges in place of the persimmons. You can use a pear in place of the apple.

# Persimmon and Black Walnut Bread

1 ¾ cups sifted all-purpose flour

1 ¼ cups sugar

1 teaspoon baking soda

¾ teaspoon fine sea salt

½ teaspoon ground mace or nutmeg

2 large eggs, at room temperature

1 cup persimmon purée (from 2 to 3 dead-ripe Hachiya or 1 quart wild persimmons)

⅓ cup bourbon

8 tablespoons (1 stick) unsalted butter, melted

1 cup black walnuts, coarsely chopped

1 cup diced dried apricots or pitted dates

This is a quick bread, similar to banana bread but made with persimmon pulp instead of mashed bananas. As with any recipe that calls for persimmon pulp, wild persimmons are best, but it's also good with the more common Hachiya variety.

This is an old recipe, so it uses liquor as both a flavoring and a way to add moisture to the bread. I'm partial to bourbon, but apricot or peach brandy goes great with the persimmons. Liquor and sweet wine were once critical components in southern fruited cakes. I've seen old recipes that instruct the cook to wrap cakes in cloths saturated in liquor or wine in preparation for long storage. Similarly, some recipes said to place a snuff glass or shot glass of spirits in the center of a ring cake stored in a closed tin. The cakes would gradually absorb the alcohol, making them keep for months, if not years, although I have my doubts about the appeal of any cake that supposedly tastes as good after a few years as it did when it was first baked.

Black walnuts are one of those foods that people either love or hate. It took me years to appreciate their strong, distinctive flavor. My grandparents adored them, and since they were plentiful in our Blue Ridge Mountains, there was usually a bushel in the basement to use through the fall and winter. Black walnuts have a rock-hard outer shell. My granddaddy would smash them open with the side of a hatchet or mallet. When he got older and had less strength, he would strew them onto the pavement of the carport and back over them a few times with his lawn tractor.

MAKES 8 SERVINGS

1. Preheat the oven to 350°F. Grease a 5 × 9-inch loaf pan, line the bottom with a piece of parchment paper, grease the paper, and dust the inside of the pan with flour, tapping out any excess.

2. Sift together the flour, sugar, baking soda, salt, and mace into a large bowl. Whisk the eggs in a medium bowl until the whites and yolks are blended, then whisk in the purée, bourbon, and butter. Make a well in the center of the flour mixture, pour in the egg mixture, and stir with a rubber spatula only until blended. Fold in the nuts and apricots. Scrape the batter into the prepared pan.

3. Bake in the center of the oven until a tester inserted into the center of the loaf comes out clean, about 1 hour. Cool in the pan on a wire rack for 10 minutes, then turn out the loaf onto the rack to cool to room temperature before slicing. Store tightly wrapped for up to 1 week or frozen for up to 3 months.

VARIATION: You can use mashed pawpaws in place of the persimmon purée in this recipe. (You can use mashed pawpaw in any baked recipe that calls for mashed bananas.) Like wild persimmons, pawpaws are an elusive tree fruit that can be found growing wild in the woods and underbrush in parts of the South and are occasionally cultivated. They are often called a poor man's banana. They are yellow and do taste a little like bananas and mangos, tropical flavors rarely found in fruits native to North America. Pawpaws were once a mainstay of the traditional Native American and pioneer diet. Some say that pawpaws kept Lewis and Clark alive during their expedition.

# PLUMS

**Plums once grew wild in most of the world, including in the South.**
Most of those wild plums were small, tart, and painfully astringent, so they
were better suited for wine and brandy making than for eating. Charleston resident Henry Laurens is credited with introducing better-tasting
Old World plums from the south of France to the colonies around 1755,
but it's unclear whether he personally undertook the effort or merely paid
for it. (He was later elected president of the Continental Congress, which
perhaps begs the same question.)

The plums we grow and eat today in the South and in the United States
come from a mixture of European, Asian, and wild American rootstock.
Small, firm plums are particularly good for making preserves. Large, plump,
juicy plums can be enjoyed raw or cooked. Wild American plums are almost always cooked. A notably delicious native plum is the beach plum.
Many plum purists believe it's the best plum, and perhaps the best fruit,
that grows on the East Coast. Beach plums thrive in the sandy dunes and
salty air. They grow in tight thickets, which were once used as hedges
and fences. The plants sent out such a profusion of sturdy shoots that
it was often easier and faster to grow an erosion-resistant fence than to
build one. ■

## Plum, Peach, and Tomato Salad

4 plums, pitted and cut into thin wedges

2 large peaches, peeled, pitted, and cut into thin wedges

2 medium tomatoes, peeled if necessary, cored, and cut into thin wedges

1 small red onion, halved lengthwise and cut into thin strips

1 to 2 jalapeño or serrano chiles, finely chopped (remove the seeds and membranes to reduce the heat)

Finely grated zest of 1 lime

Juice of 2 limes (about ⅓ cup)

1 teaspoon kosher salt

½ teaspoon ground black pepper

¼ cup lightly packed cilantro leaves, coarsely chopped

Considering that tomatoes are botanically a fruit, it makes sense that they can play well with other fruits that are in season at the same time. This salad is simple and refreshing. Any variety of firm, colorful tomato is nice in this salad, but tart green tomatoes make a nice contrast to the sweet fruit. This concoction is very good with smoked duck or grilled fish.

MAKES 4 SERVINGS

(1) Stir together all of the ingredients except the cilantro in a large bowl. Cover and let sit at room temperature for 1 hour to give the flavors time to come together, stirring occasionally.

(2) Stir in the cilantro and check the seasoning just before serving.

VARIATION: To quickly and easily transform this salad into fruit salsa, simply dice the fruit into small pieces and bump up the chile to taste. You'll get about 4 cups of salsa.

## Fresh Fruit Salad with Secret Dressing and Fresh Ginger Muffin Cakes

3 tablespoons light, floral honey, such as orange blossom, tupelo, or acacia

¼ cup Grand Marnier or other orange liqueur

1 tablespoon bitters

Finely grated zest and juice of 1 orange (about ½ cup)

8 cups fresh fruit peeled if necessary and cut into bite-sized pieces, such as plums, berries, kiwi, peaches, nectarines, figs, grapes, and oranges

Fresh Ginger Muffin Cakes, for serving (recipe follows)

This is no ordinary fruit salad. The dressing puts it over the top and no one can guess the secret ingredient: bitters, the crucial ingredient in so many classic southern cocktails, such as a Sazerac. It's fine to use tried-and-true brands such as Angostura or Pechaud's, but there are other small-batch artisanal bitters on the market, so see what you can find out there. You can vary the fruit depending on what is in season, but make sure the fruit is firm, fresh, fragrant, and colorful. Avoid apples and pears because they are too crunchy.

MAKES 6 TO 8 SERVINGS

1. Whisk together the honey, liqueur, bitters, orange zest, and orange juice in a large bowl. Add the fruit and toss gently to coat with the sauce.

2. Cover and chill for at least 30 minutes and up to 8 hours before serving with the muffins.

## Fresh Ginger Muffin Cakes

Vegetable oil spray

¼ cup peeled and finely grated fresh ginger

6 tablespoons plus ½ cup sugar

Finely grated zest of 2 lemons

2 cups all-purpose flour

½ teaspoon kosher salt

¾ teaspoon baking soda

8 tablespoons (1 stick) unsalted butter, at room temperature

2 large eggs, at room temperature

1 cup well-shaken buttermilk

I adapted this recipe from an old cookbook that focused on breakfast and brunch food. Each time I make them, I am charmed by their flavor and aroma. They are ethereal, more like little cakes than muffins. See page 310 for tips on making attractive muffins.

Ginger has always been quite popular in southern cooking and was once common in home gardens. For this recipe, the ginger must be very fresh and juicy with firm, unblemished skin. The ginger must be peeled, but don't waste your time or try your patience trying to peel those little knobs and bumps. Just cut them off and peel the main part of the piece of ginger. A rasp-style grater (such as a Microplane) works best for very fine grating.

MAKES 12 MUFFINS

1. Preheat the oven to 375°F. Mist the top of a standard 12-cup muffin tin with the spray. Mist the cups or line them with paper muffin cups. Be sure to use a light metal muffin tin. Dark metal and nonstick tins—even when lined with paper cups—make the crust too thick and dark.

2. Stir together the ginger and 4 tablespoons of the sugar in a small saucepan and cook over medium heat until the sugar has melted and the mixture is hot. Remove from the stove and let cool to room temperature, then stir in the lemon zest and 2 more tablespoons of the sugar.

3. Whisk together the flour, salt, and baking soda in a medium bowl and set aside.

4. Beat the butter and the remaining ½ cup of sugar until light and fluffy in a large bowl with an electric mixer set to high speed, about 2 minutes. Add the eggs one at a time, beating well after each addition. Scrape down the sides of the bowl with a rubber spatula. Add the flour mixture in three additions, alternating with the buttermilk, beating on low speed only until the batter is smooth after each addition. Overmixing makes the muffins tough. Fold the ginger-lemon mixture into the batter.

5. Spoon the batter into the muffin tins. Bake until a tester inserted into a muffin comes out clean, about 15 minutes. Serve warm.

## Plum Cake

This is a simple and pretty spice cake with little plum domes peeking up through the batter. Any kind of plum will work, but slightly underripe plums hold their shape when baked, and dark plums look pretty. Italian plums, the ones that are often dried to make prunes, are ideal. The cake is made in a springform pan for easy serving, but it can also be made in a standard round cake pan if you don't mind working to get the first piece out.

MAKES 8 SERVINGS

Vegetable oil spray

1 cup all-purpose flour

1 teaspoon baking powder

½ teaspoon kosher salt

2 teaspoons ground cinnamon

½ teaspoon ground allspice

½ teaspoon ground ginger

½ teaspoon ground nutmeg

8 tablespoons (1 stick) unsalted butter, at room temperature

¾ cup plus 1 tablespoon sugar

2 large eggs

1 teaspoon pure vanilla extract

6 to 8 small plums, halved and pitted (about 1 pound)

Lightly sweetened whipped cream, for serving

1. Preheat the oven to 350°F. Mist the inside of a 9-inch springform pan with the spray.

2. Whisk together the flour, baking powder, salt, cinnamon, allspice, ginger, and nutmeg in a medium bowl.

3. Beat the butter and ¾ cup of the sugar until light and fluffy in a large bowl with an electric mixer set to high speed, about 3 minutes. Scrape down the sides of the bowl with a rubber spatula. Add the eggs one at a time, beating well after each addition. Beat in the vanilla. Add the flour mixture and beat on low speed only until it disappears into the batter. Scrape the batter into the prepared pan and smooth the top. Arrange the plums cut-side down over the batter. Sprinkle the remaining 1 tablespoon of sugar over the top.

4. Bake until a tester inserted into the center of the cake comes out clean, 45 to 50 minutes.

5. Cool in the pan on a wire rack for at least 20 minutes. Serve warm or at room temperature, topped with a dollop of whipped cream.

WHAT ELSE WORKS? You can use other stone fruit, such as nectarines, peaches, or apricots.

## Spiced Stone Fruit Sauce

2 tablespoons orange
juice concentrate

½ to ¾ cup Major Grey's
chutney

1 tablespoon Madeira
or sherry

4 large plums, pitted
and thinly sliced
(about 1 pound)

2 peaches, peeled,
pitted, and thinly
sliced (about
6 ounces)

2 apricots, peeled,
pitted, and thinly
sliced (about
4 ounces)

1 cup pitted
sweet cherries

This quick, chunky sauce reminds me of that odd concoction known as hot curried fruit, a dish that was common during the 1950s and '60s and that still sometimes pops up at church dinners and family reunions. Try this aromatic sauce with baked ham, roasted duck, or pork chops. Stir it into hot cooked rice. Tuck it into a roasted sweet potato. Spoon it over cheese. If you're up for a little taste adventure, serve it over vanilla ice cream and Brown Sugar Pound Cake (page 220).

MAKES 3 CUPS

1  Stir together the orange juice concentrate, ½ cup of the chutney, and the Madeira in a large saucepan. Cook over low heat, stirring until the concentrate and chutney melt.

2  Add the fruit and gently stir to coat. The fruit should be lightly coated and moist, so stir in more melted chutney if needed. Serve warm.

WHAT ELSE WORKS? You can use other stone fruit, such as pluots or nectarines.

# POTATOES

**Culinary historians venture that potatoes** held no cachet on southern tables until Jefferson and Franklin served them after their well-known Paris sojourns. Potatoes fared better as immigrants from potato-loving cultures arrived in waves over the next century or so, bringing their favorite spud varieties, recipes, and foodways with them.

Today, home gardens and small farms are the guardians of potato diversity, as are cooks who appreciate that different recipes require different kinds of potatoes, ranging from low-starch to high-starch varieties. Low-starch, waxy potatoes hold their shape when cooked, making them good candidates for potato salad, for example. High-starch varieties have dry flesh that collapses when cooked, so they're best for fluffy mashed potatoes. Round, brown potatoes are most common, but these tubers—particularly heirloom varieties—come in a range of shapes and colors, including white, gold, red, pink, purple, and blue.

Many people find comfort in the reliable familiarity of potatoes. This short verse by John Tyler Pettee sums up the sentiment:

Pray for peace and grace and spiritual food,
For wisdom and guidance, for all these things are good.
But don't forget the potatoes. ■

# Potato, Mushroom, and Gruyère Gratin

2 tablespoons butter, divided

4 ounces wild mushrooms, stems discarded, cut into ¼-inch slices

4 ounces cremini mushrooms, cut into ¼-inch slices

¾ cup heavy cream

¾ cup whole milk

2 garlic cloves, peeled and finely chopped

1 teaspoon kosher salt

½ teaspoon pepper

½ teaspoon chopped fresh thyme

½ teaspoon finely chopped fresh rosemary

¼ teaspoon freshly grated nutmeg

1½ pounds starchy potatoes (such as russets)

1 cup freshly grated aged Gruyère cheese

When my daughter was in an early grade, the children were asked to bring in their favorite food as part of a Thanksgiving celebration, during which they would sport little Pilgrim hats and feathered headbands crafted from construction paper and too much glue. The array of foods was thought provoking and mostly centered on fish-shaped crackers. My daughter requested this. It's still one of her favorite things to eat.

There is perhaps nothing better to serve with beef tenderloin for a holiday meal.

MAKES 6 SERVINGS

(1) Position a rack in the middle of the oven and preheat oven to 400°F. Butter the bottom of a shallow 2- or 2½-quart baking dish.

(2) Melt 1 tablespoon of the butter in a large skillet over medium-high heat. Add the wild mushrooms and cook, stirring often, until they soften and any liquid evaporates, about 8 minutes. Work in batches, if necessary, to avoid crowding the mushrooms in the pan so that they can brown well and stay firm instead of getting slimy and lost in lots of liquid. Pour the cooked mushrooms onto a plate and set aside.

(3) Melt the remaining 1 tablespoon of butter in the skillet and cook the cremini mushrooms the same way. Transfer them to the plate and set aside.

(4) Stir together the cream, milk, garlic, salt, pepper, thyme, rosemary, and nutmeg in a large saucepan.

(5) Working with one potato at a time, peel the potatoes and cut into even slices that are no more than ⅛-inch thick and stir them into the cream mixture. A vegetable slicer is ideal, although the slicing can be done with a sharp knife. To make the process easier and safer when using a knife, cut a thin slice off one of the long sides of the potato so that it sits flat and does not wobble on the cutting board.

(6) Bring the potatoes just to a simmer over medium-high heat, then remove the pan from the heat. Use a slotted spoon to transfer half of the potatoes to the prepared dish, spreading them evenly. Top with the cooked mushrooms but leave any accumulated mushroom liquid behind. Spoon the remaining potatoes over the mushrooms, spreading evenly. Pour the potato cooking liquid evenly over the top and sprinkle with the cheese.

(7) Bake until the top is browned and the potatoes are tender and bubbling around the edges, 45 to 55 minutes. If the top gets too brown before the potatoes are done, lay a flat sheet of aluminum foil over the top. Let stand at least 10 minutes before serving.

WHAT ELSE WORKS? You can replace up to 8 ounces of the potatoes with thinly sliced celery root or Jerusalem artichokes. Another nice variation is to omit the mushrooms and increase the total amount of potatoes to 2 pounds, using a combination of russets and sweet potatoes.

### TIPS AND TECHNIQUES

There are four simple things that make a potato gratin thick and creamy instead of runny. First, use very starchy potatoes, such as russets. Second, slice the potatoes directly into the cream so that they don't oxidize and turn the color of wet newspaper before they're cooked. Third, heat the potatoes in the cream before layering them in the dish. This gives the potatoes a chance to release some of their starch into the cream, which helps thicken the liquid. Fourth, let the gratin rest for at least 10 minutes before serving to give it time to firm up.

## Roasted Potatoes

2 pounds low-starch potatoes, left whole or cut depending on their size

2 tablespoons extra-virgin olive oil

Coarse salt and ground black pepper, to taste

1 tablespoon chopped fresh rosemary or sage (optional)

The best potatoes for roasting are low-starch, so-called waxy varieties that stay firm and hold their shape when cooked, such as fingerlings, Yukon Gold, Bintje, Finns, and crescents. Most so-called new potatoes are low-starch.

When the potatoes are small, you can leave them whole. When cutting large potatoes, you can change the personality of the recipe by changing their shape, such as little coin-shaped rounds, wedges, cubes for home fries, or long slabs that turn out like steak fries. The pieces should be roughly the same size and shape so they'll cook at the same rate. If you want crisp potatoes, make sure they are completely dry when they go onto the pan and don't salt them until after they are roasted. The salt makes the potatoes release moisture and keeps them soft.

MAKES 6 SERVINGS

1. Preheat the oven to 400°F. Line a rimmed baking sheet with aluminum foil. (For extra crispness, roast them in a very large cast-iron skillet.)
2. Place the potatoes on the prepared baking sheet, drizzle with the oil, and toss to coat. Spread into a single layer and roast until the potatoes are tender when pierced with the tip of a knife and the cut sides are browned, 20 to 40 minutes, depending on the size of the pieces.
3. Season the hot potatoes generously with salt, pepper, and the rosemary, if using. Serve warm.

VARIATION: Season the hot potatoes with seasoned salt, either packaged or homemade. To make your own, grind two parts kosher salt and one part finely chopped fresh herbs and/or citrus zest together in a spice grinder or small food processor. Make sure the herbs are very dry so that the salt stays granular instead of turning into paste. Store in an airtight container in the refrigerator for up to 1 month.

# Roasted Fingerling Potato Salad with Lemon-Basil Vinaigrette

It is impossible to have too many different kinds of potato salad. This one is chock full of unexpected twists in texture and seasoning. The potatoes are roasted and then dressed in a tangy, savory dressing that doesn't include a speck of mayonnaise. This is a great dish for picnicking, tailgating, and dinner on the grounds. It's also beautiful and will draw people back to the bowl or platter.

MAKES 6 SERVINGS

### SALAD

- 2 pounds fingerling potatoes
- 2 tablespoons extra-virgin olive oil
- 2 large roasted red bell peppers, cut into thin strips (about 1 ½ cups) (page 314 or store-bought)
- ½ cup shallots, finely chopped
- ¼ cup lightly packed basil leaves, cut into thin ribbons
- ¾ cup coarsely grated Parmesan or Manchego cheese

  Kosher salt and ground black pepper

### LEMON-BASIL VINAIGRETTE

- Zest of 1 lemon (about 2 teaspoons)
- Juice of 2 lemons (about ½ cup)
- 4 garlic cloves, finely chopped
- ½ cup lightly packed basil leaves
- 1 tablespoon Dijon mustard
- ½ cup extra-virgin olive oil
- 2 teaspoons kosher salt, or to taste

  Ground black pepper, to taste

1. For the salad: Preheat the oven to 400°F. Line a rimmed baking sheet with aluminum foil.
2. Cut the potatoes in half lengthwise. Transfer to the prepared baking sheet, drizzle with the oil, and toss to coat. Spread the potatoes in a single layer and roast only until they are tender when pierced with the tip of a knife and the cut sides are browned, 20 to 40 minutes, depending on the size of the pieces. Do not overcook the potatoes or they will fall apart in the salad. Make the vinaigrette while the potatoes are roasting.
3. For the vinaigrette: Combine the lemon zest, lemon juice, garlic, basil, and mustard in a blender and blend until chopped. With the blender running, slowly pour in the oil and blend until the dressing is thick. Season with salt and pepper.
4. Transfer the hot potatoes into a large bowl and toss gently with the Lemon-Basil Vinaigrette. Let cool to room temperature, stirring occasionally.
5. Gently mix in the roasted peppers, shallots, basil, and cheese. Season generously with salt and pepper. Serve at room temperature.

MAKE-AHEAD NOTE: You can make the salad up to 1 day ahead, but don't add the fresh basil more than 1 hour before serving. Store covered and refrigerated. For best flavor, return the salad to room temperature before serving.

# Carolina Fish Muddle

3 ounces bacon or
side meat, diced

1 large onion, cut in half
lengthwise and thinly
sliced (about 2 cups)

1 celery stalk, thinly
sliced (about ¼ cup)

2 garlic cloves, chopped

1 (8-ounce) can
tomato sauce

1 ½ cups fish stock,
chicken stock, or
water, plus more
as needed

12 ounces potatoes,
peeled only if neces-
sary and cubed or
thinly sliced (about
3 cups)

1 small bay leaf

2 teaspoons chopped
fresh thyme

¼ cup finely chopped
flat-leaf parsley, plus
more for garnish

1 small dried hot
pepper pod or a
pinch of crushed
red pepper flakes

2 teaspoons kosher salt,
plus more to taste

1 ½ pounds fish fillets cut
into 1-inch pieces

6 large eggs

Buttered saltines or
hot bread, for serving

Muddle is a rustic fish and potato stew with deep roots in North Carolina. The word "muddle" refers not only to the stew but also to the process of making the stew, as in "let's go muddle us some muddle." A muddle can be a community event where huge vats are made and sold to raise funds for churches, marching bands headed to a big parade, volunteer fire departments, and such. I love to see what foods a community holds up as their food, the thing they make with pride and for profit as if to say, "We live here, so we made this. Come buy some."

Like any recipe rooted in home cooking and community tradition, there are countless versions of muddle, all coming down to what swims through the lo-cal waters. In the western part of the state, muddle is made from creek fish. At the coast, it's made with ocean fish. Muddle is a way to cook whatever you don't throw back. Fillet your catch and put it in a pot with plenty of potatoes, onions, tomatoes, and the seasonings you like (or at least those you have) and there you go. Curiously, authentic muddle is always finished with eggs. The eggs can be poached in the simmering stock, stirred in to thicken the soup, or boiled sepa-rately and crumbled over the top.

I was once served truly exceptional muddle on the banks of the creek where a bunch of us had been fishing all day. That evening, while the rest of us goofed around and watched our sunburns bloom, a dear friend simmered our stellar muddle in a clean bucket nestled into campfire coals. A bucket. No stove-top muddle can conjure the same effect as that magical creek fish stew cooked over a fire and under the stars, but it is possible to make a satisfying muddle at home, no bucket required.

MAKES 6 SERVINGS

1. Cook the bacon in a Dutch oven or small soup pot over medium-high heat until it renders its fat and turns crisp, stirring often, about 8 minutes. Add the onion and celery and a pinch of salt, then stir to coat in the bacon drippings. Cook, stirring often, until the vegetables soften, about 8 minutes. Stir in the garlic and tomato sauce and cook for 2 minutes.

2. Stir in the stock, potatoes, bay leaf, thyme, parsley, hot pepper, and salt. Bring to a boil, reduce the heat, and simmer until the potatoes are tender and just starting to break apart, about 40 minutes. Remove the bay leaf and stir in the fish. The liquid should be level with or slightly above the ingredi-ents, so add more stock if needed.

3. This next step depends on how you want the eggs. If you are poaching the eggs, increase the heat so that the soup comes to a low boil, then crack the eggs onto the surface of the simmering soup, spacing them evenly. Cover the pot and cook until the fish is opaque and the egg whites are set but the yolks are still soft, 8 to 10 minutes. If the egg whites are still loose when the fish is

done, baste the eggs with hot broth to set the tops. Spoon an egg into each serving bowl, ladle hot muddle over the top, sprinkle with parsley, and serve at once.

If you are stirring beaten eggs into the soup, cook the fish for 5 minutes, then vigorously whisk the eggs in a bowl until the whites and eggs are blended and stir them into the hot soup. Cook the soup, stirring often, until the fish is opaque, 3 to 5 minutes more. The eggs will thicken the broth. Ladle the hot muddle into serving bowls, sprinkle with parsley, and serve hot.

If you are using hard-cooked eggs, cook the fish until it is opaque, about 10 minutes. Coarsely chop or slice the eggs and sprinkle them over the top. Ladle the hot muddle into serving bowls, sprinkle with parsley, and serve hot.

## Heavenly Mashed Potatoes

3 pounds small russets or other high-starch potatoes, peeled

2/3 cup whole milk, warmed

6 tablespoons butter, at room temperature, divided

4 ounces cream cheese, at room temperature

1/2 cup sour cream or crème fraîche (page 388 or store-bought), at room temperature

Kosher salt, to taste

These are outstanding mashed potatoes. They are flavorful enough to stand alone but can take on gravy. They are creamy and soft as silk yet hold their shape on the plate. Although they are delicious when served as soon as they are made, they are best made in advance and refrigerated before baking, which is handy for meals when you need to prepare a few things ahead of time.

Here's a quick lesson in making top-notch creamy mashed taters. Use high-starch potatoes (such as reliable russets) about the size of a fist because they are fluffy when cooked. Salt the cooking water generously because starches cooked in plain water never taste sufficiently salted, no matter how much you add at the end. Dry the potatoes in the warm pot after they are drained so that they are primed to absorb the seasonings. Never purée a potato with anything that has to be plugged in, for it flails them into gluey paste. A ricer or an old-fashioned hand-cranked food mill is ideal because it yields fluffy, perfectly smooth potato purée. These potatoes alone justify buying one. Make sure the dairy products are warmed or at room temperature. The entire mashing and seasoning process should be completed while the potatoes are warm, so dousing hot potatoes with cold milk is not helpful.

MAKES 8 SERVINGS

1. Preheat the oven to 350°F. Butter a 9 × 13-inch glass or ceramic baking dish.
2. Place the potatoes in a large pot and cover with cold water. Bring to a boil, add 1/2 teaspoon kosher salt per cup of water, reduce the heat, partially cover the pot, and simmer just until tender enough to pierce with a fork, about 20 minutes. Do not overcook the potatoes or they will start to fall apart and get waterlogged. Drain well in a colander and return to the still-warm pot so that the potatoes can steam dry for about 3 minutes. They will look chalky around the edges.

③ Force the hot potatoes through a ricer or a food mill fitted with the medium disc into a large bowl. If you don't have a food mill or ricer, mash them as smooth as you can with a hand-held potato masher.

④ Stir the warm milk into the potatoes with a wooden spoon. Stir in 4 tablespoons of the butter and the cream cheese and sour cream and mix well. Season generously with salt. Spoon the potatoes into the prepared dish. Dot the top of the potatoes with the remaining 2 tablespoons of butter.

⑤ Bake the potatoes until they are heated through and the top is golden brown, about 30 minutes.

MAKE-AHEAD NOTE: You can make the potatoes through Step 4 up to 2 days ahead. Add enough milk to make them a little looser than usual because they will firm up overnight. Let cool to room temperature, cover the dish tightly with plastic wrap, and refrigerate. When ready to bake, remove the plastic, cover the dish with aluminum foil, and place in a preheated 350°F oven. Bake the potatoes for 30 minutes, remove the foil, and continue baking until the potatoes are hot and the top is light golden brown, about 30 minutes more. When time is tight, you can reheat the potatoes in the microwave, but this is not optimal.

## Mashed Potato Cakes with Cranberry Cumberland Sauce

I was raised on skillet cakes formed from leftover mashed potatoes, but they were sauced with ketchup if with anything at all. The Cranberry Cumberland Sauce is optional, but it elevates the humble cakes to fine-dining status. I first tasted this combination at a pub in the Temple Bar district of Dublin, Ireland. Cumberland Sauce is traditionally served cold with roasted meat, and I have never seen the recipe in a southern cookbook, but who am I to argue with the genius pub cook who ladled it warm over my potato cakes?

MAKES 4 SERVINGS

1 cup dry bread crumbs or panko

½ teaspoon kosher salt

¼ teaspoon ground black pepper

2 cups Heavenly Mashed Potatoes (page 248) or other well-seasoned mashed potatoes, chilled

1 large egg, lightly beaten

1 to 4 tablespoons all-purpose flour, as needed

2 tablespoons vegetable oil

2 tablespoons butter

Cranberry Cumberland Sauce, for serving

① Preheat the oven to 300°F. Set a wire rack inside a large rimmed baking sheet and place in the oven.

② Stir together the bread crumbs, salt, and pepper on a plate. Stir together the potatoes and egg in a medium bowl until smooth. If the potatoes are too soft to hold their shape on the spoon, stir in enough flour to make them the consistency of soft dough. Form the potato mixture into 8 equal cakes about ½-inch thick. Coat the cakes lightly and evenly with the bread crumbs and set aside in a single layer to dry a little while the pan gets hot.

3. Heat the oil and butter in a large well-seasoned cast-iron skillet or nonstick skillet over medium-high heat until the butter stops foaming. Working in batches, add the cakes to the pan, reduce the heat to medium, and cook, turning once, until warmed through and nicely browned on both sides, about 5 minutes per side. Transfer the cooked cakes to the wire rack in the oven to stay warm until all of the cakes are cooked, or up to 20 minutes.

4. Serve the cakes warm atop a pool of warmed Cranberry Cumberland Sauce.

## Cranberry Cumberland Sauce

1 orange

1 lemon

½ cup ruby port

1 cup red currant jelly

1 cup canned whole berry cranberry sauce

2 teaspoons ground ginger

2 teaspoons dry mustard

¼ teaspoon kosher salt

This traditional sauce hails from England and was surely a precursor to our Thanksgiving cranberry sauce. It keeps well for weeks and perks up potato cakes and roasted meat, particularly leftover turkey and ham. A jar of this sauce makes a great hostess gift during the holidays.

MAKES ABOUT 2 ½ CUPS

1. Use a channel zester to cut thin strips of zest from the orange and the lemon. Place the zest in a small bowl and set aside.

2. Squeeze the orange and lemon juice into a medium saucepan. Stir in the port, jelly, cranberry sauce, ginger, mustard, and salt. Bring to a simmer over medium heat. Cook, stirring occasionally, until the jelly and cranberry sauce dissolve and the sauce thickens, about 4 minutes. Remove from the heat and stir in the zest.

3. Transfer into a glass jar and refrigerate for at least 24 hours and up to 3 weeks. Serve at room temperature or gently warmed.

# Summer Vegetable Potato Salad

1 ½ pounds small waxy potatoes, left whole or cut into large bite-sized chunks

3 tablespoons dry white wine

3 tablespoons white wine vinegar or rice vinegar

8 ounces slender green fillet beans and/or yellow wax beans, ends trimmed

1 tablespoon whole-grain Dijon mustard

2 teaspoons kosher salt, plus more to taste

1 teaspoon ground black pepper, plus more to taste

½ cup extra-virgin olive oil

½ cup thinly sliced red onion

1 cup whole miniature tomatoes, as many colors as possible

¼ cup chopped flat-leaf parsley

¼ cup chopped fresh basil

This is my signature summer salad. It delivers a stunning array of colors, so serve it in a pretty bowl for all to see. Be sure to use low-starch, waxy potatoes that hold their shape when cooked, a type that is sometimes called a boiling potato. Good choices include crescents, fingerlings, bliss, creamers, and Finns. This is a recipe where potatoes with colored flesh—such as red, pink, gold, or blue—look good.

At my house, we affectionately call this Compost Salad. A few years back I co-hosted a baby shower for the manager of my beloved local farmers' market. It was a chance to invite my hardworking farmer friends over to have fun. I bought all of the ingredients at the market and spent nearly an hour digging through bins of potatoes, seeking out the smallest, most perfectly round ones, which looked like polished gemstones. I made a quadruple batch of salad to serve in a gorgeous Italian pottery bowl, arranging the vegetables just so and garnishing it with fresh herbs. I put all the peelings and such in an empty grocery bag to haul out to the compost bin. Shortly before the guests were due to arrive, my husband saw me scurrying around and asked how he could help. As I ran upstairs to change clothes, I asked him to take out the compost. When I came back down, just as the doorbell started to ring, I saw the bag of compost still sitting on the counter and hollered up the stairs, "Why didn't you take out the compost?" "I did." Just then I saw the empty bowl next to the sink. And I knew. Yep. He had dumped my salad into the compost bin. Each time I tell this story, the other husbands go home armed with an anecdote that makes their recent blunders pale in comparison.

MAKES 8 SERVINGS

(1) Place the potatoes in a large pot and cover with cold water. Bring to a boil, add ½ teaspoon kosher salt per cup of water, reduce the heat, and cook at a low boil only until the potatoes are tender when pierced with the tip of a knife, about 15 minutes. Do not overcook them or they will start to fall apart and get waterlogged. Drain them in a colander and return them to the hot pot to let any remaining moisture evaporate away. Spread the hot potatoes in a single layer on a rimmed baking sheet, sprinkle with the wine and vinegar, and let cool to room temperature. The potatoes will absorb most of the liquid as they cool. Transfer the cooled potatoes and any standing liquid into a large bowl.

(2) Fill a large bowl with ice water. Bring a medium saucepan of water to a boil. Add ½ teaspoon kosher salt per cup of water. Add the beans and cook until barely tender, 5 to 8 minutes, depending on their size. Transfer with a slotted spoon into the ice water to stop the cooking and set the color. Drain well, pat dry, and set aside.

(3) Whisk together the mustard, salt, pepper, and oil in a medium bowl. Pour over the potatoes and stir gently until the potatoes are coated. Stir in the beans, onion, and tomatoes. If the salad seems dry, drizzle in a little more oil. Season with additional salt and pepper. Just before serving, stir in the parsley and basil. Serve at room temperature.

## Colcannon

3 pounds russet potatoes, peeled and cut into 2-inch chunks

8 cups stemmed and thinly shredded kale or other sturdy greens

½ cup chicken stock

Kosher salt and ground black pepper, to taste

6 tablespoons butter, at room temperature, divided

1 cup thinly sliced leeks or scallions (white and tender green parts)

1 to 1 ½ cups whole milk, warmed

Threads of Scotch-Irish and Celtic ancestry run all through the culture and traditions of the southern Appalachian Mountains where I grew up, including some of our food. Colcannon, a savory and deeply satisfying blend of mashed potatoes and tender greens, is a perfect example. Mountain people ate it all the time, even if they didn't always call it by its original Irish name.

When I had colcannon in Ireland, it was served piping hot with a deep puddle of melted yellow Irish butter in the center, like we might make a gravy lake in our potatoes. The potatoes were eaten from outside to the inside, dipping each bite into the butter. Lord have mercy!

This is the perfect thing to serve with Braised Corned Beef and Carrots with Whiskey and Marmalade Glaze (page 71). You can thin any leftover colcannon with warm stock or milk to make wonderful soup.

MAKES 8 SERVINGS

(1) Place the potatoes in a large pot and cover with cold water. Bring to a boil, add ½ teaspoon kosher salt per cup of water, reduce the heat, and cook at a low boil only until tender when pierced with the tip of a knife, about 20 minutes.

(2) Meanwhile, place the kale and stock in a large skillet. Bring to a simmer over medium heat and cook, stirring often, until the kale is tender, about 10 minutes. Remove from the heat and season with salt and pepper.

(3) Melt 2 tablespoons of the butter in a medium saucepan. Add the leeks and a pinch of salt and cook, stirring often, until tender, about 10 minutes.

(4) When the potatoes are done, drain well in a colander and then return to the still-warm pot so that they can steam dry. Force the warm potatoes through a ricer or a food mill fitted with a medium disc into a large bowl.

(5) While stirring with a wooden spoon, slowly add enough milk to make the potatoes creamy. Stir in the kale, the leeks, the remaining 4 tablespoons of butter, and a touch more milk, if needed. Season with salt and pepper and serve warm.

## Soupy Taters

2 pounds tiny, freshly dug new potatoes, washed

2 to 4 tablespoons butter, at room temperature

½ cup well-shaken buttermilk or half-and-half

1 teaspoon kosher salt

½ teaspoon ground black pepper

1 tablespoon finely chopped fresh herbs, such as parsley or chives

Soupy taters are creamed new potatoes. You should make this recipe with the first potatoes large enough to pull up or dig. They must be tiny with skins as thin and delicate as tissue paper. Any variety of potato will do, so long as they are straight out of the ground. Freshly dug spring potatoes are sweet and delicate, quite different from the sturdy starchiness of aged potatoes.

I call these soupy taters because my family calls them soupy taters, as do many rural families across the Blue Ridge. Most people use milk or cream to make the potatoes soupy, but I like the tang of first-rate farmstead buttermilk. If you enjoy sour cream on potatoes, you'll like the buttermilk too.

This dish is the preferred accompaniment to Killed ("Kilt") Lettuce (page 164), a pairing made in Spring Heaven. The rich creaminess balances the vinegary tang of the salad.

Let me remind you that when you are a kid, you think that whatever your family does is normal, at least until you get out into the world to look around a bit and realize that much of your family's behavior was just plain odd. What this has to do with soupy taters and kilt lettuce is that my family loved them together but didn't want the vinegar to run into the potatoes and curdle the milk. So each of us would take a soup spoon and place it at the 12 o'clock position under our dinner plates, so that the top of the plate was slightly elevated. We put our potatoes at the top of the plate and the kilt lettuce at the bottom, so all the vinegar would pool at the bottom and not sully our taters. Such an odd thing to do. Such a good solution.

MAKES 4 TO 6 SERVINGS

1. Place the potatoes in a large saucepan of cold water. Bring to a boil, add ½ teaspoon kosher salt per cup of water, reduce the heat, and cook at a low boil only until the potatoes are tender when pierced with the tip of a knife, about 10 minutes. Drain the potatoes well, return them to the still-warm pan, and let them steam dry for a minute or so.

2. While the potatoes are still hot, lightly crush them with the back of a spoon or a fork, leaving the pieces fairly large. Add as much butter as your conscience will allow. Drizzle in enough buttermilk to coat the potatoes and make them a little soupy. Season generously with the salt and pepper, garnish with the herbs, and serve warm.

VARIATION: For something similar, yet completely different, season the crushed potatoes with a generous drizzle of excellent, aromatic extra-virgin olive oil in lieu of the buttermilk. Sprinkle with plenty of cracked pepper and large-crystal garnishing salt or imported truffle salt.

WHAT ELSE WORKS? You can add a generous handful of freshly shelled and lightly cooked garden peas to the potatoes just before serving. New potatoes and peas are a classic springtime dish. They are also delicious with a small handful of finely chopped spring onions, scallions, or ramps.

# RADISHES

**Radishes are easy and eager to grow.** They are one of the first things ready to harvest in a spring garden, so the earliest English colonists planted them in the South. Radishes have kept their association with spring, but there are varieties appropriate to grow and harvest in all seasons.

Because most commercial radishes are small, round, and red, many people don't realize that radishes come in a variety of shapes, colors, sizes, and flavors. Depending on the type, radishes can be enjoyed raw or cooked or used for seasoning and coloring other foods. Some varieties have a distinctive peppery punch, which reminds us that radishes are in the mustard family, while others are cooling and mild. Beyond the familiar round sorts, there are icicle-shaped radishes, from stubby to as large as baseball bats. Quirky aerial radishes are grown for their edible seedpods rather than for their roots. Radishes that usually mature in winter, such as the black radish, have a distinctive woodsy, earthy flavor and are often cooked, although they can be eaten raw when they are small with tender skins.

Beware that fresh radishes wilt quickly after they are pulled, rendering them pithy and bland. They have no shelf life, often making commercial varieties from grocery stores a disappointing choice. Moreover, most radishes sold in little plastic bags in stores have had their tasty greens removed. The proliferation of commercial radishes might explain why radishes have declined in popularity since World War II. Southern bon vivant Eugene Walter said that one of his grandmother's favorite expressions was "sad as a store-bought radish." ■

# Skillet-Roasted Radishes

1 tablespoon extra-virgin olive oil

1 pound small radishes, trimmed of leaves and rootlets

2 tablespoons butter

½ teaspoon kosher salt

¼ teaspoon ground black pepper

2 teaspoons chopped fresh thyme

Radishes are usually eaten raw but they can also be cooked. Smaller radishes yield better results, so ideally they should be no more than 1 inch in diameter. If your radishes are long and thin instead of round, cut them crosswise into 1-inch-thick slices. This dish is very pretty when made with colorful rainbow radishes. Winter varieties, such as black radishes, are usually good roasters, but be sure to peel them if the skins are tough and cut them into wedges.

MAKES 4 SERVINGS

1. Preheat the oven to 475°F. Heat the oil over high heat in a large, heavy skillet (preferably cast-iron) until shimmering hot. Add the radishes and stir or gently shake the skillet to coat the vegetables in the hot oil. Cook, stirring or shaking the skillet occasionally, until the radishes are lightly browned in spots, about 4 minutes.

2. Transfer the skillet to the oven and roast until the radishes are barely tender, 10 to 15 minutes. Gently shake the skillet or stir the radishes every 5 minutes so that the vegetables do not scorch on the bottom.

3. Add the butter, salt, and pepper and stir to coat. Sprinkle with thyme and serve warm.

WHAT ELSE WORKS? You can replace half of the radishes with whole baby turnips that are about the same size.

# Radish Sandwiches

4 tablespoons (½ stick) unsalted butter, preferably European or cultured, at room temperature

8 thin slices of crusty white bread (such as a baguette) or soft white sandwich bread

Coarse salt or kosher salt

8 small radishes, ends trimmed and very thinly sliced

This recipe salutes the European breakfast tradition of eating radishes with butter, which tames the vegetable's bite. Simple, yet sublime. This is more of a method or idea than a recipe. Although it's hard to beat really good fresh European or cultured butter on the bread, you can also use quark, herbed cheese spread, whipped cream cheese, or mayonnaise. You can add lemon zest, a few finely chopped herbs, or finely chopped radish greens to the spread, but keep this simple.

Assorted radishes in different shapes and colors are pretty, but the classic for this dish is the peppery breakfast radish. The radishes must be very crisp, so if yours are a little fatigued, soak the slices in ice water for a few minutes to wake them up, then pat them dry.

MAKES 4 SERVINGS

Generously butter the bread. Sprinkle with plenty of salt. Arrange the radish slices prettily on top. Serve open face. Enjoy within an hour.

WHAT ELSE WORKS? You can use paper-thin slices of seedless cucumber and/or sweet onion in place of some or all of the radishes.

## Nearly Instant Radish Pickles

3 cups paper-thin radish slices or ribbons

1 teaspoon fine sea salt

1 teaspoon sugar

At first glance, there seems to be little similarity between traditional southern and traditional Asian cooking, but one place of overlap is a mutual love for salty, pickled things. These quick pickles are very easy and can be served as a slawlike salad or piled onto a sandwich.

This technique works with any type of radish, but a mixture of round, oblong, and tapered (such as rainbow, breakfast, and daikon) looks nice. The only requirement is that the vegetables be extremely fresh, because the only dressing is the natural juices drawn out by the salt and sugar. When the vegetables are at their peak, this deceptively simple thing is very good.

A vegetable slicer makes quick work of this, but a vegetable peeler works too.

MAKES 4 TO 6 SERVINGS

Spread the radish slices evenly on a serving plate. Sprinkle with the salt and sugar and let sit at room temperature until moist and a little juicy, 5 to 10 minutes. Serve immediately.

WHAT ELSE WORKS? You can use this same method to pickle ribbons of cucumber, carrots, summer squash, and zucchini and very thin slices of melon and seedless watermelon. When using a combination of vegetables, prepare each one separately because each releases moisture at its own rate.

## Radish, Kohlrabi, and Potato Salad with Sour Cream and Dill Dressing

8 ounces new potatoes, scrubbed and cut into bite-sized pieces (about 2 cups)

8 ounces small kohlrabi, peeled and cut into bite-sized pieces (about 2 cups)

2 tablespoons white wine vinegar or rice vinegar

¼ cup sour cream (regular or reduced fat)

1 teaspoon whole-grain Dijon mustard

2 tablespoons finely chopped fresh dill

2 tablespoons finely chopped shallot or spring onion

Kosher salt and ground black pepper, to taste

4 ounces radishes, trimmed and thinly sliced (about 1 cup)

Cubes of cooked kohlrabi are very similar to cooked potato, so they work well in potato salad. This colorful combination pulls together a number of vegetables that are in season at the same time. Because some of the vegetables are cooked and some are raw, this salad has plenty of crunch. This salad is mayonnaise-free, which pleases those who do not like mayonnaise. (I do not understand those people.)

MAKES 4 TO 6 SERVINGS

1. Place the potatoes and kohlrabi in a large pot and cover with cold water. Bring to a boil, add ½ teaspoon kosher salt per cup of water, reduce the heat, and simmer only until tender when pierced with the tip of a knife, about 15 minutes. Drain in a colander. Return the vegetables to the pot and set aside for a few minutes so they can steam dry. Sprinkle the vinegar over the vegetables and let cool to room temperature, stirring occasionally. They will absorb the vinegar as they cool.

2. Stir together the sour cream, mustard, dill, and shallot in a large bowl. Season generously with salt and pepper. Stir in the potatoes, kohlrabi, and radishes. Cover and refrigerate until chilled, at least 30 minutes. Just before serving, stir and taste for seasoning.

WHAT ELSE WORKS? You can replace some or all of the cooked kohlrabi with raw seedless cucumber.

# Fish Tacos with Radish Slaw

2 cups finely shredded savoy cabbage or other green cabbage

1 tablespoon kosher salt

½ cup thinly sliced radishes

¼ cup thinly sliced scallions or spring onions (white and tender green parts)

1 tablespoon rice wine vinegar

1 tablespoon fresh lime juice

1 tablespoon honey

1 tablespoon extra-virgin olive oil

¼ teaspoon ground black pepper

TACOS

Vegetable oil spray

4 catfish or other thin, mild fish fillets, cut in half crosswise (about 4 ounces each)

½ teaspoon kosher salt

¼ teaspoon ground black pepper

½ cup instant or all-purpose flour

¼ cup fine cornmeal or corn flour (masa)

1 tablespoon chili powder, or to taste

½ cup mayonnaise

3 tablespoons fresh lemon or lime juice

8 small flour tortillas, warmed for serving

Sour cream or crema, for garnish

Fish tacos didn't originate in the South, but southerners took to them like fish to water. The mild farmed catfish from the Delta are good here, but other mild white fish fillets are also good. The technique for cooking the fish yields crispy, crusty fillets that aren't fried. Be sure to use fine cornmeal or corn flour because coarse meal doesn't cook as quickly as the fish and remains rough and gummy.

Fish tacos are often topped with radishes, but we southerners like our slaw, so this recipe combines the two. The slaw is a good side dish to serve with other things, even if you aren't making the tacos. Salting and draining the vegetables makes this slaw wonderfully crisp, but you can skip that step when time is short. When the radish greens are very fresh and tasty, you can add them to the slaw.

MAKES 4 SERVINGS

1. For the slaw: Toss the cabbage and salt together in a colander. Let drain for at least 2 hours at room temperature. Rinse the cabbage, pat dry, and transfer into a bowl. Add the radishes and scallions. Whisk together the vinegar, lime juice, honey, and oil in a small bowl and season with the pepper. Pour the dressing over the cabbage mixture and toss to coat. Use the slaw soon, or cover and refrigerate. Stir well before serving.

2. For the tacos: Position rack in top third of oven and preheat to 500°F. Mist a rimmed baking sheet with the spray or line with nonstick aluminum foil.

3. Season the fish on both sides with the salt and pepper. Whisk together the flour, cornmeal, and chili powder in a shallow dish. Stir together the mayonnaise and lemon juice in a small bowl. Spread a thin layer of the mayonnaise mixture on both sides of the fish, then coat with the flour mixture, shaking off any excess. Arrange the fish in a single layer on the prepared baking sheet.

4. Bake until the crust is crisp and golden and the fish is cooked through, about 10 minutes. Serve at once in the warm tortillas with a little slaw and a dollop of sour cream. Serve the rest of the slaw on the side.

MAKE-AHEAD NOTE: You can make the slaw up to 2 days ahead. Store covered and refrigerated. Stir well and check the seasoning before serving.

# RAMPS

**Ramps are native to North America** and are often associated with Appalachia, a region that is usually overlooked, dismissed, or misinterpreted in discussions of southern food. Botanically, ramps are a type of foraged wild leek, but that's misleading. Leeks are mild and ramps are anything but. The pungent taste and lingering aroma of wild ramps are immediately identifiable and unlike anything else. Trying to describe ramps is like trying to describe the taste of water—there's no adequate vocabulary for it, even though we know exactly what it is.

Wild ramp season is short, beginning in the Appalachian highlands and spreading northward into parts of New England and the upper Midwest, rarely growing in any place for more than about three weeks and disappearing altogether after about two months. Ramps are stubborn and have resisted all efforts to have their growing season manipulated. They like to hide on steep, stony slopes and moist forest floors. It's possible to cultivate ramps, and any ramps are better than no ramps, but cultivated ones just don't compare to the wild ones.

Beginning with Native Americans, many people have viewed ramps as a bracing tonic that thins the blood and strengthens the body after a long winter. Because ramps are one of the first green things to poke up through the soil each year, they can be a tonic for the mind as well. Ramp festivals are still a rite of spring in some communities. For centuries, ramps were maligned for their association with so-called hillbillies, so it's ironic that ramps are darlings of the upscale culinary world these days. ■

# Pickled Ramps

| | |
|---:|:---|
| 3 | cups trimmed ramp bulbs |
| 1 ½ | cups cider vinegar |
| 1 | cup water |
| 1 | bay leaf |
| 1 | cinnamon stick |
| 1 | small mace blade or ¼ teaspoon ground mace or nutmeg |
| ¼ | teaspoon crushed red pepper flakes |
| 1 | teaspoon coriander seeds |
| ½ | teaspoon whole cloves |
| ¼ | cup sugar |
| 1 | teaspoon pickling salt |

This is a way to hang on to the fleeting ramp season a little longer. These pickles keep in the refrigerator for a few weeks. Eat them straight out of the jar or use them in recipes that call for pickled onions, gherkins, or cornichons. You can use the brine in place of vinegar in salad dressings. A young rock star chef friend of mine taught me to thin mayonnaise with ramp brine to use as dressing for potato salad.

This recipe uses only the ramp bulbs. To trim whole ramps, cut off the rootlets and slip off the outer layer of the bulb if it is loose. Cut off the leafy greens, leaving the white bulbs attached to slender pink stems. If the leaves are fresh, pliant, and bright green, you can use them to make ramp pesto by following the recipe on page 281 and using them in place of the basil.

MAKES 1 QUART

1. Have ready a 1-quart jar that has been sterilized in boiling water or run through the dishwasher on the hottest cycle. The jar should have a sterilized tight-fitting lid. The jar and lid don't have to stay hot, but they must stay sterile.

2. Pack the ramp bulbs into the prepared jar. Bring the vinegar, water, bay leaf, cinnamon stick, mace blade, red pepper flakes, coriander, cloves, sugar, and salt to a boil in a medium saucepan, stirring to dissolve the sugar.

3. Pour the hot brine over the ramps, close the jar, and set aside to cool to room temperature. Refrigerate for at least 3 days before serving. The ramps will keep in the refrigerator for at least 3 months. (Occasionally some of the ramps will turn blue because of a reaction between their natural minerals and the acidic brine. They look peculiar but are still safe to eat. The blue often fades over time.)

WHAT ELSE WORKS? You can use this brine to pickle scallions, small spring onions, pearl onions, shallots, or small cipollini onions. It's also a great brine for green tomatoes cut into wedges.

## Ramp and Potato Soup with Scallion and Goat Cheese Muffins

1 tablespoon butter

2 cups diced ramp bulbs

1 ½ pounds starchy potatoes (such as russets), peeled and cut into 1-inch pieces

4 cups chicken stock

1 teaspoon kosher salt, plus more to taste

1 teaspoon ground black pepper, plus more to taste

½ cup well-shaken buttermilk

¼ cup finely chopped fresh chives

2 tablespoons finely chopped fresh basil

1 tablespoon finely chopped fresh dill

1 tablespoon green Tabasco sauce

½ cup chopped scallions (white and tender green parts) or additional ramps, for serving

Scallion and Goat Cheese Muffins, for serving (recipe follows)

Fresh ramps are often cooked with potatoes in the spring. The flavor of raw ramps is strong and distinct, but as with most alliums, cooking mellows their pungency and tames their aroma. Alas, even when cooked, ramps can linger on your breath. The director of an annual ramp festival confessed that festival organizers used to give out breath mints at the end of the day, but their budget couldn't allow them to continue.

MAKES 6 SERVINGS

1. Melt the butter in a large, heavy soup pot over medium heat. Add the ramps and cook, stirring frequently, until softened but not browned, about 8 minutes. Add the potatoes, stock, salt, and pepper and simmer gently until the potatoes are completely tender and falling apart, about 45 minutes.

2. Purée 2 cups of the ramp mixture in a blender and return to the pot, or purée part of the mixture directly in the pot with an immersion blender. The purée thickens the rest of the soup.

3. Stir in the buttermilk, chives, basil, dill, and Tabasco and warm through over low heat, about 5 minutes. Season with salt and pepper. Sprinkle the soup with scallions and serve warm with the muffins.

VARIATION: Nothing else in the world tastes like ramps, but if you have no access to ramps, you can still make great soup by substituting 1 ½ cups chopped spring onions and ½ cup coarsely chopped garlic.

MAKE-AHEAD NOTE: This soups tastes best made 1 day ahead. Cool to room temperature, cover, and refrigerate. Reheat gently over low heat.

# Scallion and Goat Cheese Muffins

Vegetable oil spray

1 cup whole milk, divided

4 ounces soft, fresh goat cheese (chèvre)

1 ½ cups all-purpose flour

1 tablespoon baking powder

1 ½ teaspoons sugar

½ teaspoon kosher salt

6 tablespoons butter, melted

1 large egg

¼ cup finely chopped scallions (white and tender green parts)

1 teaspoon finely chopped fresh dill

Most people eat ramps with cornbread, but now that ramps are fashionable and appear on upscale menus, their companion bread can receive an upgrade. The lemony tang of fresh goat cheese in these muffins echoes the zip of the buttermilk in the soup. Don't be tempted to use more ramps in place of the scallions in these muffins; they won't get tender in the time it takes the muffins to bake, plus enough is enough. The muffins are delicious in their own right, even without the soup.

See page 310 for tips on making attractive muffins.

MAKES 1 DOZEN

1. Position a rack in the center of the oven and preheat to 400°F. Mist the top and cups of a standard 12-cup muffin tin with the spray. Be sure to use a light metal muffin tin. Dark metal and nonstick tins—even when lined with paper cups—make the crust too thick and dark.

2. Stir together 2 tablespoons of the milk and the goat cheese in a small bowl.

3. Whisk together the flour, baking powder, sugar, and salt in a large bowl. Whisk together the melted butter and egg and the remaining milk in a medium bowl. Pour the butter mixture into the flour mixture and stir just until combined. Use a rubber spatula to gently fold in the scallions and dill.

4. Spoon half of the batter into the muffin cups. Spoon a small ball of the goat cheese mixture into the center of each cup. Spoon the remaining batter over the cheese. Bake until the tops are golden and a tester inserted into the muffin comes out clean, about 20 minutes. Be sure the tester doesn't go into the cheese because the cheese will still be soft, even when the muffins are done. Serve warm.

# Ramps in Fluffy Eggs

4 large eggs

1 tablespoon ice water

¼ teaspoon kosher salt, plus more to taste

1 tablespoon butter

4 ramps (bulbs and tender greens), finely chopped

½ cup fresh ricotta cheese

Ground black pepper, to taste

4 pieces of buttered toast or split biscuits, for serving

Scrambled eggs with ramps is a classic combination. The trick to scrambling eggs is to go low and slow because eggs suffer from rushed, high-temperature cooking, which makes them tough. The addition of fresh ricotta to scrambled eggs is something I learned in Italy. It adds great moisture and fluffiness to the eggs. However, the ricotta must be fresh, not the stiff, stabilized, commercial type often used in lasagna. Look for fresh ricotta where you would find specialty and farmstead cheeses.

MAKES 2 SERVINGS

1. Whisk the eggs in a medium bowl until the whites and yolks are blended. Add the water and salt and whisk vigorously until the long, ropey strands of egg white disappear.

2. Melt the butter in a medium nonstick skillet over medium-low heat. Add the ramps and a pinch of salt and cook, stirring, until softened, about 5 minutes. Whisk the eggs again and add to the skillet. Reduce the heat to low and let the eggs sit until the edges start to firm up. Gently and slowly drag a heatproof spatula or wooden spoon back and forth across the bottom of the pan, making sure you cover the entire surface.

3. When the eggs are barely set and still quite moist on top, remove the skillet from the heat, add the ricotta, and stir gently to incorporate. It's fine if a few clumps of ricotta remain visible. The eggs will continue cooking as you stir. Sprinkle with salt and pepper and serve at once over the toast.

VARIATION: Ramps are often in season at the same time as the earliest spring asparagus and morels. If you ever encounter this fortunate confluence, cook a handful of diced asparagus and/or sliced morels along with the ramps before you add the eggs.

# RASPBERRIES

**Brambly black raspberries are indigenous to North America.** The familiar red ones and the rare yellow ones originated in the Old World and were exported by the British to New England in the eighteenth century. When brought south, red raspberries were a failure, for the most part. Red raspberries don't like heat and humidity, so their growing area was confined to those limited parts of the South where summers stayed relatively cool. Unlike persnickety red raspberries, luscious native black raspberries were plentiful and hardy throughout most of the South. Black raspberries were not domesticated until the 1800s, when they were needed to hybridize a viable southern red raspberry. Whether red, black, purple, or yellow, raspberries are like prized jewels in the kitchen, ready to add glorious color and flavor to recipes. During their peak season, plump, velvety raspberries are an easy indulgence. ■

## Raspberry, Roasted Beet, and Walnut Salad

1 pound small to medium beets, peeled and cut into ½-inch cubes

4 tablespoons grape-seed oil or vegetable oil, divided

6 tablespoons raspberry vinegar, divided

2 tablespoons finely chopped shallot

2 teaspoons Dijon mustard

2 tablespoons walnut oil or additional grapeseed oil

Kosher salt and ground black pepper, to taste

6 cups lightly packed mixed baby lettuces

1 cup walnuts, toasted

½ cup crumbled blue cheese or goat cheese

2 cups fresh raspberries

Beets are so sweet that they are used as a source of sugar, and roasting intensifies that natural sweetness. With that in mind, it's easy to see how tiny roasted beets and berries can work together in a salad. The secret to this recipe is to let the beets cool in the raspberry vinegar so that they can soak up the fruity flavor. Any color of beet is fine, although the yellow ones are particularly striking on the plate. The ingredients are arranged on top of the greens, which makes this a composed salad rather than a tossed salad.

MAKES 4 SERVINGS

1. Preheat the oven to 400°F.

2. Place the beets on a rimmed baking sheet lined with aluminum foil. Drizzle with 2 tablespoons of the grapeseed oil and season with a little salt and pepper. Cover with aluminum foil and roast for 20 minutes. Uncover and continue roasting until tender, about 30 minutes more. Transfer into a bowl, toss gently with 3 tablespoons of the vinegar, and let sit until the beets cool to room temperature, stirring occasionally.

3. Stir together the remaining 3 tablespoons of vinegar, the shallot, and a pinch of salt in a medium bowl and let sit for 5 minutes. (This tames any sharp flavor in the shallot and makes the vinaigrette taste better.) Pour the liquid from the beets into the shallot mixture and set the beets aside. Add the mustard to the shallot mixture, then whisk in the remaining 2 tablespoons of grapeseed oil and the walnut oil. Season with salt and pepper.

4. Place the lettuces in a large bowl. Drizzle in enough vinaigrette to moisten and toss well with tongs to lightly coat the greens. Spread the greens on a serving platter or divide among serving plates. Top with the beets, walnuts, blue cheese, and raspberries. Serve soon, with any remaining vinaigrette on the side.

### TIPS AND TECHNIQUES

When a salad contains nuts, it's nice to use oil from that nut in the vinaigrette. These oils can be potent, so a little goes a long way. I usually dilute nut oils with an equal amount of neutrally flavored oil, such as grapeseed oil, vegetable oil, or very mild and fruity olive oil. I don't recommend strong olive oil because its distinct flavor often clashes with the nut oil. Because nut oils go rancid quickly, they are the only type of oil that I store in the refrigerator. Even when stored properly, they stay fresh only about six months. They can also be pricey, so I buy the smallest bottles I can find or share larger bottles with a friend.

## Berry Butter

¼ cup raspberries

¼ cup blackberries

¼ cup confectioners' sugar

½ teaspoon finely grated orange zest

¼ teaspoon pure vanilla extract

¼ teaspoon ground nutmeg or ground cinnamon

1 cup (2 sticks) butter, at room temperature

This subtly sweet butter is a great way to use berries that are overly ripe but still tasty. The confectioners' sugar adds sweetness without the grit of granulated sugar. Slather Berry Butter on biscuits, bagels, muffins, waffles, or toast for a quick treat and a bit of fruit.

MAKES ABOUT 1 ¼ CUPS

1. Combine the berries, confectioners' sugar, orange zest, vanilla, and nutmeg in a medium bowl. Crush the berries with a potato masher or the back of a spoon until fairly smooth. Add the butter and stir vigorously to combine.

2. Spoon into an airtight container and refrigerate until firm. Store in the refrigerator for up to 3 days or transfer into a freezer bag and store in the freezer for up to 3 months.

WHAT ELSE WORKS? You can use any combination of berries, including strawberries and blueberries.

## Buttermilk Pie with Raspberry Crown

1 (9-inch) pie shell (page 396 or store-bought)

2 large eggs, separated

6 tablespoons unsalted butter, at room temperature

1 cup sugar

3 tablespoons all-purpose flour

1 tablespoon raspberry vinegar or fresh lemon juice

½ teaspoon pure vanilla extract

½ teaspoon finely grated lemon zest

¼ teaspoon kosher salt

1 cup well-shaken buttermilk, at room temperature

3 to 4 cups fresh raspberries

Buttermilk pie belongs to that large and welcoming clan of custard and chess pies, standards in home kitchens across the South. This one brokers a truce between too sweet and too tart and is more airy than most. A finishing crown of perfect berries puts it over the top. You can use all ruby red berries or include yellow and black as well.

Buttermilk is indispensable in authentic southern food. In addition to its distinctive flavor, its acidity plays a crucial role in the chemistry of cooking. In other words, use liquid buttermilk, not reconstituted buttermilk powder. The powdered stuff might taste vaguely like buttermilk, but it won't deliver the goods.

MAKES 8 SERVINGS

1. Bake and cool the pie shell according to the directions on page 398.

2. When ready to make the pie, preheat the oven to 350°F. Position a rack in the center of the oven.

3. Whip the egg whites in a large, very clean glass or metal bowl until they are mixed and look cloudy with an electric mixer set to low speed. Increase the mixer speed to high and whip to soft peaks. Set aside.

4. Beat the butter and sugar until light and fluffy in a large bowl with the mixer set to high speed. Beat in the egg yolks and mix well. Beat in the flour, vinegar, vanilla, lemon zest, and salt. With the mixer on low speed, slowly add the buttermilk.

5. Use a rubber spatula to fold about one-fourth of the beaten egg whites into the buttermilk mixture to lighten the batter. Fold in the rest of the beaten whites. (The batter should be fairly smooth, but it is better to have a few visible wisps of whites than to stir so hard that you deflate the whites completely.) Pour the filling into the pie shell. The filling should come just to the inside rim of the crust, so you might have a little filling left over. You can discard it or bake it in a ramekin as a cook's treat.

6. Bake until the filling is lightly browned and a tester inserted 3 inches from the center comes out clean, about 45 minutes. (When done, custard fillings are not firm in the very center. When gently shaken, the center should jiggle slightly but no longer slosh or ripple.)

7. Cool the pie to room temperature on a wire rack. The center of the pie will fall and firm up as it cools. Cover the top of the pie with fresh raspberries arranged in pretty concentric circles. Serve at room temperature or lightly chilled.

### TIPS AND TECHNIQUES

Cold eggs are easiest to separate because cold yolks are less likely to break. Egg whites won't whip properly if they contain even a speck of yolk, so crack the eggs one at a time. Collect each white in a small cup and then pour it into the work bowl. That way, if you do break the yolk, it spoils only that one white in the cup instead of all of them in the bowl. If you drop in a bit of shell, fish it out with a large piece of shell; the little piece will almost magically cling to the larger piece.

## Easy Cake Cobbler

1 cup milk

1 cup sugar

1 cup soft southern wheat self-rising flour

1 teaspoon pure vanilla extract

8 tablespoons (1 stick) unsalted butter

4 cups raspberries (about 1 pound)

This is another in the seemingly endless cavalcade of southern cobblers and is perhaps the easiest of all. One bowl, one dish, and about five minutes and this is in the oven. The batter rises to the top as a tender cake with chewy edges reminiscent of a sugar cookie. It tastes good warm or at room temperature, so this is a handy make-ahead cobbler that travels well. This recipe requires self-rising flour, so do not substitute all-purpose flour mixed with added leavening.

MAKES 8 SERVINGS

1. Preheat the oven to 350°F.

2. Whisk together the milk, sugar, flour, and vanilla in a medium bowl until well blended and set aside.

3. Place the butter in a 9-inch square baking dish and place in the oven to melt. Remove the dish from the oven and sprinkle the berries evenly over the butter; do not stir. Whisk the batter again and pour over the fruit; do not stir.

④ Bake until the cobbler is browned on top and bubbly around the edges, 35 to 40 minutes. Let cool at least 10 minutes before serving.

WHAT ELSE WORKS? You can make this cobbler with whole blackberries, blueberries, or strawberries or with peeled, pitted, and thinly sliced peaches, apricots, or nectarines.

## Chilled Raspberry Soup with Key Lime Shortbread

This gorgeous magenta dessert soup is full of fresh berry flavor with only enough cream to make it a little indulgent. Because crème fraîche doesn't separate like sour cream or yogurt, the soup stays creamy and tasty for a few days. The soup needs to chill overnight, so plan accordingly.

If your raspberries are full of tough seeds, force the berries through a food mill or mesh sieve to remove the seeds and then transfer the purée into the blender.

MAKES 4 TO 6 SERVINGS

① Place the berries, sugar, key lime juice, crème fraîche, and cream in a blender and purée the mixture.

② Transfer into a large glass bowl or jar, cover, and refrigerate overnight. Serve chilled in chilled dessert bowls or tea cups with the cookies on the side.

WHAT ELSE WORKS? You can replace some or all of the raspberries with strawberries.

4 cups fresh red raspberries

¼ to ½ cup sugar, depending on the sweetness of the berries

3 tablespoons bottled key lime juice

¼ cup crème fraîche (page 388 or store-bought)

¼ cup light cream or half-and-half

Key Lime Short-bread, for serving (recipe follows)

## Key Lime Shortbread

These tangy melt-in-your-mouth shortbread cookies complement the touch of lime in the Chilled Raspberry Soup. If you can't find fresh key limes, then use high-quality bottled key lime juice, such as Nellie and Joe's brand. Whether fresh or bottled, the bold flavor of key lime juice is integral to the cookies. However, it's best to stick with regular Persian limes for the zest, to get the pretty bright green color not found on creamy yellow, ripe key limes.

The shortbread dough is very easy to work with and tolerates multiple rollings and cuttings. However, it does work best when it is lightly chilled and firm when it goes into the oven, so if the dough gets soft when handled, stick the cut-out cookies back into the fridge for 10 minutes or so. Round cookies are standard, but you can use intricate cookie cutters or cut the dough into rectangles or squares with a pizza cutter. Don't skip the glaze because that's where the zip of lime really shines.

COOKIES

1 ½ cups all-purpose flour

½ cup confectioners' sugar

½ cup cornstarch

1 cup (2 sticks) unsalted butter, at room temperature

1 tablespoon key lime juice

2 teaspoons finely grated lime zest

(continued on next page)

1 ¼ cups confectioners'
sugar

2 teaspoons finely
grated lime zest

2 to 3 tablespoons
key lime juice

1. For the cookies: Whisk together the flour, confectioners' sugar, and cornstarch in a medium bowl and set aside.
2. Beat the butter, key lime juice, and lime zest until creamy in a large bowl with an electric mixer set to medium speed. Add the flour mixture and beat on low speed until pea-sized clumps of dough form. Gather the clumps into a ball, place between 2 large sheets of plastic wrap, and roll to ¼-inch thickness. Refrigerate until firm, at least 2 hours.
3. Preheat the oven to 350°F. Line a baking sheet with parchment paper or a silicone baking mat.
4. Cut the dough into 2-inch rounds (or other shapes) and arrange them 1 inch apart on the prepared baking sheet. (If the dough is so firm that it breaks when you try to cut it, let it sit at room temperature for 10 minutes.) Bake the cookies until firm and slightly golden on the edges, about 12 minutes; do not let them brown on top. Let cool on the pan for 2 minutes and then use a spatula to transfer to a wire rack to cool to room temperature.
5. For the glaze: Whisk together the confectioners' sugar and lime zest in a small bowl. Gradually whisk in enough key lime juice to make a smooth glaze that is creamy and spoonable but not runny. Spoon the glaze over the tops of the cookies, spreading it to the edges. Set the cookies aside until the glaze is hardened, about 15 minutes. Store in an airtight container at room temperature.

## Simple Raspberry Sauce with Intense Chocolate Sorbet

2 ½ cups fresh raspberries

¼ cup sugar

1 teaspoon fresh
lemon juice

1 tablespoon Chambord
raspberry liqueur
or raspberry syrup
(optional)

Intense Chocolate
Sorbet, for serving
(recipe follows)

This dessert is a celebration of raspberries and chocolate. The flavors are simple and clean. Each recipe can, of course, be used separately. The sauce, sometimes called a *coulis*, is quick and easy. It's delicious with the sorbet but goes over everything from ice cream to cake to fresh fruit.

1. Purée the berries, sugar, and lemon juice in a blender. Strain through a fine mesh sieve into a large bowl, pressing on the solids with a rubber spatula to remove all the liquid. Discard the solids.
2. Taste the sauce and adjust the sugar or lemon juice, if needed. Stir in the liqueur, if using.
3. Serve over scoops of Intense Chocolate Sorbet.

WHAT ELSE WORKS? You can use strawberries in place of the raspberries.

# Intense Chocolate Sorbet

3 cups water

2 tablespoons light corn syrup

1 cup sugar

⅔ cup cocoa, sifted

2 ounces bittersweet chocolate, coarsely chopped

1 teaspoon pure vanilla extract

This sorbet can be made with or without an ice cream freezer. It's a lovely frozen treat for people who do not eat dairy products. The deep, intense chocolate flavor comes from a combination of cocoa powder and melted bittersweet chocolate.

When a recipe calls for chopped chocolate, do not be tempted to use chocolate chips. The chips usually contain paraffin to help them hold their pointy shape. That paraffin can give a waxy feel or cloudy appearance to the finished recipe. Instead, buy blocks of chocolate and chop them with a heavy knife. Do not chop chocolate in a food processor or blender because solid chocolate can break the blade. Some stores sell small buttons of pure chocolate intended for baking and cooking, which are fine to use.

MAKES 1 QUART

1. Bring the water, corn syrup, and sugar to a boil in a medium saucepan, stirring until the sugar dissolves. Remove the pan from the heat and whisk in the cocoa until smooth. Add the chocolate and vanilla and stir until the chocolate melts and is smooth. Transfer into a large glass or metal bowl, cover, and refrigerate until the mixture is very cold (under 40°F), at least 4 hours, then stir well.

2. Churn the sorbet in an ice cream freezer according to the manufacturer's instructions. The sorbet will be soft, like a thick milk shake. To freeze hard enough to scoop, transfer into an airtight container, press plastic wrap directly onto the surface, and freeze until firm

VARIATION: To make the sorbet without an ice cream freezer, pour the mixture into a shallow glass baking dish. Cover and freeze until firm. Break the sorbet into large pieces, place them in the bowl of a food processor, and pulse until smooth but not watery. Serve at once, or spoon the sorbet into an airtight container and freeze until firm.

For an even quicker version, serve the mixture as a granita. Remove the dish of frozen base from the freezer and rake it up with a fork. The ice crystals will be large, like a snow cone.

# RHUBARB

**Rhubarb was planted in the earliest colonial gardens** of New England and gradually worked its way south, but it didn't catch on until growers could produce plants that had larger stalks in proportion to the toxic leaves, which made rhubarb more useful. Rhubarb leaves contain high levels of oxalic acid, which can be lethal if consumed in large quantities. Well established in southern gardens by the mid-1800s, rhubarb continued to be appreciated more for its medicinal value than for good eating. It was often used as a spring tonic and notable purgative.

Over the years, rhubarb worked its way from the medicine chest to the pie chest. Pie is the most common destination for rhubarb, so much so that some older cookbooks and garden logs called it pie plant. It might look like red celery, but rhubarb is a member of the buckwheat family and a close relative of sorrel and dock, which might explain why it's so sour. Cooks were once taught to sweeten rhubarb pie with as much sugar as would be used in any fruit pie and then add that much again and then turn around and throw in another handful over their shoulders. ■

# Rhubarb and Strawberry Cobbler
# with Cornmeal Biscuit Crust

FILLING

Butter or vegetable
oil spray

3 cups trimmed and
thinly sliced rhubarb
(about 1 pound)

4 cups strawberries,
capped and halved
or quartered

1 teaspoon rose water
or orange flower water

½ cup sugar

1 tablespoon cornstarch

CORNMEAL
BISCUIT CRUST

1 cup all-purpose flour

⅓ cup cornmeal

3 tablespoons
sugar, divided

1 ½ teaspoons baking
powder

½ teaspoon kosher salt

5 tablespoons butter,
cut into small cubes
and chilled

⅔ to 1 cup heavy cream
Instant or all-purpose
flour, for rolling

1 large egg

1 tablespoon ice water
Unsweetened yogurt,
crème fraîche, or
whipped cream,
for serving

I had the pleasure of cooking and speaking at the Smoky Mountain Table Celebration at the beautiful Blackberry Farm in Walland, Tennessee. I shared recipes for the simple, authentic mountain food from my childhood, including this cobbler. On the final night, the participants gathered around tables along the edge of the farm's enviable garden, which is tended by true master gardeners. To close the meal and the event, we served this cobbler warm from the oven, spooned into small canning jars and topped with freshly made sheep's milk yogurt from the farm's dairy. What a night.

MAKES 8 SERVINGS

1. For the filling: Butter or spray a shallow 2-quart baking dish. Toss together the rhubarb, strawberries, and rose water in a large bowl. Add the sugar and cornstarch and toss to coat the fruit. Spread the fruit mixture into the prepared baking dish.

2. For the crust: Preheat the oven to 375°F.

3. Whisk together the flour, cornmeal, 2 tablespoons of the sugar, baking powder, and salt in a large bowl. Sprinkle the butter over the top and toss to coat. Use a pastry blender or your fingertips to work in the butter until the mixture resembles coarse bread crumbs. Use a fork to stir in enough cream to form soft dough that pulls in all of the dry ingredients.

4. Turn the dough out onto a lightly floured surface. Gently knead the dough until it is smooth, about 5 turns. Pat or roll the dough to a ½-inch thickness. Use a biscuit cutter, cookie cutter, or knife to cut the dough into the desired shapes and arrange them over the filling. Make an egg wash by whisking together the egg and ice water in a small bowl, then lightly brush the biscuit tops with the mixture and sprinkle with the remaining 1 tablespoon of sugar.

5. Bake until the biscuits are golden brown and the fruit juices are bubbling, 45 to 50 minutes. Let the cobbler cool for 15 minutes before serving. Top each serving with a small dollop of yogurt, if desired.

## Spiced Rhubarb Ketchup

4 cups trimmed and chopped rhubarb (about 1 ¼ pounds)

1 cup chopped red onion

¼ cup golden raisins

¾ cup sugar

½ cup organic unfiltered cider vinegar or white wine vinegar

2 teaspoons finely grated orange zest

Juice of 1 orange (about ½ cup)

1 tablespoon peeled and finely grated ginger

½ teaspoon ground cinnamon

⅛ teaspoon ground cloves

½ teaspoon whole yellow mustard seed

½ teaspoon kosher salt

2 tablespoons ruby port

This recipe combines two traditional approaches to rhubarb. First, it pairs rhubarb with ruby port wine. Second, it uses rhubarb to make a type of ketchup, the name once given to spiced sweet and tangy sauces made from a variety of fruits and vegetables, not just from tomatoes. Use it for dipping and drizzling when you would consider using standard tomato ketchup or fruit chutney. It's tasty on everything from french fries to fine cheeses.

MAKES 3 CUPS

1. Stir together the rhubarb, onion, raisins, sugar, vinegar, orange zest, orange juice, ginger, cinnamon, cloves, mustard seed, and salt in a large saucepan. Bring to a boil over medium-high heat. Remove the pan from the heat, cover, and set aside for 30 minutes.

2. Cook over medium heat until the rhubarb is very tender and the liquid is thick enough to coat the back of a spoon, about 10 minutes. Remove from the heat, stir in the port, and set aside to cool to room temperature.

3. Transfer into a clean glass jar, cover, and refrigerate until chilled. This keeps for up to 3 weeks.

# Pork Chops with Rhubarb Pan Dressing

Vegetable oil spray

2 cups trimmed rhubarb, cut into ½-inch pieces

4 thick slices of bread, torn into fairly small crumbs (about 2 cups)

¾ cup packed light brown sugar

½ teaspoon ground cinnamon

¼ teaspoon ground allspice

⅛ teaspoon dry mustard

2 teaspoons chopped fresh rosemary

1 teaspoon kosher salt, divided

½ teaspoon ground black pepper, divided

4 boneless pork loin chops, about ¾-inch thick

1 tablespoon vegetable oil

1 tablespoon butter

This is an old farm family recipe that has nearly faded into obscurity. That's a shame. The spiced tangy flavor of the rosy rhubarb tastes so good with pork, and this homey, filling meal is ready to serve in under an hour.

MAKES 4 SERVINGS

1. Preheat the oven to 350°F. Mist the inside of a 2-quart baking dish with the spray; set aside.
2. Stir together the rhubarb, bread crumbs, brown sugar, cinnamon, allspice, mustard, and rosemary, ½ teaspoon of the salt, and ¼ teaspoon of the pepper in a large bowl. Spoon about three-quarters of the rhubarb mixture into the prepared baking dish.
3. Season the pork chops with the remaining ½ teaspoon of salt and ¼ teaspoon of pepper. Heat the oil and butter in a large skillet over medium-high heat. Add the pork chops and cook undisturbed until they are browned on the bottom, about 3 minutes. When they are sufficiently browned, they will release from the pan easily without tugging or tearing. Turn the chops with tongs and brown the other side. Place the chops on top of the rhubarb mixture in the baking dish. Sprinkle the remaining rhubarb mixture over the chops.
4. Cover and bake for 20 minutes. Uncover and continue baking until the pork registers 150°F on a thermometer inserted into the center and the juices run clear when pricked with the tip of a knife. Serve warm.

TIPS AND TECHNIQUES

Use a combination of butter and oil when browning food in a skillet. Butter tastes great but can burn quickly over high heat. Oil tolerates higher heat but can be bland. Using equal amounts of each unites the best attributes of both: the butter adds flavor to the oil and the oil keeps the butter from burning.

# SHELL BEANS

**Nearly every bean in the world is native to the Americas,** where they have been cultivated for centuries. All beans grow in pods, but not all pods are eaten. That's the story of shell beans, the varieties that are shelled out of their pods on their way to the table.

A lot of shell beans are dried. One could argue that many of the iconic southern dishes that feature beans—soup beans of Appalachia, red beans and rice of New Orleans, country-style baked beans—are all made from dried beans, not fresh. True, but every dried bean started as a fresh bean that someone had to grow.

At one time, hundreds of different shell beans grew in the South. Perhaps the most lauded are those collectively known as butter beans. They can be speckled, green, or white. The name "butter bean" is relatively recent. Older cookbooks and garden logs call these same beans sieva, sivvy, runner beans, or Carolina beans. They are sometimes called limas, perhaps because they originated in Peru, but they are a far cry from the large, pasty, mushy limas that terrorized us in grade school cafeterias, and we take umbrage at the association. When cooked properly, the beans melt in your mouth into creamy, buttery goodness—thus the name butter beans.

Part of the lore and practice of eating shell beans is the shelling itself. For eons it was done by hand, one pod at a time. Hand shelling, even by expert hands, is slow-going, tedious work that will wear out the sides of thumbs, leaving them sore and stained. A dishpan full of pods yields only a cup or two of precious beans. (This might explain why Jack traded a whole cow for a handful of some sort of bean that was already shelled.)

Eventually mechanical shellers came along, a godsend for busy cooks and farmers who knew that shelled beans would be welcomed in the marketplace. The machines quickly crank out beans like a Gatling gun, shooting beans into a bucket and flinging spent shells out the back. Speed notwithstanding, shell bean purists insist that the machine stresses the beans and that only hand shelling will do.

Butter bean love never fades. People crave them all their days. Food writer Eugene Walter is credited with the story that on a summer evening some years ago he and two of the South's most celebrated writers, William Faulkner and Katherine Anne Porter, were dining together at a posh restaurant in Paris. As Eugene put it, "They'd gone all out. You wouldn't believe what we'd had. It was a hot summer evening, and there was that moment as we sipped our 1870 cognac or Grand Marnier or whatever we had after the coffee, when Katherine Anne Porter said something like 'Back home, butter beans'll be coming in.' And he said, 'The baby speckled ones.' After all the triumph of French cuisines. It's a warm summer evening, and they're thinking about the first butter beans back home." ■

## Basic Cooked Shell Beans

3 cups freshly
shelled beans

1 ½ teaspoons kosher salt,
plus more to taste

1 medium onion,
quartered, leaving the
root attached to hold
the wedges together

1 carrot, cut into chunks

2 stalks celery,
cut into chunks

1 bay leaf

3 short thyme sprigs

3 whole cloves

2 tablespoons extra-
virgin olive oil, butter,
or bacon drippings

Ground black
pepper, to taste

This is a reliable way to cook shell beans, whether serving them plain or preparing them to use in other recipes. The cooking time can vary considerably, depending on the size and freshness of the beans. A reliable predictor is to taste a raw bean. If it is very tender and moist, it will cook quickly. If it puts up a little resistance, it will take longer. The finished bean should be tender yet still hold its shape. If the beans start to break apart during cooking, lower the heat and cook them more gently.

You can change the personality of the beans through the fat stirred in at the end. Olive oil and butter are fairly neutral. Bacon drippings give a traditional southern bent. Keep in mind that you can mix the fats. I often blend olive oil with a wee spoonful of drippings.

You should get 3 cups (about 1 pound) of shelled beans from 3 pounds of pods.

MAKES ABOUT 3 CUPS

1. Rinse the beans thoroughly in several changes of water to remove any bits of hull and stickiness. When the water runs clear, transfer into a large saucepan and add enough cold water to cover the beans by 1 inch. Stir in the salt, onion, carrot, celery, bay leaf, thyme, and cloves. Bring to a boil, skim off the foam, reduce the heat, and simmer until tender, 15 to 40 minutes, depending on the size and freshness of the beans. The beans must stay submerged, so add a little more water if needed. Taste and add more salt if needed. Remove the pan from the heat and set aside for at least 15 minutes to give the beans time to absorb the salt. Discard the onion, carrot, celery, bay leaf, thyme sprigs, and cloves. Stir in the fat. Season with pepper and more salt, if needed.

2. If you are going to eat the beans now, you can drain them or leave them in the tasty liquid. Serve warm. If you are going to store the beans to eat later or use in another recipe, leave them in the liquid. Let cool, then cover and refrigerate for up to 3 days.

TIPS AND TECHNIQUES

The combination of onion, bay leaf, and cloves is popular in classical cooking, but finding the small leaf and tiny cloves to remove before serving is like the proverbial needle in a haystack. To simplify the search, use the whole cloves as thumbtacks to attach the bay leaf to a wedge of onion. When you fish out the onion, the small bits come with it.

## Shell Beans Braised with Sage and Tomato

3 cups Basic Cooked Shell Beans (page 278)

1 tablespoon extra-virgin olive oil, plus more to taste

1 tablespoon finely chopped garlic

2 tablespoons lightly packed chopped fresh sage

¾ cup seeded and finely chopped tomato

1 teaspoon kosher salt, plus more to taste

¾ teaspoon ground black pepper, plus more to taste

I love to finish basic cooked shell beans this way. The sage and tomato combine with the cooking liquid to make a creamy, flavorful sauce. The dish is stunning with whole, tiny tomatoes, such as red currant tomatoes, but chopped tomatoes (even canned tomatoes) are fine. You can use other herbs in place of the sage, such as marjoram, oregano, basil, or rosemary (sparingly), but adjust the amount of herb according to the intensity of its flavor.

MAKES 4 TO 6 SERVINGS

1. Drain the Basic Cooked Shell Beans, reserving the cooking liquid.
2. Heat the oil in a large, heavy skillet (preferably cast-iron) over medium-high heat. Add the garlic and sage and cook, stirring, until they begin to sizzle. Stir in the beans, tomato, salt, and pepper and 1 cup of the reserved cooking liquid. Reduce the heat and simmer until the sauce is thickened and very creamy, about 20 minutes. Add a little more of the cooking liquid if the beans get dry.
3. Check the seasoning and serve hot, drizzled generously with more oil.

## Shell Bean Gratin

MAKES 4 TO 6 SERVINGS

You can easily transform Shell Beans Braised with Sage and Tomato into a gratin by spooning the finished recipe into a shallow baking dish. Add enough chicken stock to come up level with the beans. Toss 1 ½ cups of fresh bread crumbs or crumbled cornbread with 2 tablespoons of extra-virgin olive oil, melted butter, or warm bacon drippings. Sprinkle the crumbs evenly over the bean mixture. Bake in a 350°F oven until the juices are bubbling at the edges and the crumbs are browned, about 45 minutes. Serve warm.

## Beans and Greens Bruschetta

MAKES 4 TO 6 SERVINGS

Another great way to serve Shell Beans Braised with Sage and Tomato is to spoon them onto thick, crusty slices of grilled or toasted bread, along with a big spoonful of Southern Skillet Greens (page 170) to serve as hearty, satisfying bruschetta. Top with a generous drizzle of good olive oil and a healthy pinch of crushed red pepper flakes or a few fat drops of Hot Pepper Vinegar (page 88).

## Carrboro Minestrone with Classic Basil Pesto

2 tablespoons extra-virgin
olive oil, plus more to taste

½ cup finely chopped
pancetta or bacon
(about 5 ounces)

3 cups very finely chopped
onion

4 large garlic cloves,
finely chopped

¾ cup very finely
chopped celery

1½ cups very finely
chopped carrot

2 tablespoons tomato paste

8 cups chicken stock,
plus more as needed

2 teaspoons kosher salt,
plus more to taste

4 small thyme sprigs

2 bay leaves

1 large sage sprig

2 pieces Parmigiano-
Reggiano cheese rind
(about 3 ounces)

4 cups coarsely chopped
savoy cabbage

5 cups finely chopped
Tuscan kale leaves

1½ cups fresh or canned
whole peeled tomatoes,
chopped, juices reserved

3 cups freshly shelled beans,
such as cranberry, borlotti,
or October beans

2 tablespoons
red wine vinegar

1 teaspoon ground black
pepper, or to taste

Crushed red pepper
flakes, to taste

Classic Basil Pesto (recipe
follows), for serving

The closest farmers' market to my house is my beloved Carrboro Farmers' Market. It's the pivot point of my seasonal cooking. It's also the hub of my social circle, providing dear friendships and a guaranteed good time. I do a few cooking demos for the market each year. One year in early autumn, when the days were still quite hot but the nights were beginning to cool off, I made this soup. I based it on authentic Ligurian minestrone but used local ingredients. In recipes such as this, local and seasonal ingredients should guide the recipe, not the other way around.

This recipe yields a big pot of soup and tastes best made at least one day ahead. It keeps well for up to a week and gets better each day. It also freezes well.

MAKES ABOUT 3 QUARTS

① Heat the oil in a large enameled cast-iron Dutch oven or soup pot over medium heat. Add the pancetta and cook, stirring occasionally, until it renders its fat and is lightly browned, about 8 minutes.

② Add the onion, garlic, celery, and carrot and a pinch of salt and stir to coat. Cook until softened, stirring occasionally, about 8 minutes. Push the vegetables to the edge of the pot to leave a small area bare in the center. Add the tomato paste and stir it around in the cleared spot until it sizzles without scorching, about 2 minutes. Stir to coat the vegetables in the paste.

③ Add the stock, salt, thyme sprigs, bay leaves, sage sprig, and cheese rinds. Bring to a boil, reduce the heat, and simmer for 5 minutes.

④ Add the cabbage, kale, tomatoes with their juices, and beans. Partially cover and simmer until the vegetables are completely tender, 45 minutes to 1 hour. Discard the thyme sprigs, bay leaves, sage sprig, and cheese rinds. (Some people find the softened rinds to be delicious.) Stir in the vinegar and season with salt and pepper.

⑤ Serve hot, topped with a pinch of red pepper flakes and a dollop of pesto. Another drizzle of oil is also nice.

WHAT ELSE WORKS? This soup is open to endless variations and substitutions. You can use other types of cabbage or other sturdy, leafy greens in place of the savoy and kale. You can use other types of fresh shell beans or replace some of them with snap beans.

MAKE-AHEAD NOTE: This soup tastes best made at least 1 day ahead. Cool, cover, and refrigerate for up to 1 week or transfer into airtight containers and freeze for up to 3 months. Check the seasoning when reheating the soup. It will probably need more salt and a splash of red wine vinegar to perk up the flavors.

## Classic Basil Pesto

4 cups lightly packed basil leaves

½ cup extra-virgin olive oil

⅓ cup pine nuts, lightly toasted

2 garlic cloves

¼ cup freshly grated Parmigiano-Reggiano cheese

¼ cup freshly grated Pecorino cheese or additional Parmigiano-Reggiano

1 teaspoon kosher salt

This is classic, simple pesto as made where it originated in Genoa, Italy. You can use this formula to create your own custom pesto by changing the type of herb or nut. For the smoothest texture, use a blender, not a food processor.

MAKES ABOUT 1 CUP

1. Combine the basil, oil, pine nuts, and garlic in a blender. Blend into a smooth paste, stopping often to push down the basil with a rubber spatula. Be patient; this step can take as long as 5 minutes.

2. Add the cheese and salt and blend until smooth. Serve at room temperature.

MAKE-AHEAD NOTE: You can store the pesto for up to 4 days. Transfer into an airtight container, top with a thin film of olive oil, and refrigerate. The oil helps block out air, which is what makes the pesto oxidize and darken on top. When ready to serve, return the pesto to room temperature and stir in the oil. Repeat this step each time you return leftovers to the refrigerator.

## Creamed Butter Beans

3 cups freshly shelled butter beans

Kosher salt, to taste

1 cup crème fraîche (page 388 or store-bought)

1 teaspoon coarsely ground black pepper

1 tablespoon chopped fresh thyme

Butter beans are, by far, my favorite shell bean and on my short list of favorite foods ever. I love both the meaty speckled varieties that look like creek pebbles when cooked and the tiny green butter beans no larger than a dime or, as the old-timers would say, "about the size of a squirrel's ear." Butter beans, whether large and speckled or small and pale, are all in the lima bean family. I really hate to hear that. Limas have a tarnished reputation that might dissuade people from trying butter beans. Perhaps southerners started using the term "butter beans" to give these beloved beans a fresh start under an assumed name.

I tell my loved ones that if I ever fall seriously ill, I want them to bring me a bowl of these divine beans and lift them to my lips with a silver spoon. If I still perish, well, it's just my time to go.

MAKES 6 SERVINGS

1. Thoroughly rinse and drain the beans in several changes of water until the water stays clear, discarding any bits of leaves, hulls, or vine. Place the beans in a large, heavy saucepan and cover with cold water to a depth of 1 inch. Add ½ teaspoon kosher salt per cup of water. Bring to a boil and skim off the foam. (You might need to skim once or twice more during cooking. The foam comes from the natural sugars and proteins in the beans.) Reduce the heat and simmer gently until the beans are tender but not mushy or breaking apart, 15 to 30 minutes, depending on their freshness.

②  Remove from the heat and taste one of the beans. If needed, stir in more salt. Set the beans aside for at least 15 minutes to give them time to absorb the salt. Drain and return the beans to the pan.

③  Add the crème fraîche and stir until it melts, enrobing the beans and creating a wonderful sauce. Generously season the beans with lots of black pepper and more salt, if needed. Stir in the thyme and serve warm.

## Butter Bean, Heirloom Tomato, and Cornbread Shortcakes

In this recipe, creamy beans, juicy slices of impeccable tomatoes, and crisp bacon are tucked into split piping hot wedges of cornbread, like a savory shortcake. This is reminiscent of the bean sandwiches that poor people turned to when there was little else. We've come a ways.

Excellent tomatoes—preferably a local heirloom variety that is treasured for its flavor—are as important as the beans in this recipe. The tomatoes must be fully ripe and luscious, preferably still warm from the sun and, with luck, grown within sight of the kitchen. For me, that's a Cherokee Purple. You can use any kind of butter bean, but the tiny green ones look prettiest.

Timing and sequencing are key, but not complicated, when preparing this recipe. Cook the bacon first if you will need the drippings to use in the cornbread. The shortcakes must be assembled and served while the cornbread is piping hot, so get it into the oven next. Slice the tomatoes and warm the beans while the cornbread is baking.

MAKES 6 SERVINGS

Real Skillet Cornbread (page 391), freshly baked and piping hot

12  thick bacon slices, cooked crisp and drained

12  large slices of the best local tomatoes, peeled if necessary

Coarse kosher salt or garnishing salt (such as fleur de sel or Maldon) and coarsely ground black pepper, to taste

Creamed Butter Beans (page 281), warm

①  Cut the piping hot cornbread into 6 equal wedges. Split each wedge in half. Place a bottom half on each of 6 serving plates. Top each with 2 slices of bacon and 2 slices of tomato. Sprinkle with salt and pepper. Replace the cornbread tops.

②  Spoon warm Creamed Butter Beans over the top and around the sides of each serving. Sprinkle a little more pepper on top, for looks. Serve hot.

VARIATION: When I need this humble dish to look upscale and appeal to any butter bean skeptics, I neatly stack the components to resemble the layered dessert known as napoleons. I bake thin, uniform cornbread rounds in a Lodge cast-iron drop biscuit pan. I use round slices of pancetta baked on a rimmed baking sheet instead of bacon strips. I slice tomatoes that are the same diameter as the cornbread and pancetta. Quite fancy.

## Shell Bean, Sun-Dried Tomato, and Smoked Mozzarella Salad

6 tablespoons extra-
virgin olive oil, divided

1 medium onion,
halved lengthwise and
cut into thin strips

1 fennel bulb, cut
into thin strips or
paper-thin slices

¼ cup sherry vinegar

3 garlic cloves,
finely chopped

1 teaspoon
Dijon mustard

2 teaspoons dried
oregano

3 cups Basic Cooked
Shell Beans, drained

½ cup chopped,
oil-packed, sun-
dried tomatoes

8 ounces smoked
mozzarella, cut into
½-inch cubes

2 tablespoons capers,
drained

Kosher salt and ground
black pepper, to taste

4 cups lightly
packed baby
arugula or spinach

Toasted baguette slices
topped with olive
tapenade, for serving

This is a great make-ahead salad that travels well, so it's lovely for picnics or brown bag lunches. The mixture of cooked and fresh ingredients has a great contrast of textures and colors. Crisp crostini topped with the olive relish known as tapenade make a nice accompaniment.

To transform this into a more hearty salad, stir in grilled chicken, grilled shrimp, or a jar of high-quality tuna packed in olive oil.

MAKES 8 SERVINGS

1. Heat 2 tablespoons of the oil in a large skillet over medium heat. Add the onion and fennel and a pinch of salt. Cook, stirring often, until softened and lightly browned, about 15 minutes. Set aside to cool to room temperature.

2. Whisk together the vinegar, garlic, mustard, and oregano and the remaining 4 tablespoons of oil in a large bowl.

3. Stir in the beans, tomatoes, mozzarella, and capers. Stir in the onion and fennel. Season with salt and pepper.

4. Just before serving, stir in the arugula. Serve with tapenade crostini on the side.

MAKE-AHEAD NOTE: The salad can be made up to 2 days ahead. Do not stir in the fresh greens until just before serving.

· · · · · · · · · · · · · · · · · · · · · · · · · · · · · · · · · · · · · · · · · · · · · · · · · · · · · · · · · · · · · · · · · · · · · · · · · · · · · · · ·

Edamame are the new face of boiled legumes nibbled straight out of their salty pods. Boiled peanuts remain the tried-and-true. Both are great snacks, perfect for eating riding down the road with the windows down and the music up, headed to some place you can't wait to get to.

## Boiled Edamame

1 pound small, tender soybean pods (edamame)

3 tablespoons kosher salt or coarse salt, plus more to taste

Edamame are soybeans, a crop grown for years in the South, but usually as a commercial commodity. In recent years, soybeans have appeared on the family table, probably as a result of the rise in the popularity of soy foods.

People who love boiled peanuts see the similarities in salty, briny boiled soybeans, but you probably won't find sacks of them sold in mom-and-pop shops or along back roads, at least not yet. Eat the edamame just like boiled peanuts: put the pod up to your lips and squeeze out the sweet and salty little beans. Take a swig of a cold drink. Repeat.

MAKES 4 SERVINGS

(1) Soak the pods in a large bowl of ice water for 15 minutes and drain. Sprinkle with the salt, tossing to coat well. Cover and refrigerate for 2 hours.

(2) Bring a large pot of water to a boil. Stir in the salted soybeans and cook, stirring gently once or twice, until the pods are barely tender, about 5 minutes. Drain and rinse under cold running water until cool enough to handle.

(3) Transfer into a serving bowl and sprinkle with a few grains of salt. Serve within 2 hours.

# Boiled Peanuts

3 pounds freshly
dug green peanuts
in their shells

Kosher salt, as needed

The art and ritual of boiling peanuts might not be fully understood by people not raised in the tradition. I had never heard of boiled peanuts until I had a roommate from Georgia. I lived with her upwards of four years, and the only thing I ever saw her cook outside a microwave was peanuts. She'd go home to see her folks and return bearing a sack of green peanuts held out like a grail, the holy one.

Boiled peanut people have preferences for doneness and saltiness. Some people like them completely soft and some people want them a little toothsome, but under no circumstances should they be crunchy. It's like cooking beans, which is what peanuts are. The number of servings that come from each pound of peanuts is inversely proportional to the number of beers involved.

MAKES AROUND 4 SERVINGS

1. Place the peanuts in a large stockpot. Add enough cold water to cover the peanuts by 1 inch. Add 1 tablespoon of salt for each quart of water. Bring to a boil, reduce the heat, and simmer until the peanuts are as tender as you like, 1 to 2 ½ hours. The fresher the peanuts, the more quickly they will cook.

2. Remove the pot from the heat and let the peanuts cool in the cooking liquid for 15 to 30 minutes. Taste a peanut for salt. The longer they sit in the cooking liquid, the saltier they will be. Drain well and serve warm or at room temperature.

## Cola and Boiled Peanut Baked Beans

2 tablespoons bacon drippings or flavorful peanut oil

1 large onion, finely chopped

4 cups cooked and drained fresh white beans or other similar shell beans

2 cups shelled boiled peanuts (page 285)

½ cup sorghum

2 tablespoons packed light or dark brown sugar

1 teaspoon dry ginger

2 tablespoons dry mustard

1 cup cane cola

¾ cup chopped cooked country ham, cooked bacon, or "burnt ends" of pit-cooked barbecue (about 3 ounces)

This recipe pulls together three southern traditions in a very nontraditional way. First is the tradition of eating peanuts with cola, such as pouring roasted, salted peanuts down into a glass bottle of cold drink. Second is baked beans, a classic dish for which there are a zillion recipes. Third is boiled peanuts. Peanuts are legumes, not nuts. That means that they act like beans, especially when boiled in their shells until tender.

The key to good boiled peanuts is to use freshly dug green peanuts. If you don't have access to the right kind of peanuts, buy boiled peanuts from people who do, such as The Lee Bros. at boiledpeanuts.com.

The type of cola makes a difference in this recipe. You really should use a glass bottle of cola sweetened with natural cane sugar. You'll find it in a natural food store, some gourmet markets and delis, and most tiendas. Such colas have a spicy, faintly molasseslike flavor that shines in this recipe. Diet soda won't do.

Like most homemade baked beans, these are best made at least one day ahead.

MAKES 6 TO 8 SERVINGS

(1) Preheat the oven to 325°F.

(2) Heat the drippings in a medium skillet over medium-high heat. Add the onion and a pinch of salt. Cook, stirring often, until softened, about 8 minutes. Transfer into a 2 ½-quart baking dish. Stir in the beans, peanuts, sorghum, brown sugar, ginger, mustard, cola, and ham.

(3) Bake, stirring every 30 minutes, until the sauce reduces and thickens, 1 ½ to 2 hours. Let sit for at least 30 minutes before serving slightly warm or at room temperature. For best flavor, cool, cover, and refrigerate overnight before reheating gently.

# SNAP BEANS

**Way, way, way back, all cultivated beans** shimmied up cornstalks and grew alongside squash as part of the legendary Three Sisters system of cooperative planting that formed the heart of Native American cultivated crops. Broadly speaking, beans are eaten either in their pods or shelled out of their pods. In this book, I am using the term "snap beans" to encompass the types of beans left in their edible pods. I call them snap beans because their crisp pods emit an audible snap when broken into bite-sized pieces. Other colloquial names for edible pod beans include pole beans, runner beans, bush beans, green beans, and string beans. Each name tells a little of the story of this type of bean.

Beans that grow on climbing vines—such as the original native varieties—are called pole beans or runner beans because they need to run up poles, cornstalks, or arbors for support. Low-growing varieties are called bush beans. Many snap beans are indeed green, but the name "green bean" refers not to their color, but to their immaturity because they are picked while the young pods are still edible. String beans have a sturdy, inedible string running down the sides of the pods that must be pulled off before the beans can be eaten. Because strings have been bred out of most varieties, string beans (both the name and the beans themselves) are fading into obscurity, although some people maintain that string beans are the tastiest of all and continue to grow them, hybridization and convenience be damned.

Nearly all snap beans are eaten or preserved while the pods are still fresh. One notable exception is the obscure Appalachian practice of drying snap beans in their pods and then cooking the dried beans and the leathery pods together. These beans are called shuck beans or leather britches. It's a great example of the distinct regional differences within southern cooking. Shuck beans were elemental food for generations of Appalachian people, yet most southerners have never heard of them. Beans are universal, but often adapted to local tastes.

A word about cooking beans. Few aspects of southern cooking are more maligned and misunderstood than the issue of how long to cook vegetables, particularly snap beans and greens. At one time, most snap beans were sturdy pole beans with thick, tough pods that required extensive cooking to become edible. However, subjecting the newer stringless varieties to long cooking would dissolve them into a tasteless mess. Each variety of bean requires (and deserves) the appropriate approach. If a bean pod is delicate and tender enough to eat raw, it needs quick, gentle cooking. If a bean pod is thick and has strings that must be pulled off, it needs long, slow cooking. When you know your bean, you know your cooking method. It's the same rationale behind searing steaks versus braising short ribs. ■

## Oven-Roasted Whole Beans

1 to 1 ¼  pounds slender beans, ends trimmed

1 to 2  tablespoons extra-virgin olive oil

1  teaspoon kosher salt, or to taste

½  teaspoon ground black pepper, or to taste

This is a quick and easy way to prepare whole beans. It works best with slender pods with few developed beans inside. Save sturdy bean-filled pods for recipes that bring out their flavor through long cooking.

MAKES 4 TO 6 SERVINGS

1  Preheat the oven to 450°F.

2  Put the beans on a rimmed baking sheet, drizzle with enough oil to moisten, season with the salt and pepper, and toss to coat. Spread the beans in a single layer and roast until tender with a few browned spots, 6 to 10 minutes, depending on the size and freshness of the pods.

3  Check the seasoning and serve hot.

VARIATION: You can use infused olive oil, such as garlic, lemon, basil, or mushroom, in place of the regular olive oil.

WHAT ELSE WORKS? You can replace the beans with Brussels sprouts. Trim the ends and cut them in half lengthwise, although really small ones can be left whole. Roast until tender on the inside and crisp and browned on the outside, 6 to 10 minutes. Shake the pan occasionally so they'll cook evenly.

## Cook-and-Hold Beans Finished with a Flourish

1  pound slender snap beans, stem ends trimmed

When beans are at their peak of fresh flavor, they need nothing more than a light seasoning of salt and butter or olive oil. When you've had your fill of that simple goodness, here are four ways to add a little flourish. You can cook the beans and serve them at once or keep them on hand for a few days to finish when needed. This technique works best with beans that have no strings or very few strings. The pods should be slender and tender.

MAKES 4 TO 6 SERVINGS

1  Fill a large bowl with ice water. Bring a large saucepan of water to a boil. Add ½ teaspoon kosher salt per cup of water. Add the beans and cook until just tender, as few as 5 minutes for fillet beans and up to 25 minutes for larger beans. Use a slotted spoon or strainer to immediately transfer into the ice water to stop the cooking and set the color.

2  Drain the beans and spread them in a shallow layer over a few sheets of white paper towel or a clean tea towel and roll up loosely into a log shape. Put the roll in a zip-top bag and refrigerate for up to 4 days.

## Beans with Pecans, Lemon, and Parsley

3 tablespoons butter

¼ cup pecans, chopped

1 recipe Cook-and-Hold Beans (page 289)

Zest of 1 lemon

2 tablespoons finely chopped flat-leaf parsley or chervil

Kosher salt and ground black pepper, to taste

These beans are weeknight simple with dinner party elegance. You can change the type of nuts and use an orange instead of a lemon. Although using a rasp-style grater for the zest is quick, this dish is very pretty with thin strips of zest made by a channel zester.

MAKES 4 TO 6 SERVINGS

1. Melt the butter in a large, deep skillet over medium heat. Stir in the pecans and cook, stirring often, until they are crisp and the butter is lightly browned, about 3 minutes.

2. Add the beans and toss to mix. Heat through, about 5 minutes. Mix in the lemon zest and parsley. Season with salt and pepper and serve hot.

## Beans with Crispy Parmesan Cheese

1 recipe Cook-and-Hold Beans (page 289)

Kosher salt and ground black pepper, to taste

3 tablespoons butter, cut into small pieces

½ cup freshly grated Parmesan cheese

A crisp, lacy layer of good cheese makes these simple beans tasty and attractive. Be sure to grate the Parmesan from a fresh wedge of cheese.

MAKES 4 TO 6 SERVINGS

1. Preheat the oven to 400°F.

2. Arrange the beans in a single layer in a baking dish. Season with salt and pepper. Dot with the butter and sprinkle with the cheese.

3. Bake until the cheese is bubbly and browned in spots, about 10 minutes. Serve hot.

## Beans Bundled in Country Ham

1 recipe Cook-and-Hold Beans (page 289)

8 long, very thin slices center-cut country ham

4 tablespoons butter or garlic butter, melted

These bundles are lovely and make a great addition to a holiday buffet. If you cannot find the right cut of country ham, use slices of prosciutto, speck, or Serrano ham instead.

MAKES 4 TO 6 SERVINGS

1. Preheat the oven to 400°F.

2. Divide the beans into 8 equal bundles. The beans should be parallel to one another, like cordwood. Arrange the slices of ham on a clean work surface. Place a bundle of beans at one short end of each slice and roll them up so that the ham forms a belt around the center of the bundle.

3. Place the bundles in a baking dish large enough to hold them in a single layer. Drizzle the melted butter over the bundles. Bake until the beans are warm and the ham is a little crisp on the edges, about 15 minutes. Serve warm.

## Bean Salad with Dill Vinaigrette

1 recipe Cook-and-Hold Beans (page 289)

1 small onion, halved lengthwise and cut into thin strips (about 1 cup)

1 red, orange, or yellow bell pepper, cored and cut lengthwise into thin strips (about 1 cup)

¼ cup sliced ripe black olives (such as Kalamata or Gaeta)

4 tablespoons extra-virgin olive oil

2 tablespoons white wine vinegar or sherry vinegar

2 tablespoons chopped fresh dill

1 tablespoon sugar

Kosher salt and ground black pepper, to taste

This salad reminds me of dilly beans, a classic southern way to put up whole beans. The salad tastes best at room temperature, so it's great for outdoor dining. It's tasty with grilled steak or grilled tuna.

MAKES 4 TO 6 SERVINGS

1. Stir together the beans, onion, bell pepper, and olives in a large bowl. Whisk together the oil, vinegar, dill, and sugar in a small bowl. Season with salt and pepper. Pour over the bean mixture and stir to coat. Let the salad sit for at least 30 minutes for the flavors to develop, stirring occasionally. Stir and check the seasoning before serving.

2. Serve soon or cover and refrigerate for up to 4 days. The bright green beans will fade in the vinaigrette over time. For best flavor, return to room temperature before serving.

## Mixed Summer Bean Salad with Creamy Caesar-ish Dressing

1 cup shelled green butter beans

1 tablespoon extra-virgin olive oil, divided

1 pound yellow wax beans, ends trimmed

¼ cup finely chopped shallot or scallions (white and tender green parts)

½ cup walnut pieces, lightly toasted

½ cup lightly packed flat-leaf parsley

Creamy Caesar-ish Dressing (recipe follows)

Kosher salt and ground black pepper, to taste

This is a lovely salad that combines willowy yellow wax beans with bright green butter beans. I've also made it with green beans and other fresh shell beans (such as scarlet runners or edamame) or with field peas (such as lady cream peas). The combination of beans is up to you, but stick with a nice mix of colors. I once tried snap beans with striking purple pods, but they turned green when cooked, taking the wind out of my color scheme sails.

MAKES 4 TO 6 SERVINGS

1. Place the butter beans in a large saucepan and cover with cold water. Add ½ teaspoon kosher salt per cup of water. Bring to a boil, skim off the foam, reduce the heat, and simmer until just tender, about 25 minutes. Drain in a colander and rinse under cold running water until cool. Drain well, transfer into a large bowl, and toss with a little of the oil to keep the beans moist.

2. Bring a large saucepan of water to a boil. Add ½ teaspoon kosher salt per cup of water. Add the wax beans and cook until tender, about 12 minutes. Use a slotted spoon or strainer to transfer into a colander and rinse under cold running water until cool. Drain well, pat dry, and add them to the bowl of butter beans, along with a little more oil to keep them moist.

3. Stir in the shallot, walnuts, and parsley. Pour enough dressing over the mixture to moisten and stir gently to coat. Season with salt and pepper and let sit at room temperature for 15 minutes. Just before serving, stir well and check the seasoning. Serve at room temperature.

WHAT ELSE WORKS? You can use other snap beans, other shell beans, or field peas.

## Creamy Caesar-ish Dressing

½ cup mayonnaise

⅔ cup coarsely grated
Asiago, Parmesan,
Grana Padano, or other
hard grating cheese

1 garlic clove

Finely grated zest
of 1 lemon

6 tablespoons
lemon juice

2 teaspoons Worces-
tershire sauce

1 tablespoon walnut
mustard or grainy
Dijon mustard

1 teaspoon sugar

¼ cup extra-virgin
olive oil

Kosher salt and ground
black pepper, to taste

This dressing is similar to Caesar dressing but uses mayonnaise instead of raw egg and Worcestershire sauce instead of anchovy. Worcestershire is to southern cooking what anchovy is to Mediterranean cooking and fish sauce is to Asian cooking. All three are made from fish and provide savory flavor. The dressing is good on other salads or on simple steamed vegetables.

MAKES ABOUT 1 ½ CUPS

1. Put the mayonnaise, cheese, garlic, lemon zest, lemon juice, Worcestershire, mustard, and sugar in a blender and mix until combined.

2. With the blender running, slowly drizzle in the oil. Season with salt and pepper. Serve at room temperature. Use soon or store covered and refrigerated for up to 5 days. Stir well and check the seasoning before serving.

# Fillet Bean and New Potato Lasagna

Eating and cooking in Italy has made me a better southern cook because it has taught me to see familiar ingredients in a new light, with renewed respect and passion. Here's a good example. During one visit I ate an incredible lasagna made with tender beans and paper-thin slices of potatoes nestled between the layers of pasta. It was a version of green beans cooked with new potatoes, something I've eaten my whole life. This is my re-creation of that dish.

Those tiny, delicate fillet beans that are sometimes called haricot verts or French beans work best in this recipe.

MAKES 12 SERVINGS

**PARMIGIANO-REGGIANO AND PROSCIUTTO CREAM SAUCE**

- 3 ¼ cups whole milk
- 1 small onion, peeled and coarsely chopped
- 2 garlic cloves, crushed
- 2 tablespoons chopped fresh thyme
- 6 tablespoons unsalted butter
- 3 tablespoons instant flour or all-purpose flour
- ½ cup lightly packed, freshly grated Parmigiano-Reggiano cheese
- 1 cup finely chopped prosciutto (about 4 ounces)

  Kosher salt and ground black pepper, to taste

**LASAGNA**

- 8 ounces fillet beans, stem ends trimmed and cut into 2-inch lengths (about 2 cups)
- 1 ½ pounds waxy potatoes, such as Yukon Gold, peeled and sliced ⅛-inch thick (about 6 cups)
- 12 no-boil lasagna noodles (about 8 ounces)
- 1 ½ cups freshly grated Gruyère cheese
- ½ cup freshly grated Parmigiano-Reggiano cheese

  Vegetable oil spray

1. For the sauce: Bring the milk, onion, garlic, and thyme to a simmer in a small saucepan over medium heat. Remove from the heat and set aside to steep for 1 hour. Strain though a mesh sieve into a large bowl, pressing on the solids with a spoon. Discard the solids. Return the milk to the saucepan and keep warm over low heat.

2. Melt the butter in a medium saucepan over medium heat. Whisk in the flour and cook, whisking, for 2 minutes. Do not let the flour brown, so adjust the heat as needed. Slowly pour in the warm milk, whisking continuously. Cook, stirring slowly and steadily with a heat-proof rubber spatula, until the sauce is smooth and slightly thickened, about 3 minutes. Remove from the heat and stir in the cheese and prosciutto. Season with salt and pepper. Carefully press a piece of plastic wrap directly onto the surface of the sauce to prevent a skin from forming. Set aside.

3. For the lasagna: Preheat the oven to 350°F. Butter a 9 × 13-inch glass or ceramic baking dish.

4. Bring a medium saucepan of water to a boil. Add ½ teaspoon kosher salt per cup of water. Add the beans and cook until just tender, about 5 minutes. Drain in a colander and rinse under cold running water until cool. Drain and pat dry.

5. Place the potatoes in a large saucepan and cover with cold water. Add ½ teaspoon kosher salt per cup of water. Bring to a boil, reduce the heat, and simmer until almost tender, about 8 minutes. Drain well and pat dry.

6. Remove the plastic wrap from the cream sauce and scrape any sauce stuck to the plastic back into the pan. Warm over low heat. Spread ¼ cup of the sauce over the bottom of the prepared baking dish. Cover with 4 lasagna noodles, overlapping the edges slightly as needed. Drizzle ¾ cup of sauce over the noodles. Layer in half of the beans, half of the potatoes, and half of the Gruyère. Cover with 4 lasagna noodles and drizzle with ¾ cup of sauce. Layer in the rest of the beans, the potatoes, and the Gruyère. Top with the remaining 4 lasagna noodles. Pour the rest of the sauce over the top. Sprinkle with the Parmigiano-Reggiano.

⑦ Mist the shiny side of a sheet of aluminum foil with vegetable oil spray and cover the dish, sprayed side down. Bake for 20 minutes, remove the foil, and continue baking until the top is golden and the edges are bubbling, about 25 minutes more.

⑧ Let stand for at least 10 minutes before serving hot.

WHAT ELSE WORKS? You can use asparagus spears in place of the fillet beans.

## Slow-Simmered Beans with Tomatoes and Bacon

1 ½ pounds sturdy string beans

3 ounces high-quality slab or sliced bacon, cut into ½-inch cubes or strips

1 medium onion, halved lengthwise and cut into thin strips

2 garlic cloves, thinly sliced

2 cups peeled, seeded, and chopped fresh tomatoes or canned whole peeled tomatoes, chopped, juices reserved

1 teaspoon kosher salt, plus more to taste

½ teaspoon ground black pepper, plus more to taste

The only way to coax the deep and delicious flavor of old-fashioned, sturdy beans is to cook them until they are meltingly tender and army green. That does not happen quickly. These beans simmer in bacon drippings alongside onions and tomatoes, resulting in beans that are true to their southern roots. This is a recipe for beans that must be strung, such as pole beans, broad beans, romano, half runners, and greasy cut shorts—the old-time varieties that bean aficionados believe have the best flavor. Subjecting a fragile bean to this type of long cooking will ruin it.

Stringing and breaking beans is like yoga for me, deeply relaxing and meditative. I cannot begin to guess how many summer evenings my family spent out on the porch, working on beans until it got too dark to see. Each year we worked through bushel after bushel of beans and canned dozens of quarts in an old pressure cooker with a persnickety rubber gasket. The lid of that cooker blew off every few years, leaving a Rorschach blot on the kitchen ceiling, a stain common across the rural South before the advent of safe pressure cookers. We ate fresh beans all summer and home-canned beans all winter. I did not taste a store-bought bean from a tin can until I was in college.

MAKES 4 TO 6 SERVINGS

① Break off the ends of the beans and use them like pull tabs to pull off the strings that run down the seams of the pods. No amount of cooking will make those strings edible. Snap (break) the beans into bite-sized lengths.

② Cook the bacon in a large saucepan over medium heat until it is browned and has rendered its drippings, stirring often, about 10 minutes. Stir in the onion, garlic, and tomatoes. Bring to a simmer, stirring and scraping up the browned bits from the bottom of the pan.

③ Stir in the beans, salt, and pepper and bring to a boil. Reduce the heat and simmer, stirring occasionally, until the beans are completely tender, about 2 hours. The beans must stay very moist in a little gently bubbling sauce, so add water as needed. Check the seasoning and serve hot. Store cooled leftovers covered and refrigerated for up to 4 days. They get better each day.

# STRAWBERRIES

**Explorers and colonists** found huge fields carpeted in wild strawberries growing in the South and over much of eastern North America. There were stories of riders and horses emerging from those fields so covered in red strawberry juice that they looked wounded. The profusion and variety of native berries astounded the colonists, who shipped specimens back to Europe to bolster the viability and flavor of Old World varieties.

Strawberries are not actual berries because they carry their seeds on the outside. The plants spread through self-propagation. They send out runners that take hold and send out even more runners, spreading by leaps and bounds. Perhaps this ability to strew themselves about led to the name "strawberry," as a derivation of "strewberry." Another common notion is that the name came from the common practice of mulching the plants with straw.

Most strawberries are scarlet red, but there are also white and yellow varieties. They can range from tiny to large and from lumpy to smooth, but all good specimens are unmistakably redolent. Their botanical name, *Fragaria*, means fragrance, which suggests the sweet perfume that wafts from perfectly ripe strawberries. People accustomed to only long-hauled fruit are often awestruck by the intense flavor of strawberries left to fully ripen on the plants, where the warm sun can coax every bit of natural sweetness from the berries. ■

# Fresh Strawberries and Shortcake Cream Biscuits with Chocolate Gravy

**SHORTCAKE CREAM BISCUITS**

1 ½  cups all-purpose flour

¾  cup cake flour

3  tablespoons granulated sugar

2  teaspoons baking powder

½  teaspoon kosher salt

6  tablespoons unsalted butter, chilled

1  cup heavy cream, plus more for brushing

4  teaspoons turbinado, demerara, or raw sugar

**BERRIES**

4  cups capped and sliced strawberries

2  tablespoons granulated sugar

**CHOCOLATE GRAVY**

¼  cup cocoa powder

1  cup granulated sugar

3  tablespoons instant flour or all-purpose flour

2  cups whole milk

4  tablespoons (½ stick) butter, cut into 4 pieces

This is my version of strawberry shortcake: hot shortcake biscuits and ripe berries under a blanket of the warm, silky, rich chocolate sauce known as chocolate gravy. The term comes from the old southern practice of using the word "gravy" to describe any flour-thickened sauce made in a skillet, whether savory or sweet. Chocolate gravy, also known as Soppin' Chocolate, is traditional in parts of the central Appalachian Mountains but practically unknown elsewhere. It's made from ingredients that could be found in even the humblest of country stores and quickly brought together by resourceful mamas who wanted to make a little sweet treat for their families.

MAKES 6 SERVINGS

1. For the biscuits: Preheat the oven to 400°F. Line a baking sheet with parchment paper or a silicone baking mat.

2. Whisk together the all-purpose flour, cake flour, granulated sugar, baking powder, and salt in a large bowl. Use a pastry blender or your fingertips to work in the cold butter until the pieces are the size of small peas. Stir in the cream until shaggy dough forms.

3. Turn the dough out onto a very lightly floured surface and knead 2 or 3 times, just until it comes together. Roll or pat the dough into a rectangle about ¾-inch thick. Stamp out 5 biscuits with a 3-inch cutter. Press straight down without twisting the cutter so that the biscuits can rise evenly to their full height. Gently gather and roll the scraps of dough and cut out the sixth biscuit. You might have enough scraps for an oddly shaped bonus biscuit.

4. Transfer the biscuits to a baking sheet. Brush the tops lightly with cream and sprinkle with the turbinado sugar. Bake until golden, about 25 minutes. Cool to room temperature on a wire rack.

5. For the strawberries: Toss the berries with the granulated sugar in a large bowl and set aside for at least 15 minutes, stirring occasionally.

6. For the gravy: Sift the cocoa, granulated sugar, and flour into a large skillet (preferably cast-iron). Slowly add the milk, whisking until smooth. Cook over medium heat, stirring continuously with a heatproof spatula until the gravy thickens to the consistency of thin pudding, about 8 minutes. The gravy will thicken around the edge first, so keep it stirred up from the bottom and sides. Remove the pan from the heat and add the butter one piece at a time, stirring until it melts before adding the next.

7. Split the biscuits in half and divide among the serving plates. Top with the berries and their juice. Ladle a generous amount of warm gravy over the top and serve hot.

MAKE-AHEAD NOTE: You can make the shortcake biscuits up to 2 days ahead. Store at room temperature in an airtight container.

## TIPS AND TECHNIQUES

Many biscuit and pie crust recipes say to add cold butter to the dry ingredients. That's because when the bits of cold butter suspended in the dough go into the hot oven they melt and release steam, which makes biscuits light and pie crust flaky. You can cut the butter into small cubes and chill them, but I prefer to grate the butter on the large holes of a box grater, dipping the end of the stick of butter into the flour occasionally to keep it from sticking and smearing on the grater. The short shards of grated butter blend into the dough quickly, before it has a chance to warm up.

## Sonker and Dip

PASTRY

3 cups all-purpose flour

¾ teaspoon kosher salt

1 cup lard or vegetable shortening, chilled

1 large egg

2 tablespoons cider vinegar

4 to 6 tablespoons ice water

Instant flour or additional all-purpose flour, for rolling

2 tablespoons butter, melted

2 tablespoons sugar

(continued on next page)

Sonker is a well-known name in and around Surry County, North Carolina, but no one seems to know how it originated. Sonker—a sweet fruit filling in a pastry crust—is one of the countless versions of southern cobbler. As with other cobblers, it probably originated one day when a thrifty cook simply put together whatever was on hand and made something good from it. The sweetened milk topping is called "dip," a term as obscure as "sonker." Perhaps at one time people spooned it out of the pan with a metal ladle known as a dipper. We'll never know for sure.

Traditional sonker was made in a bread pan, an enormous metal baking pan some four inches deep that filled the oven of a woodstove. Sonker was designed to feed a group, such as the hired hands who brought in the harvest. This version of the recipe is scaled to be reasonable but still generous.

Sonker is usually topped with strips of pastry woven into a lattice crust. It's lovely but tedious. You can simplify the recipe by replacing the lattice with small free-form pieces of pastry or rounds cut with a biscuit cutter.

MAKES 8 TO 12 SERVINGS

(1) For the pastry: Whisk together the flour and salt in a large bowl. Use a pastry blender or your fingertips to work in the lard until the mixture resembles wet sand. Whisk together the egg and vinegar in a small bowl and pour over the flour mixture. Sprinkle 4 tablespoons of ice water over the flour and stir with a fork until the pastry comes together in large clumps. If the dough is too dry for all of the flour to mix in, sprinkle in more water 1 tablespoon at a time. Pour the pastry onto a large piece of plastic wrap and gently gather and knead

⅓ cup all-purpose flour

1 cup sugar

1 teaspoon ground
cinnamon

½ cup water

8 tablespoons (1 stick)
butter, melted

1 teaspoon pure
vanilla extract

8 cups capped and
sliced strawberries

DIP

¼ cup sugar

2 tablespoons
cornstarch

2 cups whole milk

½ teaspoon pure
vanilla extract

into a ball. Divide in half. Flatten each piece into a disk about ½-inch thick, wrap well, and refrigerate until chilled, at least 30 minutes. This gives the pastry time to rest so the flour can continue to absorb the liquid and the pastry will be easier to handle.

2. For the filling: Whisk together the flour, sugar, and cinnamon in a large bowl. Whisk in the water, melted butter, and vanilla. Add the strawberries, mix well, and set aside.

3. To assemble: Preheat the oven to 350°F.

4. Press one of the disks of pastry evenly over the bottom of a 9 × 13-inch baking pan. Bake until the pastry is dry but not browned, about 10 minutes. Meanwhile, use a floured rolling pin to roll the other disk of pastry to a 9 × 13-inch rectangle. If you are making a lattice crust, use a pastry wheel or pizza cutter to cut the pastry into 1-inch-wide strips. Otherwise, cut the pastry into free-form pieces of any shape or into rounds with a biscuit cutter.

5. Remove the pan from the oven and increase the oven temperature to 375°F. Spread the strawberry filling over the bottom crust. Arrange the strips of pastry over the filling, crisscrossing them into a lattice design if you wish. Otherwise, arrange the pieces evenly over the filling. Leave a little space between some of the pieces so the juicy filling can bubble up through them. Brush the pastry with melted butter and sprinkle with sugar.

6. Bake until the pastry is browned and the filling is bubbling, about 40 minutes. Let the sonker sit for at least 10 minutes before serving. Meanwhile, make the dip.

7. For the dip: Whisk together the sugar and cornstarch in a medium saucepan. Whisk in the milk. Cook over medium heat, stirring constantly, until the sauce thickens enough to coat the back of a spoon. Remove the pan from the heat and stir in the vanilla.

8. Serve the sonker warm or at room temperature, topped with warm dip.

WHAT ELSE WORKS? You can replace the strawberries with raspberries, blackberries, blueberries, cherries, ground cherries, thinly sliced peaches, or thinly sliced cooked sweet potatoes.

## Strawberry Compote with Aged
## Balsamic Vinegar and Cracked Pepper

4 cups capped and
   quartered strawberries

¾ to 1 cup sugar (depending
   on the sweetness of
   the berries)

2 tablespoons water

3 tablespoons aged
   balsamic vinegar
   (at least 8 years old)

2 teaspoons cracked
   or coarsely ground
   black pepper

My favorite way to use aged balsamic vinegar is over fresh berries or peaches. As balsamic ages, it gets thick, sweet, and complex, more like syrup than vinegar, so it enhances the natural sweetness of foods. This recipe is not successful with young, thin balsamic that tastes too sharp and acidic. The cracked pepper adds a little mystery to the compote. It keeps well in the refrigerator for up to one month.

For an easy party dish, unwrap a wheel or wedge of premium Brie, Camembert, or other similar cheese and cover the top generously with compote. Garnish the top with a sprinkling of whole pink peppercorns.

For an easy and elegant dessert, make a sundae by spooning the compote over premium vanilla gelato or ice cream.

MAKES ABOUT 2 CUPS

(1) Bring the strawberries, sugar, and water to a boil in a medium saucepan. Reduce the heat and simmer, stirring occasionally and skimming off any foam that collects on the surface, until thickened to the consistency of jam, about 15 minutes.

(2) Remove the pan from the heat and cool to room temperature. Stir in the vinegar and pepper. Pour into a clean glass jar with a tight-fitting lid and refrigerate for up to 1 month.

WHAT ELSE WORKS? You can replace the strawberries with raspberries, blackberries, or a combination of berries.

## Roasted Beet and Goat Cheese Stacks
## with Strawberry Compote

6 red and/or
   golden beets
   (about 3 inches
   in diameter)

1 (4-ounce) log
   soft, fresh goat
   cheese (chèvre)

½ cup Strawberry
   Compote with
   Balsamic Vinegar
   and Cracked Black
   Pepper

The fruity sweetness of the strawberry compote is wonderful with the earthy sweetness of roasted beets. Rounds of tangy goat cheese make a lovely counterpoint to both flavors. These little stacks are stunning, particularly if you use both magenta and golden beets. For best results, use beets that are about the same diameter as the log of goat cheese. The stacks, which resemble napoleons, can be served on their own or atop a few leafy salad greens.

MAKES 4 SERVINGS

(1) Roast the beets according to the directions on page 31. When the beets are cool enough to handle, peel and cut into ¼-inch-thick rounds. Use only the center slices of similar size; discard the end pieces or save them for another use.

2. Let the cheese sit at room temperature for 15 minutes. Cut the log of cheese crosswise into ¼-inch-thick rounds with a knife dipped into warm water or with a length of unflavored dental floss. (Place the string under the cheese, cross the ends over the top and pull gently to contract the loop; the string will easily cut through the cheese with little breakage or mess.)

3. To assemble, make 4 stacks of alternating roasted beet slices and goat cheese slices on serving plates. Spoon about 2 tablespoons of compote around each stack and serve at room temperature.

## Strawberry Tiramisu Trifles

1 cup strawberry preserves

6 tablespoons Grand Marnier, Cointreau, or other orange liqueur

6 tablespoons fresh orange juice

1 cup chilled whipping cream

8 ounces mascarpone cheese, at room temperature

⅓ cup sugar

1 teaspoon pure vanilla extract

7 ounces crisp ladyfingers or *biscotti savoiardi*

4 cups capped and sliced strawberries

6 perfect whole berries, for garnish

Trifle is an old-fashioned recipe made by layering cake, custard, and cream in a fancy glass bowl and sometimes dousing the whole thing with alcohol. This trifle features crisp ladyfingers and mascarpone, ingredients found in Italian tiramisu, but paired with berries and orange liqueur instead of chocolate and espresso.

These lovely, delicious little treats are assembled in glasses so that everyone gets an individual serving, which always makes people feel special and well tended. Glasses with 9-ounce capacities and sides about the same height as an upright ladyfinger are ideal, such as parfait glasses, short drinking glasses, or wine glasses that are not tapered at the top. However, if you prefer to make one big trifle, you can use a standard trifle bowl, a deep serving bowl, or even a 9 × 13-inch baking dish for times when looks are no big deal.

MAKES 6 SERVINGS

1. Whisk together the strawberry preserves, liqueur, and orange juice in a small bowl.

2. Beat the whipping cream to very soft peaks in a medium bowl. Add the mascarpone, sugar, and vanilla and continue beating until soft peaks form.

3. Divide half of the whipped cream mixture evenly among the six serving glasses. (A small spring-loaded scoop makes this easier and neater.) Stand 4 ladyfingers upright inside each glass, spacing them evenly. The whipped cream mixture should hold them in place. Divide half of the strawberry preserve mixture evenly among the glasses. Divide the sliced strawberries among the glasses. Top with the rest of the preserve mixture, followed by the remaining cream mixture. Cover and refrigerate for at least 4 hours and up to overnight. Just before serving, garnish each parfait with a whole berry.

Liqueurs add flavor, liquid, and sweetness to recipes. However, if you do not want to use alcohol, use flavored drink syrups instead, such as those used in fancy coffee concoctions. Match the flavor of the syrup to the liqueur, such as coffee for Kahlúa, hazelnut for Frangelico, orange for Grand Marnier, and raspberry for Chambord. These syrups are available in coffee shops, gourmet shops, and many grocery stores.

## Crisp Green Salad with Fresh Strawberry Vinaigrette

This lovely, simple salad is a refreshing way to enjoy strawberries in something other than dessert. It is particularly nice with brunch. Crunchy butter lettuce is a better choice than delicate greens that would get soggy under the thick dressing. The light flavor and pleasant aroma of almond oil are great with the berries and complement the almonds in the salad, but you can use neutral grapeseed oil. The strong flavor of olive oil would mask the berries.

MAKES 4 TO 6 SERVINGS

STRAWBERRY
VINAIGRETTE

2 cups capped and sliced strawberries

¼ cup raspberry vinegar

1 tablespoon floral honey

¼ cup almond or grapeseed oil

Kosher salt and ground black pepper, to taste

SALAD

1 small head butter lettuce, Bibb lettuce, or other crunchy lettuce

12 strawberries, capped and halved or quartered

½ cup slivered almonds, lightly toasted

Coarsely ground black pepper, to taste

1. For the vinaigrette: Purée the berries, vinegar, and honey in a blender. With the machine running, add the oil in a steady stream. Season with salt and pepper.

2. For the salad: Core the lettuce and tear the leaves into bite-sized pieces. You should have about 6 lightly packed cups. Divide the lettuce among serving plates.

3. Drizzle the salads with vinaigrette, then scatter the strawberries and almonds over the top. Sprinkle with pepper and serve at once.

# SUMMER SQUASH

**When Europeans first landed on the continent,** they found Native
Americans cultivating a variety of edible gourds, including summer
squashes. From the beginning, summer squashes were distinguished from
winter squashes. They take their name from *askutasquash*, a Narragansett
word meaning "green thing eaten uncooked." Summer squash are picked
in warm weather before they mature, so their skins and seeds are edible,
even when raw. In contrast, winter squashes aren't harvested until they
mature and develop the hard shell that makes them suitable for long keeping through cold weather.

The most common varieties of summer squash in the early southern
kitchen garden were yellow crooknecks and cymlings. Crookneck squash
often overshadowed all other types of squash because they were prolific,
if not always the tastiest. Cymling is the traditional name for the flying
saucer–shaped varieties we now often call patty pans or scallops. Many
squash connoisseurs consider cymlings to be the most flavorful summer
squash, and their popularity is once again on the rise. Many gardens and
markets now offer a bounty of squashes in assorted shapes and colors.

As any gardener can attest, many types of summer squash flourish in
the South. Do they ever. Trying to grow only a few summer squash is like
trying to grow only a little kudzu. ■

# Summer Squash Gratin

2 pounds mixed summer squashes (such as crooknecks, zephyrs, and cymlings)

6 tablespoons butter, divided

1 large onion, chopped

2 garlic cloves, finely chopped

3 cups fresh bread crumbs, divided (page 389)

1 cup grated Gruyère cheese

1 cup sour cream

1 tablespoon chopped fresh thyme

2 large eggs, lightly beaten

1 ½ teaspoons kosher salt

½ teaspoon ground black pepper

Nearly every good southern cook has a squash casserole that has become a beloved family favorite. This is mine. You'll notice that I call it a gratin, not a casserole. That's because in my experience people are wary of anything called a casserole but gobble up anything called a gratin. Thus the title is a marketing ploy.

The key to this recipe, and to all squash casseroles, is to never boil the squash, a vegetable prone to soaking up water like a dry sponge, making an entire dish a soggy mess with diluted flavor. Here, the squash is steamed in the microwave, but you can use a standard steamer. The more types and colors of squash you use in this dish, the prettier and more interesting it will be.

MAKES 8 SERVINGS

1. Preheat the oven to 350°F. Butter a shallow 2 ½-quart baking dish.
2. If the skin of the squash is tough, peel it. If the squash has large, wet seeds, scoop them out and discard them. Trim and dice the firm squash flesh into ½-inch pieces. There should be about 6 cups. Transfer it into a large glass bowl and add a splash of water. Cover with plastic wrap and microwave on high until the squash is tender, about 5 minutes. Drain off any standing liquid. (You can also cook the squash in a steamer basket set over a saucepan of simmering water.) Use a potato masher or fork to coarsely mash about half of the squash; leave the rest in larger pieces.
3. Melt 2 tablespoons of the butter in a medium skillet over medium-high heat. Add the onion and a pinch of salt. Cook, stirring often, until softened, about 8 minutes. Add the garlic and cook, stirring, until fragrant, about 1 minute. Add to the bowl of squash. Stir in 1 ½ cups of the crumbs and the cheese, sour cream, and thyme.
4. In a small bowl, whisk the eggs until the whites and yolks are blended, then stir into the squash mixture. Season with the salt and pepper. Spoon the mixture into the prepared baking dish.
5. Wipe out the skillet. Melt the remaining 4 tablespoons of butter and sauté the remaining 1 ½ cup of the crumbs in the butter until golden. Scatter the toasted crumbs over the squash mixture.
6. Bake uncovered until the gratin is golden brown and firm in the center, about 30 minutes. Serve hot.

WHAT ELSE WORKS? You can use a mixture of summer squashes and zucchini or all zucchini.

# Squash and Onions Redeemed

3 tablespoons
butter, divided

1 large onion,
finely chopped

4 cups thinly sliced
summer squash,
peeled if necessary
(about 1 pound)

Kosher salt and ground
black pepper, to taste

John Bartram, eighteenth-century naturalist, called boiled squash "poor enter-tainment." That's the heart of the problem with most old-fashioned squash and onion recipes that call for little beyond boiling them into a soggy heap. In this recipe, the vegetables are simmered in their own juices, concentrating and pro-tecting their delicate flavors. The texture of the finished dish is like soft, buttery mashed potatoes. The butter is traditional, but you can substitute extra-virgin olive oil for a more Mediterranean approach, or use equal amounts of both.

Served hot, this is a great side dish. Served at room temperature, it makes tasty bruschetta topping. Leftovers work well in omelets.

MAKES 4 TO 6 SERVINGS

1. Heat 1 tablespoon of the butter in a large skillet over medium-high heat. Add the onion and a pinch of salt, stir to coat, and cook, stirring often, until the onion is very soft and golden, about 10 minutes.

2. Stir in the squash, a pinch of salt, and 1 tablespoon of butter. Reduce the heat to medium-low, cover, and cook for 15 minutes, stirring occasionally. The squash should release enough liquid to stay very moist.

3. Uncover, increase the heat to high, and cook, stirring constantly, until the excess liquid cooks away and the squash is the consistency of rustic mashed potatoes, about 5 minutes. Most of the squash should be smooth with a few larger, tender pieces mixed in.

4. Remove from the heat, stir in the remaining 1 tablespoon of butter, and season generously with salt and pepper. Serve hot or at room temperature.

## Squash Blossom Soup with Mixed Herb Pesto

6 tablespoons butter

1 large onion, chopped

2 pounds summer squash, thinly sliced (about 6 cups)

2 medium carrots, thinly sliced (about 1 cup)

1 medium russet potato, peeled and chopped (about 1 cup)

4 to 5 cups chicken or vegetable stock

1 ½ teaspoons kosher salt, plus more to taste

½ teaspoon ground black pepper, plus more to taste

24 large squash blossoms (each about 3 inches long), divided

Mixed Herb Pesto, for serving (recipe follows)

Gardeners can have short memories. Come planting time, they forget that the year before they had vowed they would never again set out more than one or two hills of squash and zucchini, if that much. (Some thought that one or two hills per county would be plenty.) Instead, they plant several hills, and by midsummer those plants have taken hold and begun to produce. And produce. And produce. So the gardeners begin to share their surplus. A few weeks later, neighbors that once received baskets of squash with open arms start pulling the drapes and acting like they aren't home.

One way to stave off a surfeit of squash is to nip it in the bud. Literally. The bright, perky blossoms are as tasty as the squash themselves. Using female blossoms thins the crop. Using male blossoms is like a bonus second harvest from the same plants.

In this recipe, the blossoms also add wisps of color, like short strands of golden ribbon swirled through the soup. It reminds me of the old practice of people eating the blossoms of the speckled day lilies that grew along fencerows, far from the dusty road and certainly never sprayed with anything.

MAKES 2 QUARTS

1. Melt the butter in a large saucepan over medium-high heat. Add the onion and a pinch of salt and cook, stirring often, until softened but not browned at all, about 5 minutes. Add the squash and carrots and a pinch of salt. Cook, stirring often, until the vegetables are tender, about 8 minutes. Add the potato and enough stock to just cover the vegetables. Season with the salt and pepper. Bring to a boil over high heat, then reduce the heat to medium-low and simmer until the potato is tender, about 10 minutes.

2. Meanwhile, clean the blossoms by gently rinsing them in a bowl of cool water. Break off and discard the stems and the short green sepals at the base of the flower. Gently cut or tear open the blossoms and break loose and discard their fuzzy centers. Cut the blossoms crosswise into ¼-inch strips. Stir half of the blossom strips into the soup and simmer for 3 minutes.

3. Purée the soup in a blender (working in batches to not fill the blender more than half full) or directly in the pot with an immersion blender. Add more stock if the soup is too thick. Season with additional salt and pepper. Just before serving, stir in the remaining blossoms and simmer only until they soften into golden ribbons. Serve hot, topped with a drizzle of Mixed Herb Pesto.

WHAT ELSE WORKS? You can use thinly sliced spinach leaves in place of the squash blossoms.

## Mixed Herb Pesto

½ cup lightly packed flat-leaf parsley

½ cup lightly packed baby arugula

½ cup lightly packed basil leaves

½ cup lightly packed mint leaves

1 tablespoon chopped fresh thyme

1 tablespoon fresh lemon juice

½ cup freshly grated Parmesan cheese

¼ cup slivered almonds, lightly toasted

⅓ to ½ cup extra-virgin olive oil

Kosher salt and ground black pepper, to taste

Pesto can be made from more than just basil. This recipe combines a variety of green leafy herbs into a tasty pesto that perks up soups, sandwiches, or simple steamed vegetables. It's also good tossed with pasta and cheese.

Feel free to play with the combination and proportion of herbs to suit your taste and to use whatever you have on hand. Same with the nuts; try everything from pine nuts to walnuts to pecans to hazelnuts.

MAKES ABOUT 1 CUP

1 Pulse the herbs, lemon juice, cheese, and nuts in the bowl of a food processor fitted with the metal blade until finely chopped.

2 With the machine running, slowly add enough of the oil to make a thick, coarse paste. Season with salt and pepper. Serve at room temperature.

MAKE-AHEAD NOTE: You can store the pesto for up to 4 days. Transfer into an airtight container, top with a thin film of olive oil, and refrigerate. When ready to serve, return the pesto to room temperature and stir in the oil. Repeat this step each time you return leftovers to the refrigerator.

## Herbed Summer Squash and Pasta Salad with Crispy Chicken Thighs

8 ounces pearl couscous

4 tablespoons lemon-infused olive oil, divided

1 medium onion, diced

2 cups diced assorted summer squashes (about 1 ½ pounds)

½ cup coarsely grated Parmesan cheese

¼ cup lightly packed chopped fresh basil

¼ cup lightly packed chopped flat-leaf parsley

Zest and juice of 1 lemon (about ¼ cup)

¼ cup pine nuts, toasted

Kosher salt and ground black pepper, to taste

Crispy Chicken Thighs, for serving (recipe follows)

Served on its own, this hearty salad makes a great all-purpose side dish or light meal. For the taste of Sunday dinner in one bowl, serve the salad with the crispy chicken. The moist, meaty chicken is capped with crisp golden skin and is full of flavor.

The more colorful the squash, the prettier the dish, so try to include a variety of tender squashes that don't have to be peeled. I'm partial to the firm texture and pretty scalloped edges of patty pans (cymlings) cut into thin wedges and to thinly sliced young striped zephyrs. I like to use pearl couscous (also known as Israeli couscous) in this salad, but other small pasta—orzo, riso, stelline, or ditalini—will also work.

MAKES 4 TO 6 SERVINGS

1. Cook the couscous according to package directions. Drain well, pour into a large bowl, toss with 2 tablespoons of the oil, and set aside, stirring from time to time.

2. Heat the remaining 2 tablespoons of oil in a large skillet over medium heat. Add the onion and a pinch of salt and cook, stirring often, until softened, about 8 minutes. Add the squash and cook until crisp-tender, about 5 minutes. Add to the couscous.

3. Stir in the cheese, basil, parsley, lemon zest, lemon juice, and pine nuts. The salad should be quite moist, so drizzle with more oil if needed. Season with salt and pepper.

4. Serve slightly warm or at room temperature, with the chicken if you wish.

## Crispy Chicken Thighs

6 large bone-in chicken thighs with skin (about 2 ¼ pounds total)

2 to 3 teaspoons kosher salt

I am suspicious of any recipe that claims to be oven-fried chicken. So far as I'm concerned, fried chicken is either fried or it isn't. However, this recipe shows that frying isn't the only way to get crisp, golden chicken skin and moist, well-seasoned meat. The trick is to salt the chicken pieces and let them dry overnight in the refrigerator. The salt brings the excess moisture to the surface so that high heat can cook it away. It works like magic. Make sure the skin on each thigh completely covers the meat because any loose edges will shrink and roll up like a window shade when cooked, exposing and drying out the meat. You can use this technique with other chicken parts (so long as they have skin), but thighs will deliver the juiciest, tastiest meat. For best results, use organic chicken that has never been frozen.

MAKES 4 TO 6 SERVINGS

1. Rinse the chicken and pat it completely dry with paper towels. Gently pull the loose skin so that it covers the rounded top and sides of each thigh, taking care not to rip or tear the skin. Arrange the thighs in a single layer with sides not touching on a wire rack set inside a rimmed baking sheet. Generously and evenly salt the chicken. Place the chicken, uncovered, in the refrigerator for at least 4 hours and preferably overnight. The more time the skin has to dry, the crisper it will be when cooked.

2. Position a rack in the upper third of the oven and preheat the oven to 450°F. (Use the convection roast setting if you have it.) Roast until the meat is cooked through and the skin is very crisp and golden, 15 to 20 minutes. When the meat is pierced with the tip of a small knife, the juices should have no traces of pink. An instant-read thermometer inserted into the thickest part of a thigh (avoiding the bone) should register 165°F. Serve hot.

## Yellow Squash Muffins

| | |
|---|---|
| | Vegetable oil spray |
| 2 ½ | cups all-purpose flour |
| ½ | cup granulated sugar |
| ¼ | cup firmly packed light brown sugar |
| 1 ½ | teaspoons baking powder |
| ¼ | teaspoon baking soda |
| ¾ | teaspoon fine sea salt |
| 1 ½ | teaspoons ground cinnamon |
| ¾ | teaspoon ground ginger |
| ¼ | teaspoon ground nutmeg |
| ⅓ | cup golden raisins |
| ⅓ | cup chopped walnuts |
| 2 | large eggs |
| ¾ | cup water |
| ⅓ | cup vegetable oil |
| 1 | cup lightly packed grated yellow summer squash |

These muffins deliver everything I love about a good muffin. They are tender, cakey, light, and not too sweet. They are quick and easy to make without needing to pull out a mixer. They work for breakfast, snacks, and lunchboxes and keep well for several days.

The flavor of the squash is very subtle, so only the little yellow flecks in the muffins suggest its presence. The squash makes the muffins moist, but it is important that it not be too soggy. If your squash has large, wet seeds, discard them before grating the firm flesh on the large holes of a box grater or zipping it through the shredding disc of a food processor. Short shredded pieces work best in the muffins, so cut large squash lengthwise into halves or quarters before grating.

MAKES 1 DOZEN

1. Preheat the oven to 400°F. Mist the top of a standard 12-cup muffin tin with the spray. Mist the cups or line them with paper muffin cups. Be sure to use a light metal muffin tin. Dark metal and nonstick tins — even when lined with paper cups — make the crust too thick and dark.

2. Whisk together the flour, granulated sugar, brown sugar, baking powder, baking soda, salt, cinnamon, ginger, nutmeg, raisins, and walnuts in a large bowl.

3. In a small bowl, whisk the eggs until the whites and yolks are blended, then whisk in the water and oil. Pour the egg mixture into the flour mixture and stir with a rubber spatula only until the dry ingredients disappear into the batter. Fold in the squash.

④ Divide the batter among the muffin cups. Bake the muffins until a tester inserted into the center of a muffin comes out clean, about 20 minutes.

⑤ Serve warm or at room temperature. Turn the muffins out onto a clean tea towel and let them cool upside down.

WHAT ELSE WORKS? You can use grated zucchini, apples, sweet potatoes, or carrots in place of some or all of the squash. You can use pecans in place of the walnuts.

### TIPS AND TECHNIQUES

There are a few easy steps to making attractive muffins that rise well and are not shot through with holes. First, don't overmix the batter; stir only until the dry ingredients disappear. To make muffins uniform in size with pretty rounded tops, use a spring-loaded scoop to plop the batter into the muffin tin. Next, even if you are using paper liners in the tin, mist the top of the tin with vegetable oil spray. The edges that rise out of the cup and touch the top of the pan will release without tearing.

## Squashy Joes

2 teaspoons
vegetable oil

½ cup finely
chopped onion

½ cup finely
chopped carrot

2 cups diced summer
squash (peeled only
if the skins are tough)

1 pound lean ground
beef or turkey

1 tablespoon ground
ancho chile or mild
chili powder

1 teaspoon sweet
paprika or smoked
paprika (*pimentón*)

2 teaspoons
ground cumin

(continued on
next page)

I raise my eyebrows at recipes that seem to be a gimmick to trick kids (or the vegetable averse of any age) into eating something. But when I saw an article in a parenting magazine about slipping vegetables into familiar recipes, such as sloppy joes, I couldn't stop thinking about it. I gave it a try, and here we are. I like the nubby texture of diced squash, but you can also grate it into unidentifiable pieces if the squash needs to remain incognito. My family usually eats this on Texas toast or buns, but I've also spooned it over nachos and rolled it up in burritos.

MAKES 6 SERVINGS

① Heat the oil in a large skillet over medium-high heat. Add the onion and carrot and a pinch of salt and cook, stirring often, until beginning to soften, about 5 minutes. Stir in the squash and another pinch of salt and cook until crisp-tender, about 3 minutes more. Transfer into a medium bowl.

② Add the meat to the skillet and cook, breaking up the meat with the spoon, until no longer pink. Stir in the ancho chile, paprika, and cumin and cook, stirring, for 30 seconds. Stir in the tomato sauce, water, barbecue sauce, Worcestershire, brown sugar, and squash mixture. Simmer, stirring occasionally, until the mixture is very thick, about 10 minutes. Season with salt.

③ Spoon over the Texas toast, top with slices of cheese, and serve hot.

1   (8-ounce) can
    tomato sauce

1   cup water

¼   cup barbecue sauce
    or ketchup

1   tablespoon
    Worcestershire sauce

1   tablespoon packed
    light brown sugar

    Kosher salt, to taste

6   hot slices of Texas
    toast or garlic bread
    or 6 buns, for serving

6   slices provolone or
    other sandwich cheese

WHAT ELSE WORKS? You can use strands of spaghetti squash in place of the diced summer squash. Cut 1 (3 ½- to 4-pound) spaghetti squash in half lengthwise and discard the seeds. Cook the spaghetti squash in the microwave or in the oven.

To microwave: Place the halves cut-side down in a glass or ceramic baking dish. Pour ½ cup of water around the squash and cover the dish tightly with plastic wrap. Microwave on high until the squash shell is soft when pierced with a knife, about 12 minutes. Carefully remove the hot squash from the microwave and pierce the plastic wrap so that the steam can escape, then let sit until cool enough to handle. Use a fork to pull out and separate the strands of squash.

To roast: Preheat the oven to 350°F. Place the halves cut-side down on a rimmed baking sheet lightly coated with vegetable oil spray. Roast until you can easily pierce the shell with a knife, 45 to 60 minutes. Use a fork to pull out and separate the strands of squash.

## Mirliton and Seafood Gratin

1 ½  pounds pale green,
     thin-skinned mirlitons

4    tablespoons (½ stick)
     butter, divided

1 ½  cups fresh bread
     crumbs (page 389)

1    medium onion,
     chopped

1    green bell pepper,
     cored and chopped

2    celery stalks,
     thinly sliced

1    pound shrimp,
     peeled and deveined

8    ounces lump
     crabmeat, picked
     over for bits of shell

3    tablespoons
     finely chopped
     flat-leaf parsley

1    teaspoon Creole
     seasoning, or to taste

The squash that some people call chayote is called mirliton in southern Louisiana. I'm told that how people pronounce "mirliton" depends on where they live. It's "me-lay-taw" in the country and "murl-uh-tahn" in town. In other parts of the South, these squash are sometimes called vegetable pear, which describes their shape and smooth, pale green skin. They have a clean, crisp texture and mild flavor, which people compare to summer squash and cucumber. (As their hard, inedible seeds suggest, mirlitons are actually a type of winter squash, but most people use their flesh like summer squash, so I'm including them in this section.) There is another variety of mirliton (often called alligator pear) that has a dark green, spiny shell, which is nearly impossible to peel unless you boil the whole thing until tender, so it's not a good choice for this recipe.

In the seafaring Deep South, mirlitons are often stuffed with seafood and shellfish. In this recipe, I've combined mirliton with shrimp and crabmeat and baked the mixture under a crisp topping of buttered crumbs, like a classic gratin. You can use 12 ounces of cooked crawfish meat in place of the shrimp.

MAKES 6 SERVINGS

1  Preheat the oven to 400°F. Butter or spray a shallow 2 ½-quart baking dish.

2  Peel, pit, and cut the mirlitons into 1-inch chunks. (By the way, when slippery mirliton juice dries on your hands, it leaves a thin residue that makes fingertips tight and shiny, as though they had been dipped in school glue and allowed to dry. It washes off easily, or you can wear gloves.) Put the chunks

into a large saucepan and cover with cold water. Add ½ teaspoon kosher salt per cup of water. Bring to a boil, reduce the heat, and simmer until very tender, about 30 minutes. Drain well, transfer into a large bowl, and coarsely mash with a potato masher or large spoon.

③ Melt 2 tablespoons of the butter in a large skillet over medium-high heat. Add the bread crumbs and cook, stirring often, until golden. Transfer into a small bowl.

④ Melt the remaining 2 tablespoons of butter in the skillet. Stir in the onion, bell pepper, and celery and cook, stirring often, until softened, about 10 minutes. Depending on the size of the shrimp, leave whole or cut into large bite-sized pieces. Stir the shrimp into the onion mixture and cook until they just turn opaque, about 1 minute. Stir in the crabmeat and parsley and ½ cup of the buttered crumbs. Transfer into the bowl of mirlitons and stir gently to mix. Season with the Creole seasoning.

⑤ Transfer into the prepared baking dish. Sprinkle the remaining 1 cup of buttered crumbs over the top. Bake until the filling is bubbling and the crumbs are browned, about 20 minutes. Serve hot.

## Sufficient Grace Summer Squash with Buttered Crumbs

4 tablespoons (½ stick) butter, divided

1 cup fresh bread crumbs (page 389) or crushed saltine cracker crumbs

2 pounds mixed tiny summer squashes, trimmed and thinly sliced

Kosher salt and ground black pepper, to taste

This is, hands down, my favorite way to eat summer squash. It reminds me of the squash fried in the black skillet my grandmother used to make, but it's lighter and easier. The secret is to use only the tiniest of squash, no larger than an inch thick with skin so tender that you can nick it with a thumbnail. Larger squash are too wet and seedy.

Do not be tempted to add anything, not even herbs. The grace of the squash and buttered crumbs is sufficient.

MAKES 4 TO 6 SERVINGS

① Melt 2 tablespoons of the butter in a large, heavy skillet (preferably cast-iron) over medium-high heat. Stir in the crumbs and cook until crisp, golden brown, and fragrant, stirring often, about 5 minutes. Transfer into a medium bowl.

② Melt the remaining 2 tablespoons of butter in the skillet over medium-high heat. Add the squash and a pinch of salt and stir to coat. Cover and cook, stirring often, until the squash is barely tender and not at all mushy or watery, 5 to 8 minutes. Season with salt and pepper. Sprinkle the crumbs over the squash and serve hot.

# SWEET PEPPERS

**The vegetables that we often call peppers** are actually chiles. The misnomer started with a persistent case of mistaken identity and wishful thinking on the part of the early Spanish explorers. Christopher Columbus's expedition came across Native Americans using chiles to season food, which led them to confuse chiles with peppercorns, one of the profitable spices the explorers had hoped to discover during their travels. Chiles, whether mild or hot, are capsicums, and they are botanically unrelated to the plants that produce peppercorns. Some cooks and gardeners continue to use the words "peppers" and "chiles" interchangeably, but in this book the mild and sweet capsicums are called sweet peppers and the hot capsicums are called chile peppers.

Sweet and mild peppers carry a recessive gene that keeps them from forming the fiery capsaicin common to hot chile peppers. Sweet peppers tend to be much larger than hot chiles. For example, a bell pepper is huge compared to a Thai bird chile. Sweet peppers are green while unripe and change into colors (usually red, orange, yellow, or purple) and continue to sweeten as they mature. They also become more digestible as they ripen, which is why colored peppers cause fewer troubles than green peppers for most people.

Sweet peppers are common in southern recipes, both traditional and ethnic. Bell peppers, along with onions and celery, make up the so-called holy trinity used to season many Creole and Cajun recipes. Many of the South's iconic relishes and pickles—chow chow, piccalilli, chile sauce, and pickled peppers—would not exist without sweet peppers. And without sweet red peppers, there would be no pimento cheese. Nuff said. ■

## Roasted Peppers

Perhaps no vegetable benefits from roasting more than ripe sweet peppers, such as bells or frying peppers. Roasting intensifies their natural sweetness and removes their thin, tough skins. It's very easy to do. You can roast a single pepper or a whole batch at once. The only requirement is a source of direct high heat, such as the open flame of a gas burner on your stove, a grill, or a broiler.

The heat caramelizes the sugars in the peppers, so they must be ripe enough to have developed sugars. In other words, don't try this with an unripe green pepper because all you will get is an acrid, burned green pepper. (This caveat doesn't apply to green chiles because the point of roasting them is to char the skins, not sweeten the flesh.)

Leave the peppers whole and do not oil them. If using a broiler, arrange the peppers on a foil-lined baking sheet. If using a gas burner or grill (either gas or charcoal), place them directly on the grate as close to the heat source as possible. (Turn on the vent fan if doing this on your gas stove in the kitchen.) Roast the peppers until they are blistered and blackened all over, turning as needed with tongs. They should look ruined. Transfer the charred peppers into a large bowl and cover with a plate or plastic wrap. You can also tuck them inside a zip-top plastic bag. Let the peppers rest until they are cool enough to handle. The captured steam will finish cooking them. Gently pull out the stem and core of each pepper; most of the seeds will come out still attached to the core. Gently rub or peel off the blackened skin. It's fine if a few bits stay stuck to the flesh. Do not rinse the peppers or you will wash away their great flavor.

Use the peppers at once, or cover and refrigerate for up to 3 days. You can also freeze the peppers in airtight containers for up to 3 months. The frozen peppers retain their flavor, but they soften, so they are best used in cooked dishes.

## Roasted Red Pepper Dip

1 cup chopped roasted sweet red peppers (page 314)

1 (15-ounce) can chickpeas or cannellini beans, drained and rinsed

¼ cup well-stirred tahini

2 tablespoons fresh lemon juice

3 garlic cloves, finely chopped

2 teaspoons dried Italian blend herbs

⅓ cup lightly packed basil leaves

1 tablespoon tomato paste

1 teaspoon smoked paprika (*pimentón*)

3 tablespoons sherry vinegar or red wine vinegar

1 teaspoon kosher salt, or to taste

¼ teaspoon cayenne pepper

2 to 4 tablespoons extra-virgin olive oil

I used to call this hummus but learned that most people expect hummus to be beige and bland. This is neither. It's brick red and packed with flavor. I like to serve this with pita crisps, but you can use any scooper, from chips to crackers to raw vegetables. It also makes a tasty spread to perk up sandwiches. Because it's best made at least one day ahead and served at room temperature, it's a great choice for leisurely parties and lunchboxes.

MAKES 8 SERVINGS

1. Combine the peppers, chickpeas, tahini, lemon juice, garlic, Italian herbs, basil, tomato paste, smoked paprika, vinegar, salt, and cayenne in the bowl of a food processor fitted with the metal blade and process until coarsely chopped.

2. With the machine running, drizzle in enough of the oil to make the mixture smooth and thick. Taste and adjust the seasoning as needed.

3. Transfer into a large bowl and let sit at room temperature for at least 30 minutes to allow the flavors to develop. For best results, cover and refrigerate overnight. Return to room temperature and stir well before serving.

## Old-Fashioned Pimento Cheese

1 cup finely diced roasted pimentos or other sweet red peppers (page 314)

1 pound extra-sharp yellow cheddar cheese, coarsely grated

1 pound sharp or extra-sharp aged white cheddar cheese, coarsely grated

¼ cup very finely grated onion

2 tablespoons dill pickle juice or fresh lemon juice

¼ teaspoon dry mustard

¼ teaspoon sugar

¾ to 1¼ cups homemade mayonnaise (recipe follows) or high-quality store-bought mayonnaise

½ teaspoon kosher salt, or to taste

¾ teaspoon ground black pepper, or to taste

¼ teaspoon cayenne pepper, or to taste

When they are in season, I make pimento cheese with fresh pimentos or other sweet red peppers instead of jarred. It's easy to forget that those little bits of pimento in those tiny jars were once fresh.

A word about pimento cheese. There are many ways to divide the peoples of the so-called New South, but one way is to cull off those who don't eat pimento cheese. You can divvy up the rest by separating those who eat only their mama's pimento cheese from those who'll eat most any kind of pimento cheese (but secretly wish it was their mama's).

Proper pimento cheese is a dish of texture and decorum, not runny neon goo from a plastic deli cup. For some, pimento cheese is a tasty filling for celery stalks. For others, it's the best thing to smear on a cracker or up the middle of a folded-over piece of cottony white bread. For us true connoisseurs, pimento cheese gives our poor hearts ease. Pimentos are heart-shaped. Coincidence?

MAKES ABOUT 4 CUPS

1. Stir together the pimentos, cheese, onion, pickle juice, mustard, and sugar and mix well. Stir in enough mayonnaise to make a chunky paste that just holds together. Season with the salt, pepper, and cayenne.

2. Refrigerate for at least 1 hour before serving. Serve at room temperature or lightly chilled.

## Homemade Mayonnaise

2 large egg yolks, chilled

3 teaspoons fresh
lemon juice

2 teaspoons
white wine vinegar

½ teaspoon Dijon
mustard

1 teaspoon kosher salt,
plus more to taste

1 ½ cups vegetable oil
or mild extra-virgin
olive oil (or a combi-
nation), divided

Because I value homemade pimento cheese highly, I sometimes pull out all the stops and make it with homemade mayonnaise. I'll admit up front that this is not easy to make, but the results are incomparable. It requires a lot of determined, diligent whisking, so I recommend tag teaming this task with a friend. Another option is to use the whisk attachment on an immersion blender. I have no luck with standard blenders or food processors, although I've seen it done.

In addition to its role in pimento cheese, a jar of homemade mayonnaise in the fridge during The High Holy Days of Tomato Sandwich Season is a blessing.

MAKES ABOUT 1 ½ CUPS

1. Place a medium glass or metal bowl in the freezer to chill for 10 minutes.
2. Whisk together the egg yolks, lemon juice, vinegar, mustard, and salt in the chilled bowl. Whisk until blended and bright yellow, about 30 seconds.
3. Whisking constantly, add ½ cup of the oil a few drops at a time to the yolk mixture, taking about 4 minutes to do so. Add the remaining 1 cup of oil in a very slow, very thin, steady stream, whisking constantly until the mayonnaise is thick and lighter in color, 8 to 15 minutes, depending on your fortitude. (Putting the oil in a squeeze bottle with a small opening helps control the flow.)
4. Cover and let sit at room temperature for 1 hour, then refrigerate for up to 1 week.

## New-Fangled Stuffed Peppers

8 large red and/or yellow bell peppers or other large sweet variety

8 ounces tuna packed in olive oil, preferably fillets in a jar

2 tablespoons raisins or currants, soaked in hot water for 10 minutes, then drained

1 cup large fresh bread crumbs from very crusty bread (page 389)

¼ cup ripe black olives, such as Kalamata, pitted and chopped

3 tablespoons pine nuts, toasted

3 tablespoons chopped fresh basil

3 tablespoons chopped flat-leaf parsley

2 tablespoons capers, drained

2 garlic cloves, finely chopped

2 teaspoons finely grated orange zest

1 tablespoon fresh orange juice

½ teaspoon kosher salt, or to taste

¼ teaspoon ground black pepper, or to taste

Extra-virgin olive oil, as needed

¼ cup coarsely grated Asiago, Pecorino, or Parmesan cheese

Any community cookbook and most recipe boxes passed down through a southern family contain at least one recipe for stuffed peppers, usually green bells filled with a meat mixture and topped with a little tomato sauce. I take a completely different approach. I start with roasted peppers and fill them with Mediterranean tuna stuffing. You can serve them as an entrée or as an appetizer atop grilled bread or salad greens. They are good warm or at room temperature.

The type and quality of the tuna is key. It must be packed in olive oil, not in water. Tuna preserved in a little oil is silky and deeply flavored, not bland and watery. Not even fresh tuna is as good in this recipe. Oil-packed tuna fillets in jars imported from Spain or Italy are best, but canned tuna in oil will also work. If you cannot find oil-packed tuna, skip the tuna and use cooked white beans and olive oil instead.

MAKES 4 TO 6 SERVINGS

1. Preheat the oven to 350°F.

2. Roast the peppers according to the directions on page 314. When the peppers are cool enough to handle, carefully remove the stems. Make a long slit down one side of each pepper and open like a book. Remove the seeds and arrange the peppers in a single layer on a work surface.

3. Drain the oil from the tuna into a small bowl and set it aside. Place the tuna in a large bowl and fold in the raisins, bread crumbs, olives, pine nuts, basil, parsley, capers, garlic, orange zest, and orange juice and 3 tablespoons of the reserved tuna oil. Season with the salt and pepper.

4. Divide the filling among the peppers. Fold the peppers closed or roll them up to enclose the filling, depending on their shape. Place the peppers in a 9 × 13-inch glass or ceramic baking dish. Drizzle the remaining 3 tablespoons of tuna oil over the tops. If there is not enough tuna oil, make up the difference with olive oil. Sprinkle with cheese and bake until the cheese melts and the filling is warm, about 15 minutes. Serve warm or let cool to room temperature.

MAKE-AHEAD NOTE: You can fill the peppers up to 1 day ahead. Store covered and refrigerated. Increase the baking time by about 5 minutes.

# Pepper Poppers with Chipotle Chicken Salad

1 cup whipped cream cheese, at room temperature

Finely grated zest and juice of 1 lime (about 3 tablespoons)

½ teaspoon dried Mexican oregano

½ teaspoon kosher salt

¼ teaspoon ground black pepper

2 canned chipotle chiles in adobo sauce, or to taste

1 ½ cups finely chopped grilled chicken

¼ cup finely diced red bell pepper

½ cup corn kernels

¼ cup finely diced red onion

12 miniature sweet peppers, halved lengthwise and cored

Chopped cilantro or parsley, for garnish

These no-cook pepper poppers provide plenty of flavor, color, and crunch, so they are great party food or a light meal. The chicken salad is a real departure from standard pickle-and-mayonnaise stuff because it gets a little smoke and heat from chipotle chiles in adobo sauce.

For something completely different, use the chicken salad to make a clever club sandwich. Spread the salad on thin slices of toasted cornbread or sandwich bread and top with bacon, lettuce, tomato, and sliced avocado.

MAKES 24

1. Combine the cream cheese, lime zest, lime juice, oregano, salt, and pepper in a medium bowl. Stir until well combined. Purée the chipotles with a fork, add to the cream cheese mixture, and mix well. Fold in the chicken, bell pepper, corn, and onion. Refrigerate the mixture until slightly chilled.

2. To assemble, spoon about 1 tablespoon of salad into each pepper half, garnish with cilantro, and serve at room temperature.

WHAT ELSE WORKS? You can use jalapeños or other chiles instead of the miniature sweet peppers for even more kick. You can also use larger sweet peppers cut into curved wedges.

MAKE-AHEAD NOTE: You can prepare the salad up to 2 days ahead, covered tightly and refrigerated.

## Romesco Sauce

1½ cups toasted and cubed Italian or French bread

½ cup blanched almonds, preferably Marcona almonds

½ cup hazelnuts

6 garlic cloves

1 cup seeded and chopped tomatoes

1 teaspoon crushed red pepper flakes, or to taste

1 cup coarsely chopped roasted sweet red peppers (page 314)

1 tablespoon chopped fresh rosemary

1 tablespoon chopped fresh oregano

1 teaspoon sugar

1 teaspoon kosher salt, plus more to taste

¼ teaspoon ground black pepper, plus more to taste

1 teaspoon smoked paprika (*pimentón*)

¼ cup sherry vinegar

¼ to ½ cup extra-virgin olive oil

There is a long southern history of making pepper sauces and relishes that have subtle sweetness and a bit of heat. This recipe honors that tradition, although it's Spanish rather than southern. However, Spanish cuisine was one of the earliest influences of what would evolve into southern cuisine, so this recipe has credible ancestry. As is common in many Spanish recipes, the sauce is thickened with toasted bread and ground nuts. Trust your palate when making this sauce. It should be a balanced blend of tangy, sweet, hot, and smoky.

Romesco sauce is versatile and makes a nice finish to roasted and grilled meats and vegetables such as Blasted Asparagus and the options under "What Else Works?" (page 20) and Roasted Potatoes (page 245). It's also good on top of a frittata and on fritters. For a quick entrée, sauté shrimp in olive oil and then coat them in Romesco sauce just before serving.

MAKES ABOUT 3 CUPS

(1) Place the bread, almonds, hazelnuts, garlic, and tomatoes in the bowl of a food processor fitted with a metal blade and pulse to break them up roughly.

(2) Add the red pepper flakes, roasted peppers, rosemary, oregano, sugar, salt, pepper, smoked paprika, and vinegar. Pulse until the nuts are finely ground.

(3) With the machine running, gradually pour in enough of the oil to make the sauce the consistency of very thick salad dressing that can hold its shape on a spoon. Do not overprocess; small bits of nuts should remain visible. Taste to make sure the sauce has plenty of piquancy and enough salt and adjust the seasoning if needed.

MAKE-AHEAD NOTE: The sauce can be made up to 3 days ahead. Store tightly covered and refrigerated for up to 1 week. Stir well, check the seasoning, and return to room temperature for serving.

## Pressed Sandwich

1 large loaf good-quality, sturdy, crusty bread, such as ciabatta or French loaf

¼ cup olive tapenade

3 roasted red, yellow, or orange bell peppers, cut into wide strips (page 314)

4 ounces soft, fresh goat cheese (chèvre)

6 tablespoons Balsamic Vinaigrette (page 385) or bottled Italian dressing, divided

8 ounces marinated artichoke hearts, drained

6 ounces thinly sliced ham

4 ounces thinly sliced peppered salami

1 large handful of leafy greens, such as baby spinach or arugula

8 large basil leaves, shredded

This is my favorite way to serve an interesting picnic sandwich. A loaf of crusty bread is stuffed with roasted peppers, cheese, meat, and vegetables and bathed in vinaigrette. The stuffed loaf is wrapped tightly and pressed under a weight for at least an hour before serving. How perfect! A sandwich that tastes best after it's been mashed in the bottom of the cooler.

This recipe is really more of a procedure. You can change the fillings to suit your own taste. Note that one sandwich feeds four to six people. It takes a bit of time to make one, but you probably won't have to make many.

MAKES 4 TO 6 SERVINGS

1. Halve the bread horizontally and hollow out the soft bread from the top and bottom, leaving a ½-inch-thick shell of crust. (Discard the crumbs or reserve for another use.)

2. Spread the tapenade in the bottom shell and cover with the roasted red pepper strips. Crumble the goat cheese over the peppers and drizzle with 3 tablespoons of the vinaigrette. Arrange the artichoke hearts, ham, and salami over the goat cheese. Toss the greens and basil with the remaining 3 tablespoons of vinaigrette in a small bowl and then add them to the sandwich.

3. Close the sandwich with the top bread shell, tucking in the fillings so they are enclosed. Wrap the sandwich tightly in plastic wrap and put in a shallow baking pan. Set something heavy (such as large soup cans, a cast-iron skillet, or full wine bottles) on top of the sandwich and chill for at least 1 hour and up to 6 hours. The weighting and pressing compacts all of the ingredients and melds the flavors. To serve, cut the sandwich into manageable slices.

## Chow Chow Slaw

1 small green cabbage, cored and grated or finely chopped (about 6 cups)

1 large green bell pepper, cored and finely chopped (about 1 cup)

1 large red bell pepper, cored and finely chopped (about 1 cup)

1 small red or yellow onion, finely chopped (about ½ cup)

1 medium green tomato, cored and finely chopped (about 1 cup)

1 tablespoon kosher salt

¾ cup sugar

¾ cup cider vinegar

1 teaspoon whole yellow mustard seed

½ teaspoon dry mustard

¼ teaspoon ground turmeric

½ teaspoon celery seed

¼ teaspoon ground ginger

Chow chow is a classic southern pickled vegetable relish used to perk up simple foods, such as a pot of soup beans. Many cooks put up huge batches each summer to use through the winter. This fresh slaw captures those same flavors and textures but is made in small batches that can be used quickly instead of preserved in canning jars.

This slaw tastes best when served within a few days after it's made, but it also holds in the freezer up to three months. Honest. In the freezer. When packed into airtight containers, it retains much of its crunch when thawed, like magic.

Chow chow slaw is good on hot dogs, grilled brats, and burgers.

MAKES 6 TO 8 SERVINGS

1. Toss together the cabbage, green pepper, red pepper, onion, tomato, and salt in a colander that is set inside a large bowl. Cover and set aside at room temperature for 1 hour or refrigerate overnight. Discard the accumulated liquid. Transfer the vegetables into a large bowl.

2. Bring the sugar, vinegar, mustard seed, dry mustard, turmeric, celery seed, and ginger to a boil in a small saucepan over high heat, stirring until the sugar dissolves. Boil for 1 minute. Remove from the heat and cool to room temperature. Pour over the vegetables and mix well. Cover and refrigerate until chilled, at least 4 hours and up to 3 days. For longer storage, pack the slaw into airtight containers and freeze up to 3 months. Thaw and stir well before serving.

### TIPS AND TECHNIQUES

The pieces of chopped vegetables should be small, from ¼- to ½-inch pieces. You can coarsely grate the vegetables on a box grater or chop them in the bowl of a food processor fitted with the metal blade. (The processor's shredding disc leaves the pieces too long and stringy.) Do not fill the bowl more than halfway and use short pulses so that the vegetables bounce up and down onto the blade to be chopped instead of ground into mush.

## Skirt Steak and Peppers with Orange-Chipotle Glaze

3 red, orange, and/
or yellow sweet
peppers, cored and
cut lengthwise into
¼-inch strips

1 large onion, halved
lengthwise and cut
into ¼-inch strips

2 pounds skirt steak

2 teaspoons kosher salt

1 teaspoon ground
black pepper

½ cup Orange-Chipotle
Glaze (recipe follows),
plus more for serving

In this recipe, skirt steak is roasted on a bed of peppers and onions, then finished with a sweet-hot citrus glaze. The dish looks like fajitas, so I sometimes serve it on tortillas garnished with sour cream and lime wedges. But the flavor of the dish reminds me of orange beef from Chinese take-out, so other times I serve it over rice, garnished with scallions and mandarin oranges.

If you cannot find skirt steak, substitute flat-iron or flank steak that is less than 1 inch thick. For any of these flavorful but relatively tough cuts, the trick is to slice the roasted meat thinly on the diagonal against the grain, so always start on a corner. If you make cuts straight across, you can use the strips as shoelaces.

MAKES 6 SERVINGS

1. Preheat the oven to 450°F.
2. Spread the peppers and onion on a foil-lined baking sheet. Season the meat with the salt and pepper and lay it on top of the peppers and onions. The meat should cover most of the vegetables.
3. Roast for 10 minutes. Remove the pan from the oven, turn the steak over, and spread the glaze over the top of the meat. Return to the oven and roast for approximately another 10 minutes for medium rare or 15 minutes for medium. Cover the meat loosely with foil and let rest for 5 minutes before slicing.
4. Starting on a corner and cutting on the diagonal against the grain, cut the meat into thin slices.
5. Place the peppers and onions on a serving platter. Arrange the slices of steak over the top. Serve warm, serving the rest of the glaze on the side.

WHAT ELSE WORKS? You can replace some of the sweet peppers with chiles.

## Orange-Chipotle Glaze

⅓ cup fresh orange juice

¾ cup red wine vinegar

½ cup soy sauce

1 ½ cups sugar

2 tablespoons canned chipotle chiles in adobo sauce, finely chopped, or to taste

1 ½ cups sweet orange marmalade

This sweet-hot glaze is wonderful on any cut of steak. This recipe makes more than you need for one recipe of Skirt Steak and Peppers, but it keeps well for weeks, giving you plenty of time to use it up.

MAKES ABOUT 2 CUPS

1. Combine the orange juice, vinegar, soy sauce, and sugar in a large saucepan. Mash the chipotles with a fork until smooth and add to the orange juice mixture. Bring to a boil over high heat, stirring to dissolve the sugar. Reduce the heat and simmer until the sauce has reduced by half, about 30 minutes.

2. Stir in the marmalade and cook until melted, about 2 minutes. The sauce should thickly coat the back of a spoon. Serve warm or let cool, cover tightly, and refrigerate for up to 1 month. Reheat gently for serving.

Zesty Black-Eyed Pea Salsa and
Chunky Tomatillo Guacamole

Roast Beef, Boursin, and Asparagus Bundles

Mixed Summer Bean Salad with Creamy Caesar-ish Dressing

Grilled Vegetable Ratatouille Salad

Pancetta Crisps with Chèvre and Fresh Pear

Butter Bean, Heirloom Tomato, and Cornbread Shortcakes

OPPOSITE: Buttermilk Pie with Raspberry Crown

Whole Stuffed Cheese Pumpkin

# SWEET POTATOES

**Sweet potatoes were domesticated in the Americas** more than 2,000 years ago and became a standard crop of Native Americans, particularly the Cherokees, who were expert farmers. The earliest explorers shipped sweet potatoes back to Europe, where they became one of the first New World foods adopted by the Europeans. Sweet potatoes quickly developed a sensational reputation as both an exotic food and a potent aphrodisiac. They were a particular favorite of Henry VIII, who certainly married often if not well.

Some people use the terms "sweet potato" and "yam" interchangeably, but the two root vegetables are actually unrelated. Sweet potatoes are native to the Americas. Yams are native to Africa. The entrenched misnomer and confusion are the result of at least three things. Spanish explorers came across sweet potatoes growing in the Caribbean and called them *batata*, the same word they used for yams and white potatoes. About the same time, Portuguese explorers encountered sweet potatoes in Brazil and shipped them to Africa, where they were grown to provision Portuguese ships headed to the New World. Some enslaved Africans called them yams, probably from the West African word *unyamo*, which means "to eat." And in the 1930s, a moist orange sweet potato from Puerto Rico was marketed as a Louisiana yam to distinguish it from other sweet potatoes.

A sweet potato by any other name would taste as sweet. ■

## Roasted Sweet Potatoes

6 medium sweet
potatoes (about
8 ounces each)

This is the way to roast sweet potatoes to eat or to make purée for recipes. I am a huge fan of roasting sweet potatoes because it intensifies their flavor and concentrates their considerable natural sugars. As old-time cooks would say, roasting a sweet potato "brings out the candy." In contrast, boiling sweet potatoes makes them gluey and soggy and washes away much of their flavor and nutrients. That's why I've never understood why so many recipes—from casseroles to pies to cakes—start with boiled sweet potatoes. I respectfully and vehemently disagree. No matter what the recipe says, I always start with roasted sweet potato flesh.

MAKES 6 SERVINGS

1. Preheat the oven to 350°F. Pierce each potato a few times with a fork or the tip of a knife.
2. Place on a rimmed baking sheet lined with foil to catch the inevitable drips. Roast until tender, about 40 minutes. If it matters to you, you can rotate them a quarter turn every 15 minutes so they don't get that scorched wet spot on the bottom.

NOTE: Here are some quick ways to season a hot, split, roasted sweet potato:

- salt, butter, and sour cream
- brown sugar and cinnamon
- a praline (just let it melt)
- Fresh Pineapple Salsa (page 97) or other fruit salsa
- a squeeze of fresh lime juice and sprinkling of ground chiles
- a spoonful of orange marmalade, apple butter (page 13), or Sassy Pepper Jam (page 88)
- Spiced Stone Fruit Sauce (page 242)

To make purée to use in recipes, set the potatoes aside until they are cool enough to handle and then pull off the skins. Force the potato flesh through a food mill fitted with the medium disc or push through a mesh sieve into a medium bowl. You can use any color or variety of sweet potato for purée, but avoid the potatoes that are huge and look like footballs because they will be watery and stringy when cooked. To be suitable for recipes, the finished purée must have the smooth, thick consistency of canned pumpkin. If the purée needs to be drained, transfer into a large sieve lined with a double thickness of white paper towels or overlapping paper coffee filters set over a large bowl. Press a piece of plastic wrap directly onto the surface of the purée to keep it from drying out and refrigerate for at least 2 hours. Discard the accumulated liquid. Cover and refrigerate the purée and use within 3 days or freeze in airtight containers for up to 3 months.

One 8- to 10-ounce sweet potato should yield about 1 cup of purée.

## Twice-Baked Sweet Potatoes

4 medium sweet
potatoes (about
8 ounces each)

¼ cup heavy
cream, warmed

4 thick bacon slices, cut
crosswise into ¼-inch
strips (about 4 ounces)

1 cup chopped onion

2 garlic cloves,
finely chopped

3 cups stemmed and
thinly shredded kale
or other similar
leafy green

½ cup chicken or
vegetable stock

¾ cup freshly grated
aged Gouda or
Gruyère cheese,
divided

¼ teaspoon freshly
grated nutmeg

Kosher salt and ground
black pepper, to taste

Just like russet baking potatoes, roasted sweet potatoes can be stuffed and twice baked. The potato flesh is scooped out of the shells, seasoned with greens, bacon, and cheese, and then stuffed back into the shells for a second baking. This is a great make-ahead way to serve baked sweet potatoes, which would get gummy if just left sitting.

Most sweet potatoes have orange, pink, or red flesh. However, there are varieties with deep purple flesh or white flesh. White sweet potatoes tend to be a little drier and less sweet, which makes them a nice choice for this recipe.

The cheese sprinkled on top of the potatoes should bake into a browned crust, so use a type of cheese that doesn't separate when heated. The classic cheese to use in this way is Gruyère, the cheese that crowns French onion soup. I am also quite fond of aged Gouda, such as UnieKaas Reserve. As it ages, Gouda develops a deep caramel and butterscotch flavor that is wonderful with sweet potatoes and winter squash. Another good choice, although it can be hard to find, is Pleasant Ridge Upland Reserve, one of the finest farmstead cheeses in the country.

MAKES 4 ENTRÉE SERVINGS OR 8 SIDE DISH SERVINGS

1. Preheat the oven to 350°F. Pierce the potatoes in several places with a fork. Place in a single layer on the oven rack with a sheet of foil on the rack below to catch any drips. Roast the potatoes until tender, about 40 minutes. When cool enough to handle, cut each in half lengthwise and use a melon baller or small spoon to scoop out the flesh into a medium bowl, leaving a ¼-inch-thick shell. Arrange the shells in a baking dish large enough to hold them upright in a single layer.

2. Mash the potato flesh until smooth with a fork. Stir in the cream.

3. Cook the bacon in a skillet over medium heat until crispy. Transfer with a slotted spoon to paper towels to drain.

4. Pour off all but 1 tablespoon of the drippings and add the onion to the skillet. Cook, stirring often, until softened, about 8 minutes. Add the garlic and cook for 30 seconds. Stir in the kale and stock. Cover the pan and cook, stirring occasionally, until the kale is tender, about 15 minutes. Uncover and cook until any remaining liquid evaporates.

5. Stir the kale mixture into the mashed sweet potatoes. Gently stir in the reserved bacon and ¼ cup of the cheese. Season with the nutmeg, salt, and pepper. Divide the sweet potato mixture evenly among the 8 shells. Sprinkle the tops with the remaining ½ cup of cheese.

6. Bake until the potatoes are heated through and the cheese is melted, about 30 minutes. Serve warm.

VARIATION: You can omit the bacon and cook the vegetables in butter instead.

# Mashed Sweet Potatoes

3 pounds medium sweet potatoes (about 8 ounces each)

2 tablespoons firmly packed light brown sugar

⅓ cup peach preserves

2 tablespoons dry sherry

4 tablespoons (½ stick) butter, melted

2 tablespoons fresh lemon juice

2 teaspoons finely grated lemon zest

½ teaspoon freshly grated nutmeg

¼ teaspoon ground cinnamon

½ teaspoon ground ginger

½ teaspoon kosher salt, or to taste

This deceptively simple recipe is a knockout way to serve sweet potatoes. It's on the opposite end of the continuum from those over-the-top casseroles crammed full of sugar, nuts, and marshmallows. Here, naturally sweet roasted sweet potatoes get to have their say. The lack of sugar is made up for with a generous amount of seasoning. Restraint may have its place, but so does reward.

I love the silkiness of potatoes puréed with a food mill. However, they are also tasty when coarsely mashed by hand. (Lumpy potatoes aren't sloppy, they're rustic.) Under no circumstances should they be mashed with a mixer or in a food processor because they will get runny and later set up in the bowl like mortar.

For a lovely presentation, make this with half orange and half white sweet potatoes. Cook and season each color separately, then swirl them together for a marbleized effect in the serving bowl. White sweet potatoes are very starchy and soak up liquid like a dry sponge, so you might need more butter for them.

MAKES 6 TO 8 SERVINGS

① Position a rack in the center of the oven and preheat to 350°F. Butter a 2 ½ quart baking dish.

② Pierce the potatoes in several places with a fork and arrange them in a single layer on the oven rack with a sheet of foil on the rack below to catch any drips. Roast until tender, about 40 minutes. When cool enough to handle, peel the potatoes and force them through a food mill or potato ricer into a large bowl, or mash them with a potato masher until smooth.

③ Add the brown sugar, preserves, sherry, melted butter, lemon juice, lemon zest, nutmeg, cinnamon, ginger, and salt to the potatoes and beat with a wooden spoon until well mixed.

④ Spoon the mixture into the prepared dish and bake until heated through, about 20 minutes. Serve warm.

VARIATION: For a more straightforward and less sweet way to season the purée, use browned butter instead of the other ingredients. You'll need 8 tablespoons (1 stick) unsalted butter. Melt the butter in a small, heavy saucepan over medium heat. Cook, gently swirling the pan often, until the butter is covered in white foam and begins to brown in the center, 2 to 3 minutes. Lift the pan off the heat and continue swirling until the butter is deep golden brown throughout and smells toasty and nutty. Fold the browned butter into the sweet potato purée. If it is too stiff, add ¼ to ½ cup warm whole milk to make the purée soft and spoonable. Season with salt and pepper and serve warm.

MAKE-AHEAD NOTE: You can make the potatoes up to 1 day ahead. Cool, cover, and refrigerate. You can reheat them in the oven, covered, but increase the baking time to about 30 minutes.

## Sweet Potato Home Fries

6 medium sweet potatoes (about 2 ½ pounds)

3 tablespoons extra-virgin olive oil

1 teaspoon coarse salt or kosher salt

1 tablespoon chopped fresh rosemary

2 to 4 tablespoons honey

This is the quickest way I know to serve roasted sweet potatoes. The bite-sized cubes become tender in the center with caramelized edges. A little honey brings out their sweetness, while salt and fresh rosemary keep the dish from turning into one of those cloying casseroles. For that matter, it's fine to skip both the rosemary and the honey to let the flavor of the potatoes stand on its own merit. If you want the pieces to look more like french fries than home fries, cut the potatoes into sticks instead of cubes.

I do not salt sweet potatoes or other root vegetables before roasting because the salt makes them release their moisture and start to fall apart. To help them hold their shape, don't salt them until right after they come out of the oven. Likewise, be sure to keep the pieces in a single layer on the baking sheet so that they roast instead of steaming into soft blobs.

When roasting the potatoes to use in other recipes, omit the rosemary and honey.

MAKES 6 SERVINGS

1. Preheat the oven to 375°F.
2. Peel the potatoes and cut into uniform ¾-inch cubes. Toss with the oil to coat and spread in a single layer on a foil-lined rimmed baking sheet. Roast until tender when pierced with a knife and the edges are beginning to brown, about 30 minutes.
3. Season the potatoes with the salt while they are still hot so that it will stick. Sprinkle with the rosemary and drizzle with the honey to taste. Serve warm, although they are fine at room temperature.

WHAT ELSE WORKS? You can cook nearly any root vegetable, or a medley of roots and tubers, with this technique. Good candidates for this method are beets, turnips, carrots, parsnips, rutabagas, pumpkin, and winter squash.

### TIPS AND TECHNIQUES

When deciding how much of an herb sprig to use, ask yourself how much of it is chewable. Nearly all of any herb plant is edible, but not all of it is necessarily pleasant to eat. For herbs with soft stems (such as parsley and cilantro), you can use all of the leaves, the short stems that hold the leaves, and as much of the larger stems as are tender. You do not have to painstakingly pluck off individual tiny leaves. For herbs with hard, deciduous stems (such as rosemary), you obviously do not want to be adding sticks to your food, so strip off the leaves.

## Sweet Potato Salad with Cranberry Vinaigrette or Peanut and Sorghum Vinaigrette

4 medium sweet potatoes (about 2 pounds)

2 tablespoons extra-virgin olive oil

Kosher salt, to taste

2 tart apples, cored and thinly sliced or cut into matchsticks

½ cup flat-leaf parsley, coarsely chopped

1 cup toasted pecan pieces or chopped peanuts, depending on the vinaigrette

Cranberry Vinaigrette or Peanut and Sorghum Vinaigrette (recipes follow)

Ground black pepper, to taste

Where I live in central North Carolina, summer doesn't release its grip easily. Even into late October, our chilly mornings can turn into hot days. Children trundle off to school all bundled up and come home trailing clothing behind them like they were molting. Food cravings can be equally mercurial. We're so ready to taste the fall crops, but it's still too hot to embrace simmering comfort food. That's when I make sweet potato salad, a summer recipe made with fall ingredients.

Early in sweet potato season, I make this with the Peanut and Sorghum Vinaigrette, particularly when I can get freshly made sorghum. As it gets close to Thanksgiving and fresh cranberries come around, I switch to the Cranberry Vinaigrette. Both vinaigrettes are quite good on other salads.

This is a great way to use up leftover Sweet Potato Home Fries (page 329), or you can start with fresh potatoes. You can also grill the sweet potatoes using the directions for the potatoes on page 105.

MAKES 6 SERVINGS

1. Preheat the oven to 425°F.

2. Peel the potatoes and cut them into bite-sized chunks. Toss the potatoes with the oil to coat and spread in a single layer on a foil-lined baking sheet. Roast until tender and the edges are beginning to brown, about 20 minutes. Season with salt while the potatoes are still hot so it will stick. Set aside to cool to room temperature.

3. Transfer the potatoes into a large bowl. Add the apples, parsley, and nuts. Pour enough vinaigrette over the salad to moisten the ingredients and toss lightly to coat. Season with salt and pepper and serve at room temperature.

## Cranberry Vinaigrette

½  cup fresh cranberries

2  tablespoons chopped shallot

2  teaspoons grainy Dijon mustard

¼  cup white wine vinegar

   Zest and juice of 1 lime (about 3 tablespoons)

2  tablespoons light brown sugar

6  tablespoons grapeseed oil or vegetable oil

   Kosher salt and ground black pepper, to taste

This bright and cheerful red vinaigrette is pretty. You can use any leftovers on a simple salad of orange and grapefruit sections.

MAKES ABOUT 1 CUP

1. Place the cranberries, shallot, mustard, vinegar, lime zest, lime juice, and brown sugar in a blender and blend until chopped.
2. With the blender running, slowly add the oil and blend until the dressing is mixed. Season with salt and pepper.
3. Use soon or transfer into a glass jar with a tight-fitting lid and refrigerate for up to 3 days. Return to room temperature, shake vigorously, and check the seasoning before serving.

## Peanut and Sorghum Vinaigrette

¼  cup roasted peanuts

2  tablespoons chopped shallot

¼  cup sorghum

¼  cup organic unfiltered apple cider vinegar

½  cup flavorful peanut oil

   Kosher salt and ground black pepper, to taste

To make sure the dressing tastes like peanuts, be sure to use flavorful organic or Asian peanut oil, not the bland kind used to deep-fry turkeys. If your oil doesn't have a strong peanut flavor and aroma, you can boost it with toasted sesame oil.

What many southerners call molasses is actually sorghum. Real molasses comes from sugarcane, and sorghum comes from, well, sorghum, an annual reed-shaped grass that has roots in Africa, as does so much of our southern culinary heritage. If you cannot find sorghum, use maple syrup or cane syrup instead. Do not use dark molasses, such as blackstrap molasses, because it is too strong for this recipe.

MAKES ABOUT 1 CUP

1. Place the peanuts, shallot, sorghum, and vinegar in a blender and blend until chopped.
2. With the blender running, slowly add the oil and blend until the dressing is mixed. Season with salt and pepper. If you use salted peanuts, you might not need more salt.
3. Use soon or transfer into a glass jar with a tight-fitting lid and refrigerate for up to 3 days. Return to room temperature, shake vigorously, and check the seasoning before serving.

# Chicken and Sweet Potato Stew

3 thick bacon slices, cut crosswise into ¼-inch strips (about 3 ounces)

4 boneless, skinless chicken thighs, cut into 2-inch pieces

1 teaspoon kosher salt, plus more to taste

½ teaspoon ground black pepper, plus more to taste

1 tablespoon peanut oil or vegetable oil

1 cup chopped onion

1 cup chopped celery

1 cup chopped bell pepper

2 garlic cloves, thinly sliced

2 tablespoons instant or all-purpose flour

1 tablespoon red curry powder or garam masala

1 cup chicken stock

1 (14 ½-ounce) can whole peeled tomatoes

2 cups peeled sweet potato cut into ¾-inch cubes

3 tablespoons golden raisins or currants

¼ cup peanut butter

½ cup well-stirred coconut milk (lite or regular) or half-and-half

½ cup hot mango chutney

½ cup coarsely chopped roasted peanuts

Hot cooked long-grain white rice, for serving

Cooked bacon, thinly sliced scallions, coconut, and additional chutney, for serving

The somewhat unusual combination of chicken, sweet potatoes, peanuts, tomatoes, coconut, chutney, and curry has deep roots in the South, particularly in the Lowcountry, where there was ready access to imported spices and where expert cooks from many cultures stirred their own familiar ingredients into the pots.

This stew is similar to both West African groundnut (peanut) stew and chicken country captain. Both of those dishes call for an even longer list of ingredients slowly cooked together. I've streamlined the process by using ingredients (such as chutney and good curry powder) that deliver many flavors from one jar. The stew should be a little spicy and very aromatic. Don't skip the condiments. They are integral to the look and flavor of the dish. Plus, everyone will have fun doctoring up custom bowls of stew.

MAKES 8 TO 10 SERVINGS

1. Cook the bacon in a small Dutch oven or soup pot over medium-high heat, stirring often, until browned and crispy. Transfer with a slotted spoon to paper towels to drain. Leave the drippings in the pot.

2. Season the chicken with the salt and pepper and brown in the bacon drippings, about 5 minutes. Transfer to a plate and set aside.

3. Add the oil to the pot. When it's hot, stir in the onion, celery, bell pepper, garlic, and a pinch of salt. Cook, stirring often, until the vegetables are softened, about 8 minutes. Sprinkle the flour and curry powder over the vegetables and stir well. Cook, stirring constantly, for 2 minutes. Slowly pour in the stock, stirring to scrape up the browned bits from the bottom of the pot. Add the tomatoes and break them up with the side of the spoon. Cook, stirring constantly, until the mixture is smooth and slightly thickened, about 2 minutes.

4. Stir in the chicken, sweet potato, and raisins. Cover and simmer, stirring occasionally, until the chicken is cooked through and the sweet potatoes are tender, about 8 minutes.

5. Stir in the peanut butter, coconut milk, chutney, and peanuts and heat through, about 5 minutes. Season with salt and pepper. Serve hot over the rice, topped with the condiments.

## Sweet Potato Rum Cake

### CAKE

¾ cup golden raisins or currants

⅓ cup dark rum

4 large eggs, at room temperature

2 cups granulated sugar

1 cup vegetable oil

2 teaspoons pure vanilla extract

2 cups roasted sweet potato purée (page 326)

3 cups all-purpose flour

1 teaspoon baking powder

1 teaspoon baking soda

½ teaspoon fine sea salt

1 ½ teaspoons ground cinnamon

½ teaspoon ground nutmeg

¾ cup well-shaken buttermilk

### GLAZE

½ cup tightly packed dark brown sugar

4 tablespoons (½ stick) unsalted butter

3 tablespoons whipping cream

Leftover rum from soaking the raisins for the cake (about ¼ cup)

Rum cake is popular around the holidays, but it is often little more than a generic yellow cake made from a mix and soaked in enough rum that it could detonate if left too near the Yule log. This one starts with really good cake, a step in the right direction. Most of the strong rum flavor is in the glaze. For a milder cake, use the buttermilk glaze that goes on the Ocracoke Fig Cake (page 133). Or, you can reduce the overall sweetness of the cake by not using any glaze and simply dusting with confectioners' sugar.

MAKES 12 TO 16 SERVINGS

1. For the cake: Preheat the oven to 350°F. Grease and flour a 10-inch Bundt pan or tube pan.

2. Stir together the raisins and rum in a small bowl and let sit for at least 30 minutes for the raisins to plump up.

3. Beat the eggs and granulated sugar in a large bowl with an electric mixer set to high speed until the mixture is thick and pale, about 4 minutes. Beat in the oil and vanilla. Stir in the sweet potato purée and mix well. Scrape down the sides of the bowl with a rubber spatula.

4. Sift the flour, baking powder, baking soda, salt, cinnamon, and nutmeg together into a large bowl. Add the flour mixture to the egg mixture in three additions, alternating with the buttermilk, beating each time only until the batter is smooth.

5. Drain the raisins, reserving the rum for the glaze. Fold the raisins into the batter.

6. Scrape the batter into the prepared pan. Bake in the center of the oven until a tester inserted into the cake comes out clean, 1 hour to 1 hour 20 minutes. Remove from the oven and let cool in the pan on a rack for 10 minutes. Meanwhile, make the glaze.

7. For the glaze: Bring the brown sugar, butter, and cream to a boil in a heavy saucepan over high heat, stirring until the sugar dissolves. Continue cooking until the mixture begins to thicken, about 3 minutes, stirring often. Remove from the heat and stir in the rum.

8. Turn out the cake and set it upright on a wire rack set over a baking sheet or large plate to catch the excess glaze. Poke holes all over the top of the cake with a wooden skewer or chopstick. Spoon half of the warm glaze over the cake. Let the rest of the glaze rest at room temperature for 15 minutes so that it will thicken. Pour this glaze over the cake, letting it dribble down the sides. Cool the cake completely before serving.

## Sweet Potato Biscuits

2 ½ cups all-purpose flour

1 tablespoon baking powder

1 teaspoon fine sea salt

¼ cup packed light brown sugar

¾ teaspoon ground cinnamon

½ teaspoon ground ginger

½ teaspoon ground allspice

½ teaspoon mace

½ cup vegetable shortening

1 cup roasted sweet potato purée (page 326)

1 cup heavy cream

Instant flour or additional all-purpose flour, for rolling

These biscuits are very tender and a little sweet, much like a good cream scone. Unlike most biscuits, they are better served the next day at room temperature. The night's rest makes them less crumbly and gives the flavors time to meld. They are a welcome addition to any fall or winter meal, particularly around the holidays. They make incredible ham biscuits. If you use a 1 ½-inch cutter, little ham biscuits are a crowd-pleasing hors d'oeuvre or buffet dish.

MAKES FIFTEEN 2 ½-INCH BISCUITS, TWELVE 3-INCH BISCUITS, OR TWENTY-FOUR 1 ½-INCH BISCUITS

(1) Preheat the oven to 350°F. Line a baking sheet with parchment paper or a silicone baking mat.

(2) Mix together the flour, baking powder, salt, brown sugar, cinnamon, ginger, allspice, and mace in a large bowl. Use a pastry blender or your fingertips to work in the shortening until the mixture is crumbly. Stir in the sweet potatoes with a fork. Slowly add the cream and stir until the dough comes together and pulls in all of the dry ingredients. Add more cream, 1 tablespoon at a time, if needed.

(3) Pour the dough onto a lightly floured surface and gently knead until smooth and supple, about 8 turns. Roll or pat the dough to a ¾-inch thickness. Cut out the biscuits with a round cutter. If the dough sticks, dip the cutter into some flour. Push the cutter straight down without twisting so that the biscuits can rise to their full potential. Place the biscuits on the prepared baking sheet.

(4) Bake until the biscuits are firm and spring back when lightly touched on top, about 15 minutes for 1 ½-inch biscuits, 20 minutes for 2 ½-inch biscuits, and 25 minutes for 3-inch biscuits. Transfer to a wire rack to cool to room temperature. Store at room temperature in an airtight container overnight before serving.

## Sweet Potato Biscuit Bread Pudding
## with Bourbon-Pecan Caramel Sauce

3 large eggs

¾ cup sugar

1 tablespoon pure
vanilla extract

2 cups half-and-half

4 cups loosely crumbled
Sweet Potato Biscuits
(6 to 8 biscuits)

¼ cup dried cherries
or golden raisins

Bourbon-Pecan
Caramel Sauce, for
serving (recipe follows)

The point of bread pudding is to use leftover bread, whatever that daily bread might be. I've made biscuit pudding for years, but one day I decided to use left-over sweet potato biscuits, and a new family favorite was born. Unlike pudding made from crusty yeast bread, the tender biscuits nearly dissolve in the sweet custard, so biscuit pudding is very soft. With the Bourbon-Pecan Caramel Sauce, it's ethereal. Really, really sweet, but ethereal.

MAKES 8 SERVINGS

1. Preheat the oven to 350°F. Butter a 1 ½-quart baking dish. The pudding bakes in a water bath, so set the dish inside a large baking pan.

2. Whisk the eggs in a large bowl until the yolks and whites are blended. Whisk in the sugar, vanilla, and half-and-half. Stir in the biscuits and cherries. Pour into the prepared baking dish. Add enough very hot tap water to the baking pan to come halfway up the outside of the baking dish. Bake until the top is puffed and the pudding is just set, about 50 minutes. A thin knife inserted about 1 inch from the center should come out moist but not wet.

3. Remove the pudding from the oven and let it sit in the hot water bath for 5 minutes before serving warm with Bourbon-Pecan Caramel Sauce.

## Bourbon-Pecan Caramel Sauce

1 ¼ cups sugar

½ cup water

¼ cup light corn syrup

1 ¼ cups whipping cream

1 cup coarsely chopped
pecans, toasted

2 tablespoons bourbon

½ teaspoon large-crystal
garnishing salt, such
as fleur de sel or
Maldon, or kosher salt

This sauce is a liquid praline, and it is almost too good. There are people who will pretend they hear something in the backyard and offer to be an intrepid investi-gator, when they are actually sneaking into the kitchen to eat this straight from the jar by the spoonful. Or so I am told.

MAKES ABOUT 2 CUPS

1. Stir together the sugar, water, and corn syrup in a large, heavy saucepan. Cook over medium heat without stirring until the sugar dissolves and turns the color of amber, about 7 minutes. Use a pastry brush dipped in cold water to wash down any sugar crystals on the side of the pan. Immediately remove the pan from the heat and carefully pour in the cream; it will bubble vigorously and the caramel will harden. Stir over low heat until the mixture is smooth.

2. Bring the sauce to a boil and cook until it thickens enough to lightly coat the back of a spoon, stirring often, about 3 minutes. Remove from the heat and stir in the pecans, bourbon, and salt. Serve warm or let it cool, then cover and re-frigerate for up to 1 week. Reheat gently for serving.

## Sliced Sweet Potato Pie

### FILLING

1 ½  cups evaporated milk or half-and-half (about 12 ounces)

2  pounds small to medium sweet potatoes

4  large eggs

½  cup packed light brown sugar

¼  cup granulated sugar

¾  teaspoon fine sea salt

½  teaspoon ground nutmeg

¾  teaspoon ground cinnamon

2  teaspoons pure vanilla extract

1  tablespoon fresh lemon juice

### STREUSEL TOPPING

½  cup all-purpose flour

½  cup granulated sugar

¼  teaspoon ground cinnamon

⅛  teaspoon fine sea salt

5  tablespoons unsalted butter, cut into small cubes and chilled

½  cup chopped pecans

A pecan streusel topping makes this pie quite similar to a sweet potato casserole, but it is far less sweet than most southern versions. It is considered a pie because it bakes in a pie plate, even though it doesn't have a pastry crust. This style of pie was once common in rural farm households that had plenty of potatoes but little money to purchase refined flour for a crust. The cooks sometimes baked these pies in pottery pie plates made from ruddy clay. The brown rims of these "dirt dishes" resembled the edge of a baked crust.

The thinly sliced sweet potatoes are simmered in canned evaporated milk, once a staple in many southern kitchens. I love the stuff, but what I love even more is the canned milk poem I recite whenever I get the chance. I do not know who wrote it, but dearly wish it were me. I studied literature for decades and consider myself reasonably well read, yet this is the only poem I know by heart.

> Carnation milk is the best in the land.
> Here I stand with a can in my hand.
> No tits to pull, no hay to pitch,
> You just poke a hole in the son of a bitch.

MAKES 8 SERVINGS

1. For the filling: Pour the evaporated milk into a medium saucepan. Working one at a time, peel the sweet potatoes and cut into very thin slices that are no more than ⅛-inch thick. Add the slices to the milk to prevent them from darkening. Bring the potatoes and milk to a gentle simmer over medium-low heat, cover, and cook until the slices are tender but not falling apart, about 8 minutes.

2. Meanwhile, whisk the eggs in a medium bowl until the whites and yolks are blended. Whisk in the brown sugar, granulated sugar, salt, nutmeg, cinnamon, vanilla, and lemon juice and set aside.

3. For the streusel: Whisk together the flour, granulated sugar, cinnamon, and salt in a medium bowl. Use a pastry blender or your fingertips to work in the butter until the pieces are the size of peas. Squeeze together about one-third of the streusel into balls the size of marbles, but leave the rest crumbly. Add the pecans and toss lightly to combine.

4. Use a slotted spoon to transfer the potatoes into a deep 9-inch pottery, ceramic, or glass pie plate, spreading them evenly over the bottom. Whisk the cooking liquid into the egg mixture and pour it slowly over the potatoes. Sprinkle the streusel over the top.

5. Bake until a knife inserted into the center comes out moist but not wet, about 45 minutes. Cool on a wire rack for at least 15 minutes before serving warm.

VARIATION: You can bake the filling in a 9-inch deep-dish pie shell that has been baked and cooled according to the directions on page 398.

# TOMATOES

**The tomato-eating world can be divided into two camps:** people who will eat only vine-ripened, sun-warmed, about-to-burst-open tomatoes, preferably from a vine not too far from the kitchen table, and people who will settle for the hard-as-plastic, uniform spheres found year-round in stores. The first camp hopes to convert the second.

A tomato renaissance is happening in our gardens and on our plates. Tomatoes are the most popular of all home garden plants. There is a variety perfectly suited for nearly any location, from an acre plot to a sunny spot on the sill. People who grow nothing else will hover and fuss over their tomatoes so that they can indulge their passions and cravings for a richer, truer, tastier tomato—the real thing. Few culinary pleasures are both so deeply satisfying and so readily accessible as eating a warm-from-the-vine tomato. There's nothing like a lean-over tomato, a tomato that causes you to lean over to eat it because its juice will run down your arm and drip off your elbow.

Both growers and eaters often include so-called heirloom tomatoes in their quest for taste perfection. Some experts insist that a variety must be at least fifty years old before it can be designated as an heirloom. Others contend that some younger varieties qualify, so long as they are grown from a series of saved seeds until no deviations show up in the plant. In either case, heirlooms must be grown from seeds that are saved from year to year. Growers save the seeds because these beloved tomatoes have attributes worth saving and handing down to the next generation, particularly flavor and suitability to the local growing conditions.

Tomato passion runs deep, but it wasn't love at first sight for everyone. Tomatoes are native to Central and South America, where they first grew wild and were eventually domesticated and cultivated for food since pre-Columbian times. The word "tomato" comes from the Aztec *tomatl*. Spanish and Portuguese explorers took tomatoes back to Europe, where they were used as ornamentals. As a nightshade, tomatoes were suspected of causing madness, if not death. Other people thought them to be aphrodisiacs, so even if tomatoes were not poisonous they were still too racy for cultured folk, who had no need for love apples.

Tomatoes were introduced to the South around the turn of the eighteenth century. Some historians claim that Portuguese slave traders introduced tomatoes to West Africa, so that some Africans brought to America during the era of slavery already knew how to cook with them. Those cooks are certainly credited with combining okra, tomatoes, and rice — foundations of classic Lowcountry cuisine.

Most early written recipes called for cooking tomatoes for hours, perhaps a holdover from the notion that they were poisonous. In *The Carolina Housewife* (1847), Sarah Rutledge wrote: "The art of cooking tomatoes lies mostly in cooking them enough. In whatever way prepared, they should be put on some hours before dinner. This vegetable is good in all soups and stews where such a decided flavoring is wanted."

It's possible that no one can say enough about the glory of real tomatoes, the ones that will eventually slay the dragon of the sorry-ass storebought stuff. But songwriter Guy Clark came close when he wrote:

Homegrown tomatoes, homegrown tomatoes
What would life be without homegrown tomatoes?
Only two things that money can't buy
That's true love and homegrown tomatoes. ■

Some of the recipes in this chapter (and many old southern recipes) call for peeling tomatoes, an idea that might seem odd to those who have never enjoyed old-fashioned, homegrown tomatoes. Some tomatoes, particularly the heirloom varieties that are grown for flavor instead of looks, often have thick, chewy skins that can slough off into tough pieces when cooked, so it's a good idea to peel them before they go into the pot. Even some raw tomatoes are better when peeled. The decision of whether to peel a tomato comes down to whether that peel is something you want to eat. Whether raw or cooked, tomato skin should never be a distraction.

To peel only a few tomatoes, use a serrated knife or serrated vegetable peeler. For larger batches, use this method: Use a serrated knife to cut a shallow X just through the skin on the bottom of each tomato; do not cut deeply into the flesh. Bring a large pot of water to a boil. Fill a large bowl with ice water. Working with only 2 or 3 tomatoes at a time, lower them into the boiling water just long enough for the scored skin to split a little, 20 to 30 seconds. (Do not put all of the tomatoes into the boiling water at once or the last ones pulled out will have started to cook and will be mealy and messy when peeled.) The riper the tomatoes, the less time this will take. Immediately transfer them into the ice water to cool. Remove them from the ice water and peel off the skin. The skin should slip off in large strips; if not, return the stubborn tomato to the boiling water for a few more seconds. Cut out the cores and any bruised spots made apparent by the hot water.

# Pasta with No-Cook Tiny Tomato Sauce

3 cups ripe miniature tomatoes, the more colors the better (about 1 pound)

2 garlic cloves, chopped

Pinch of crushed red pepper flakes

1 tablespoon drained capers or chopped ripe olives

1 teaspoon finely grated orange zest

1 tablespoon balsamic or sherry vinegar

¼ cup excellent extra-virgin olive oil

Kosher salt and ground black pepper, to taste

8 ounces dried pasta, preferably a short, chunky shape

½ cup lightly packed basil leaves, torn or coarsely chopped

¼ cup lightly packed flat-leaf parsley, coarsely chopped

2 teaspoons chopped marjoram

¾ cup cubed ricotta salata or freshly grated Parmigiano-Reggiano

Those tiny but mighty tomatoes that grow in cascading clusters, such as tiny red Sweet 100s, yellow pears, and brilliant orange Sungolds, flourish in the summer heat. For this light, fresh, uncooked sauce, lusciously ripe specimens are essential. They should be firm yet dissolve into sweet pulp when you pop them into your mouth. A colorful combination looks beautiful on the plate.

Pull out the best extra-virgin olive oil you have. Since this sauce isn't cooked, the character of the oil really comes through. Enjoy this sauce the day it is made. It doesn't keep well because the acidity of the tomatoes chemically cooks the flavor and color out of the herbs. Moreover, refrigeration ruins fresh tomatoes.

This concoction also makes great bruschetta topping. Stir in the herbs and cheese just before piling it onto slices of toasted or grilled crusty bread that have been rubbed with a garlic clove.

MAKES 4 SERVINGS

① Leave any tiny tomatoes whole and cut the rest in half. Place them in a bowl and stir in the garlic, red pepper flakes, capers, orange zest, vinegar, and oil. Season with salt and pepper. Let sit at room temperature while the pasta cooks, or up to 2 hours.

② Cook the pasta to al dente according to package directions. Drain the pasta, add to the tomato mixture, and stir gently to combine. Let sit for 2 minutes to allow the pasta to absorb some of the liquid. Sprinkle the herbs and cheese over the top and stir gently to combine. Check the seasoning and serve at once.

## Yellow Tomato Gazpacho

2 ½ pounds yellow
tomatoes

2 yellow or orange
bell peppers

1 jalapeño or other chile

3 Persian cucumbers or
1 English cucumber or
other variety with thin
skins and minimal
seeds (about 1 pound)

1 medium red onion

1 ½ cups 1-inch cubes
crustless Italian or
French bread

2 garlic cloves

1 tablespoon kosher salt

1 teaspoon ground
black pepper

½ teaspoon sweet or
hot paprika

1 teaspoon ground
cumin

1 teaspoon sugar

2 tablespoons sherry
vinegar, divided

4 tablespoons extra-
virgin olive oil, divided

Gazpacho is a welcome thing during the days of high summer when walking out-side feels like being hit in the face with a blowtorch. There's a lot of stuff called gazpacho out there, and some of it is barely recognizable. My version harks back to the beginnings of gazpacho in Spain, when it was a way to salvage stale bread with vinegar and a few vegetables. Tomatoes, which have become common in most recipes, didn't appear in gazpacho until they were brought back from the New World and deemed safe to eat uncooked, which wasn't that long ago in the grand scheme of things. Gazpacho isn't new to the South. There's a recipe for "Gaspacho" in Mary Randolph's *The Virginia Housewife* (1824).

Yellow tomatoes give this soup a lovely golden hue, but the recipe works with ripe tomatoes of any color or stripe. The key is to serve it well chilled, to bring out the contrast between the smooth, creamy base and the tiny cubes of crunchy vegetables. Taking the time to neatly dice all of those little cubes of vegetables is worth it. They just taste better.

MAKES 2 QUARTS

1. Core the tomatoes, cut into large chunks, collecting the juices, and place in a large bowl.

2. Core the bell peppers. Finely dice one of the peppers and set it aside in a medium bowl. Coarsely chop the other pepper and add it to the tomatoes.

3. Trim the stem end from the jalapeño. (To reduce its heat, cut it in half length-wise and trim away the seeds and inner membranes.) Coarsely chop the jalapeño and add to the tomatoes.

4. Peel the cucumbers. Finely dice 1 cup of cucumber and add to the finely diced bell pepper. Coarsely chop the remaining cucumbers and add to the tomato mixture.

5. Finely dice ½ cup of onion and add to the finely diced pepper and cucumber. Coarsely chop the rest of the onion and add to the tomato mixture.

6. Place the bread in a small bowl and cover with cold water. Let sit for 1 minute, then drain off the water, squeeze the bread dry, and add to the tomato mixture.

7. Transfer half of the tomato mixture into a blender. Add the garlic, salt, pepper, paprika, cumin, and sugar. Add 1 tablespoon of the vinegar and 2 tablespoons of the oil. Blend on the lowest speed to finely chop the vegetables. Increase the speed to high and blend until very smooth, at least 1 minute. Pour the purée into a fine-mesh sieve set over a large bowl. Use a rubber spatula to push the purée into the bowl, extracting as much liquid as possible. Discard the solids. If the vegetables were sufficiently puréed, there should be little more than seeds and bits of tomato skin.

8. Repeat with the remaining coarsely chopped tomato and vegetable mixture, 1 tablespoon of vinegar, and 2 tablespoons of oil.
9. Taste the gazpacho to check the seasoning. Stir in the finely diced vegetables.
10. Cover and refrigerate until well chilled, at least 4 hours and preferably overnight. Whisk the gazpacho and taste again to check the seasoning just before serving.

## Cherry Tomato and Mozzarella Salad with Pesto Vinaigrette

2 cups cherry tomatoes or other miniature tomatoes (red or mixed colors)

2 cups bite-sized fresh mozzarella balls, drained

½ cup Pesto Vinaigrette (recipe follows)

Coarse or large-crystal garnishing salt, to taste

Cracked or coarsely ground black pepper, to taste

There was little mozzarella cheese or pesto in traditional southern cooking, but now both items are so commonplace that we can't imagine a tomato season without them. This combination of small round tomatoes and white balls of cheese topped with emerald green pesto vinaigrette looks fantastic in a glass serving bowl. Another option is to pile the tomatoes and cheese on a platter of spinach or arugula and drizzle the vinaigrette over the top. This dish is easily doubled or tripled or more for serving a crowd. Because it is served at room temperature, it's great for a picnic or buffet.

The combination of tomatoes and basil shows that what grows together goes together. Things that flourish under the same growing conditions and come into season at the same time almost always taste great served together. Nature is a savvy menu planner.

Fresh mozzarella cheese is sometimes formed into small bite-sized balls called bocconcini or ciliegine. They come packed in liquid, and you'll find them in most well-stocked grocery stores, but you can substitute a regular size ball of fresh mozzarella cut into bite-sized cubes. Large-crystal garnishing salt such as fleur de sel or Maldon is a great finishing touch because it doesn't dissolve when wet, retaining a pleasant crunch.

MAKES 4 SERVINGS

Gently stir together the tomatoes and bocconcini in a serving bowl.
Pour the vinaigrette over the top. Season generously with salt and pepper.
Serve at room temperature.

## Pesto Vinaigrette

1 cup basil pesto
(page 281 or
store-bought)

3 tablespoons
champagne vinegar
or white wine vinegar

Finely grated zest
and juice of 1 lemon
(about ¼ cup)

¼ cup extra-virgin
olive oil

Kosher salt and ground
black pepper, to taste

Use this gorgeous and brightly colored vinaigrette on any salad that contains tomatoes. It is also good tossed with pasta.

MAKES 1 ½ CUPS

1. Combine the pesto, vinegar, lemon zest, lemon juice, and oil in a small glass jar with a tight-fitting lid. Close the jar and shake vigorously to combine the ingredients. Season with salt and pepper.

2. Use soon or refrigerate for up to 4 days. Return to room temperature, shake vigorously, and check the seasoning before serving.

## Tomato Biscuits with Basil Butter

4 hot freshly baked
biscuits (page 394)

Basil Butter (recipe
follows)

1 large or 2 medium
sun-ripened tomatoes

Coarse salt and ground
black pepper

I'm from the mountains of western North Carolina, a place where people eat paper-thin slices of fresh tomato tucked inside hot, generously buttered biscuits. These biscuits are so beloved that local biscuit-centric fast food places serve off-the-menu, unadvertised 'mater biscuits during the summer. The only updating I'm giving to this tradition is to put a little basil in the butter, but there's nothing wrong with using plain ole butter, particularly a lush, full-flavored cultured butter.

Tomato biscuits are good for breakfast or lunch. Small biscuits with dainty slices of peeled tomato make an elegant hors d'oeuvre.

MAKES 2 TO 4 SERVINGS

Split the hot biscuits and slather the insides with some of the Basil Butter. Core the tomato, peel it if necessary, and cut into very thin slices. Tuck the slices inside the biscuits and sprinkle them generously with salt and pepper. Close the biscuits and press lightly so that the melting butter mingles with the tomato juice. Eat them while they're hot.

## Basil Butter

8 tablespoons (1 stick) butter, at room temperature

2 tablespoons finely chopped fresh basil

1 teaspoon fresh lemon juice

¼ teaspoon kosher salt

Keeping flavored butters, often called compound butters, stashed in the freezer is an easy way to add flavor when cooking time is limited. A pat or two perks up plain vegetables and sauces. It's simple to make a double or triple batch of this butter, so make extra while the basil is plentiful. How nice it will be to open the freezer next winter and pull out a little taste of summer.

MAKES 8 SERVINGS

1. Beat the butter in a medium bowl with a wooden spoon until smooth. Add the basil, lemon juice, and salt and mix well.

2. Spoon the butter into a log the size of a stick of butter down the center of a piece of plastic wrap. Tightly roll up the butter in the plastic and twist the ends closed like a Tootsie Roll. The taut plastic will smooth the surface of the butter and make the log nice and round. Refrigerate until firm. Serve at room temperature. The butter can be refrigerated for up to 1 week or placed in a freezer bag and frozen for up to 6 months.

WHAT ELSE WORKS? In place of the basil, you can use other leafy herbs, such as parsley, cilantro, mint, lovage, chives, or chervil, or edible flower petals. Some herbs are more flavorful than others, so adjust the amount accordingly. For other compound butter combinations, see pages 100–102.

## Fresh Tomato Pie

1 (9-inch) deep-dish
  pie shell (page 396
  or store-bought)

1 ½ pounds large
  sun-ripened tomatoes

½ teaspoon kosher salt,
  plus more to taste

¼ cup lightly packed
  basil leaves, coarsely
  chopped

½ cup crisp bacon pieces
  (optional)

¼ teaspoon celery salt
  or celery seed

¾ cup high-quality
  mayonnaise

  Zest and juice of
  1 lemon (about ¼ cup)

1 ¼ cups grated Asiago
  cheese, divided

½ teaspoon ground
  black pepper, plus
  more to taste

⅓ cup crushed saltine
  cracker crumbs

Nothing less than perfect vine-ripened tomatoes will do for this pie. Be creative and mix tomatoes of different varieties and colors. The tomatoes are seasoned with lemon, an old southern tradition. The lemon heightens the natural acidity found in many heirloom tomato varieties, a characteristic that many people seek in a fresh tomato.

It's up to you whether to peel the tomatoes. However, keep in mind that heirloom and other old-fashioned tomatoes often have skins as tough as tarpaper and are unpleasant to chew whether raw or cooked. See page 339 for tips on how to peel ripe tomatoes.

Homegrown tomatoes inspire swagger, bluster, and (mostly) friendly competition among gardeners. Perfect tomatoes are the queen of the garden, the *'mater familia*. One year, my daddy grew a sorry bunch of tomato plants that never produced diddly-squat. His next-door neighbor, only a few steps away, had a bumper crop. One night the neighbor tied two of his perfect tomatoes onto the withered vines in my daddy's garden, out of a combination of empathy and good-natured ribbing. During the coming days, he tied a series of objects to those vines, including tennis balls, Christmas ornaments, plastic Easter eggs, and empty tomato soup cans—always under the cloak of darkness and with a straight face.

MAKES 8 SERVINGS

1. Bake and cool the pie shell according to the directions on page 398.
2. When ready to bake the pie, preheat the oven to 350°F.
3. Use a serrated knife to cut the tomatoes into ¼-inch-thick slices. Cover a wire rack with several layers of paper towels and set the rack over the sink to catch the drips. Arrange the tomatoes in a single layer on the rack. Sprinkle them with the salt and let drain for at least 10 minutes. Pat the tomatoes dry with fresh paper towels.
4. Arrange half of the tomatoes over the bottom of the pie shell. Scatter the basil and bacon, if using, over the tomatoes and arrange the rest of the tomatoes on top.
5. Stir together the celery salt, mayonnaise, lemon zest, and lemon juice in a small bowl. Stir in ¾ cup of the cheese and season with salt and pepper. Spread the mayonnaise mixture over the tomatoes.
6. Toss together the remaining ½ cup of cheese and the crumbs in a small bowl; sprinkle over the top of the pie.
7. Bake until the top of the pie is nicely browned, 30 to 35 minutes. Place on a wire rack to cool to room temperature before serving.

# Tomato and Bread Salad

4 cups 1-inch cubes Italian or French bread

¼ cup extra-virgin olive oil, plus more as needed

2 tablespoons red wine vinegar

2 tablespoons capers, drained

¾ teaspoon dried Italian herb blend or dried oregano

2 large roasted red or yellow bell peppers or other sweet peppers, cut into thin strips (about 1 cup) (page 314 or store-bought)

1 small sweet onion, halved lengthwise and cut into thin strips

3 cups diced tomatoes or halved miniature tomatoes

1 teaspoon kosher salt, or to taste

½ teaspoon ground black pepper, or to taste

½ cup lightly packed basil leaves, cut into thin ribbons

This is my favorite tomato salad. It's little more than top-notch tomatoes and good bread in a tangy dressing. In Italy this salad is known as panzanella, where it originated as a way to use up day-old bread, so Italian bread is a great choice, as are a baguette or a crusty country loaf. Avoid sourdough bread—although the texture is right, the sourness doesn't work here. Thin-sliced soft sandwich bread quickly dissolves into a soggy mess, so that's out of the question. For a more southern twist, use toasted cubes of cornbread, such as Black Pepper Cornbread Croutons (page 128). This salad is gorgeous when made with an array of colorful tomatoes, both red and yellow peppers, and both green and purple basil.

Around Pensacola, Florida, there is a similar dish called gaspachee (also spelled gazpachi, gaspachee, and gauspachi). It is a cross between thick soup and a very moist salad. It's made from hardtack, tomatoes, mayonnaise, and sometimes cucumbers, green bell pepper, garlic, and herbs. Local legend has it that the recipe grew from the custom of Spanish and Italian sailors softening their rocklike hardtack in gazpacho soup made from the fresh produce they enjoyed while in port.

Transform this into an entrée salad by adding grilled chicken shredded into bite-sized pieces.

MAKES 4 TO 6 SERVINGS

1. Preheat the oven to 350°F.
2. Spread the cubes of bread in a single layer on a baking sheet. Place in the oven and bake until the cubes are crisp on the outside but still a little chewy on the inside, about 10 minutes; do not let the bread brown.
3. Whisk together the oil, vinegar, capers, dried herbs, peppers, onion, tomatoes, salt, and pepper in a large bowl. Let sit for 5 minutes so that the tomatoes can release a little juice.
4. Stir in the bread cubes and let sit for about 5 minutes more, stirring occasionally so that the bread can soak up some of the juice. The salad should be moist but not so wet that the bread gets soggy. Add more oil, if needed.
5. Stir in the basil, check the seasoning, and serve soon. Leftovers might taste good the next day, but the salad won't look as appealing. The bread gets quite soft and the tomatoes languish in the refrigerator, so it's best to enjoy this salad the day it's made.

The easiest way to cut basil is to make a stack of leaves with the largest leaves on the bottom. Starting on one long edge, roll the stack into a cylinder. The large outer leaves will hold the smaller ones in place. Cut the cylinder crosswise with a sharp knife. The closer the cuts, the narrower the pieces will be. Shake them loose and the basil will fall into neat ribbons, sometimes called a chiffonade. This same technique works with large leafy vegetables such as collards, kale, and chard.

## Skillet-Roasted Cherry Tomatoes

1 tablespoon extra-virgin olive oil

2 cups cherry or other miniature tomatoes

2 tablespoons butter

2 tablespoons chopped fresh basil

Kosher salt and ground black pepper, to taste

This nearly instant recipe is part side dish, part sauce. It's a great strategy for using all those small tomatoes when they start coming in so fast they need to be picked twice a day. These warm, juicy, buttery tomatoes are great alone, but they also make a great topping for cheese grits, pasta, bruschetta, sautéed vegetables, or grilled chicken and seafood. They are a tasty accompaniment to the Savory Smoked Ham, Spinach, and Cheese Bread Pudding (page 173).

MAKES 4 SERVINGS

1. Stir together the oil and tomatoes in a medium bowl.
2. Heat a large, heavy skillet (preferably cast-iron) over high heat. Carefully pour in the tomatoes; they will sizzle and pop. Cook, stirring or gently shaking the pan to roll them around, until their skins begin to shrivel and are browned in spots, about 3 minutes.
3. Remove the skillet from the heat, add the butter and basil and swirl the pan to melt the butter. Season generously with salt and pepper and serve warm.

# Parmesan-Crusted Green Tomatoes

4 medium green
tomatoes (each
about 4 ounces)

1 teaspoon kosher salt,
or to taste

½ teaspoon ground black
pepper, or to taste

½ cup coarsely grated
Parmesan cheese

Not everyone in the South grew up eating fried green tomatoes, but when that hit movie gave this humble dish a title role, fried green tomatoes began popping up in restaurants all over the place. Some versions succumbed to the excesses of Hollywood, dolled up beyond all recognition. The appeal of a green tomato is in that greenness, with its astringent flavor and crisp flesh. I believe no recipe should mask those qualities, and this one does not. You get warm, firm, tangy tomatoes with a wisp of crispy crust, ready to serve in minutes.

Eating unripe green tomatoes is a tasty strategy to enjoy the very first and very last tomatoes of the season. However, avoid large green tomatoes because of their tough skins and woody cores.

These crusty tomatoes make a great side dish and can do wonders for a sandwich. For a delicious treat, top the piping hot tomatoes with Roasted Garlic Mayonnaise (page 148), Pickled Okra Rémoulade (page 197), or a generous spoonful of Old-Fashioned Pimento Cheese (page 316).

MAKES 4 SERVINGS

1. Preheat the broiler.
2. Core the tomatoes and use a serrated knife to cut them crosswise into ⅓-inch-thick slices. Sprinkle both sides with the salt and pepper. Arrange them in a single layer on a rimmed baking sheet lined with parchment paper. Cover the tops with a thin, even layer of cheese.
3. Broil until the cheese is melted and golden brown, 8 to 12 minutes, depending on the distance between the tomatoes and the broiler. Serve hot.

## BLT Chicken

6 boneless, skinless
chicken breast halves
(each about 6 ounces)

2 cups well-shaken
buttermilk

Vegetable oil spray

1 cup dry plain or
Italian-flavored
bread crumbs

2 teaspoons kosher salt

½ teaspoon ground
black pepper

1 to 2 tablespoons melted
butter or extra-virgin
olive oil

6 large slices
fresh tomato

6 bacon slices,
cooked and diced
(about 6 ounces)

6 sandwich slices
cheddar cheese

6 to 8 cups shredded
romaine lettuce or
other crunchy lettuce

1 cup bottled Creamy
Italian or Ranch
dressing, or to taste

This one-dish dinner delivers all of the flavors we love in a good BLT sandwich. It's a hit with families with varying preferences (read "picky eaters"). If you have an eater who doesn't like tomato, just leave it off one piece. If you have an eater who doesn't eat bacon, just leave it off one piece. If you have an eater who wants only chicken nuggets, leave all the toppings off one piece. Honest, this chicken made through Step 4 is a great way to make homemade chicken fingers or nuggets.

The buttermilk soak is crucial; it's what makes the chicken so moist and tender. Regular milk cannot do that.

MAKES 6 SERVINGS

1. Place the chicken in a large bowl or zip-top plastic bag. Pour in enough buttermilk to submerge and coat the chicken, cover or close, and refrigerate for at least 1 hour and up to overnight.

2. Preheat the oven to 400°F. Set a wire rack inside a large rimmed baking sheet lined with aluminum foil. Mist the rack with the spray.

3. Pour the crumbs onto a shallow plate and season with the salt and pepper. Working with one piece at a time, remove the chicken from the buttermilk, let any excess drip off, and coat in the crumbs. Arrange the coated chicken in a single layer on the rack and drizzle the butter over the tops.

4. Bake until the chicken is cooked through and the crumbs are golden, 20 to 25 minutes. The chicken is done when an instant-read thermometer inserted into the thickest part of a breast registers 165°F and the juices show no traces of pink.

5. Remove the pan from the oven and place a tomato slice on each piece of chicken. Top the tomato with bacon, followed by a slice of cheese. Return the pan to the oven until the cheese melts, about 2 minutes.

6. Toss the lettuce with the dressing and arrange on a serving platter. Top with the warm chicken and serve promptly.

## Tomato Gravy

3 cups finely chopped tomatoes

1 teaspoon kosher salt, plus more to taste

2 tablespoons bacon drippings (see note) or butter

½ cup finely chopped onion

3 tablespoons instant or all-purpose flour

½ cup whole milk

Ground black pepper, to taste

Tomato gravy means different things across the South. In some places it describes a spicy tomato sauce that resembles marinara sauce or Creole sauce. Where I'm from, tomato gravy is a quick pan sauce made in the skillet after frying bacon (although I've seen recipes that use the drippings du jour, such as from frying pork chops, country ham, sausage, chicken, or fish). It's wonderful spooned over biscuits, rice, grits, cheese toast, eggs, and whatever came out of that skillet. You can make gravy with fresh tomatoes all summer and with premium canned tomatoes all winter.

To transform tomato gravy into flavorful cream of tomato soup, thin with more milk.

MAKES 4 TO 6 SERVINGS

1. Stir together the tomatoes and salt in a medium bowl and set aside to give the tomatoes time to release some juice.

2. Meanwhile, heat the drippings in a large, heavy skillet (preferably cast-iron) over medium-high heat. Stir in the onion and cook, stirring often, until softened, about 5 minutes.

3. Sprinkle in the flour and cook, stirring continuously, for 2 minutes; reduce the heat as necessary to prevent the flour from scorching.

4. Stir in the tomatoes and their juices. Reduce the heat to low and simmer, stirring often, for 5 minutes.

5. Stir in the milk and simmer, stirring slowly and continuously, until the gravy is thick enough to coat the back of a spoon, about 5 minutes. Season with salt and pepper. Serve hot.

NOTE: If you need to fry bacon to get drippings to make this gravy, you'll need about 4 thick slices. Cut the bacon crosswise into thin strips and cook over medium heat in the skillet until crisp. Use a slotted spoon to transfer to paper towels to drain, leaving the drippings in the skillet. Stir the cooked bacon into the gravy just before serving.

## Slow-Roasted Tomatoes

3 pounds ripe Roma or
  other paste tomatoes

1 tablespoon kosher salt

¼ cup extra-virgin
  olive oil

Slow-roasted tomatoes are tomatoes with their flavor volume turned up as high as it will go. A leisurely roast at low temperature cooks out much of the water, leaving petals of sweet, rich, intensely flavored tomato flesh. Romas (also called plum tomatoes, paste tomatoes, or sauce tomatoes) are ideal for roasting because they are meaty with few seeds. Roasted tomatoes keep far longer than dead-ripe fresh tomatoes, letting you enjoy a little taste of summer on a cold, cold night.

MAKES ABOUT 3 CUPS

1. Preheat the oven to 250°F. Line a rimmed baking sheet with parchment paper.
2. Core the tomatoes, cut them in half lengthwise, and use your fingers to scoop out the seeds. (A small tool called a tomato shark is the best way to remove only the core without lopping off the end of the tomato.)
3. Place the tomatoes cut-side up in a single layer on the prepared baking sheet. Sprinkle with the salt and drizzle with the oil. Roast until the tomatoes have collapsed and their centers are mostly dry, yet still slightly soft and plump, 2 to 4 hours, depending on the size and moisture content of the tomatoes. The pieces should have the texture of a moist prune. Let the tomatoes cool to room temperature on the pan. Gently pull off and discard the skins.

MAKE-AHEAD NOTE: The cooled tomatoes can be transferred into an airtight container and refrigerated for up to 3 days.

For longer refrigerated storage, transfer the cooled tomatoes into a jar that has been sterilized in boiling water or run through the dishwasher on the hottest cycle. The jar should have a sterilized tight-fitting lid. The jar and lid do not have to stay hot, but they must stay sterile. Submerge the tomatoes in extra-virgin olive oil, close the jar, and refrigerate for 1 hour. Open the jar and run the handle of a small spatula or wooden chopstick around the inside of the jar to release any air bubbles. Top off with more oil, if needed. The tomatoes must remain submerged. Cover and refrigerate for up to 2 weeks.

To store in the freezer, pack the tomatoes into a freezer bag, squeeze out the excess air, close, and freeze for up to 3 months. The flavor will be protected, but the texture declines, and they are best used in cooked recipes such as sauces.

## Roasted Roma Tart

½ recipe Basic Pastry I (page 396)

½ cup crème fraîche (page 388 or store-bought)

2 tablespoons whole-grain Dijon mustard

2 tablespoons chopped fresh thyme, divided

¾ cup crumbled soft, fresh goat cheese (chèvre)

3 cups Slow-Roasted Tomatoes (page 351)

There are three distinct components to this tart. First is the tomatoes, which are slowly roasted into little pillows of tomato velvet with very concentrated flavor. Second is the simple filling, with no ingredients that will upstage those tomatoes. And third is the crust, which is made from flaky, flavorful, old-fashioned lard pastry. (If the lard is a deal breaker for you, see page 397 for another delicious pastry. You should also read the ingredients of most commercial pie crusts.)

The Slow-Roasted Tomatoes are divine. The recipe makes just enough for this tart, so I suggest making extra to allow for the ones you are bound to eat before the tart is assembled, or to have a few left over.

MAKES 8 SERVINGS

1. Fit the pastry into a 10-inch tart pan with a removable bottom. Bake and cool to room temperature according to the directions on page 398.

2. Preheat the oven to 350°F.

3. Mix the crème fraîche and mustard and 1 tablespoon of the thyme in a small bowl. Use the back of a small spoon to spread 2 tablespoons of the mixture evenly over the bottom of the tart crust and set the rest aside. Sprinkle the cheese into the crust.

4. Cover the cheese with the tomatoes. Working from the outside of the crust toward the center, arrange the pieces in concentric circles and overlap their edges so that very little of the filling shows.

5. Bake the tart until the tomatoes are just beginning to lightly brown, about 15 minutes. Sprinkle with the remaining 1 tablespoon of thyme. Cut into wedges and serve warm or at room temperature with a spoonful of the remaining crème fraîche mixture on the side.

# Simmered Tomato Sauce

6 tablespoons extra-virgin olive oil

1 cup finely chopped onion

¼ cup thinly sliced garlic

¾ teaspoon dried oregano

¾ teaspoon dried basil

¾ teaspoon dried marjoram

3 pounds ripe plum tomatoes, peeled, seeded, and coarsely chopped

¼ cup red wine

½ teaspoon kosher salt

1 teaspoon sugar

1 tablespoon sherry vinegar or balsamic vinegar

¼ cup chopped fresh basil, lightly packed

2 to 3 tablespoons tomato paste, if needed

When the tomatoes are coming in at a fever pitch, it's time to make sauce to stash away for winter. Good sauce relies on the right type of tomato: paste tomatoes, also known as plum tomatoes, Roma tomatoes, or sauce tomatoes. These small, oblong tomatoes have more flesh and fewer gloppy seeds, so they yield more sauce with deeper, richer flavor. To greatly reduce the chance of bitter sauce, take the time to peel and seed the tomatoes before the cooking begins. See page 339 for tips on peeling tomatoes.

Taste the finished sauce and adjust the seasoning to your personal taste, but keep in mind that if the sauce will be used as an ingredient in other recipes it should be neutral enough to not interfere with those recipes.

MAKES ABOUT 4 CUPS

1. Heat the oil in a large pot over medium heat. Add the onion and garlic and a pinch of salt and cook, stirring often, until the onion is softened and the garlic is golden, about 8 minutes. Do not let the garlic scorch. Add the oregano, basil, and marjoram. Cook, stirring continuously, for 30 seconds. Stir in the tomatoes, wine, and salt. Simmer, stirring occasionally, until the tomatoes are very soft and have started to break down, about 1 hour.

2. Purée in a blender (working in batches to not fill the blender more than half full) and return to the pot, or purée the sauce directly in the pot with an immersion blender. Simmer the sauce until it reduces to 4 cups, about 30 minutes.

3. Stir in the sugar, vinegar, and basil. Taste the sauce and adjust the seasoning. If the sauce tastes flat, add more salt. If it still tastes flat, add more vinegar because the acidity will perk up the flavors. If the sauce is too acidic, stir in a pinch of baking soda because the alkalinity will balance the acidity. If the sauce is correctly seasoned but still tastes puny, add enough tomato paste to punch up the tomato flavor.

4. Cool the sauce to room temperature, then cover and refrigerate for up to 3 days or freeze in airtight containers for up to 3 months. Taste the thawed sauce and adjust the seasoning before serving.

## TIPS AND TECHNIQUES

Always check the seasoning of a dish that's been frozen. Freezing subdues seasoning, particularly salt. That's why dishes that were great before they were frozen often taste a little flat when thawed and reheated. Start by adding more salt. If the dish still tastes flat, try adding acidity, such as a splash of vinegar or citrus juice, ideally using an ingredient that is in the dish already.

# Tomato Jam

2 tablespoons extra-
virgin olive oil

¼ cup finely chopped
onion

¼ cup peeled and grated
fresh ginger

3 garlic cloves,
finely chopped

1 teaspoon ground
cinnamon

1 teaspoon ground
coriander

½ teaspoon ground
cumin

⅛ teaspoon ground
cloves

⅛ teaspoon ground
allspice

⅛ teaspoon cayenne
pepper, or to taste

¼ cup sherry vinegar

½ cup packed light
brown sugar

6 cups peeled, seeded,
and chopped tomatoes
(about 2 ½ pounds)

1 teaspoon kosher salt

½ teaspoon ground
black pepper

¼ cup honey

2 tablespoons
lemon juice

This is a little sweet, so it's jam in my book. It's also spicy, so it perks up foods that could use a little zip. Think of it as a sophisticated combination of ketchup, chile sauce, and chutney. It's good on sandwiches, on vegetables (especially field peas), on crispy fried things, on meatloaf, and with cheese. This small batch will keep in the refrigerator for a few months without sealing the jars.

MAKES ABOUT 3 CUPS

1. Heat the oil in a large saucepan over medium heat. Add the onion and a pinch of salt and cook, stirring occasionally, until softened, about 5 minutes. Stir in the ginger and garlic and cook, stirring, for 1 minute. Stir in the cinnamon, coriander, cumin, cloves, allspice, and cayenne and cook, stirring, for 30 seconds. Stir in the vinegar, brown sugar, and tomatoes.

2. Reduce the heat and simmer, stirring occasionally, until the tomatoes break down and almost all of the liquid cooks away, about 1 ½ hours. Stir in the salt, pepper, and honey, increase the heat and boil until the jam is shiny and thick, about 2 minutes. Remove the pan from the heat and stir in the lemon juice. Let the jam cool to room temperature, stirring occasionally.

3. Transfer the jam into a clean glass jar with a tight-fitting lid. Store covered and refrigerated for up to 3 months.

## Sweet and Spicy Green Tomato Pie

Pastry for double-crust 9-inch pie (page 396 or store-bought)

2 to 2 ½ pounds small to medium green tomatoes

1 teaspoon finely grated lemon zest

1 tablespoon fresh lemon juice

¾ cup granulated sugar

½ cup packed light brown sugar

½ cup all-purpose flour

½ teaspoon kosher salt

¼ teaspoon ground allspice

½ teaspoon ground cinnamon

4 tablespoons (½ stick) butter, cut into small cubes

1 egg beaten with 1 tablespoon cold water

Cinnamon ice cream or vanilla ice cream, for serving

Firm, tart, green tomatoes make a pie that is remarkably similar in flavor and texture to pie made from firm, tart, green apples. Recipes for green tomato pie have been around for decades. I suspect these pies were invented by creative cooks who had little access to tree fruit, so they turned to the tomato fruit growing in the garden. The pies might also have been a strategy to salvage any green tomatoes still on the vine just before the first killing frost.

Be sure to use small green tomatoes because large ones have unpleasant woody cores. This is a good way to use green tomatoes that are as hard as rocks — riper tomatoes make the filling too juicy.

MAKES 8 SERVINGS

1. Position a rack in the center of the oven. Place a rimmed baking sheet in the oven and preheat to 400°F.

2. To make the pie shell, use a lightly floured rolling pin to roll half of the pastry into an 11-inch round on a lightly floured piece of waxed paper or parchment paper. Fit it into a 9-inch pie plate, cover with plastic wrap, and refrigerate for at least 30 minutes. (See page 398 for tips on rolling pastry.)

3. To make the pastry top, use a lightly floured rolling pin to roll the other half of the pastry into an 11-inch round on a lightly floured piece of waxed paper or parchment paper. Slide it onto a baking sheet, cover with plastic wrap, and refrigerate for at least 30 minutes.

4. Peel and core the tomatoes. Use a vegetable peeler or small serrated knife to peel the tomatoes. (Because they are very firm, the blanching and shocking method used for large amounts of ripe tomatoes will not work.) Use a serrated knife to cut the tomatoes in half from top to bottom and then cut each half crosswise into very thin slices, no more than ⅛-inch thick. There should be about 6 cups of sliced tomatoes. Place them in a large bowl.

5. Whisk together the lemon zest, lemon juice, granulated sugar, brown sugar, flour, salt, allspice, and cinnamon in a small bowl. Pour over the tomatoes and toss to coat. Pour the tomato mixture into the pie shell and mound it up in the center. Scatter the cubes of butter over the filling. The shell will be very full but the tomatoes will cook down as the pie bakes.

6. Cover the filling with the pastry top. Lightly press the edges of the pastry together and trim off any excess to leave a ½-inch overhang. Fold under the edge to be even with the rim of the pie plate and crimp to seal. Brush the top lightly with the egg wash, making sure it doesn't pond up around the edge of the crimped crust. Cut a few slits on top to allow steam to escape.

7. Place the pie on the baking sheet in the hot oven. The hot sheet will help cook the bottom pastry and will also catch the inevitable drips. Bake for 15 minutes. Reduce the oven to 350°F. Lay a flat sheet of foil over the pie if it is browning

too quickly. Continue baking until the crust is golden and any juices that come up through the slits are thick and bubbling, about 35 minutes more. Take the pie off the baking sheet and place on a wire rack to cool to room temperature before cutting.

## Smoked Tomato Soup with Herbed Beans

Smoke 'em while you've got 'em. Smoked tomatoes keep well in the freezer, making this soup a possibility during the winter, long after fresh tomatoes have disappeared from the garden. The soup's wonderful aroma will linger in your kitchen for hours. It is thickened with bread and served with a generous scoop of piping hot beans, so it's hearty and very satisfying. The beans are braised in garlic and stock until they are bathed in thick, creamy sauce and then finished with a handful of fresh herbs that add color, flavor, and aroma. You can start with home-cooked or canned beans, but save their liquid because it thickens the sauce.

This is a great way to enjoy a bottle of excellent extra-virgin olive oil. The warmth of the soup will release the oil's aroma.

MAKES 2 QUARTS

### SOUP

- 2 tablespoons extra-virgin olive oil
- 1 large onion, diced (about 3 cups)
- 1 finely chopped anchovy fillet, 2 teaspoons anchovy paste, or 2 teaspoons Worcestershire sauce
- 4 garlic cloves, sliced
- 1 tablespoon chopped fresh rosemary
- 4 cups coarsely chopped smoked tomatoes and their juices (recipe follows)
- 2 to 2 ½ cups chicken or vegetable stock
- 2 cups 1-inch cubes crusty, country-style white bread or baguette
- 1 teaspoon kosher salt, or to taste
- ¾ teaspoon ground black pepper, or to taste
- 1 teaspoon smoked paprika (*pimentón*), or to taste

Freshly shaved Parmesan cheese and extra-virgin olive oil, for serving

(continued on next page)

1. For the soup: Heat the oil in a large pot over medium-high heat. Add the onion and cook, stirring often, until softened, about 8 minutes. Add the anchovy, garlic, and rosemary and cook, stirring constantly, for 1 minute. Stir in the tomatoes and 2 cups of the stock and bring to a boil. Stir in the bread. Reduce the heat and let the soup simmer gently until the bread is soft, about 5 minutes.

2. Purée the soup in a blender (working in batches to not fill the blender more than half full) and return it to the pot, or purée it directly in the pot with an immersion blender. The soup should be thick but pourable, so thin it with additional stock if needed. Season with the salt, pepper, and smoked paprika. Taste the soup; if your tomatoes aren't as smoky as you like, you can boost their flavor with a little extra paprika. Keep the soup warm over low heat while you make the beans.

3. For the beans: Heat 2 tablespoons of the oil in a skillet over medium-high heat. Add the garlic and cook, stirring, until you can smell the aroma, about 30 seconds.

4. Add the beans with their liquid and 1 cup of the stock. Simmer over low heat, stirring often, until the beans are hot and bathed in thick, creamy sauce, about 20 minutes. Add more stock as needed. Season with the salt and pepper.

¼ cup extra-virgin
olive oil, divided

2 garlic cloves,
finely chopped

6 cups home-cooked
shell beans (such as
cannellini or pinto)
with 1 cup cooking
liquid or undrained
canned beans

1 to 2 cups chicken stock,
divided

1 teaspoon kosher salt

¾ teaspoon ground
black pepper

½ cup chopped
flat-leaf parsley

½ cup chopped
fresh basil

5 Just before serving, stir in the parsley and basil and the remaining 2 tablespoons of oil. Keep warm over low heat until ready to serve, stirring often
and adding more stock if needed.

6 To serve, ladle the soup into shallow bowls. Spoon some of the hot beans
into the center of each serving, topping with the cheese and a generous
drizzle of oil. Serve hot.

## Smoked Tomatoes

3 pounds fresh
tomatoes

You can smoke the tomatoes on a grill, in an outdoor smoker, or in a stove-top smoker pan. Whichever method you choose, consider making extra because the tomatoes freeze well and are nice to have on hand to make more soup or to use in other recipes. The tomatoes are smoked whole, so small, firm tomatoes—particularly paste tomatoes—work best. The tomatoes should be fully ripe but not juicy.

MAKES ABOUT 4 CUPS

1. Prepare an outdoor grill with a lid, a stove-top smoker, or an outdoor smoker for smoking according to the manufacturer's instructions. Lighter-flavored wood chips, such as oak, alder, and apple, are good choices. Arrange the tomatoes in a single layer on the grate or in a disposable aluminum roasting pan. Smoke the tomatoes until they are browned and soft and their skins are starting to shrivel, 1 to 3 hours, depending on the type of smoker. Do not let the heat source get so hot that the tomatoes char on the bottom or become crispy. Adjust the heat source and vents and replenish the chips as needed to maintain the smoke.

2. Set the tomatoes aside until cool enough to handle. Peel off and discard the skins. Working over a medium bowl to catch the juice, core the tomatoes and cut them in half lengthwise. Scoop out the seeds with your fingers and drop the tomatoes into the bowl. If there is a lot of pulp clinging to the seeds, drain them in a fine sieve set over a small bowl and add the collected juice to the tomatoes. You can store the smoked tomatoes covered and refrigerated for up to 3 days or frozen in airtight containers for up to 6 months.

# TURNIPS

**The turnip, an ancient food that has been cultivated** for thousands of years, was one of the first foods brought to America by colonists because turnips kept well in cold weather and could be fed to both humans and animals.

Although southerners eat turnip roots, they have never been as popular in the South as they are in the North. Southerners, particularly in the upper regions of the South, took to the greens. In some communities, even now, the term "turnip greens" describes all edible greens. Outsiders occasionally suggest that southerners eat the part that should be thrown away and throw away the part that's meant to be eaten. Actually both the sharp, spicy greens and the sweet, earthy roots are delicious and enjoyable.

A "mess" is an old-time southern unit of measurement for certain foods, particularly greens. It's more of a guideline or notion than a fixed amount. Some people say it's what will fit in a large metal dishpan, an empty flour sack, or an outstretched apron. Some get into specifics and say that a mess weighs five pounds. The essence of a mess o'greens is that it's the amount needed to feed those who need to be fed. ■

# Mashed Root Vegetables

1 pound root vegetables, such as turnips, parsnips, rutabagas, celery root, carrots, and/or sweet potatoes

2 pounds starchy potatoes (such as russets)

1 to 2 tablespoons butter, at room temperature

½ to 1 cup half-and-half or whole milk, warmed

2 teaspoons kosher salt, plus more to taste

¼ teaspoon ground black pepper

This is a versatile, rustic mash up. The combination of vegetables is up to you, so mix and match to highlight the flavors you enjoy most, or simply to use up what you have on hand. Having said that, the dish is most successful when it's at least half potatoes because some root vegetables can be a little wet when mashed. Similarly, it's best to mash the mixture coarsely rather than spinning it into a purée that might get gluey. Depending on the combination, the flavor can range from mild to strong and the color from creamy white to orange.

MAKES 6 SERVINGS

1. Peel the root vegetables and potatoes and cut them into 1-inch pieces. It's important that all of the pieces be the same size so that they will cook at the same rate. Place them in a large saucepan and cover with cold water. Add ½ teaspoon kosher salt per cup of water. Bring to a boil over medium-high heat, reduce the heat, and simmer gently only until the vegetables are tender when pierced with the tip of a knife, about 30 minutes. Do not let the vegetables cook until they begin to fall apart or they will be too waterlogged to mash. Drain the vegetables in a colander, then return them to the still-warm pan to steam dry, about 2 minutes. The chunks of potato should look chalky along the edges.

2. Gently mash the vegetables with a handheld potato masher or the back of a large spoon. Leave them fairly coarse.

3. Gently stir in the butter and warm half-and-half. Season with the salt and pepper and serve soon.

MAKE-AHEAD NOTE: This dish is best served as soon as it is made, but you can keep it warm for up to 2 hours by transferring the mixture into a large glass or metal bowl. Cover the bowl with plastic wrap or foil and set the bowl over (not in) a pan of gently simmering water. If the mixture gets dry, stir in more warmed half-and-half or stock. If you must, you can make the mash up to 1 day ahead. Spoon into a buttered casserole dish and dot the top with butter. Store covered and refrigerated. Reheat in a 350°F oven for about 20 minutes or in the microwave.

## Creamy Baby Turnip Soup
## with Smoked Trout Butter

2 tablespoons butter

2 leeks (white and tender green parts only), cleaned and sliced (about 1 ½ cups)

1 medium onion, peeled and diced (about 1 ½ cups)

2 pounds very small and mild turnips, trimmed and sliced (about 5 cups)

1 medium russet potato, peeled and diced (about 2 cups)

4 cups chicken stock

1 ½ teaspoons kosher salt, plus more to taste

1 cup whole milk or half-and-half

¼ teaspoon ground nutmeg

½ teaspoon ground black pepper, plus more to taste

Smoked Trout Butter, for serving (recipe follows)

This soup is silky, soothing, and mild. I like to use those little thin-skinned white Japanese turnips about the size of a ping-pong ball, but any variety will do so long as they are not so large that they are pithy, woody, or strong smelling. The effect of swirling the richly flavored butter into the soup when it's served is amazing. The heat of the soup melts the butter and releases its aroma, and the smokiness of the trout and bacon make the soup complete.

Be sure to use hot-smoked fish in the butter. That means that the fish is fully cooked, meaty, and deeply flavored. I use trout because North Carolina's rivers yield some of the world's best trout, but you can use hot-smoked salmon or whatever the specialty is where you live. This butter is good in other simple soups, such as potato soup or corn chowder. It's also good as a spread for crackers. It does wonders for a plain baked potato.

MAKES 2 QUARTS OF SOUP AND 1 ½ CUPS OF BUTTER

1. Melt the butter in a large pot over medium heat. Add the leeks and onion and a pinch of salt and stir to coat. Cook, stirring occasionally, until softened, about 8 minutes. Add the turnips, potato, stock, and salt. Bring to a boil, reduce the heat, partially cover the pot, and simmer until the vegetables are completely tender, about 25 minutes.

2. Purée in a blender (working in batches to not fill the blender more than half full) and return it to the pot, or purée the soup directly in the pot with an immersion blender. Stir in the milk and heat through. Season with the nutmeg and pepper, plus more salt if needed.

3. To serve, ladle the hot soup into serving bowls. Top each serving with 3 tablespoons of Smoked Trout Butter and serve at once.

MAKE-AHEAD NOTE: You can make the soup up to 1 day ahead; cool, cover, and refrigerate. Stir well and check the seasoning when you reheat it for serving.

## Smoked Trout Butter

MAKES 1 ½ CUPS

8 tablespoons (1 stick) butter, at room temperature

¼ cup finely chopped cooked bacon (from about 3 thick slices)

¾ cup skinless hot-smoked trout, crumbled (about 3 ounces)

2 tablespoons chopped fresh dill

Beat the butter in a medium bowl with a wooden spoon until smooth. Fold in the bacon, trout, and dill. Wrap well and chill until firm.

MAKE-AHEAD NOTE: You can make the butter up to 4 days ahead. Store covered and refrigerated.

## Turnip and Potato Galette

Vegetable oil spray

6 tablespoons butter, melted and divided

2 pounds waxy potatoes, peeled and sliced paper-thin

1 teaspoon kosher salt, or to taste

½ teaspoon ground black pepper, or to taste

1 pound small turnips, peeled and sliced paper-thin

1 cup chicken stock, warmed

As the wispy layers of turnip and potato cook, they collapse into a thin cake that is silky and buttery in the center with edges that are a little chewy and browned. I like to make this in a skillet to encourage those edges, but a pie plate also works. Use not-too-starchy potatoes that hold their shape when cooked, something like a Kennebec, Yellow Finn, or Yukon Gold. Look for small turnips that have no woody interiors. But, most important, slice the vegetables paper-thin. The slicing disc on a food processor or a vegetable slicer works well, but it's possible with a sharp knife and patience.

MAKES 6 SERVINGS

(1) Position a rack in the center of the oven and preheat to 425°F. Mist the inside of a 9- or 10-inch cast-iron skillet or glass pie plate with the spray, then brush the bottom with 1 tablespoon of the butter.

(2) Spread half of the potatoes evenly in the skillet, drizzle with 2 tablespoons of the butter, and sprinkle with half of the salt and pepper. Add the turnips to the skillet. Add the rest of the potatoes, arranging the top slices in a pretty circle with the edges overlapping like fish scales. Pour the stock evenly over all. Drizzle with the remaining 3 tablespoons of butter and sprinkle with the rest of the salt and pepper.

(3) Cover tightly with foil and bake for 30 minutes. Uncover and bake until the top is well browned and there is very little liquid around the edges, 30 to 35 minutes more. Run a thin knife around the inside edge and let sit for 5 minutes before cutting into wedges and serving warm.

WHAT ELSE WORKS? You can use either the potatoes or the turnips alone. You can also replace the turnips with rutabagas.

# Glazed Baby Turnips and Apples

1 pound baby turnips (about 2 pounds if the greens are still attached)

1 tablespoon rendered duck fat, bacon drippings, or extra-virgin olive oil

1 tablespoon butter

1 firm, sweet-tart apple, peeled, cored, and cut into thin wedges

2 teaspoons sugar

Kosher salt and ground black pepper, to taste

1 teaspoon chopped fresh thyme or rosemary

This is a simple fall dish, perfect for when the second harvest of turnips coincides with the start of apple season. The texture of the turnips reminds me of home fries with just a touch of sweetness to balance the earthiness. The duck fat makes the turnips extra crispy and flavorful. This side dish is fantastic with Pan-Roasted Duck Breasts with Cherries (page 79), which will yield the fat to use in the recipe.

MAKES 4 SERVINGS

1. Trim the greens and rootlets from the turnips. (Discard the greens or use them in another recipe.) Cut any turnips larger than 1 inch in diameter into halves or quarters to make all of the pieces roughly the same size. (You can also cut them into sticks that resemble french fries.) Bring a large saucepan of water to a boil. Add ½ teaspoon kosher salt per cup of water. Add the turnips, reduce the heat, and simmer until crisp-tender, about 5 minutes. Drain well.

2. Heat the fat and butter in a large, heavy skillet (preferably cast-iron) over medium-high heat. Stir in the drained turnips and the apples. Sprinkle with the sugar, salt, and pepper and stir to coat. Spread the turnips and apples in a single layer with most of the cut sides on the bottom of the skillet and let cook undisturbed until browned on the bottom, about 8 minutes. Turn the pieces over or gently stir and continue cooking until tender, about 7 minutes more. Check the seasoning, sprinkle with the thyme, and serve warm.

VARIATION: You can use a firm pear instead of the apple.

# Smothered Turnips and Greens

1 ½ pounds small turnips with their greens

2 tablespoons extra-virgin olive oil

1 tablespoon bacon drippings or additional olive oil

2 tablespoons water

1 teaspoon kosher salt, or to taste

½ teaspoon ground black pepper, or to taste

This is a classic southern way to quickly cook turnips with their greens. Unlike turnips slowly cooked in enough liquid to make potlikker, these are cooked until tender in flavorful oil and only a splash of water and then browned for intensified flavor. This method goes by many names: smothered, seethed, suffocated, and drowned. What violent monikers for such a gentle dish.

If you wind up with turnips that have had their greens cut away, you can replace the greens with a bunch of chard, which is a member of the beet family. Do not be alarmed about the huge mound of uncooked greens — they cook down to very little, leaving just a few bits of green interspersed through the white cubes of turnip. This is a very pretty dish.

MAKES 4 TO 6 SERVINGS

(1) Cut off the greens from the turnips and discard any discolored leaves. Coarsely chop the greens. Wash them to remove any grit and drain in a colander. It's fine if water clings to the leaves because it will help them cook later. Trim the turnips and cut them into scant ½-inch cubes.

(2) Heat the oil and drippings in a large skillet (preferably cast-iron) over medium-high heat. Add the greens to the skillet one large handful at a time, tossing with tongs to help them wilt a little before adding more. Be careful, the water on the leaves might pop a little when it hits the hot oil. When all of the greens are in the skillet, stir in the turnips and the 2 tablespoons of water. Reduce the heat, cover, and cook, stirring occasionally until the turnips are tender, 10 to 15 minutes.

(3) Uncover, increase the heat, and cook, stirring often, until the liquid cooks away and the cubes of turnips are lightly browned, 5 to 8 minutes. Season with the salt and pepper and serve hot.

WHAT ELSE WORKS? You can use this method to cook baby beets with their greens.

# Turnips in Maple Cream Sauce

1 pound small turnips, peeled and cut into ¼-inch slices

3 tablespoons real maple syrup, preferably Grade B

1 tablespoon whole-grain Dijon mustard

3 tablespoons crème fraîche (page 388 or store-bought)

Kosher salt and ground black pepper, to taste

2 teaspoons chopped fresh thyme

½ cup coarsely chopped pecans, toasted

In this recipe, tender slices of gently cooked turnip are bathed in a creamy, flavorful sauce that is lightly sweetened with real maple syrup. I like to use Grade B syrup because it has stronger flavor than Grade A pancake syrup. I realize that cane syrup, molasses, and sorghum are more authentically southern than maple syrup, but I've tried all three in this recipe and frowned at the results with each. Those dark sweeteners bully the delicate turnips and turn the sauce the color of motor oil dripped from under a car onto snow.

MAKES 4 TO 6 SERVINGS

1. Bring a large saucepan of water to a boil. Add ½ teaspoon kosher salt per cup of water. Add the turnips and cook until just tender, 5 to 10 minutes. Drain and return to the pot.

2. Stir in the maple syrup, mustard, and crème fraîche and cook over medium heat, stirring often, until the sauce reduces and coats the turnips, about 2 minutes. Season with salt and pepper, stir in the thyme and pecans, and serve warm.

## TIPS AND TECHNIQUES

Toasting enhances and refreshes the flavor of nuts, particularly when they have been stored in the freezer and their flavorful oils have gone dormant. The easiest way to toast nuts is to spread them in a single layer on a rimmed baking sheet. Place in a preheated 350°F oven until you can just begin to smell the nuts. Do not let them darken more than one shade. Immediately pour the nuts onto a very lightly dampened tea towel or a few layers of dampened paper towels. Even when removed from the oven, the nuts will continue to cook for about a minute because of the very hot oil inside them, so they must come off the hot pan at once or risk burning. Any bits of shell or dust will stick to the damp towel. Toasting time depends on the size, type, and freshness of the nuts. Chopped nuts and pale nuts (such as pine nuts and blanched almonds) take about 5 minutes. Whole nuts, halves, and dark nuts (cashews, pecans, walnuts, whole almonds, and hazelnuts) take about 10 minutes. Keep a close watch because they can go from perfect to burned in seconds. Burned nuts are ruined. Pitch them out to the squirrels, accept the situation, and start over.

# WINTER SQUASH

**In the beginning, there was squash.** One of the first crops cultivated in North America, squash was a staple crop so essential that some Native Americans considered it holy. Colonists found Native Americans cooking fresh squash, drying the flesh and the seeds for long storage, and weaving thin, desiccated strips of rind into mats. The most common type of winter squash grown by the Native Americans was pumpkins, so early colonists tended to call all squashes by that name. Although it seems like a cliché, pumpkin was almost certainly served at the first Thanksgiving, probably in pies and as a sweet made by stuffing them with honey and spices and roasting them in embers.

Both summer squash and winter squash are gourds. The difference between them is mainly a matter of maturity, which affects how and when we use them. Summer squash is harvested when young, so the skins and seeds are soft and edible. We eat them soon after harvest, usually during the summer. Winter squash is harvested when fully mature, so the skins and seeds are hard and thick. Thanks to those sturdy shells, winter squash are good keepers, so they can be eaten after harvest in warm weather and also kept through the winter.

Cooks are rediscovering that winter squash, which includes edible pumpkins, are inexpensive, easy to prepare, and full of flavor. Heirloom pumpkins, many with curious shapes and colors, are also capturing our imaginations and charming our taste buds. ■

# Cushaw Pie

2/3 cup firmly packed
light brown sugar

1/2 cup granulated sugar

2 tablespoons
all-purpose flour

1/2 teaspoon kosher salt

1/2 teaspoon ground
cinnamon

1/8 teaspoon ground
allspice

1/8 teaspoon ground
cloves

1/8 teaspoon ground
ginger

1/8 teaspoon ground
nutmeg

3 large eggs

1 cup heavy cream

1 1/2 cups roasted
cushaw purée

1 (9-inch) deep-dish
pie shell (page 396
or store-bought)

Lightly sweetened
whipped cream,
for serving

Cushaw is an ancient variety of winter squash that was vitally important in the Native American diet. When we read of the Three Sisters practice of growing corn, beans, and squash together, that squash was often a cushaw. They are grown in limited numbers all over the South but have a strong association with the Appalachian Mountains. A cushaw is shaped like an enormous green striped pear with a longer, curved neck. The story is told that mountain farmers favored cushaws because a round punkin might roll down the hill and break their necks or, even worse, hurt their mules. The hooked neck of a cushaw would grab hold of something on its way down and stay put.

Cushaws have firm, sweet-smelling flesh that works beautifully in recipes that would usually be made with canned pumpkin, such as pie. Some cushaws are quite large, yielding enough roasted purée to make pies all winter. Use the directions for Winter Squash Purée (page 368) to prepare the cushaw.

MAKES 8 SERVINGS

1. Preheat the oven to 450°F. Place a rimmed baking sheet in the oven.

2. Whisk together the brown sugar, granulated sugar, flour, salt, cinnamon, allspice, cloves, ginger, and nutmeg in a small bowl.

3. Whisk the eggs in a large bowl until the whites and yolks are blended. Whisk in the cream and cushaw purée. Whisk in the brown sugar mixture until the filling is smooth but not frothy. Pour the filling into the pie shell. The filling should come just to the rim of the crust, so discard any excess.

4. Place the pie on the baking sheet and bake for 20 minutes. Reduce the oven temperature to 325°F and bake until the sides of the filling begin to puff and the center is nearly set but still jiggles oh-so-slightly when shaken gently, about 20 minutes more. Avoid testing the doneness with a knife, which can cause the filling to crack as it cooks. Take the pie off the baking sheet and place on a wire rack to cool to room temperature. The filling will continue to firm as it cools. Cover with plastic wrap and refrigerate for at least 1 hour and up to a day. Serve chilled or at room temperature, topped with a dollop of whipped cream.

WHAT ELSE WORKS? You can replace the cushaw with purée from a pie pumpkin, a sugar pumpkin, or another dense winter squash such as kabocha, red kuri, or blue Hubbard. Roasted sweet potato purée is also good.

## Winter Squash Purée

Use this method to prepare winter squash, including pumpkins, to use in recipes. It can also be eaten on its own. Be sure to use a type of squash or pumpkin that is meant to be cooked. It should have a relatively small seed cavity and thick, dense, dry flesh. Do not try to eat your jack-o'-lantern or other ornamental pumpkin. They are meant for carving, not cooking. Their flesh is very wet and flavorless, and no amount of draining or seasoning will redeem it.

Preheat the oven to 375°F. Depending on size, cut the squash into halves, quarters, or large wedges and scrape away the seeds and fibers. Place the pieces cut-side up on a rimmed baking sheet or inside a roasting pan. Brush the cut surface with vegetable oil. Roast until the flesh is very soft, 30 to 60 minutes, depending on the type of squash and the size of the pieces. When cool enough to handle, use a spoon to scrape the roasted flesh away from the skin. Purée the pulp in a food processor fitted with the metal blade or by running through a food mill fitted with the medium disc.

To be suitable for recipes, the finished purée must have the smooth, thick consistency of canned pumpkin. If the purée needs to be drained, transfer it into a large sieve lined with a double thickness of white paper towels or overlapping paper coffee filters set over a large bowl. Press a piece of plastic wrap directly onto the surface of the purée to keep it from drying out and refrigerate for at least 8 hours. Discard the accumulated liquid. Cover and refrigerate the purée for up to 3 days or freeze in airtight containers for up to 3 months.

One pound of whole pumpkin or squash yields about ½ cup of purée.

## Pasta with Roasted Winter Squash in Browned Butter, Sage, and Hazelnut Sauce

3 pounds winter squash, such as red kuri or butternut, peeled and seeded

2 tablespoons extra-virgin olive oil

Kosher salt and ground black pepper, to taste

1 pound uncooked orecchiette pasta (or other short, ridged pasta)

10 ounces baby spinach

8 tablespoons (1 stick) unsalted butter

3 tablespoons chopped fresh sage

½ cup coarsely chopped, skinned hazelnuts, toasted

1 cup freshly grated aged Gouda or Parmesan

This is one impressive pasta dish. It has layers of flavor and bright colors that look gorgeous served in a big pasta bowl. Browned butter is a classic sauce for pasta filled with winter squash, such as tortellini, cannelloni, or ravioli. This dish captures those same flavors.

Perhaps the only thing better than butter is browned butter. Butter is made up of water, milk solids, and butterfat. When it's browned, the water cooks away and the milk solids turn toasty brown and aromatic. This magic can happen only with real butter, so don't try it with margarine or butter blends.

I love to use aged Gouda cheese in this recipe. The flavor of the amber-colored cheese is rich and nutty with hints of caramel and butterscotch. It's delicious with the sweet squash and hazelnuts. It's easy to find in well-stocked stores, but the familiar, reliable flavor of excellent Parmesan is also good.

MAKES 6 TO 8 SERVINGS

① Preheat the oven to 400°F.

② Cut the squash into ¾-inch cubes and spread them in a single layer on a baking sheet lined with foil. Drizzle with the oil. Roast until tender, about 45 minutes. Season with salt and pepper, cover with foil to keep warm, and set aside.

③ Cook the pasta according to the package directions. Drain and return to the pot. Add the spinach and toss with tongs so that the heat of the pasta wilts the spinach. Add the squash and gently toss to combine. Season with salt and pepper, cover with foil to keep warm, and set aside.

④ Melt the butter in a small, heavy saucepan over medium heat. Let the butter cook, gently swirling the pan often, until the butter is covered in white foam and begins to brown in the center, 2 to 3 minutes. Lift the pan off the heat and continue swirling until the butter is deep golden brown throughout and smells nutty and toasty. Drop in the sage and nuts, which will bubble furiously at first. As soon as the sizzling stops, pour the browned butter over the pasta and squash and toss gently to combine. Sprinkle with the cheese and serve at once.

VARIATION: You can replace both the winter squash and the pasta with spaghetti squash. The larger and more mature the squash, the more the flesh will look like spaghetti. See page 311 for directions on how to cook spaghetti squash. Use a fork to pull out the strands into a large bowl. Toss the hot squash with the spinach and finish the recipe as usual, picking up with Step 3.

## Black Bean and Winter Squash Chili

2 tablespoons vegetable oil

1 medium onion, chopped (about 1 ¼ cups)

4 large garlic cloves, chopped

2 teaspoons dried Mexican oregano

2 teaspoons ground ancho chile

2 teaspoons smoked paprika (*pimentón*)

4 teaspoons ground cumin

½ teaspoon ground cloves

½ teaspoon ground coriander

1 teaspoon ground cinnamon

1 tablespoon brown sugar

1 tablespoon cocoa powder

1 to 2 cups vegetable stock or vegetable juice

1 (28-ounce) can whole fire-roasted tomatoes

2 cups home-cooked or canned black beans, drained and rinsed

3 cups peeled and seeded winter squash, cut into ¾-inch cubes

¼ cup peanut butter

1 teaspoon kosher salt, or to taste

1 ½ teaspoons hot sauce, or to taste

1 cup coarsely chopped cilantro or flat-leaf parsley leaves

*Pepitas* (roasted and salted pumpkin seeds), sour cream, and lime wedges, for serving

This is my vegetarian chili. It features beans and squash, one of the oldest ingredient combinations in Native American cookery, a cornerstone of what would evolve into southern cuisine. The chili cooks quickly, so it gets its depth of flavor from a generous dose of spices and seasonings reminiscent of *mole* sauce. It might seem odd to use all of these ingredients together, but this is really good chili, meatless or otherwise.

The chili tastes best when made at least one day ahead. It keeps for up to four days. It gets better each day.

MAKES ABOUT 2 QUARTS

1. Heat the oil in a large pot over medium heat. Add the onion and a pinch of salt and cook, stirring often, until softened, about 8 minutes.

2. Stir in the garlic, oregano, chile, smoked paprika, cumin, cloves, coriander, cinnamon, brown sugar, and cocoa. Cook, stirring constantly, for 1 minute. Reduce the heat if the spices begin to scorch. Stir in 1 cup of the stock, then add the tomatoes, beans, squash, and peanut butter. Break up the tomatoes with the side of the spoon.

3. Bring the soup to a boil, reduce the heat, and simmer, stirring occasionally, until the squash is tender and the flavors blend, about 20 minutes. If the chili gets too thick, stir in more stock as needed.

4. Season with the salt and hot sauce. For the best flavor, cool, cover, and refrigerate overnight. Just before serving, stir in the cilantro and check the seasoning. Serve hot, topped with *pepitas*, sour cream, and a squeeze of lime.

## Butternut Squash and Caramelized Onion Gratin

1  medium butternut squash (about 2 ½ pounds)

2  cups fresh bread crumbs (page 389)

2  cups freshly grated aged Gouda or Gruyère cheese

2  tablespoons chopped fresh rosemary

2  teaspoons chopped fresh thyme

4  tablespoons (½ stick) butter

4  cups thinly sliced onions (about 1 pound)

2  tablespoons sugar

½  teaspoon kosher salt

½  teaspoon ground black pepper

½  cup chicken stock

This is a wonderful fall dish. At the food-laden Thanksgiving table, everyone will appreciate the light texture and fresh herbs as a contrast to heavily sweetened and spiced casseroles.

Butternut squash is often the type of winter squash that is easiest to find, but feel free to experiment with other varieties. However, because the squash must be peeled and cubed, avoid thin-walled bumpy varieties that require a whole lot of work for very little flesh. To make peeling a butternut squash easier, start with a small, squat squash with a very thick neck. Most of the squash's bulbous bottom is filled with seeds, so a stout neck will yield the most usable squash.

MAKES 8 SERVINGS

1. Preheat the oven to 350°F. Butter a 9 × 13-inch glass or ceramic baking dish.

2. Cut the neck away from the base of the squash. Cut the stem end off the neck and then stand the neck upright on the cutting board, using its flat bottom to steady it. Use a heavy knife to cut away the hard skin in downward strokes. Trim away any remnants of skin with a sharp vegetable peeler. Cut the peeled neck into ½-inch-thick planks. Cut each plank into ½-inch cubes. Cut the walls of the base from around the seeds. Peel the pieces with the vegetable peeler and then place them flat-side down on the cutting board to cut into ½-inch cubes.

3. Mix the bread crumbs, cheese, rosemary, and thyme in a small bowl.

4. Melt the butter in a large skillet over medium-high heat. Add the onions and cook, stirring often, until softened, about 15 minutes. Stir in the squash, sugar, salt, and pepper and cook, stirring often, until the squash is tender and the onions are golden, about 10 minutes. Spread the squash mixture into the prepared baking dish. Pour the stock evenly over the top.

5. Cover the dish tightly with foil and bake for 15 minutes. Increase the oven temperature to 400°F. Uncover the squash, sprinkle the bread crumb mixture over the top and bake uncovered until the top is golden brown and crisp, about 20 minutes. Let the gratin rest for 10 minutes before serving warm.

# Whole Stuffed Cheese Pumpkin

1  medium cheese pumpkin (about 5 pounds)

Vegetable oil

1½  teaspoons kosher salt

¾  teaspoon ground black pepper

2  cups 1-inch cubes day-old Italian or French bread

½  cup half-and-half or heavy cream

4  thick bacon slices, cut crosswise into ¼-inch strips (about 4 ounces)

1  large onion, halved lengthwise and cut into thin strips (about 3 cups)

4  garlic cloves, thinly sliced

1  tablespoon chopped fresh thyme or sage

4  ounces aged cheese, such as Gruyère, cheddar, or Gouda, thinly sliced or crumbled

It's not unusual to see recipes for stuffing those little mini pumpkins or halved winter squashes, but here we're going large. In this recipe, the roasted pumpkin encases a rich filling that is similar to savory bread pudding. The practice of using a big pumpkin as both an ingredient and a cooking vessel dates back to Native American cooking and colonial hearth cooking. This stunning entrée dish is impressive enough to use as a centerpiece. If you omit the bacon, it can be the focal point for a vegetarian holiday meal.

Be sure to use a roasting pumpkin, not a carving pumpkin. I am fond of the cheese pumpkin, so named for its light brown, round, squat, flat-bottomed shape that resembles the wooden boxes once used to store cheese. There are other heirloom pumpkins with similar shape and texture.

MAKES 8 SERVINGS

1. Preheat the oven to 350°F.

2. To carve out the lid, use a short, sharp knife (preferably serrated) to cut out a circle midway between the stem and the outer edge of the pumpkin, as though starting a jack-o'-lantern. Use short strokes and a sawing motion. Lift out the lid and set it aside. Use your hands or a small sharp spoon to scoop out and discard the seeds and wet fibers. Rub a little oil over the outside of the pumpkin and set it in a baking pan or Dutch oven to catch the drips and the rare surprise collapses. Generously season the inside of the pumpkin with the salt and pepper.

3. Place the bread in a medium bowl. Pour the half-and-half over the bread and set aside to soak until needed.

4. Cook the bacon in a large skillet over medium-high heat, stirring often, until well browned. Stir in the onion and a pinch of salt and cook, stirring often, until the bacon is crisp and the onion is soft, about 5 minutes. Stir in the garlic and thyme and cook for 30 seconds.

5. Spoon half of the bacon mixture into the pumpkin. Top with half of the bread and half of the cheese. Repeat the layers. The pumpkin should be full, but not packed hard with stuffing. Replace the lid.

6. Bake until a thin paring knife easily pierces the shell of the pumpkin, about 90 minutes. Remove from the oven and let sit for 15 minutes before serving hot. You can serve it by slicing the pumpkin into wedges, or simply dig in with a giant spoon, making sure to scoop out some tender pumpkin flesh as part of each serving. The pumpkin and filling will stay warm for at least 1 hour, but the outside of the pumpkin starts to wrinkle as it cools and looks like Cinderella's carriage in the wee hours after the ball.

## Roasted Winter Squash Wedges and Rings

2 pounds winter squash

3 tablespoons extra-virgin olive oil

1 teaspoon kosher salt, or to taste

½ teaspoon ground black pepper, or to taste

2 to 3 tablespoons honey, cane syrup, molasses, sorghum, pomegranate molasses, maple syrup, or aged balsamic vinegar, for serving

When cut into simple rings, chunks, or wedges, winter squash cooks quickly and makes a reliable go-to side dish. To spruce it up just a little, drizzle on a simple, subtly sweet seasoning just before serving. Large pieces of roasted squash are good warm or at room temperature, which makes them great for entertaining or buffets. They are also good on simple green salads dressed with vinaigrette and topped with shaved Manchego cheese and chopped Medjool dates.

MAKES 4 SERVINGS

1. Preheat the oven to 425°F.

2. Depending on the shape and size of the squash, cut in halves, quarters, wedges, or rings. Scoop out and discard the seeds and strings. Peel the pieces if you wish.

3. Arrange the pieces in a single layer on a lightly oiled, rimmed baking sheet. Brush the cut sides with the oil and sprinkle with the salt and pepper. Roast until the squash is tender, 20 to 40 minutes, depending on the size of the pieces.

4. Serve warm or at room temperature, left plain or drizzled with 2 to 3 tablespoons of one of the sweet toppings.

# ZUCCHINI

**Its name is Italian, but, like its squashy cousins,** zucchini is a native
of Central America and arrived in the South through northward migra-
tion and with immigrating colonists from Europe. The word means "little
squash" in Italian, but zucchini are notorious shape shifters, exploding
from too small to notice to monstrous, seemingly in an instant and certainly overnight. For centuries, gardeners avoided this problem by cultivating zucchini solely for its delicious blossoms, never giving the vegetables
a chance to become overgrown. It was also a strategy to stave off the onslaught of excess zucchini. The vegetable itself didn't gain widespread popularity until there were cooks and eaters who appreciated that zucchini,
unlike more demure and delicate summer squashes, can hold their own
with stronger, bolder seasonings such as garlic and chile peppers.

As a type of summer squash, zucchini can be eaten raw or cooked. The
skins and seeds are fully edible, although those prospects lose their appeal
as they grow. Not all zucchini are long, slender, and dark green. Zucchini
can also be round or bulbous and can come in light green, gold, and yellow and have stripes and spots. Small zucchini can resemble other summer squashes to the point that any differences might be only in the eye
of the beholder. ■

# Dark Chocolate Zucchini Cake with Ganache Glaze

## CAKE

- 4 ounces high-quality bittersweet chocolate, coarsely chopped
- ¼ cup vegetable oil
- 1 ¼ cups sifted all-purpose unbleached flour
- ¼ cup unsweetened cocoa powder
- 1 teaspoon baking powder
- 1 teaspoon baking soda
- ½ teaspoon fine sea salt
- 4 tablespoons (½ stick) unsalted butter, at room temperature
- ¾ cup sugar
- 2 large eggs
- 1 teaspoon pure vanilla extract
- ¼ cup well-shaken buttermilk
- 1 ½ cups peeled, seeded, and grated zucchini

## GANACHE GLAZE

- ⅓ cup heavy cream
- 6 ounces fine-quality bittersweet chocolate, coarsely chopped
- 1 tablespoon light corn syrup

This is a very good chocolate cake. It's moist and tender with dark chocolate intensity glazed with a shiny coat of rich ganache. Oh, and it happens to contain grated zucchini. The vegetable is undetectable, so if you don't tell, they won't ask.

Be sure to use a high-quality bittersweet chocolate that is smooth and shiny with no dull gray residue on the outside. The gray bloom indicates that at some point the chocolate got warm enough for part of its cocoa butter to melt, rise to the surface, and solidify. This doesn't affect the taste of the chocolate, but it can make the ganache dull and cloudy.

MAKES 8 SERVINGS

1. For the cake: Preheat the oven to 350°F. Grease and flour a 9-inch cake pan.
2. Heat the chocolate and oil in a small saucepan over low heat until the edges of the chocolate begin to soften and melt. Remove from the heat and stir until the chocolate is completely melted and smooth. Set aside.
3. Sift together the flour, cocoa, baking powder, baking soda, and salt into a large bowl. In another large bowl, beat the butter and sugar until light and fluffy with an electric mixer set to high speed, about 3 minutes. Scrape down the sides of the bowl with a rubber spatula. Add the eggs one at a time, beating well after each addition, then beat in the vanilla. With the mixer set to low speed, add the flour mixture in thirds, alternating with half of the buttermilk and beating each time only until the batter is smooth. Stir in the melted chocolate mixture. Use a rubber spatula to fold in the zucchini.
4. Scrape the batter into the prepared pan and bake until a tester inserted in the center comes out clean, 35 to 40 minutes. Cool the cake in the pan on a wire rack for 10 minutes, and then turn it out onto the rack to cool to room temperature before glazing.
5. For the ganache: Bring the cream to a simmer over medium heat in a saucepan. Remove the pan from the heat and add the chocolate and corn syrup. Stir until the chocolate is melted and smooth. Let cool for 3 minutes.
6. Leave the cake on the rack and set the rack in a rimmed baking sheet to catch the drips. Pour the ganache over the cake, smoothing with a spatula and letting the excess drip down the sides. Let the cake sit until the ganache is set, at least 1 hour. Serve the cake at room temperature.

## Crispy Zucchini and Potato Skillet Cakes

2 small zucchini
(about 8 ounces)

1 medium russet potato
or other starchy
potato, peeled
(about 8 ounces)

½ small red onion
(about 2 ounces)

¼ cup finely crushed
saltine cracker crumbs

1 large egg,
lightly beaten

1 teaspoon kosher salt,
plus more to taste

½ teaspoon ground
black pepper

Vegetable oil,
for pan-frying

These little cakes are as crisp as chips on the edges with slightly creamy centers, just like good latkes. They make a great side dish, but they also make a lovely little appetizer when topped with the sour cream and caviar or smoked fish, or with something zesty like Tomato Jam (page 354) or Sassy Pepper Jam (page 88).

MAKES ABOUT 1 DOZEN

1. Grate the zucchini, potato, and onion into long, thin strands on the large holes of a box grater or with the shredding disc of a food processor. Transfer into a colander and let drain for 3 minutes. Press the vegetables to extract as much liquid as possible and let drain for another 2 minutes. Pick up the vegetables in small handfuls, squeeze out as much liquid as possible and then transfer into a large bowl. Stir in the crackers, egg, salt, and pepper.

2. Pour oil to a depth of ¼ inch into a large, heavy skillet (preferably cast-iron) and heat over medium-high heat until shimmering hot. Cover a wire rack with several layers of paper towels and keep near the stove to drain the cakes. (See page 106 for tips on pan-frying.)

3. Working in batches of 4 or 5 cakes at a time, spoon rounded tablespoons of the vegetable mixture into the skillet and gently flatten the mound into a cake that is about ½-inch thick in the center. Cook the cakes until the edges are golden brown and they are set in the center, about 2 minutes, then flip them over. (If they bend in the center when you try to turn them, they're not ready.) Brown the other side, about 2 minutes more. Transfer the cakes to the paper towels to drain. Add a little more oil to the skillet between batches if needed.

4. Sprinkle the hot cakes with a little more salt and serve hot.

WHAT ELSE WORKS? You can replace the zucchini with summer squash or more potato. Do not omit the potato because its starch helps keep the cakes intact.

# Italian Sausage and Tortellini Soup

2 teaspoons extra-virgin olive oil

1 pound sweet or hot Italian sausage

1 medium onion, peeled and chopped (about 2 cups)

2 large garlic cloves, finely chopped

2 teaspoons dried Italian herb blend

½ cup dry red wine

4 cups chicken stock

1 (28-ounce) can crushed tomatoes

1 (8-ounce) can tomato sauce

2 small zucchini, sliced (about 2 cups)

1 large carrot, sliced (about 1 cup)

1 medium red bell pepper, diced (about 1 cup)

1 teaspoon kosher salt, plus more to taste

12 to 16 ounces cheese tortellini

Ground black pepper, to taste

Pinch of crushed red pepper flakes

Grated Asiago or Parmesan cheese, for serving

I have made untold gallons of this hearty soup over the years. It is one of those prized recipes that nearly everyone gobbles up with rave reviews. It's quick, easy, homey, and filling. Served with hot garlic bread, it's a complete meal. Doubled or tripled, it's an easy and economical way to serve a crowd. The next time you need to take food to someone, take this.

This soup does not keep well after the tortellini are added. As the soup sits, even in the refrigerator, the cooked tortellini soak up all of the liquid, leaving them soggy and the rest of the soup too dry. So if you plan to serve leftovers for a few days, cook and store the tortellini separately and stir them into the soup when reheating.

MAKES ABOUT 2 QUARTS

1. Heat the oil in a large, heavy saucepan or small Dutch oven over medium-high heat.

2. Slit the sausage casings open lengthwise with the tip of a knife, pull out the sausage, and discard the casings. Break the sausage into pieces the size of small meatballs and add to the pot. Cook the sausage, stirring occasionally, until the pieces are browned, about 10 minutes. Transfer into a medium bowl.

3. Drain off all but 1 tablespoon of the drippings from the pan. Stir in the onion and a pinch of salt and cook, stirring often, until beginning to soften, about 5 minutes. Stir in the garlic and herbs and cook, stirring, until fragrant, about 1 minute.

4. Stir in the wine, scraping up any browned bits from the bottom of the pan. Stir in the stock, tomatoes, tomato sauce, zucchini, carrot, bell pepper, and salt. Bring to a boil, reduce the heat, and simmer until the vegetables are almost tender, about 15 minutes.

5. Stir in the sausage and tortellini and simmer until the pasta is al dente. (The cooking time depends on the type of tortellini; follow the package directions.) Season with salt, pepper, and crushed red pepper flakes. Serve hot, topped with a sprinkling of cheese.

# Easy Cheesy Zucchini Squares

Vegetable oil spray

3 cups grated zucchini, peeled and seeded if necessary

2 teaspoons kosher salt

1 ½ cups all-purpose flour

1 tablespoon baking powder

3 large eggs

½ cup vegetable oil

1 teaspoon high-quality lemon pepper

2 teaspoons chopped fresh thyme

1 cup finely chopped onion

2 cups grated sharp cheddar cheese

These savory, cheesy squares can be served hot or at room temperature, and they reheat well in the microwave. I've served them as part of dinner, for brunch, in a picnic lunch, and as a hearty snack. They are also tasty cut into small bite-sized squares and served as hors d'oeuvres. To dress them up a little, top with a bit of chopped fresh tomato or olive tapenade.

The squares are seasoned with lemon pepper, an old-fashioned spice blend often used in seafood dishes. In addition to dried lemon peel and black pepper, high-quality brands contain a variety of aromatic spices that quickly add flavor to green vegetables.

MAKES 8 SERVINGS OR 36 HORS D'OEUVRES

1. Preheat the oven to 350°F. Mist the inside of a 7 × 11-inch glass baking dish with the spray.

2. Stir together the zucchini and salt in a colander and let drain for 15 minutes. Press out the liquid and let drain another 15 minutes. Pick up the zucchini in small handfuls and squeeze out as much liquid as possible, transferring into a small bowl.

3. Whisk together the flour and baking powder in a large bowl. In a small bowl, whisk the eggs until the whites and yolks are blended, then whisk in the oil, lemon pepper, and thyme. Pour the egg mixture into the flour mixture and mix well. Use a rubber spatula to fold in the zucchini, onion, and cheese. The batter will be very stiff. Scrape it into the prepared baking dish and press it evenly into the corners.

4. Bake until the top is golden brown, about 30 minutes. Cool on a wire rack for at least 5 minutes before serving.

## Baked Zucchini Blossoms
## Stuffed with Cheese

2 ounces soft, fresh
  goat cheese (chèvre)

1 teaspoon kosher salt

½ teaspoon ground
  black pepper

¼ teaspoon paprika

24 zucchini blossoms

2 tablespoons extra-
  virgin olive oil, divided

The idea of eating edible flowers sounds better than it usually turns out. It's hard to find flowers that are actually safe to eat — and even then most don't taste very good. The major exceptions are zucchini, squash, and pumpkin blossoms. In some gardens, the plants are grown for the flowers instead of the full-size vegetable. The blossoms have a subtle, pleasant flavor, like a whispered version of the vegetable. Although you can harvest female blossoms as a way to stave off the onslaught of too much zucchini, most people think the male blossoms taste better, and using the males doesn't decrease the vegetable yield.

The challenge when stuffing blossoms is to get the soft, gooey filling inside without ripping them apart. I use firm little balls of chilled goat cheese that can be tucked neatly into the blossoms. The blossoms bake quickly, and although they collapse into tender pillows, they retain their bright, appealing color.

MAKES 4 TO 6 SERVINGS

1. Form the cheese into 24 small balls the size of marbles. Stir together the salt, pepper, and paprika on a plate. Roll the balls in the salt mixture to season them. Cover loosely and refrigerate until the cheese is firm.

2. Preheat the oven to 425°F. Lightly oil a glass pie plate or shallow baking dish.

3. Gently rinse the blossoms in a bowl of cool water and pat dry. Trim and discard the green stems and short green sepals without cutting into the base of the blossom. Gently pry open the blossoms and break off and discard the fuzzy centers. If the petals stubbornly refuse to separate, use a small sharp knife to cut a small incision in one side of the blossom. Tuck a ball of cheese inside the blossoms and gently twist or fold the petals to enclose the cheese. Place the stuffed blossoms in a single layer in the prepared dish, working from the outside in to make a pretty spiral if you wish. Drizzle with 1 tablespoon of the oil and cover the pie plate with aluminum foil.

4. Bake until the blossoms are soft, about 15 minutes. Carefully remove the foil because steam will billow out. Drizzle with the remaining 1 tablespoon of oil and serve at once.

WHAT ELSE WORKS? You can use blossoms from summer squash, winter squash, or pumpkins. Vary the size of the cheese balls according to the size of the blossoms. You can use soft herbed cheese, such as Boursin, instead of the goat cheese, but omit the salt, pepper, and paprika. You can also use cream cheese instead of the goat cheese, but increase the salt, pepper, and paprika.

# Raw Zucchini Salad with Tomato Vinaigrette

SALAD

4 small zucchini (about 1 pound total), ends trimmed

2 teaspoons kosher salt

¼ cup high-quality ripe olives (such as Kalamata or Manzanilla), pitted and coarsely chopped

¼ cup coarsely chopped Marcona almonds or whole pine nuts, lightly toasted

10 small basil leaves

TOMATO VINAIGRETTE

1 ½ cups peeled, seeded, and chopped fresh tomato

1 garlic clove

1 tablespoon fresh orange juice or lemon juice

¼ cup extra-virgin olive oil

Kosher salt and ground black pepper, to taste

When zucchini are small and tender, they can be shaved into paper-thin rounds or long ribbons and served raw as a salad. Thin-skinned zucchini doesn't need to be peeled, so the ribbons are bordered with stripes of color. This is a pretty way to take advantage of zucchini of different sizes, shapes, and colors.

The salad is dressed with tomato vinaigrette and a smattering of crunchy almonds, salty olives, and fragrant basil. The tomato vinaigrette can also be used on other salads. You can transform the vinaigrette recipe by changing the variety and color of the tomatoes, from tart green to mild yellow.

MAKES 4 TO 6 SERVINGS

1. For the salad: Use a vegetable slicer or vegetable peeler to shave the zucchini into long, paper-thin ribbons or rounds. Transfer into a colander, toss with the salt, and let drain while you make the vinaigrette.

2. For the vinaigrette: Purée the tomato, garlic, and orange juice in a blender. With the blender running, slowly add the oil in a thin stream. Season with salt and pepper.

3. To assemble the salad, pat the zucchini dry with paper towels and arrange on a serving platter. Drizzle with just enough tomato vinaigrette to moisten. (You might not need all of it.) Scatter the olives, almonds, and basil over the top and serve immediately.

WHAT ELSE WORKS? You can replace some or all of the zucchini with summer squash.

## Zucchini Frittata with Smoky Roasted Red Pepper Sauce

2 tablespoons extra-virgin olive oil

2 cups thinly sliced or grated zucchini

8 large eggs

4 scallions, thinly sliced (white and tender green parts)

1 teaspoon kosher salt

½ teaspoon ground black pepper

5 ounces Boursin garlic-herb cheese

Smoky Roasted Red Pepper Sauce, for serving (recipe follows)

A frittata is a concept or technique more than a fixed recipe. It's an easy one-pan meal that is open to endless variations by changing the vegetable. Any single vegetable or medley that tastes good with eggs is a candidate. You can change the type of cheese or skip the cheese. You can also add cooked or cured meat. You can add fresh herbs. You get the picture. Although it is often served warm, a frittata is also good served at room temperature. In Italy, frittata is served between slices of good bread as a sandwich.

The Smoky Roasted Red Pepper Sauce is a nice finish, adding both flavor and color, but it is optional. Other possible sauces for a frittata are Skillet-Roasted Cherry Tomatoes (page 347) or your favorite tomato sauce, pesto, or tapenade.

MAKES 4 SERVINGS

1. Preheat the oven to 350°F.

2. Heat the oil in a 9- or 10-inch well-seasoned cast-iron or ovenproof nonstick skillet over medium-high heat. Add the zucchini and cook, stirring often, until softened, about 5 minutes.

3. Whisk the eggs in a medium bowl until the whites and yolks are blended, then whisk in the scallions, salt, and pepper. Pour the eggs over the vegetables. Reduce the heat to medium-low and cook without stirring until the eggs start to set around the edge, about 2 minutes. Use a heatproof rubber spatula to lift the edge, and then gently tilt the pan so that the uncooked egg runs underneath. Continue until the eggs are mostly set but still moist on top, about 3 minutes. Crumble the cheese over the top.

4. Transfer the skillet to the oven and bake until the eggs are set on top, about 3 minutes. Let the frittata cool in the skillet for 5 minutes, then run the spatula around the edge and slide the frittata onto a serving plate. Cut into wedges and serve warm or at room temperature, topped with a spoonful of Smoky Roasted Red Pepper Sauce.

WHAT ELSE WORKS? You can use nearly any vegetable in a frittata, just adjust the cooking time in Step 2 as needed. This is also a good way to use leftover cooked vegetables.

## Smoky Roasted Red Pepper Sauce

4 tablespoons extra-virgin olive oil

1 large yellow onion, finely chopped (about 2 cups)

4 garlic cloves, thinly sliced

2 cups chopped roasted red bell or other sweet pepper (page 314 or store-bought)

¼ cup sherry vinegar

1 teaspoon smoked paprika (*pimentón*)

1 tablespoon tomato paste

1 teaspoon sugar

Kosher salt and ground black pepper, to taste

This sauce tastes like silky, sophisticated, smoky ketchup. It is great on eggs, potatoes, and grilled meat, particularly steak. The secret ingredient is smoked paprika, also known as *pimentón*. Smoked paprika is made from peppers that are dried for weeks over smoldering oak before they are ground, which gives them a deep, natural smokehouse flavor. It comes in three varieties: sweet (*dulce*), medium (*agridulce*), and hot (*picante*), although even the hot isn't fiery.

MAKES ABOUT 2 CUPS

1. Heat the oil in a large skillet over medium-high heat.
2. Add the onion and cook, stirring occasionally, until softened, about 8 minutes. Add the garlic and peppers and cook, stirring occasionally, for 5 minutes. Add the vinegar, smoked paprika, tomato paste, and sugar.
3. Purée in a blender (working in batches to not fill the blender more than half full) and return it to the pot, or purée the sauce directly in the pot with an immersion blender. Season with salt and pepper and balance the flavors with more vinegar, smoked paprika, or sugar, if needed. Serve warm or at room temperature. Store covered and refrigerated for up to 3 days. Stir well and check the seasoning before serving.

## Grilled Vegetable Ratatouille

1 medium zucchini

1 medium summer squash

1 medium, slender Asian eggplant

1 large red, yellow, or orange bell pepper or other sweet pepper

1 large red onion

4 Roma tomatoes

Vegetable oil, for brushing

3 tablespoons extra-virgin olive oil

2 tablespoons red wine vinegar

6 basil leaves, cut into thin ribbons

1 teaspoon dried oregano or marjoram

Kosher salt and ground black pepper, to taste

Ratatouille is a classic medley of cooked zucchini, summer squash, eggplant, peppers, onions, and tomatoes. It's a great way to use up vegetables that surge into ripeness during the height of summer. In this recipe, the vegetables are grilled instead of roasted or simmered. (Note: We southerners grill, not barbecue. Barbecue is a noun, not a verb.) This recipe is written for outdoor grilling. You can also cook the vegetables indoors on a ridged grill pan or an electric countertop grill, but the flavor is not the same.

When I grill vegetables, I season them with dressing after they are cooked instead of marinating them beforehand. Raw vegetables are hard and solid, so they can't absorb the liquid. It's like trying to marinate ping-pong balls—they get wet on the surface, but nothing soaks in. In contrast, cooked vegetables are soft enough to absorb the dressing.

MAKES 6 SERVINGS

(1) Preheat a gas grill or charcoal grill for direct cooking over medium heat. For a gas grill, preheat the burners on high, covered, for 10 minutes and then reduce the heat to medium. For a charcoal grill, open the vents in the bottom of the grill and light the charcoal. (Natural hardwood charcoal is best.) When the coals are covered in gray ash (about 15 minutes after lighting), spread them in an even layer. When you can hold your hand 5 inches above the grate for 5 seconds, the heat is medium.

(2) While the grill preheats, trim the vegetables. Cut the zucchini, squash, and eggplant crosswise or on the diagonal into ⅓-inch-thick slices. Keep them about the same thickness so they'll cook at the same rate. Cut the pepper into wide planks from around the core. Cut the onion into ½-inch-wide wedges, leaving a small piece of the root attached to hold the wedge together. Cut the tomatoes in half lengthwise. Brush the vegetables with only enough vegetable oil to barely moisten them. (Excess oil will drip off the vegetables and cause flare-ups.)

(3) To keep the vegetables from falling through the grate, place them in a vegetable basket or on a mesh grilling screen. Grill the vegetables, turning frequently with tongs, until they begin to soften and are lightly charred in spots, about 5 minutes. Transfer the cooked vegetables into a large bowl and cover to hold in the steam. The steam should finish cooking the vegetables; if it doesn't, spread them onto a rimmed baking sheet and finish cooking them in a 400°F oven.

(4) Whisk together the olive oil, vinegar, basil, and oregano in a small bowl. Season generously with salt and pepper. Pour over the hot vegetables and toss to coat. Serve the vegetables warm or at room temperature. Store covered and refrigerated for up to 4 days.

WHAT ELSE WORKS? You can vary the combination or proportion of the vegetables, but you need a total of 2 to 2 ½ pounds. You can replace the olive oil mixture with your favorite bottled vinaigrette or marinade.

## GRILLED VEGETABLE RATATOUILLE REDUX

· · · · · · · · · · · · · · · · · · · · · · · · · · · · · · · · · · · · · · · · · · · · · · · · · · · · · · · · · · ·

Because Grilled Vegetable Ratatouille is so useful, I like to make extra so I'll have leftovers to use in one or more of these recipes.

## Grilled Vegetable Ratatouille Salad

This salad is beautiful and full of flavor. It tastes best served at room temperature, so it's great for buffets or outdoor events. This is really good with steak.

MAKES 6 SERVINGS

6 lightly packed cups leafy salad greens

Balsamic Vinaigrette (recipe follows) or Pesto Vinaigrette (page 343)

1 recipe Grilled Vegetable Ratatouille, at room temperature (page 383)

1 cup small marinated mozzarella balls, crumbled goat cheese, or coarsely grated Parmesan cheese

¼ cup pine nuts, toasted

½ cup brine-cured ripe black olives, such as Kalamata

3 tablespoons chopped fresh basil

2 tablespoons chopped fresh chives or scallions

1 tablespoon chopped fresh marjoram

(1) Toss the salad greens with enough vinaigrette to moisten in a large bowl and then spread on a large serving platter. Spoon the ratatouille over the greens.

(2) Scatter the cheese, pine nuts, olives, basil, chives, and marjoram over the top.

(3) Drizzle with the rest of the vinaigrette and serve at room temperature.

## Balsamic Vinaigrette

3 tablespoons balsamic vinegar

2 teaspoons Dijon mustard

1 garlic clove, finely chopped

½ cup extra-virgin olive oil

½ teaspoon kosher salt, or to taste

¼ teaspoon ground black pepper, or to taste

A few years ago, few people had heard of balsamic vinaigrette. Now it's indispensable. I often make vinaigrette in a jar so that I can shake the ingredients into an emulsion instead of whisking. Plus, any leftovers are already in a container to stash in the fridge. See page 163 for tips on making vinaigrette.

MAKES ABOUT ¾ CUP

1. Place the vinegar, mustard, garlic, and oil in a small glass jar with a tight-fitting lid. Close the jar and shake vigorously to blend. Season with the salt and pepper. Shake again just before serving.

2. Use soon or refrigerate for up to 1 week. Return to room temperature, shake vigorously, and check the seasoning before serving.

## Fish Fillets Baked in Grilled Vegetable Ratatouille Sauce

1 recipe Grilled Vegetable Ratatouille (page 383)

1 (14 ½-ounce) can tomato purée or crushed tomatoes

1 tablespoon finely chopped garlic

2 tablespoons red wine vinegar

2 tablespoons extra-virgin olive oil

6 skinless, boneless, mild fish fillets (each about 6 ounces and 1 inch thick)

1 teaspoon kosher salt, or to taste

½ teaspoon ground black pepper, or to taste

Hot, freshly cooked rice, pasta, or bread, for serving

If you grill the ratatouille on the weekend so that it's ready and waiting in the refrigerator, this is a quick weeknight meal. For best results, use thick, firm fillets that hold their shape when cooked.

MAKES 6 SERVINGS

1. Preheat the oven to 375°F.

2. Combine the ratatouille, tomatoes, garlic, and vinegar in the bowl of a food processor fitted with the metal blade. Pulse until the vegetables are finely chopped but not puréed.

3. Heat the oil in a large skillet over high heat until shimmering hot. Add the ratatouille mixture. It will bubble and sizzle furiously at first. Cook, stirring, until the vegetables are very soft and the mixture has the consistency of thick pasta sauce. Transfer into a 9 × 13-inch glass or ceramic baking dish.

4. Sprinkle both sides of the fillets with salt and pepper and arrange them in a single layer in the dish, pushing them down into the sauce.

5. Bake until the fish is just opaque in the center, 15 to 20 minutes. Serve hot over rice, pasta, or thick slices of grilled or toasted bread.

# Grilled Vegetable Ratatouille Meatloaf

1 ½ cups Grilled Vegetable Ratatouille (page 383)

1 cup fresh bread crumbs (page 389)

¼ cup whole milk or evaporated milk

2 large eggs, lightly beaten

3 tablespoons finely chopped flat-leaf parsley

1 ½ tablespoons Worcestershire sauce

2 tablespoons grainy Dijon mustard

½ teaspoon Tabasco sauce

2 teaspoons kosher salt

1 teaspoon pepper

1 ½ pounds meatloaf mix or ground chuck

½ cup ketchup

2 tablespoons cider vinegar or distilled white vinegar

1 tablespoon brown sugar

Good meatloaf is prime comfort food. This is one of my favorites, for several reasons. First, it's moist and tasty and doesn't need to be swamped with ketchup. Second, the meat is formed into individual loaves and baked on a baking sheet, so the entire surface has that same rich, slightly caramelized crust that pan loaves get only on top. Third, the loaves freeze well, so you can make extra and pull out only the number of servings you need at the time, just right for busy families eating on different schedules or small families that can't finish a full-size loaf in one meal.

The meat mixture also makes really good stuffed peppers.

MAKES 6 SERVINGS

1. Preheat the oven to 400°F. Line a baking sheet with foil.
2. Place the ratatouille in the bowl of a food processor fitted with the metal blade. Pulse until the vegetables are finely chopped but not puréed.
3. Stir together the bread crumbs, milk, eggs, parsley, Worcestershire, mustard, Tabasco, salt, and pepper in a large bowl. Add the meat and ratatouille. Mix gently with your hands just until combined; don't overwork the meat. The mixture should be very moist but not drippy.
4. Using a 1-cup measuring cup, drop 6 equal mounds of the meat mixture onto the prepared baking sheet and pat gently to form loaves about 1 ½-inches thick with flat tops.
5. Stir together the ketchup, vinegar, and brown sugar in a small bowl and spoon over the tops and sides of the loaves. Bake until the meat is no longer pink and an instant-read thermometer inserted into the center of a loaf registers 155°F, about 20 minutes.
6. Turn on the broiler and place the loaves about 3 inches from the heat to broil until the glaze slightly caramelizes, 1 to 2 minutes. Serve warm.

MAKE-AHEAD NOTE: To freeze, let the loaves cool to room temperature. Wrap them individually in plastic wrap and freeze on a flat surface so that they'll hold their shape. When solid, you can put them in a freezer bag. To reheat, unwrap the frozen loaves and place on a baking sheet. Bake in a 350°F oven until heated through, about 25 minutes. You can also gently thaw the loaves and reheat in the microwave, but it tends to make them dry and unattractive.

# BASICS

## Crème Fraîche

2 cups heavy cream (36 to 40 percent butterfat), preferably not ultra-pasteurized

½ cup well-shaken buttermilk, plain yogurt with live cultures, or cultured sour cream (not regular sour cream)

I cannot cook without crème fraîche. I love how it tastes and how it performs in recipes. Crème fraîche has a delicate flavor that is more cultured than fresh cream but less tangy than sour cream. Its thick, smooth, velvety consistency is midway between yogurt and cream cheese. Unlike volatile heavy cream or acidic sour cream, it does not curdle when heated. When sweetened and whipped, it can be used on desserts in place of whipped cream. One cheese expert said that comparing crème fraîche to commercial sour cream is like comparing foie gras to luncheon meat.

Despite its overly accented name, crème fraîche is a very simple dairy product. In the days before pasteurization and instant refrigeration, the natural cultures found in fresh cream caused it to thicken when left sitting out. Cooks did this deliberately to create what old cookbooks often called soured cream or clabber. With today's pasteurized, refrigerated cream, we have to kick-start the thickening with buttermilk, cultured yogurt, or cultured sour cream. The benign live cultures multiply and protect the cream from any harmful bacteria.

Although you can buy containers of crème fraîche at well-stocked grocery stores, it's easy to make. If at all possible, use cream that has not been ultra-pasteurized. This type of cream usually comes from nearby farmstead dairies because it doesn't have the long shelf life required for wide commercial distribution.

MAKES ABOUT 2 ½ CUPS

(1) Bring the cream and buttermilk to room temperature by letting them sit on the counter for 1 to 2 hours before you begin. Chilled ingredients take much longer to thicken or might not thicken properly. Pour the cream into a clean glass jar or bowl. Whisk in the buttermilk. Close the jar or cover the bowl with plastic wrap and let sit in a warm, draft-free place (ideally 78°F to 84°F) until the cream thickens to the consistency of soft custard, 24 to 36 hours. The colder the room, the longer it takes to thicken.

(2) Stir well, cover tightly, and refrigerate to stop the cultures from growing. Store refrigerated for up to 3 weeks. The crème fraîche will get tangier as it ages. If any whey collects on the surface, either pour it off or whisk it back in.

NOTE: After the first batch of crème fraîche, you can use some of it instead of the buttermilk as the starter in subsequent batches. If you continue this way, each batch will be a little thicker, a little creamier, and a little more flavorful.

## Fresh Bread Crumbs

If a recipe specifies fresh versus dry bread crumbs, there's a good reason. Each type of crumb serves a different purpose. Dry crumbs eliminate moisture and add crunch. Fresh crumbs help retain moisture and add bulk. Fresh crumbs are best when made from fresh or slightly stale crusty bread, such as a baguette. The bread crumbs should be fairly large, about the size of green peas.

For a small amount of crumbs to use at once, just tear the bread into small pieces by hand. To make enough to keep on hand, fill the bowl of a food processor fitted with a metal blade about half full with small chunks of bread. Pulse the processor until the crumbs are the right size. The pulsing makes the bread bounce around so that it gets chopped evenly. Store the crumbs in a glass jar with a tight-fitting lid (such as a 1-quart canning jar) in the refrigerator for up to two weeks. The glass jar keeps the crumbs usable longer than does a plastic container or bag. Avoid the temptation to freeze the crumbs. Even when stored in airtight containers, they usually wind up tasting freezer burned.

## Crispy Bacon with Rendered Drippings

This technique yields very crisp bacon and plenty of delicious drippings to use in other recipes. Start with the highest quality bacon you can find. (I am devoted to Allan Benton's bacon, available from bentonshams.com.) A standard 12- to 16-ounce package of sliced bacon yields about 2 cups cooked bacon and ½ cup drippings, depending on the fattiness of the meat.

While the bacon is still cold and firm from the refrigerator, place the entire stack of slices on a cutting board and use a large, sharp knife to cut it crosswise into ½-inch strips. Don't worry about separating the pieces; they'll come apart as they cook. Place the bacon in a large cast-iron skillet and cook over medium-high heat, stirring occasionally, until the bacon releases most of its fat, about 5 minutes. Reduce the heat to medium-low and continue cooking, stirring occasionally, until the pieces of bacon are very crisp and browned, about 15 minutes more. Taste the bacon as soon as it gets firm; some heavily smoked bacons taste better when left less crisp because additional cooking can turn them a little bitter. The fat in the skillet should be warm enough that it is covered in small white bubbles (like the foam on a glass of soda pop) but not so hot that it pops, sizzles, or scorches.

Use a slotted spoon to transfer the bacon to paper towels to drain. Carefully pour the drippings into a clean jar, leaving any sediment in the skillet. Or pour the drippings through a funnel lined with a paper coffee filter into the clean jar. Cover and refrigerate indefinitely. (Truth is, I never saw anyone refrigerate drippings until I was grown. Most cooks I knew kept bacon drippings in a little canister, a jar, or even a coffee mug within easy reach of the stove. Yes, some canister sets included one piece specifically for straining and keeping bacon grease.)

## A Pork Fat Manifesto

A word about pork, especially pork fat. Few aspects of southern vegetable cookery stir up more debate than traditional pork seasoning. Some people never cease to praise it, and some people never cease to condemn it. There are a lot of social and culinary issues tied up in the use of pork fat in the South, but it all started with an elemental need for fat to use for cooking and seasoning.

Every culture in the world cooks with the fat of the land, the type easiest to find, afford, and store. For centuries, the South did not have a ready source of vegetable fat, so people turned to animal fat. For people who had to produce or find everything they ate, pigs were the logical choice. Compared to cows and sheep, pigs were easier and less expensive to raise. Nearly all of a pig was edible, yielding lots of tasty fat and meat that kept well. Pork was the optimal choice for smoking, salting, and curing. Even now, the most prized and celebrated cured meats are made from pork.

The availability of pig fat notwithstanding, efforts to cultivate a source of vegetable fat in the South date back to the colonists. There were repeated attempts to grow sesame seeds (benne) and olive trees in the seventeenth and eighteenth centuries. Sesame seeds yielded too little oil to make them a viable commercial crop. Olive trees grew well in the balmy coastal climate, but the soil was so rich that the trees didn't bear fruit. (Olives, like grapes and some people, need to struggle to reach their full potential.) Imported olive oil was available in some colonial cities but was so expensive that it was mostly used as a condiment or as medicine, not for cooking. By the late eighteenth century, animal fat, mostly pork fat, was used more than any other kind of fat. The technologies for mass-producing vegetable oil and shortening were more than 100 years away.

By the time pork fat was no longer the only choice, it had often become the preferred choice. There will always be southern cooks and eaters who turn to pork seasoning because they like how it tastes and because it is traditional. For some reason, the combination of vegetables and pig fat is what sets off the critics, as though a preference for beans with a spoonful of bacon drippings is inherently more sinister or misguided than a preference for pizza with pepperoni.

The South isn't the only place on earth where people add a little pork to a pot. It is equally popular in Italy and Spain, where cooks have had olive oil all along. Tell your meat-eating foodie friends that you just bought some world-class Italian *guanciale* and they'll run right over. Invite them to stop by for some hog jowls and they'll just run. Pig parts by any other name — that's the only way some people are going to eat them, particularly if that other name sounds good in a foreign language.

# Real Skillet Cornbread

4 tablespoons bacon
drippings

1 ½ cups coarse or
medium stone-
ground cornmeal

½ cup all-purpose flour

1 teaspoon kosher salt

½ teaspoon
baking powder

½ teaspoon baking soda

1 large egg,
lightly beaten

1 ½ cups well-shaken
buttermilk

This is my cornbread, the one I offer up as what real cornbread ought to be: skillet-born, sugar-free, and bacon-blessed. Heating the bacon drippings in a cast-iron skillet is important. When the batter hits the hot fat, it sizzles and starts forming a deeply browned, crispy bottom crust that tastes like a good hushpuppy. Some people omit flour from their cornbread, but I find that it helps hold the cornbread together when it's cut, particularly when I use coarse stone-ground cornmeal.

My sweet daddy and I grind our own cornmeal on a 1923 Meadows Mill that my great-grandfather, Papa Will Reece, bought new. The mill is considered portable, but it weighs several hundred pounds and must be hauled on a stout trailer. It's powered by a hit-or-miss engine, one of the first machines used in farming. Daddy hauls the mill and engine to heritage festivals and such all over the country. The whole operation is really something to see.

For your cornbread, seek out the best whole-grain stone-ground cornmeal available in your community or order it from ansonmills.com. Fresh whole-grain meal is quite perishable, so store it in an airtight container in the refrigerator or freezer.

MAKES 8 SERVINGS

1. Place the drippings in a 9-inch cast-iron skillet. Place the skillet in the oven as the oven preheats to 450°F.

2. Whisk together the cornmeal, flour, salt, baking powder, and baking soda in a large bowl. In a small bowl, whisk together the egg and buttermilk, pour into the cornmeal mixture, and stir just until blended.

3. Remove the skillet from the oven and scrape in the batter. It will sizzle and pop, so be careful. Return the skillet to the oven and bake until the cornbread is firm in the middle and golden brown on top, about 25 minutes. Serve hot.

VARIATION: You can replace the bacon drippings with 2 tablespoons of butter and 2 tablespoons of vegetable oil, although the crust will not be as crisp or flavorful. Do not preheat the butter and oil in the oven or they will burn. Instead, heat them on top of the stove until the butter stops foaming and the oil is sizzling hot, just before adding the batter.

# Creamy Stone-Ground Grits

2 cups milk

2 cups water

2 teaspoons kosher salt, plus more to taste

2 small garlic cloves, finely chopped

1 cup stone-ground quick grits

4 ounces cream cheese, at room temperature

4 tablespoons (½ stick) butter, at room temperature

Ground black pepper, to taste

These are my house grits, the ones I rely on regularly and the ones I always make on Christmas morning. They are quite creamy but still have discernible texture. Stone-ground grits made from whole dried hominy have excellent flavor and fragrance, yet they are neutral enough to be an amenable side dish. Grits are companion food meant to go with other things on the plate, but they shouldn't be bland. Watery, gluey, or tasteless grits are the result of poorly cooking the wrong kind of grits, not an inherent shortcoming of grits.

Most old-fashioned stone-ground grits are "quick" grits, which cook in about half an hour. There are also coarse stone-ground grits, which are delicious but can be hard to find and take considerably longer to cook. Alas, there are also paper packets of instant grits, which shouldn't be called grits at all. They have the flavor and texture of wet talcum powder with none of the appeal.

I cook breakfast grits in equal parts milk and water because I love the texture it gives the grits. All milk is too rich and cloying. All water is too meager. For supper grits to serve with a vegetable or entrée, I sometimes use well-seasoned stock for the liquid.

Anson Mills makes the world's best grits, hands down. They are sold in a few stores and online at ansonmills.com. Their website teaches how to cook their products with finesse.

MAKES 6 SERVINGS

1. Bring the milk, water, salt, and garlic just to a boil over medium-high heat in a heavy, medium saucepan. Whisking constantly, add the grits in a slow, steady stream. Return to a boil, whisking constantly, and let boil for 1 minute. Reduce the heat and gently simmer the grits, stirring occasionally with a wooden spoon. (Use a long-handled spoon to avoid being burned by bubbling and popping hot grits.) Stir more often when the grits start to thicken. Cook the grits until they are tender and thick enough to hold their shape on the spoon, about 25 minutes.

2. Add the cream cheese and butter and stir until they blend into the grits. Season generously with salt and pepper; grits love salt.

3. Serve at once, or cover the saucepan and keep the grits warm over low heat up to 30 minutes, stirring occasionally. If the grits are too thick when you are ready to serve them, thin with a little warm milk or stock.

VARIATION: To make cheese grits, stir in ½ cup or more of grated cheese when you add the cream cheese and butter. The type of cheese will affect the personality of the grits. For example, aged white cheddar is assertive, Parmesan is subtle, goat cheese is tangy, and aged Gruyère is nutty.

## Miracle Drop Biscuits

2 cups soft southern wheat self-rising flour

1 ¼ cups well-chilled heavy cream

2 tablespoons butter, melted

I call these miracle biscuits because it is a miracle that anybody can make a decent biscuit with only three ingredients. These drop biscuits are billowy and unruly, so they aren't ideal for splitting and filling, but they are wonderful eating out of hand, for gravy, or for simple soppin'. This recipe requires self-rising flour, so do not substitute all-purpose flour mixed with added leavening.

MAKES 6 BISCUITS

1. Preheat the oven to 475°F. Line a baking sheet with a silicone baking mat or parchment paper.
2. Place the flour in a medium bowl and make a well in the center. Pour the cream into the well and stir with a fork to make soft, slightly wet dough. If necessary, finish bringing the dough together with your hands or a rubber spatula, but handle the dough as little as possible.
3. Drop the dough into 6 equal lumps on the prepared baking sheet. Brush the tops with the melted butter. Bake until the tops are golden, about 12 minutes.
4. Serve hot, although they're not bad at room temperature, even for the next day or two. Store at room temperature in an airtight container.

VARIATION: One of the charms of these biscuits is that they do not have to be rolled and cut—but they can be. For biscuits that look a little neater, use lightly floured hands to shape individual biscuits. You can also pat the dough into a 1-inch-thick slab on a lightly floured work surface and cut out biscuits with a lightly floured knife, pizza cutter, or biscuit cutter. Use all-purpose or instant flour for shaping and rolling, never self-rising, and brush away any excess from the biscuits before baking.

## Buttermilk Biscuits

3 cups soft southern wheat self-rising flour

4 tablespoons (½ stick) butter, cut into small pieces and chilled

4 tablespoons vegetable shortening or lard, cut into small pieces and chilled

¾ to 1 cup well-shaken buttermilk

Instant flour or all-purpose flour, for rolling

2 tablespoons butter, melted

Too much has been made about the art (or knack) of making good biscuits, so much so that novices are often afraid to try. Much of the problem is that it is quite difficult to describe the process on paper. It's like trying to teach someone to drive a straight shift car by having him read the instructions. At some point, the novice just has to get in the car and kill the motor and grind the gears a few times in order to learn how to take off smoothly each time, even on hills. To learn to make good biscuits, a novice has to risk making some bad biscuits.

These are cut biscuits, but you don't always need to cut them the same way. For standard round biscuits, use a 2 ½- or 3-inch round cutter. To use up all the dough, you will need to gather and reroll the scraps, which might create a few slightly uneven biscuits.

You can also pat the dough into a rectangle and use a sharp knife or pizza cutter (or even a strand of unflavored dental floss) to cut the biscuits into squares. No rolling, no biscuit cutters, no gathering scraps to reroll. The dough is handled less, so the biscuits stay light. Square biscuits are unorthodox, but the method is quick and easy.

MAKES ABOUT 1 DOZEN

1. Preheat the oven to 475°F. Line a baking sheet with parchment paper or a silicone baking mat.

2. Place the flour in a large bowl. Scatter the pieces of butter and shortening over the flour and toss to coat. Use your fingertips or a pastry blender to work the butter and shortening into the flour until the pieces are in thin flakes no larger than grains of rice. The fat will no longer be sticky. If you press some of the mixture against the back of your thumb, it should cling like a small leaf.

3. While stirring with a fork, add enough buttermilk to make soft dough that pulls in all of the dry ingredients from the bottom of the bowl. If necessary, use your hands or a rubber spatula to finish bringing the dough together. The dough should not be gloppy wet, but it is better to be a little sticky than too dry.

4. Pour the dough onto a work surface that is lightly dusted with instant or all-purpose flour. (Never roll biscuits with self-rising flour.) Gently gather and knead the dough only until it is smooth and supple, about 8 turns. Add only enough flour to keep the dough from being too sticky to handle. Excess flour makes the outside of the biscuits chalky and tough.

5. Use lightly floured hands or a lightly floured rolling pin to roll the dough to a ¾-inch thickness. Cut the biscuits into squares with a sharp knife or pizza cutter, or stamp out as many biscuits as possible with a round cutter. Do not twist the cutter so that the biscuits can rise evenly to their full potential.

Dip the cutter in flour if the dough sticks. Gather any scraps and gently knead until smooth, then roll and cut the remaining biscuits.

6. Transfer the biscuits to the prepared baking sheet. Arrange them with the sides touching for softer sides or about 1 inch apart for firmer sides. Brush the tops with the melted butter and bake until golden brown on top and bottom, 12 to 15 minutes. Serve at once or cover with a clean tea towel for up to 15 minutes.

### TIPS AND TECHNIQUES

A word on self-rising flour. Nearly every southern biscuit recipe calls for self-rising flour, which is code for a few specific brands made from low-protein soft southern wheat specially milled for biscuits. As the name implies, self-rising flour contains leavening. Some experts believe that this perfectly uniform blend of ideal leaveners in the ideal flour make self-rising flour ideal for biscuits. Even scratch-baking purists who would never consider using a mix admit that self-rising flour makes a magnificent biscuit. However, it can be difficult to find outside the South, so if the only thing standing between you and a recipe is the lack of self-rising flour, you can try this. It's not the same, but it will do in a pinch. To replace 1 cup of self-rising flour, combine the following in a bowl and whisk for a full 30 seconds:

¾ cup bleached all-purpose flour

¼ cup cake flour or instant flour

1 ½ teaspoons very fresh baking powder

¼ teaspoon fine sea salt

### TIPS AND TECHNIQUES

A word on instant flour, a type of bleached flour sold under the brand names Shake & Blend and Wondra. It comes in slender canisters, and you'll find it in most grocery stores near the other types of flour. It is extremely useful.

Instant flour is a godsend when rolling biscuits or pie pastry. It doesn't build up on the dough like all-purpose flour often does, so the dough stays light.

Unlike regular flour, instant flour doesn't get gummy when applied to moist food, so it's perfect for lightly coating chicken cutlets and fish fillets before they are sautéed or dredged in egg and crumbs.

You cannot get instant flour to lump, so it is indispensable when making sauces and gravies that are thickened with flour.

# Basic Pastry I

2 ½ cups all-purpose flour, divided

1 teaspoon kosher salt

2 tablespoons sugar

12 tablespoons (1 ½ sticks) unsalted butter, cut into small cubes and chilled

½ cup lard, cut into small cubes and chilled (about 4 ounces)

4 tablespoons vodka, chilled

2 to 4 tablespoons ice water

Instant flour or additional all-purpose flour, for rolling

Each time I talk about this recipe, it sounds like the start of a bad joke or a description of a drinking game: "Take some vodka and lard and . . . ." But the keys to this flaky, flavorful pastry are indeed chilled vodka and lard.

Let me explain the vodka. Pastry is flaky when its chilled liquid evaporates quickly in the oven, leaving little steam pockets between the grains of flour. Because vodka evaporates even more quickly than water, this pastry is more flaky than most.

Let me explain the lard, a contentious substance. Some people swear that it's an express ticket to the cardiac ward. Others believe that lard rendered from well-tended and well-fed pigs is preferable to chemically altered shortening from a lab. What no one questions is that lard makes a delectable pastry that is flaky, moist, and true to its southern roots. Try to find leaf lard, which is the highest grade of lard. It has very little pork flavor, making it the best choice for delicate baked goods. Many small-scale premium pork producers and gourmet markets sell this type of lard. If you can't (or won't) use lard, substitute solid vegetable shortening.

If you do not have a food processor, use a pastry blender or your fingertips to work in the fat.

PASTRY FOR ONE DOUBLE-CRUST 9-INCH PIE, TWO 9-INCH REGULAR OR DEEP-DISH PIE SHELLS, OR TWO 9- OR 10-INCH TART SHELLS

1. Place 1 ½ cups of the flour and the salt and sugar in the bowl of a food processor fitted with the metal blade or pastry blade and pulse to combine. Scatter the cubes of butter and lard over the flour and pulse until the pieces of fat are the size of small peas. Add the remaining 1 cup of flour and pulse until the mixture looks like coarse cornmeal. Transfer into a large bowl.

2. Sprinkle the vodka and 2 tablespoons of the ice water over the flour mixture and stir with a fork or rubber spatula to form large clumps that pull in all of the dry ingredients. Squeeze a small handful of dough; if it doesn't hold together, stir in more ice water, 1 tablespoon at a time. Although the pastry should not be wet, it works best when it is a little sticky.

3. Gather the clumps into a smooth ball of pastry. Divide the pastry in half and shape each piece into a ball. Flatten each ball into a disk and wrap tightly in plastic wrap. Refrigerate for at least 30 minutes and up to 3 days. This gives the pastry time to rest, so the flour can continue to absorb the liquid and the pastry will be easier to handle. For longer storage, place the wrapped pastry in a freezer bag and freeze for up to 2 months. Thaw in the refrigerator overnight before using.

## Basic Pastry II

3 cups all-purpose flour

1 teaspoon kosher salt

1 teaspoon sugar

8 tablespoons (1 stick) unsalted butter, cut into small cubes and chilled

½ cup vegetable shortening, cut into small cubes and chilled (about 4 ounces)

1 large egg

1 tablespoon distilled white vinegar

5 to 8 tablespoons ice water

Instant flour or additional all-purpose flour, for rolling

Before the lard and vodka pastry (Basic Pastry I) came into my life, this was my favorite for years. I still recommend it as a great pastry for beginners. The egg and vinegar make the dough very easy to handle, and it's forgiving of rough treatment.

If you do not have a food processor, use a pastry blender or your fingertips to work in the fat and use a fork to stir in the liquid.

PASTRY FOR ONE DOUBLE-CRUST 9-INCH PIE, TWO 9-INCH REGULAR OR DEEP-DISH PIE SHELLS, OR TWO 9- OR 10-INCH TART SHELLS

1. Place the flour, salt, and sugar in the bowl of a food processor fitted with the metal blade or pastry blade and pulse to combine. Scatter the cubes of butter and shortening over the flour and pulse until the mixture resembles wet sand with a few pieces of fat the size of small peas.

2. Whisk together the egg and vinegar and 5 tablespoons of the ice water in a small bowl, whisking until well-blended. Pour over the flour mixture and pulse to form large clumps that pull in all of the dry ingredients. Squeeze a small handful of dough; if it doesn't hold together, sprinkle in more ice water, 1 tablespoon at a time, and pulse only until incorporated.

3. Gather the clumps into a smooth ball of dough. Divide the pastry in half and shape each piece into a ball. Flatten each ball into a disk and wrap tightly in plastic wrap. Refrigerate for at least 30 minutes and up to 3 days. This gives the pastry time to rest, so the flour can continue to absorb the liquid and the pastry will be easier to handle. For longer storage, place the wrapped pastry in a freezer bag and freeze for up to 2 months. Thaw in the refrigerator overnight before using.

### To Roll Pastry for a Pie or Tart Shell

When you are ready to use the pastry, unwrap the disk and let it sit at room temperature for 30 minutes to warm up just enough that it won't crack when you roll it. Use a lightly floured rolling pin to roll the pastry into an 11-inch circle (a 12-inch circle for deep dish) on a lightly floured piece of waxed paper or parchment paper placed on a smooth, solid work surface. I like to use instant flour for rolling because it is less likely to make the pastry gummy or excessively floured. If you use all-purpose flour, brush away any excess with a dry pastry brush.

Place the pin in the center of the disk and press down and roll out with firm, even pressure. Give the round a quarter turn between each roll. Start each roll from the center. Add a tiny bit more flour if the dough begins to stick. If the dough gets too soft and stretchy, cover it and refrigerate for a few minutes.

Invert the pie plate or tart tin over the center of the pastry. Slide your hand under the paper and quickly flip the whole thing over. Peel off the paper and press the dough into the plate, pinching closed any cracks. For a single-crust pie, turn under the pastry that sticks up beyond the pie plate and crimp the edge. For a double-crust pie, do not trim the excess pastry until after the shell is filled and topped with the second piece of pastry. For a tart, use your fingers to press the pastry against the metal edge of the tin to make it even with the top.

Wrap the shell in plastic wrap and refrigerate for at least 30 minutes or up to 1 day. For longer storage, place the wrapped shell in a freezer bag and freeze for up to 2 months. Thaw in the refrigerator overnight before using.

The pastry should be chilled and firm because cold fat going into a hot oven is what makes the pastry flaky. Plus, chilled pastry shrinks less during baking.

### To Bake an Empty Pie or Tart Shell

Sometimes empty shells are partially or fully baked before they are filled. This is appropriate for a pie or tart that has a filling that is not cooked or a filling that will get done more quickly than the crust. This technique is sometimes called blind baking.

Place a baking sheet in the oven and preheat the oven to 400°F. Use the tines of a fork to prick (dock) the pastry in several places. These tiny holes let steam escape so that the pastry doesn't puff up into a dome as it bakes. Line the pastry with a sheet of parchment paper or aluminum foil large enough to cover the edges. Fill with pie weights or uncooked dried beans or rice. Bake for 10 minutes. Carefully remove the parchment and weights. If the pastry is to be partially baked, continue baking until the crust looks dry but does not color, about 8 minutes longer. If the shell is to be fully baked, continue baking until it is light golden brown, about 12 minutes longer. Place on a wire rack to cool to room temperature.

## STOCKS

Flavorful stock is the heart and soul of many recipes. Although there are some acceptable stocks for sale in grocery stores, few of them compare to the home-cooked thing. Homemade stock keeps for days in the fridge and months in the freezer.

Stock should be cooled to room temperature before it is refrigerated. To speed the cooling process for stock (or for any hot liquid, such as brine), here's what I do. I fill a reusable metal or hard plastic drinking bottle with water and freeze it solid. I pour the hot stock into a large bowl and set the bowl in the sink filled with ice, like an ice bath. I stir the stock with the frozen water bottle, which cools the liquid quickly without diluting it like ice would do. When done, I wash the bottle thoroughly and refreeze it for the next time.

When refrigerated, the fat in the stock rises to the surface and solidifies. That fat seals the surface and protects the flavor and freshness of the stock, so leave it in place until you are ready to use or freeze the stock.

I freeze stock in 1-cup or 4-cup containers (the amounts I use most often in recipes) so that I can thaw only as much as I need. To save space in the freezer, I ladle the stock into freezer bags, close them tightly, and freeze them flat on a baking tray. When they are frozen hard, I stack several bags into a small space.

See pages 180 and 181 for Smoked Pork Stock, Smoked Poultry Stock, and Smoked Vegetable Stock.

## Traditional Chicken Stock

4 pounds chicken parts and/or meaty bones (such as backs, necks, wings, or carcasses)

12 cups cold water

2 large onions, quartered

4 stalks celery, roughly chopped

3 medium carrots, roughly chopped

2 garlic cloves, crushed

3 bay leaves

¼ cup lightly packed flat-leaf parsley

3 short thyme sprigs

2 teaspoons black peppercorns

1 teaspoon kosher salt

This is traditional, slow-simmered chicken stock, a workhorse in the kitchen. You can use this recipe to make turkey stock as well.

MAKES ABOUT 2 QUARTS

1. Rinse the chicken parts, pat dry, and place in a large stockpot. Add the cold water and bring to a boil over high heat, stirring occasionally and skimming off the foam that accumulates on top of the stock. Stir in the onions, celery, carrots, garlic, bay leaves, parsley, thyme sprigs, peppercorns, and salt. Reduce the heat to low, partially cover the pot, and gently simmer the stock until the meat falls off the bones, the bones separate, and the liquid reduces to about 8 cups, about 3 hours.

2. Strain the stock through a fine-mesh sieve into a large bowl. The stock can be used immediately, but for best results, let it cool to room temperature and then cover and refrigerate until chilled. Just before using or freezing, remove the solidified fat from the stock. Discard the fat or save it to use in other recipes, such as in place of bacon drippings. The stock can be refrigerated for up to 1 week or frozen in airtight containers for up to 6 months.

## Shortcut Chicken Stock

Bones, skin, and scraps from 1 roasted or rotisserie chicken

4 cups store-bought organic, low-sodium chicken stock

6 cups cold water

This is the stock I make most often at my house, particularly if the recipe also calls for cooked chicken meat. Compared to traditional chicken stock, it's quick and it's certainly easy. The roasted bones from a plain rotisserie chicken (or home-roasted chicken) give the stock great flavor and body. If you don't have time to make stock as soon as the chicken is picked clean, freeze the bones and skin until needed. You can also accumulate carcasses to make multiple batches of stock at once.

This stock usually sets up like gelatin when it is chilled, a sign that every speck of flavor has been leached from the bones. It might seem odd to use store-bought stock as part of the liquid, but that provides the vegetable seasoning you'd have to add if you used only water. Plus, this stock is more flavorful than most stock you can buy in a box or can.

MAKES ABOUT 2 QUARTS

1. Place the bones, skin, and scraps in a stockpot or large soup pot. Add the stock and cold water. Bring to a boil, reduce the heat to low, partially cover the pot, and simmer the stock gently until the carcass falls apart and the liquid reduces to about 8 cups, about 1 hour.

2. Strain the stock through a fine-mesh sieve into a large bowl. The stock can be used immediately, but for best results, let it cool to room temperature and then cover and refrigerate until chilled. Just before using or freezing, remove the solidified fat from the stock. Discard the fat or save it to use in other recipes, such as in place of bacon drippings. The stock can be refrigerated for up to 1 week or frozen in airtight containers for up to 6 months.

## Vegetable Stock

| | |
|---|---|
| 2 | large onions, quartered |
| 2 | large carrots, roughly chopped |
| 2 | medium leeks, trimmed and roughly chopped |
| 2 | celery stalks, roughly chopped |
| 2 | small parsnips, peeled and roughly chopped |
| 2 | small white turnips, peeled and roughly chopped |
| 3 | garlic cloves, smashed |
| 1 | cup mushrooms or mushroom stems |
| ¼ | cup extra-virgin olive oil |
| 12 | cups cold water, divided |
| ½ | cup (lightly packed) flat-leaf parsley |
| 5 | short thyme sprigs |
| 1 | bay leaf |
| 10 | peppercorns |
| ¼ | cup white wine |
| 2 | teaspoons kosher salt |
| 1 | tablespoon white wine vinegar |

Although it sounds like it ought to be the easiest of all stocks, vegetable stock can be persnickety. You can use a few vegetable parings and trimmings, but stock needs some whole, fresh vegetables to keep it from tasting like dishwater. That's also why I start by roasting the vegetables, to intensify and concentrate their flavors. I don't use tomatoes because their color makes the stock orange, which might discolor a recipe. This often happens with store-bought vegetable stock.

You can use different vegetables from those listed here, to take advantage of what you have on hand, but avoid cruciferous vegetables such as broccoli, cauliflower, and cabbage, which can make the stock smelly. If your stock turns out bitter, simmer a couple of washed collard leaves in it for 10 minutes—they can magically sweeten it up.

I add a little salt to my stock, but use a very light hand so that it won't interfere with the seasoning of the recipe that uses the stock.

MAKES ABOUT 2 QUARTS

1. Preheat the oven to 400°F.
2. In a large roasting pan, stir together the onions, carrots, leeks, celery, parsnips, turnips, garlic, and mushrooms. Drizzle the oil over the vegetables and toss to coat. Roast, stirring occasionally, until the vegetables are lightly browned, about 45 minutes. Transfer the vegetables into a large stockpot. Pour 2 cups of the water into the warm roasting pan and scrape up the browned glaze from the bottom of the pan; pour this mixture into the stockpot. Add the remaining 10 cups of water and the parsley, thyme sprigs, bay leaf, peppercorns, wine, and salt to the pot. Bring to a boil, reduce the heat to low, partially cover the pot, and gently simmer the stock until the vegetables are very soft and the liquid reduces to about 8 cups, about 1 hour.
3. Strain the stock through a fine-mesh sieve into a large bowl and stir in the vinegar. The stock can be used immediately, but for best results, let it cool to room temperature and then cover and refrigerate until chilled. The stock can be refrigerated for up to 1 week or frozen in airtight containers for up to 6 months.

# Index